Popular Music Studies

Popular Music Studies

Edited by

David Hesmondhalgh

Lecturer in Sociology, Open University

and

Keith Negus

Senior Lecturer in Media and Communications,
Goldsmiths College, University of London

A member of the Hodder Headline Group
LONDON
Distributed in the United States of America by
Oxford University Press Inc., New York

First published in Great Britain in 2002 by
Arnold, a member of the Hodder Headline Group,
338 Euston Road, London NW1 3BH

http://www.arnoldpublishers.com

Distributed in the United States of America by
Oxford University Press Inc.,
198 Madison Avenue, New York, NY10016

© 2002 Arnold
Chapter 13 © 2002 Patria Román-Velázquez

The advice and information in this book are believed to be true and
accurate at the date of going to press, but neither the authors nor the publisher
can accept any legal responsibility or liability for any errors or omissions.

British Library Cataloguing in Publication Data
A catalogue record for this book is available from the British Library

Library of Congress Cataloging-in-Publication Data
A catalog record for this book is available from the Library of Congress

ISBN 0 340 76247 0 (hb)
ISBN 0 340 76248 9 (pb)

2 3 4 5 6 7 8 9 10

Typeset in 11/11.2 Times by Integra Software Services Pvt. Ltd, Pondicherry, India
Printed and bound in India by Replika Press Pvt. Ltd., Kundli 131 028

What do you think about this book? Or any other Arnold title?
Please send your comments to feedback.arnold@hodder.co.uk

Contents

Section III: Production, institutions and creativity **143**

Section IV: Place, space and power **205**

List of contributors

Christopher Ballantine is the L. G. Joel Professor of Music at the University of Natal, in Durban, South Africa, and a Fellow of the University of Natal. His publications have covered a wide range of issues in the fields of popular music studies, ethnomusicology and musicology. Among his books are *Marabi Nights: Early South African Jazz and Vaudeville* (1993), and *Music and its Social Meanings* (1984).

David Brackett is Associate Professor of Music at the State University of New York (SUNY) at Binghamton. He is the author of *Interpreting Popular Music* (1995) and a past president of the United States branch of the International Association for the Study of Popular Music (IASPM).

Dai Griffiths is Principal Lecturer in Music at Oxford Brookes University. He has completed papers on historical and theoretical aspects of pop music: on 'the high analysis of low music', the history of pop music since punk, and the role of words in pop songs. He has published studies of songwriters including Bruce Springsteen, Anton Webern and John Cale.

Jocelyne Guilbault is Professor of Ethnomusicology at the Music Department of the University of California, Berkeley. Since 1980 she has done extensive fieldwork in the Creole- and English-speaking islands of the Caribbean on both traditional and popular music. She has published several articles on interpretive theory and methodology in ethnographic writings, aesthetics and world music. Author of *Zouk: World Music in the West Indies* (University of Chicago Press, 1993), she recently completed a book-length manuscript on *The Calypso Music Scene. Politics and Aesthetics of a Caribbean Music Industry*.

David Hesmondhalgh is a Lecturer in Sociology in the Faculty of Social Sciences at the Open University (UK). He is the author of *The Cultural Industries* (2002) and co-editor (with Georgina Born) of *Western Music and* *its Others: Difference, Representation and Appropriation in Music* (2000). He was formerly treasurer of the International Association for the Study of Popular Music.

Shuhei Hosokawa is Associate Professor in the Department of Humanities and Social Sciences at the Tokyo Institute of Technology. He is the co-editor of *Karaoke around the World* (1998) and the author of articles on Japanese popular music and the Japanese–Brazilian community. His articles have been published in many journals, including *Cultural Studies, Popular Music* and *Japanese Studies*.

Rupa Huq is Lecturer in Leisure Management at the University of Manchester and is a Leverhulme Special Research Fellow. She is working on a book provisionally titled *Rethinking Youth Culture*.

Anahid Kassabian is Associate Professor of Communications and Media Studies, and a member of the program faculty in Women's Studies and Literary Studies at Fordham University (USA). She is the author of *Hearing Film* (2001), co-editor (with David Schwarz) of *Keeping Score: Music, Disciplinarity, Culture* (1997), and a past editor of the *Journal of Popular Music Studies*. She currently serves as chair of the International Association for the Study of Popular Music.

Lorraine Leu is a Lecturer in Portuguese and Brazilian Studies at the University of Bristol and an Editor of the *Journal of Latin American Cultural Studies*. She has published articles on Brazilian popular music and on popular culture in Trinidad and Tobago. She is the author of *Brazilian Popular Music: Caetano Veloso and the Regeneration of Tradition* (forthcoming in Spring 2003).

Ian Maxwell trained as an actor and theatre director at the Victorian College of the Arts in Melbourne, Australia, before completing his Ph.D. on hip-hop culture in Australia, to be published as *Phat Beats, Dope Rhymes: Hip Hop Down Under Comin' Upper*. He is currently a Lecturer in Performance Studies at the University of Sydney, where he teaches theories of acting, sociology of culture and critical theory.

Keith Negus is Senior Lecturer in the Department of Media and Communications, Goldsmiths College, University of London. A coordinating editor of the journal *Popular Music*, he is the author of *Producing Pop* (1992), *Popular Music in Theory* (1996) and *Music Genres and Corporate Cultures* (1999).

Michael Pickering is Reader in Culture and Communications in the Department of Social Sciences at Loughborough University. His two most recent books are *History, Experience and Cultural Studies* (1997) and *Stereotyping: The Politics of Representation* (2001). He is also co-author with David Deacon, Peter Golding and Graham Murdock of *Researching Communications: A Practical Guide to Methods in Media and Cultural Analysis* (1999).

Motti Regev is Senior Lecturer in Sociology in the Department of Sociology, Political Science and Communication at the Open University of Israel. He is author of *Rock: Music and Culture* (1995, in Hebrew) and (with Edwin Seroussi) of *Popular Music and National Culture in Israel* (2002).

Patria Román-Velázquez is Lecturer in Communication and Media Studies at City University, London. She has published articles in a number of journals and edited collections and is the author of *The Making of Latin London: Salsa Music, Place and Identity* (1999).

Will Straw is Associate Professor of Communications at McGill University. He is a co-editor of *The Cambridge Companion to Pop and Rock* (2001), and the author of numerous articles on film, popular music and Canadian culture. His current research focuses on urban culture in Canada.

Luiz Tatit is a musician and Professor of Semiotics and Linguistics in the Faculty of Philosophy, Arts and Social Sciences at the University of Sao Paulo, Brazil. He is the author of *Semiótica da canção: melodia e letra* (1994); *O cancionista: composição de cançoes no Brasil* (1996); *Musicando a semiótica: ensaios* (1997) and *Análise semiótica através das letras* (2001). He has also released the CDs *Felicidade* (1997) and *O Meio* (2000), both on the Dabliú label.

Jason Toynbee is Senior Lecturer in Communication, Culture and Media in the School of Art and Design at Coventry University (UK). He is the author of *Making Popular Music: Musicians, Creativity and Institutions* (2000).

Nabeel Zuberi is Senior Lecturer in Film, Television and Media Studies at the University of Auckland, Aoteroa-New Zealand. He is the author of *Sounds English: Transnational Popular Music* (2001).

Acknowledgements

The editors would like to thank Richard Smith for his invaluable assistance in preparing the index.

Luiz Tatit, the editors and the publisher would like to acknowledge the following copyright holder for permission to publish The Girl from Ipanema (Garota de Ipanema), original words by Viniclus de Moraes, music by Antonio Carlos Jobim, English words by Norman Gimbel, © 1963 Duchess Music Corporation/New Thunder Music Company, USA. Universal/MCA Music Limited, 77 Fulham Palace Road, London W6 (25%)/Windswept Music (London) Limited, Hope House, 40 St Peter's Road, London W6 (41.67%) for all English speaking territories, Europe, French overseas territories, Israel and Japan. Used by permission of Music Sales Ltd. All rights reserved. International copyright secured.

Introduction

Popular music studies: meaning, power and value

David Hesmondhalgh and Keith Negus

The study of popular music is at an exciting moment in its development. The pioneers of popular music analysis spent many years having to justify paying serious attention to a cultural form and medium of communication which was often dismissed for its association with entertainment and pleasure. But now university courses and units in popular music are proliferating, and the study of popular music is an established, though still relatively marginal, academic area. Dozens of books, chapters and journal articles appear every year. Whereas the early years of popular music studies were dominated by a few specific genres, there is now a healthy pluralism in research in the area. The writers who did so much to establish popular music as a legitimate field of study have now been joined by new researchers, who may have grown up in very different musical cultures (punk, salsa, hip-hop and indie, rather than rock, son, blues and folk, for example). Partly through the work of the International Association for the Study of Popular Music (IASPM), there is an encouraging – though still insufficient – degree of international dialogue amongst researchers and a strong comparative emphasis in influential published work. Those journals which regularly publish work on popular music (*Popular Music, Perfect Beat, Popular Music and Society, Cultural Studies, Black Music Research Journal, Media, Culture and Society*, to name a few) feature writers from many different geographical backgrounds and locations. The study of popular music is, at its best, a uniquely interdisciplinary area of research, drawing significant contributions from writers within a number of academic fields, including musicology, media and cultural studies, sociology, anthropology, ethnomusicology, folkloristics, psychology, social history and cultural geography.

This collection is very much intended to build on these traditions of pluralism, internationalism and interdisciplinarity. An enormous range of sounds are covered here, from bossa nova to funk to Hindi film music. The authors come from a great variety of places, from Wales to Puerto Rico to South Africa to Japan to Brazil to Australia. Although we have brought together writers with backgrounds in musicology, ethnomusicology, media, communication and cultural studies, sociology and performance studies, all share a commitment to interdisciplinarity. While we intend here to encapsulate something of the vibrancy of past dialogues and debates, we are also very definitely seeking to suggest new directions for the further development of the field. The editorial material in this volume combines these two goals in the following way. First, in this introduction, we survey the development of popular music studies, arguing that what ultimately connects people across the field is a concern with questions about the relationships between musical meaning, social power and cultural value. We show how various key disciplines have contributed to an understanding of these issues and how a certain amount of convergence has been achieved. Then, in the section introductions, we address some of the key shifts that have been taking place in popular music theorising since the early 1990s, offer some comments on theoretical strengths and limitations in the field, and outline how the authors of this collection are stimulating debate and dialogue whilst contributing to a more extensive range of viewpoints, perspectives and research agendas.

It was not too long ago that any text of this type would begin by offering a definition of popular music, and inevitably come to a halt by concluding that popular music, like popular culture, is almost impossible to define coherently, because of the many conflicting meanings clustered around the word 'popular'. These days the problem not only concerns what is meant by the 'popular', but what we mean by the very notion of music. First, questions have been raised about music as a category. As anthropologists, philosophers and enthnomusicologists have pointed out, music is not a universal category (Cook and Everist, 1999). Not all cultures have separate categories for music as a distinct activity and form separate from other social practices and rituals, and not all cultures use the same categories when referring to music. Second, the boundaries of what is categorised as music have been continually changing. The distinctions between speech, sound and music are often blurred (van Leeuwen, 1999), as is the distinction between music and noise. Numerous composers and performers, particularly in the twentieth-century experimental music tradition, have sought to challenge assumptions about the boundaries between music and non-music, whilst a number of theorists have pointed to the close connection between the 'soundscape' and the style of music made and appreciated in a given place (Schafer, 1977; Tagg, 1994). Many writers use the term 'popular music' to designate music which is mediated electronically and which comes to its listeners via the playback of audio and video recordings, or via the internet, or through performance on film or television, or in amplified live performance. Yet, the electronic technologies which are assumed to 'define' popular music as a commodified form have also undermined the meaning of 'popular'. Technologies of recording and circulation have enabled a huge variety of sounds from other times and places to *become* popular, in the sense of 'widely experienced and/or enjoyed'. The huge diversity of traditions that are often reductively labelled as 'world music' have become part of popular music, and so has 'serious' (or 'art' or 'classical') music. It is no longer at all clear that we can draw hard and fast distinctions between popular and traditional, and between serious and popular – nor is it indeed clear that we ever really could. No longer can 'popular music' be thought of as a residual category, referring to what is left over, after art and folk music are excluded (cf. Richard Middleton, 1990: 4). The practices of popular musicians and their fans actively transform, draw from and feed into art musics and folk musics. Yet the categories remain and are a continual source of musicological disagreement and ideological dispute as Simon Frith notes in *Performing Rites* (1996). In studying popular music we are dealing with an unstable, contested and changing category.

One of the most remarkable aspects of music in the twentieth century was the proliferation of discourse around it – not just academic analysis, of course, but also commentary, criticism, biography, fan writing, publicity, gossip and fiction. A huge amount was written about popular music before it began to emerge as a recognisable field of academic study in 1981, with the establishment of the International Association for the Study of Popular Music and the launch of the academic journal *Popular Music*. Fan magazines were prevalent from the 1950s onwards, as pop music began to rival film as an entertainment industry. There were trade journals, most notably *Billboard* in the United States, and literally thousands of biographies and autobiographies of popular musicians. Jazz journalism and, from the 1960s onwards, rock journalism, were particularly important in circulating knowledge and mediating values and beliefs about the creation, characteristics and influence of recorded music. Journalism helped folk, blues, jazz and rock fans make sense of their music, but inevitably on very particular terms. Rock criticism, for example, evaluated rock as a sincere and meaningful expression of the aspirations of 'youth', and as a music which supposedly transcended cultural boundaries by being transmitted and shared by peoples of many different nations and backgrounds. By the late 1960s and early 1970s, the publishing industry was commissioning influential and serious studies of the history, social significance and aesthetics of popular music, often from writers bridging the journalism/academic divide (e.g. Laing, 1969; Gillett, 1971; Marcus, 1975).

Meanwhile, in the academy, there were two significant currents of interest in popular music up until the late 1970s. Musicology and ethnomusicology ignored popular music almost entirely, but some mavericks, such as Wilfred Mellers (1964) and John Blacking (1973), were willing to pay attention to the full range of musical experience within historical and contemporary societies. In the amalgam of social history and ethnomusicology sometimes known as folkloristics, significant efforts were spent on collecting and interpreting folk musics which were increasingly perceived to be under threat from social change. Alan Lomax (1964) in the US and Paul Oliver (1969) in the UK were two notable writers here. Blues was a particularly important area for early work (e.g. Jones, 1963; Keil, 1966; Middleton, 1972). There were increasing efforts to theorise musical meaning in a manner informed by a recognition of the importance of popular music (see John Shepherd's contributions to Shepherd et al., 1977). Inspired by theoretical developments in structuralism and semiotics, which saw all cultural expression as worthy of analysis, some musicologists began exploring neglected types of popular song. Particularly significant was the work of Philip Tagg (1979, 1991) on musical signification in theme tunes, film music and pop songs, and Franco Fabbri's work on rock and *canzone* (1982a, 1982b, 1989).

In the United States, sociologists interested in 'mass culture' and so-called deviant subcultures had begun publishing studies of popular music from the late 1940s and into the 1950s (e.g. David Riesman, 1950), and Howard Becker (1963) pioneered the sociology of popular musicians with his study of dance musicians. Philosopher and social theorist Theodor Adorno (1903–1969) issued various denunciations of popular music but his serious interest in the close relations between social change, mode of production and aesthetic form helped to legitimise, and set an agenda for, the sociology of popular music – one which endures to this day (see Adorno and Horkheimer, 1979; Adorno, 1976, 1991). By the 1970s popular music was sufficiently respectable as an area of study for younger sociologists to publish articles and books, mainly on blues, country and rock. The music industry became a particular focus of concern, whether from organisational sociologists such as Paul Hirsch (1972), Richard A. Peterson (1976, 1978) or left radicals such as Steve Chapple and Reebee Garofalo (1977). In the UK, Simon Frith's *The Sociology of Rock* (1978) addressed industry and audience, and was widely read in schools and by non-academic music fans. Progressive educationalists began to argue for the pedagogic value of paying attention to the teaching of popular music in schools (e.g. Vulliamy and Lee, 1976; Small, 1977). The contribution of education studies to the field has been developed further by Lucy Green (1997, 2001) in her imaginatively researched studies of how popular music is taught and learnt.

These were the main currents informing the study of popular music as it gained momentum at the turn of the 1980s, established through dialogues amongst scholars mainly based in Europe and North America. For many years the only thing unifying these different disciplines was their object of study: popular music. No single theoretical formulation emerged to dominate or homogenise the field. While this was in many respects a blessing, in that it allowed for continuing eclecticism and multidisciplinarity, it made it difficult for popular music writers to find a means of assessing the implications of each other's work. The study of popular music was still, in other words, in search of a set of theoretical paradigms which would allow *inter*disciplinary dialogue. Gradually, in the 1980s and early 1990s, a set of key themes and concepts crystallised, to some extent shared across the different disciplines with significant input into popular music analysis, but with different inflections. One way of understanding these themes, and their unifying features, is to explain what the main disciplines that constitute popular music studies were *reacting against* in their own disciplinary histories.

Writers from musicology were reacting against the particular types of formalist analysis that characterised much of the work in their field and, in turning against this formalism, musicologists made important contributions to understanding the relationships of musical sound to social power. A number of researchers began to show how a range of social and cultural experiences is encoded in, and reformulated by, particular genres of music, and how musical sound can therefore have certain kinds of political agency. The result, exemplified in the work of many writers, has been the development of a *critical musicology*. 'Critical' here has a double sense: the aim is an approach that is critical of musicology's traditional formalism, and a musicology that is critical in looking for the social implications of any music. Critical musicologists have challenged the low value ascribed to popular music, relative to the established canon of great works in that discipline, by emphasising the distinctive properties of popular music, pointing to the importance and neglect of timbre and rhythm, and by developing new ways of analysing these distinctive properties. Major contributions to the critical musicology of popular music include Philip Tagg's monumental studies of the *Kojak* theme tune (1979) and of Abba's 'Fernando' (1991); various essays by John Shepherd, attempting to span the divide across musicology and sociology (see Shepherd, 1991); Robert Walser's study of heavy metal (1993) and musical analysis of rap (1995); and Richard Middleton's impressive 'search for a theory of gesture' which has taken him across a very wide range of rock and pop styles (see Middleton, 2000). Others showed that music was neither an autonomous nor an innocent cultural domain, which was the way it was often treated in traditional music studies, but was often expressive or suggestive of potent social and political meanings. Susan McClary (1991), for example, worked across the serious/popular music divide to show how gender and sexual politics were present in a whole range of genres, composers and performers, from Mozart to Madonna. The project of a feminist critical musicology has most notably been continued by Sheila Whiteley (1997, 2000) via her analysis of the work of individual women musicians.

Writers in ethnomusicology had always paid close attention to the social and historical conditions of music which had generally been marginalised, or under-analysed, by musicologists. But ethnomusicologists had traditionally tended to deal with music as far away (geographically and aesthetically) as possible from the technologically mediated musics of the West. From the 1970s onwards, they began to pay much closer attention to urban popular music, not only in the 'non-Western' settings which were traditionally the focus of ethnomusicology, but also in 'advanced' industrial societies. Many writers were keen to avoid the implicit functionalism of much ethnomusicology, which tended to assume music's role in maintaining the cohesion of societies. Instead they drew attention to conflict, and to ways in which popular music might challenge dominant features of the societies in which it is practised. The new ethnomusicology has produced some significant studies in popular music analysis, combining treatment of musical sound and social context in particular societies and genres. If popular music studies have covered a wide range of genres in many different geographical settings, many of the key studies of popular musics outside northern Europe and North America have come from ethnomusicologists. Notable contributions include those by Steven Feld (e.g. 2000), Jocelyne Guilbault (1993), Charles Keil (1994/1986), Peter Manuel (1993), Mark Slobin (1993), Martin Stokes (1992) and Christopher Waterman (1993).

Writers from sociology were reacting against the structuralist-functionalist approach and behaviourism that had been the dominant paradigms in much social science (especially in the USA) in the 1950s and 1960s. Often implicit in US sociological functionalism was the conservative notion that social phenomena contributing to the maintenance of the social system as a whole were generally positive. Amidst the social and cultural conflicts of the late 1960s, many sociologists were in revolt against such consensualist notions. In the new cultural sociology of the 1970s, influenced by interactionism, ethnomethodology and Marxist thought, much attention was paid to youth subcultures, but from a more sympathetic point of view than before. This helped to shape the agenda of cultural studies, as it developed as a separate (inter)discipline in the late 1970s and early 1980s, emphasising the agency of audiences and celebrating the creativity of young people, whose cultural experiences had often been dismissed or despised by journalists and social scientists. The concept of 'subculture', developed in the early twentieth century by interactionist sociologists, and revived in the wake of a new interest in 'deviance' in the 1970s, became crucial to the orientation of sociologists concerned with rock and pop music. Even though popular music was tangential – or even incidental – to much of the work, subcultural studies (e.g. Hebdige (1979) on mods and punks; McRobbie (1980) on girl subcultures) became staples of popular music courses. In parallel, organisational sociologists challenged simplistic pictures of the music industry as a production line and produced a more optimistic account, which attempted to account for some of the contradictions of rock, as 'a mass-produced music which carries a critique of its own means of production' and as a 'mass-consumed music that constructs its own "authentic" audience', in Simon Frith's formulation (Frith, 1981: 11).

Having schematically noted their separate lineages, let us now return to the question of what unifies, or at least connects, the various key disciplines contributing to popular music studies, and what makes this a distinctive area of study. Contributions from these various disciplines are nearly always oriented towards a general goal: to rescue popular music from being treated as trivial and unimportant, whether as music (which some would see as trivial because of its 'merely' ritual or entertainment function) or as popular culture (which some would see as debased because of its commercial origins, supposed lack of complexity and dubious aesthetic merit). The study of popular music has tended to effect this rescue operation in a certain way, via a commitment to a *politicisation* of music: by attempting to show that music is often – some would say always – bound up with questions of social power. In this respect, popular music studies gained their impulse from broader trends in intellectual life in the middle and late twentieth century, and in particular from the politicisation of culture apparent in the wake of the 1960s. Neo-Marxism, feminism and 'identity politics' all had an important role in raising questions about the politics of culture, and the influences of these political movements and theoretical discourses can be found throughout a great deal of the work on popular music of the period, and since. For many writers, questions of social power are in turn closely bound up with questions of cultural value, about who has the authority to ascribe social and aesthetic worth to what kinds of music, and why. A key aim of popular music studies has often been to make interventions into such questions of cultural value: to argue, for example, that the devaluation of certain forms of music is bound up with the denigration of the social groups identified and associated with these musical forms, whether hip-hop fans, disco dancers or teeny-boppers; or to understand why groups of fans come to value the music they love, and to take seriously the kinds of beliefs about society and culture which inform their thinking. Such questions of value and authority have become a concern within the many disciplines which now feed into cultural studies.

So, to summarise the argument and to restate the position we outlined earlier, a distinctive feature of popular music studies has been the willingness of participants to address the relationships between musical meaning, social power and cultural value. What is more, popular music studies have developed distinctive ways of treating these issues, addressing popular music as a multitextual cultural phenomenon (cf. Born, 1995: 16–28, building on Laing, 1985). The field has built up a cumulative analysis of popular music culture in its many different textual and technological forms, by analysing recordings, videos, television, film, radio, the internet and other media to show how music is mediated to its public, and how these different forms can produce considerable complexity and ambivalence in meaning. These characteristic qualities of theorising and analysis mean that the study of popular music has much to contribute to central debates within media and cultural studies, and in related disciplines.

Our discussion of the distinctive features of popular music studies – interdisciplinary, relatively pluralist and internationalist, concerned with power and value in relation to musical meaning, focused on the various texts that comprise popular music culture – does not imply a cosy consensus within the field, however. Even if such a consensus were desirable, it would scarcely be possible, given the wide range of disciplines and perspectives contributing to the area. In closing this introduction, we briefly identify the main concepts, debates and controversies concerning the relationships between musical meaning, social power and cultural value and how these concepts and debates are changing. The section introductions then expand on this outline structure, and explain how the work collected in each section contributes to a greater understanding of these key issues and concepts.

This collection inevitably involves debates which gained momentum during the 1990s, a period which saw the study of popular music in its second decade of institutionalisation. The beginning of this era was marked by the publication of the first major reader/textbook (Frith and Goodwin, 1990); an agenda-setting theoretical *tour-de-force* overview of the field (Richard Middleton's *Studying Popular Music*); and the launch of a major monograph series (Wesleyan University Press's Music/Culture series). By the mid-1990s, a steady stream of textbooks, readers and edited volumes was flowing out of publishing companies, and a number of dominant topics and themes could be identified, along with a number of significant (and by no means complementary or consensual) theoretical approaches. A range of concepts and themes could be found on popular music course units, whether in departments of music, sociology and ethnomusicology or media, communication and cultural studies. In broad terms, and for the purposes of clarity and convenience, we would identify four key themes in this literature.

First, there has been a focus on questions of musical meaning. This has been more prevalent in musicology than in other areas of the field. In many respects, musicologists have been responding to calls from sociologists who have often felt uneasy and incapable of knowing quite how to write about musical sound. The desire for a shared vocabulary has fed into an increasing confidence amongst those critical musicologists who have been willing to move beyond the constraints of 'the work' and formal musical notation.

This is reflected in a combination of analysis of musical style with (often historical) analysis of social and political processes.

Second, attention has been directed towards popular music audiences. This has been influenced by developments in media and cultural studies and in sociology, notably a trajectory of theorising which wished to reclaim youth subcultures from the 'social problem' perspective of the sociology of deviance, along with an emphasis, derived in many cases from post-structuralist and postmodern theory, on issues of appropriation, style and the instability of meaning. An interest in audiences and 'reception' has also accompanied a more general preoccupation (in the academy and industry) with questions of consumer culture. During the 1990s it became possible to detect an increasing dissatisfaction with the focus on subcultures as the primary window through which to understand the audiences for popular music, even if the concepts of youth had remained central to many books and courses and informed attempts to develop the less bounded concept of a music 'scene'.

Third, there was a continuing interest in the music industries, and in questions of production. The most significant work on the music industry has owed an enduring debt to Marxism (in its various permutations), and systems-oriented occupational sociology. Although initially tending to stress the constraints imposed by corporate structures and organisational routines, there has been a shift away from an equation of production with the recording industry towards a concern with the contexts within which the industries operate, the broader dynamics which inform the creativity of musical producers and a more plural sense of the range of industries, institutions and practices which might constitute the 'music business'.

Fourth, there has been a growing interest in questions of place (whether the nation, city or neighbourhood) and the dynamics and consequences of the time-space processes that, often confusingly, go by the name of globalisation. Here, developments in theorising have been paralleled by the increasingly international character of popular music, and signalled in the adoption of the category of 'world music', and the increasing borrowing, exchange and exploitation of other sounds in pop music, electronic dance music and hip-hop. A key feature has been a move away from the nation as the prime focus for understanding the relationship of popular music to places, and a growing emphasis on both the minutiae of locality, and on international musical movements. This has been accompanied by a growing realisation that popular music forms are no longer integrally tied to specific ethnic groups (assumptions that link white American males to rock music, Latin identities to salsa, and African-Americans to rhythm and blues). Instead, musical forms are increasingly being theorised as the result of a series of transforming stylistic practices and transnational human musical interactions. Linked to these changes has been a dissatisfaction with prevailing assumptions about theoretical approaches to how power is exercised, maintained and resisted, which have in turn informed writings about the character of individuals, collectivities and places.

In the section introductions we develop these ideas a little further and also briefly outline how the contributors to this volume advance our understanding of music in their individual chapters. In commissioning new articles by writers based in five different continents, and from many different cultural and musical backgrounds, our aim is to provide a stimulating introduction for those entering the field for the first time, and to make a contribution to the rich diversity of popular music studies. We hope that the debates contained within these pages will encourage further dialogue and diversification in the field.

References

ADORNO, THEODOR, 1976: *Introduction to the Sociology of Music*. New York: Seabury Press.

——, 1991: *The Culture Industry*, ed. Jay Bernstein. London: Routledge.

ADORNO, THEODOR AND MAX HORKHEIMER, 1979: *Dialectic of Enlightenment*. London: Verso.

BECKER, HOWARD, 1963: *Outsiders*. New York: Free Press of Glencoe.

BLACKING, JOHN, 1973: *How Musical is Man?* Seattle: University of Washington Press.

BORN, GEORGINA, 1995: *Rationalizing Culture*. Berkeley and London: University of California Press.

CHAPPLE, STEVE AND REEBEE GAROFALO, 1977: *Rock 'n' Roll is Here to Pay*. Chicago: Nelson-Hall.

COOK, NICHOLAS AND MARK EVERIST (eds), 1999: *Rethinking Music*. Oxford: Oxford University Press.

DENORA, TIA, 2000: *Music in Everyday Life*. Cambridge: Cambridge University Press.

FABBRI, FRANCO, 1982a: 'What Kind of Music?' *Popular Music* 2: 131–43.

——, 1982b: 'A Theory of Music Genres: Two Applications', in Philip Tagg and David Horn (eds), *Popular Music Perspectives*. Gothenburg and Exeter: International Association for the Study of Popular Music, 52–81.

——, 1989: 'The System of Canzone in Italy Today', in Simon Frith (ed.), *World Music, Politics and Social Change*. Manchester: Manchester University Press.

FELD, STEVEN, 2000: 'The Poetics and Politics of Pygmy Pop', in Georgina Born and David Hesmondhalgh (eds), *Western Music and its Others*. Berkeley and London: University of California Press, 254–79.

FRITH, SIMON, 1978: *The Sociology of Rock*. London: Constable.

——, 1981: *Sound Effects*. New York: Pantheon.

——, 1996: *Performing Rites*. Oxford: Oxford University Press.

FRITH, SIMON AND ANDREW GOODWIN (eds), 1990: *On Record*. London: Routledge; New York: Pantheon.

GILLETT, CHARLIE, 1971: *The Sound of the City*. London: Sphere.

GREEN, LUCY, 1997: *Music, Gender, Education*. Cambridge: Cambridge University Press.

——, 2001: *How Popular Musicians Learn: The Way Ahead For Music Education*. Ashgate: Aldershot.

GROSSBERG, LAWRENCE, 1999: 'Same As It Ever Was? Rock Culture. Same As It Ever Was! Rock Theory', in Karen Kelly and Evelyn McDonnell (eds), *Stars Don't Stand Still in the Sky*. London: Routledge; New York: New York University Press.

GUILBAULT, JOCELYNE, 1993: *Zouk*. Chicago: University of Chicago Press.

HEBDIGE, DICK, 1979: *Subculture*. London: Methuen.

HIRSCH, PAUL M., 1990/1972: 'Processing Fads and Fashions: An Organization-Set Analysis of Cultural Industry Systems', in FRITH AND GOODWIN (1990).

JONES, LEROI, 1963: *Blues People*. New York: Morrow Quill.

KEIL, CHARLES, 1966: *Urban Blues*. Chicago: University of Chicago Press.

——, 1994/1986: 'Participatory Discrepancies and the Power Of Music', in KEIL AND FELD (1994).

KEIL, CHARLES AND STEVEN FELD, 1994: *Music Grooves*. Chicago: University of Chicago Press.

LAING, DAVE, 1969: *The Sound of Our Time*. London: Sheed and Ward.
——, 1985: *One Chord Wonders*. Buckingham: Open University Press.
LOMAX, ALAN, 1964: *The Penguin Book of American Folk Songs*. Harmondsworth: Penguin.
MANUEL, PETER, 1993: *Cassette Culture*. Chicago: University of Chicago Press.
MARCUS, GREIL, 1975: *Mystery Train*. New York: Dutton.
MCCLARY, SUSAN, 1991: *Feminine Endings, Music, Gender and Sexuality*. Minneapolis: University of Minnesota Press.
MCROBBIE, ANGELA, 1980: 'Settling Accounts with Subcultures: A Feminist Critique'. *Screen Education* 34: 37–49.
MELLERS, WILFRID, 1964: *Music in a New Found Land*. London: Barrie and Rockcliff.
MIDDLETON, RICHARD, 1972: *Pop Music and the Blues*. London: Gollancz.
——, 1990: *Studying Popular Music*. Buckingham: Open University Press.
——, 2000: 'Popular Music Analysis and Musicology: Bridging the Gap', in Richard Middleton (ed.), *Reading Pop*. Oxford: Oxford University Press.
OLIVER, PAUL, 1969: *The Story of the Blues*. London: Barrie and Rockcliff.
PETERSON, RICHARD, 1976: 'The Production of Culture. A Prolegomenon', in Richard A. Peterson (ed.), *The Production of Culture*. London and Beverley Hills: Sage.
——, 1978: 'The Production of Cultural Change: The Case of Contemporary Country Music'. *Social Research* 45 (2): 293–314.
RIESMAN, DAVID, 1950: 'Listening to Popular Music'. *American Quarterly* 2: 359–71.
SCHAFER, R. MURRAY, 1977: *The Tuning of the World*. New York: Alfred A. Knopf.
SHEPHERD, JOHN, 1991: *Music as Social Text*. Cambridge: Polity Press.
SHEPHERD, JOHN, PETER VIRDEN, GRAHAM VULLIAMY AND TREVOR WISHART, 1977: *Whose Music?* New Brunswick and London: Transaction Books.
SLOBIN, MARK, 1993: *Subcultural Sounds*. Hanover and London: Wesleyan University Press.
SMALL, CHRISTOPHER, 1977: *Music, Society, Education*. London: J. Calder.
STOKES, MARTIN, 1992: *The Arabesk Debate*. Oxford: Clarendon Press.
TAGG, PHILIP, 1979: *Kojak: 50 Seconds of Television Music*. Göteborg: Skrifter fran Musikvetenskapliga institutionen, 2.
——, 1991: 'Fernando the Flute'. Institute of Popular Music Research Report. University of Liverpool.
——, 1994: 'Subjectivity and Soundscape, Motorbike and Music', in Helmi Järviluoma (ed.), *Soundscapes: Essays on Vroom and Moo*. Tampere: Department of Folk Tradition.
VAN LEEUWEN, THEO, 1999: *Speech, Music, Sound*. Basingstoke and London: Macmillan.
VULLIAMY, GRAHAM AND EDWARD LEE, 1976: *Pop Music in School*. Cambridge: Cambridge University Press.
WALSER, ROBERT, 1993: *Running with the Devil*. Hanover: Wesleyan University Press.
——, 1995: 'Rhythm, Rhyme And Rhetoric in the Music of Public Enemy'. *Ethnomusicology* 39 (2): 193–229.
WATERMAN, CHRISTOPHER, 1993: *Jújù*. Chicago: University of Chicago Press.
WHITELEY, SHEILA (ed.), 1997: *Sexing the Groove*. London and New York: Routledge.
—— (ed.), 2000: *Women and Popular Music*. London and New York: Routledge.

SECTION I

Musical meaning and history

EDITORS' INTRODUCTION

How has musical meaning been addressed in relation to social power and cultural value? By the early 1990s, the work of some critical musicologists had put musical meaning firmly on to the agenda, even if many contributions (for example, those influenced by media and cultural studies, and by sociology) tended to ignore music and treat meaning in terms of visual, spoken and written texts. Traditional musicology had rested on a certain kind of approach informed by 'structural listening', whereby musical 'works' were analysed in terms of their internal coherence and development; critical musicologists of popular song emphasised other types of experience of music. Examples of such work included Philip Tagg's ambitious and broad range of studies of musical meaning which seek to connect insights from musical analysis, social theory and studies of human perception and physiology (1987, 1993, 1997); Richard Middleton on different kinds of repetition in popular music (1986); and Robert Walser (1993) on the centrality of texture in heavy metal. By the mid-1990s, then, there was a canon of major studies (see also Moore, 1993 and the pieces collected in Middleton, 2000), which suggested a distinctive mode of analysis of the sound of popular music, focused on rhythm and texture as much as melody, harmony and structure.

An important development in recent years has been the increasing willingness of non-musicologists to engage with issues surrounding the specific ways in which music communicates. Lawrence Grossberg (1999) has suggested that, unless popular music studies addresses these specifics, then it risks being merely a subdivision of cultural studies. Grossberg's complaint draws attention to the need for popular music studies as a whole to take seriously the particularity of musical meanings – even if those sonorial significations might never be fully detached from other levels of textual meaning. Yet, as David Brackett points out in his contribution to this book, what is surprising about Grossberg's view is that he feels that popular music studies have failed to address this specificity, in spite of the existence of a rich vein of work which explicitly addresses that issue, most notably from musicologists such as Richard Middleton and Philip Tagg, but also from other quarters. Simon Frith's *Performing Rites* (1996), for example, builds on his earlier suggestion that sociologists need to address the aesthetics of popular music (Frith, 1987); anthropologist Georgina Born (1995: 16–23) has developed a theory of musical meaning influenced by social semiotics; and the project of a theory of sound has recently been elaborated by semiotician Theo van Leeuwen (1999). Music studies, then, has much to offer cultural studies in terms of how to understand the particularities of musical expression and meaning.

If the analysis of musical meaning were to become detached from related questions of social power and cultural value, then critical musicology would be back in the formalist trap it originally sought to flee. The contributions to this section make important advances in the study of these relationships; and all, in different ways, suggest the rewards of musicology's engagement with questions of history – socio-cultural, political and musical. Christopher Ballantine analyses South African popular music of the 1950s in relation to gender relations in South African society and in the music industries. Ballantine's chapter shows how the songs of the time reflected the breakdown of relations between men and women under the apartheid state's repressive pass laws. But he also argues that the musical accompaniments to songs by the Manhattan Brothers undercut and work against the nostalgic, misogynistic and bleakly morbid sentiments expressed in lyrics. They do this through their use of international and cosmopolitan idioms, and by suggesting alternatives to contemporary life through musical settings characterised by simplicity, gentleness and unity. Luiz Tatit provides an overview of the history and development of Brazilian popular song, in relation to its social, technological and institutional contexts. Tatit shows that two types of song prevailed in Brazil from the mid-1930s onwards: faster songs, associated with carnival; and slower songs, known as 'mid-year' songs. But Tatit's analysis, like Ballantine's, transcends the particular era under discussion, in suggesting a method that will allow for an analysis of the articulation of lyrics to accompaniment – a relationship which defines song itself. Fast songs, for example, rely on the rapid development of themes, and an emphasis on reiteration; this is paralleled in the lyrics by a strong emphasis on collective identity (appropriate to carnival). In slower songs, thematic development is slow, and there is a searching impulse. This is matched lyrically in love songs, where the subject needs an 'other' for completion. Tatit exemplifies his approach by analysing 'The Girl from Ipanema'.

Dai Griffiths' chapter also demonstrates that close listening need not be confined to issues of structure, but that it can expose social meaning. Griffiths compares a wide and eclectic mix of versions of the same song, to show that musicology can reveal the nuances of how ethnicity, gender and location are expressed by, and are constituted in, moments of musical style and performance. For example, he cites versions, by various women singers, of Bob Dylan's song 'Just Like a Woman', and he suggests that these covers reflect the impact of feminism, and that they help to draw attention to issues of concern raised by feminists. When Aretha Franklin covers songs by white songwriters borrowing from gospel ('Bridge Over Troubled Water', 'Let it Be') she makes a powerful political statement by taking such songs 'back to church', and re-gospelising them. In such cases, claims Griffiths, cover versions act as a form of public debate.

David Brackett's earlier studies of four songs (2000/1995) set a new standard for the combination of historical and social analysis with a close reading of details of music style. He extends this work here, by showing how difficult it was in the 1980s for black artists employing certain stylistic traits to cross over into the 'mainstream' of the Billboard Hot 100 from the 'margins' of black radio and recorded-music markets. Brackett thus combines close analysis of 'the details of musical style' with sensitivity to industrial conditions of the time, and indeed the contemporary socio-economic situation (this important idea of 'the mainstream' is also discussed by Toynbee, later in this volume). Brackett's work is exemplary, as are all the contributions here, of the potentially vital contribution that musicology can make to popular music studies; and of the interdisciplinary nature of the best popular musicology.

References

BORN, GEORGINA, 1995: *Rationalizing Culture*. Berkeley: University of California Press.

BRACKETT, DAVID, 2000/1995: *Interpreting Popular Music*. Berkeley: University of California Press.

FRITH, SIMON, 1987: 'Towards an Aesthetic of Popular Music', in Richard Leppert and McClary (eds), *Music and Society*. Cambridge: Cambridge University Press.

——, 1996: *Performing Rites*. Oxford: Oxford University Press.

GROSSBERG, LAWRENCE, 1999: 'Same As It Ever Was? Rock Culture. Same As It Ever Was! Rock Theory', in Karen Kelly and Evelyn McDonnell (eds), *Stars Don't Stand Still in the Sky: Music and Myth*. New York: New York University Press, 99–121.

MIDDLETON, RICHARD, 1986: 'In the Groove, or Blowing your Mind? The Pleasures of Musical Repetition', in Tony Bennett, Colin Mercer and Janet Wollacott (eds), *Popular Culture and Social Relations*. Buckingham: Open University Press.

—— (ed.), 2000: *Reading Pop*. Cambridge: Cambridge University Press.

MOORE, ALLAN F., 1993: *Rock: The Primary Text*. Buckingham: Open University Press.

TAGG, PHILIP, 1987: 'Musicology and the Semiotics of Popular Music'. *Semiotica* 66 (1–3): 279–98.

——, 1993: '"Universal Music" and the Case of Death'. *Critical Quarterly* 35 (2): 54–98.

——, 1997: 'Understanding Musical Time Sense: Concepts, Sketches and Consequences'. Institute of Popular Music, University of Liverpool. www.tagg.org

VAN LEEUWEN, THEO, 1999: *Speech, Music and Sound*. Basingstoke: Macmillan.

WALSER, ROBERT F., 1993: *Running with the Devil*. Hanover: Wesleyan University Press.

1

Music, masculinity and migrancy under early apartheid: gender and popular song in South Africa, *c.* 1948–1960

Christopher Ballantine

I tell here a story about South African popular music.[1] Or not quite: all stories – at least, all those worth the effort of telling – are 'about' more than just the flows, tensions and details of their own narrative. They also open upon broader perspectives, provide ways of thinking about more general issues, support or undermine related arguments developed elsewhere, in other narratives. Because these wider or more universal concerns help us to understand particular instances – because they have explanatory value – they become our theories. They may challenge other ways of making sense of the world or, in turn, be challenged themselves.

Implicitly, the story I tell is also a dialogue with several such theories. One of these, most fully developed by Adorno, is that we cannot seriously hope to explain the features of any music, or explicate its meaning in history, without precisely grounding it within a social context – including, importantly, its political economy. Related to this is another issue that I engage here very centrally: the argument that popular music tends to be deeply fractured along gender lines. What this implies is that music becomes associated with gendered identities – that gender roles, or stereotypes, are embodied in the numerous practices that make the performance of music possible, that give it audibility and visibility, that bring it to its audiences and to other musicians. These practices include, for instance, the music's own micro-economics (patterns of ownership, power and exploitation), as well as the discourses in which it is situated and in which it participates (the media, the utterances of fans, and of course its own songs and dances). Thus the character of music's gender relations at any particular time and place cannot be accounted for by looking only at the music itself: rather, we need also to look beyond the domain of music, to a broader socio-political history – a macrocosm against which the musical microcosm becomes intelligible.

But here I also involve another set of considerations: that music plays a role that is neither passive nor neutral. While it is true that music's own gender relations are clearly shaped by its socio-political context – by, in the instance discussed in this chapter, a system of labour migrancy during the early apartheid era in South Africa and the political and domestic campaigns surrounding it – it is also the case that music can, in turn, be an important role-player, itself making potent, highly visible, and sometimes even unexpected contributions. This is a vital point. It is easy to grasp how, as commercial entertainment, popular music might readily reinforce the gender stereotypes surrounding it. Yet, as I hope to show, popular music can in some senses go beyond the constraining conditions that make it possible – can, in a dialectical moment, turn towards those very conditions and have something of its own to 'say'.

In thinking through these issues – and here is yet another general issue, or theory – it is never enough to focus on the lyrics only. If we are to take popular song seriously, we will have to allow the *music* of any song to complicate the picture sketched by the lyrics – even if (as in the examples I shall discuss) this introduces the paradoxical, or the incongruous. Sheerly by virtue of its presence, music anyway always adds, or changes, meaning: it might relate to the lyrics through a process of selective emphasis; or frame the text in a particular way (ironically, for example); or raise matters not directly addressed by the lyrics (such as, in this chapter, the topic of globalisation); or point beyond – transcend – the words; or insist on something else altogether, even to the point of contradicting the words. And music is likely to make available a dimension of subjectivity, of feeling and emotion, whether or not that dimension is expressed by the lyrics themselves. In my story I discuss ample examples of musical strategies such as these.

What all this amounts to is the signal idea that popular song is not simply a 'mirror' of any particular time, place, space or social moment. Rather, it is itself a constitutive part of these, and it plays an active role in helping people to create, imagine or resist their world. When we try to understand such 'worlds', therefore – whether our own or those of people in other times and places – music can, and should, be one of our important sources of information.

My story has three parts. In the first part, I very briefly sketch some striking developments in the performance of popular music during the 1950s; in the second, I attempt to understand these as inseparable from a broad, and tragic, socio-political history; and in the third I present the evidence of the music itself. This story contains a serious contradiction, to which I later point, and to which I also offer a solution.[2]

I

The first part of the story begins in May 1952, when a commentator in the famous black South African popular magazine *Drum* drew attention to what he believed was a matter of real concern. 'Musical circles are worried', he told his readers: 'our women seem to have lost the ability to sing, act, dance or even mimic. They all clamour for equality with men, but they seem to make no effort nowadays to prove their worth against men – on the stage, anyway.' He went on to name various prominent female acts of the 1930s. By contrast, 'nearly every singing troupe today is all-male' (*Drum*, May 1952).

The anonymous writer – almost certainly the eminent popular-music critic and jazzman Todd Matshikiza – was of course writing from memory, but a scrutiny of the historical record confirms his insights. To begin with, vaudeville troupes consisting only of women, and run by women, had been a familiar feature of the musical landscape during the previous two decades. Notable all-women troupes from the thirties included the Merry Makers, the Rhythm Girls, the Movietone Cabaret Girls and the Pretoria Raven Girls; while among those from the forties were the Monte Carlo Follie Girls and the Streamline Sisters – a group that reaped praise in the black press for 'proving what non-Europeans can do in art' (*Ilanga Lase Natal*, 30 March 1946).

Though all-female groups flourished in the South Africa of the 1930s, women had played a highly visible role on the black vaudeville stage for several decades before that – as members of mixed-sex groups. Prominent mixed groups from the 1930s and 1940s included the Showboat Vaudeville Entertainers, the Gipsy Melody Makers, the Broadway Melodians, the Synco Fans, the African Minstrels and the illustrious Pitch Black Follies. For all their diversity, nothing detracts from what fundamentally unites these various combinations: they gave expression to a particular genre, a broadly common repertoire and a shared aesthetic, in which women and men participated if not on a basis of full equality, then at least on the assumption of significant parity – a real continuum that enabled women and men in principle to take part in the same kinds of ways. It was precisely the rupture of this unity that caught Todd Matshikiza's eye in 1952. Women now seemed to be disappearing from the black musical stage; or, when they did appear, they did so on a qualitatively different basis. Their involvement now largely depended on their allure: as mixed and women-only groups faded away, the primary route for an aspirant female singer or dancer was to be adopted by a male group for her sexy, decorative qualities. It was a turn of events that not only foreclosed opportunities for women and confined them to a particular stereotype on the musical stage; it also infantilised them.

Easily the most famous group of this era was the Manhattan Brothers, a male quartet whose members had been singing together since 1935. In 1953, they decided to take advantage of the special attraction that would be gained through the addition of a female singer. They chose Emily Kwenane; but within a few months she was to be replaced by a woman whom the group were to dub their 'Nut-brown Baby', with 'the voice of a nightingale'. The recipient of these diminishing metaphors – infant and bird – was none other than the young Miriam Makeba. Although she had already sung with the Cuban Brothers for two years, Makeba declared herself 'discovered' by the Manhattans, a term which does justice to the helplessness she felt as a young woman subject to powerful, collective masculine will: 'they were all gunning for me', she recalled later, 'and I guess a lady doesn't stand much chance against five he-men'.

Meanwhile, back on the stages and in the halls of the land, the gender dynamic was evolving in ways that continued to bolster masculine power, and place women ever more in the role of weak, passive victims. This manifested itself perhaps most strikingly through a dialectic: to the extent that women's musical autonomy was increasingly circumscribed, in the same measure what was increasingly 'liberated' was their availability for use as symbols of masculine prowess: women were there to be fought over, so that the male victor could then flaunt his prize as a kind of trophy. A story that illustrates this is one told by *Drum* journalist Casey Motsitsi, in which the main players were Nathan Mdledle of the Manhattan Brothers, and Miriam Makeba, their striking, recent adoptee. The year was 1956. Motsitsi relates that:

> the job of keeping off the wolves fell on Nathan Mdledle, a peace-loving character who can get hot all over if you needle him on the wrong. During a performance at the BMSC [Bantu Man's Social Centre] – the Manhattan Brothers were celebrating their 21st anniversary on the stage – Miriam came close to being riddled with bullets. While they were singing, one guy walked towards the stage and told her that that night he would 'skep' her (take her to his hide-out). When the show ended, the same guy went backstage with a few side-kicks and told Miriam that if she was ready, he was ready. To prove that he meant business, he pulled a gun and levelled it at her. Nathan Mdledle, at the risk of his own life, stood between the gunman and his Nut-brown Baby. 'Over my dead body,' he told the gunman.

> (*Drum*, May 1960)

Stories of this kind are replicated again and again – in the media of the time, in recent interviews which have sought to probe that era, and in other accounts.

Such aggressive, public displays were mirrored by other, more genteel intimations of a powerful, even irresistible, masculinity, and its effect on what were presumed to be hordes of women bursting with willingness and nubility. Here the print media played an important role, building images and conjuring fantasies around the leading male groups and their principal male singers. Matshikiza, for instance, frequently seemed agog with admiration for Nathan Mdledle's sexual power – on such occasions invoking the singer's nickname ('Dambuza') in a particularly chummy abbreviation. Thus, 'I said to Dam-Dam yesterday: "Dam-Dam, I bet you my last shirt you're the biggest playboy going on… What happened to the juicy berries I've seen hanging on you?" For Dam-Dam knows a nice dame when he sees one.' (*Drum*, December 1953.)

Attitudes such as these not only accorded women a highly circumscribed use-value: they also involved a kind of amnesia – an implicit denial of a time when the role of women in show business was somewhat different. With moments of greater musical co-operation and more equal interaction between men and women well forgotten by the male groups of the 1950s, there was little to halt their habit of gender stereotyping. And when these groups found that women could also serve them usefully off-stage (the Manhattan Brothers particularly enjoyed women's cooking and the tears of affirmation they shed), this stereotyping, and the power relations that underpinned it, were simply reinforced.

In sum, my narrative has shown that by the 1950s popular music performance in South Africa had undergone a process of profound masculinisation. This is evinced in the roles allotted to women in the production and reproduction of close-harmony performance – roles that, in comparison to the previous decades, were severely circumscribed. Women were useful for the allure of sexual frisson they could bring to a (male) group's public image and performance style – provided this sexuality was kept in check through tactics of disablement and infantilisation. They were useful for the confirmation they could bring to performers' masculine sexual identity through rituals of male contestation and female display – provided this did not carry any implication of a secure or lasting partnership. And they were useful for what they could bring to a group by way of domestic or emotional nurturance – provided this was always kept at a safe distance.[4]

II

How is the deterioration in gender relations described in this narrative to be explained? The explanation is, I believe, to be found outside the domain of music performance, in a broader socio-political history. For the overwhelming majority of South Africans of the time, the contemporary historical reality that had the greatest impact on the relationship between men and women was a complex network of legislation perfected by the apartheid state after the accession to power of the Nationalist government in 1948. This legislation controlled the entire migrant labour process: it affected the movement, access to employment, and residence of millions of people. A discussion of this system and its consequences – 'the most iniquitous system that could be visited on a people', in the words of one commentator (Ramphele, 1992: 15) – forms my second narrative.

The government had in fact come to power on a manifesto which promised to prevent further African urbanisation and remove the 'surplus' black population from the towns. This it would do through the mechanism of labour bureaux, making it compulsory for all Africans to register with these in order to find work. Only those Africans who legally obtained work would gain access to housing and services, and only then while they remained employed: those no longer employed would be removed. To this end, the government introduced legislation which consolidated those pass laws that already existed, and required all Africans to carry a uniform pass book. Linked to this was a key mechanism made possible under section 10 of the Urban Areas Act, in terms of which no African could stay in a 'prescribed area' for longer than 72 hours without official permission. The effect of such influx-control laws was to make all Africans in the towns guilty until they could prove their innocence: the police could, and did, challenge Africans at any time, and those who failed to produce a properly endorsed pass book would immediately be arrested. The entire system of influx control – including the pass laws and the nearly 600 labour bureaux that had been created by the end of the 1950s – not only prevented the growth of surplus labour in the towns; by sending people back to the rural areas, it also acted as efflux control, making it possible for labour surpluses to be redirected to the farms.[5]

For families, and for partnerships generally, the consequences of the system of labour migrancy were disastrous. In rural areas – now effectively labour reserves – poverty and ever scarcer resources meant that fewer and fewer able-bodied African men would be able to escape the scourge of becoming migrant workers, for at least some period of their lives; and, as the rural situation worsened, women increasingly fell under the same imperative. Thus during the 1950s the numbers of Africans living in the urban areas at any one time grew from 27.2 per cent of the total African population, to 31.8 per cent (in real terms, a growth from 2.3 million to 3.4 million people). In the reserves, families were in disarray, as wives and children were abandoned by husbands and fathers in search of work in the cities. Those left behind simply had to cope as best they could. This not only put relationships under a very severe strain: with many men leaving and never returning, it also steadily undermined marriage. In the towns, similarly, even for those migrants who had managed to have their families join them or who had formed new relationships, the situation was no better: here too, the role of husband or father offered women and children little security in an environment in which men could be summarily jailed for pass-law offences, or sent back to the reserves (see Walker, 1991 [1982]: 146–8; Hindson, 1987: 53; Posel, 1991b: 125–7).

It was clear by the 1950s that the reserves were scarcely able any longer to meet the needs either of those migrants who continued to view them as the place of a viable homestead to which they could return, or of the women who stayed behind and tried to eke out an existence for themselves and their families. It was a desperate situation: mired in chronic poverty, abused by the state, home to disproportionate numbers of old people, children and women, over-populated, over-grazed and eroded, the reserves had become enormous rural slums. The infant mortality rate is an index of this decay: 453 in every 1000 births (according to a survey in one district), while of the survivors 40 per cent died before reaching the age of ten. And these were the places that, by 1951, were home to nearly a third (31.09 per cent) of all South African women (Walker, 1991 [1982]: 146–67). The hardship of these women's lives was relentless and acute, as Cherryl Walker (ibid.) has shown.

This hardship drove women out of the reserves, and into the towns, in ever larger numbers. And it is a remarkable fact that, wherever they were, women courageously shouldered their burdens and strove to find ways of turning their shattered lives to creative advantage. In the reserves, for instance, they took over the management of agriculture: a government report for 1953/4 estimated that more than two-thirds of all African 'small farmers' were women. In the towns, the details might have been different but the consequences were similar. Increasingly unstable relationships between men and women, a rise in the numbers of children born outside marriage, routine imprisonment of men for pass-law offences, or expulsion from town altogether – all these meant that mothers and wives were often compelled to be the sole, or at least the primary, providers of financial and emotional support in their households.

Moreover, with two-fifths of urban households now being headed by women (in the figures of one survey), it was clear that by the 1950s a new form of family had to be reckoned with: a matrifocal, or female-headed, family. But this was not all. What was also clear was a tendency for families 'to extend in a multigenerational form on the matriline – a woman, her daughters (legitimate or illegitimate) and their daughters' (Walker, 1991 [1982]: 149). Far from this implying that women were somehow failing to take seriously their 'real' family commitments, it demonstrates, rather, that women had adjusted to the fact that men were now mainly ephemeral figures: thus women had redefined the scope of their family responsibilities, 'with the maternal role taking precedence over the conjugal' (Walker, 1990: 20).

So women redefined their relationship to men and their own position in the homestead. For men, and for masculine identity, the consequences of these shifts were deeply problematic. Had women been forced only to take on greater responsibilities as providers, it would perhaps not have mattered to men in the same way. But it went beyond this as, in the process, women also usurped some of men's power and authority, displacing them as head of the household. New research is beginning to reveal the extent to which men took this to be a usurpation of what they believed was theirs, legitimately, traditionally, even intrinsically: a usurpation of masculinity itself. As a result, some of the basic ideas of masculinity were put into question (see Moodie, 1997).

As women in the 1950s assumed greater degrees of responsibility, authority and power, it is surely no coincidence that they also became more politically powerful than ever before. For African women, this was, in fact, a decade of unprecedented political activism, of both a spontaneous and an organised kind; moreover, theirs added up to what has been called one of the decade's 'most militant and disciplined political movements' (Lodge, 1983: 150).[6]

How did men cope with all this? More precisely: Given that their world had changed so fundamentally and that this had led to a severe crisis of masculinity, what steps did men take to heal their shattered male identity? In a word, they embarked upon a strategy of gender re-empowerment. Men were wounded patriarchs; the available evidence indicates that they therefore tended to use violent and other means to redefine and reassert their authority over women. And in doing so, as Ramphele and Boonzaier have argued, they followed two legitimating paradigms: the example given by an oppressive state through the suffering it caused African men in the wider society, and, somewhat more mythically, an African 'tradition' which was held 'to justify practices that are said to be central to "African culture" (Ramphele and Boonzaier, 1988: 166).

Nowhere was this more starkly portrayed than in the subculture of black male youth gangs (*tsotsis*) that took root so widely in South Africa's towns during the later 1940s and the 1950s. The *tsotsis* created, and celebrated, an aggressive masculinity which, crucially for our present purposes, involved power over women. A gang member's 'success' with women – a triumph often inseparable from the threat or the reality of violence towards women – was a key marker of his male identity (Glaser, 1992: 47). But such attitudes were by no means confined to the gangs. For instance, an elite, middle-class magazine such as *Drum* regularly gave expression to similar attitudes; in so doing, of course, it also participated ideologically in the quest to revivify masculinity. (It hardly needs to be said that *Drum* was male-owned and managed, and was produced virtually exclusively by male writers and photographers.) *Drum* was, says Dorothy Driver, 'part of a signifying system whereby patriarchy manfully reasserted itself in the face of the destabilisation of its traditional rural form' (Driver, 1996: 232–8).

A range of other forces joined in this campaign, too. Perhaps one of the most surprising of these, at least at first sight, was the state itself. The state had, however, long sought to reinforce African male authority in the towns, and this tendency became decisive after the onset of Nationalist rule in 1948. Worried at the breakdown of African family life in the cities, the apartheid planners diagnosed the problem as lying in the fact that men no longer had 'traditional' authority over their women. So patriarchy had to be propped up: the laws governing influx control and access to housing were designed, at least in part, to buttress male power. They accomplished this in a number of ways. It was easier for a woman to stay legally in town if she was married to a legal resident; the law treated African women as minors, deprived them of rights of inheritance, and made fathers the sole guardians of their children; and in legal disputes between African men and women, customary, rather than common, law usually applied. As if this were insufficient, there were also 'official' vilifications of single women (see Posel, 1991a: 20–1).

I contend that the context sketched by this second narrative allows us to understand the principal features of the first. Indeed, what I have presented here is a socio-political history: a macrocosm against which the microcosmic account presented in my first narrative becomes intelligible. This narrative has tried to reveal a system of almost unimaginable brutality that swept everything before it. The South African migrant labour system devastated families, marriages and partnerships, produced deepening immiseration in the rural reserves, and caused women to become increasingly desperate. Women responded creatively, taking over the position of household heads, embarking upon an era of unprecedented women's activism, and developing a fierce anger towards men for what they perceived to be their selfishness and impotence.

And we have observed a final twist: that in an era in which powerful women exacerbated the crisis of male identity, men set about rehabilitating their masculinity by reifying women and displaying their power over them – an effort in which they were assisted by various forces. It is precisely here – in this last twist – that the features of my first narrative fall into place. We saw there how by the 1950s popular music performance in South Africa had undergone a process of profound masculinisation: this made men supremely dominant at the same moment that it handicapped and infantilised women, making them bearers of sexual allure for a male group's image, requiring them to confirm performers' masculine sexual identity through rituals of male contestation and female display, and restricting them to nurturing roles. The dialectics of the migrant labour system produced a crisis of masculinity which was addressed by a campaign to enable men and disable women. To this campaign, popular music performance made a vital and highly visible contribution.

III

Clearly, this second narrative not only explains the first: it also far exceeds the first in richness and complexity. On the evidence presented so far, we might say that popular music practice in the late 1940s and 1950s appears to resonate with just one aspect of the concurrent history of labour migrancy: namely, that final twist in the dialectic, the aspect having to do with the strategies for rehabilitating masculinity. And this provokes an important question: could any of this complex socio-political history have been taken up in the *aesthetic production* of the popular-music groups? Or to put this another, more provocative, way: as the music of commercial entertainment, could the music of these groups have been anything more than a superficial symptom, or a simple epiphenomenon of social reality? In what constitutes my third, and final, narrative, I answer these questions emphatically in the affirmative. I argue that the songs of the most famous and prolific group of the time – the Manhattan Brothers – do indeed engage profoundly with these social issues. This close-harmony group dealt copiously with the migrant-labour system or its consequences; and did so in a constellation of songs that is, significantly, the largest in their output.[7]

Of the songs the Manhattan Brothers recorded – probably 141 in all – 36 must be excluded from consideration immediately, in some cases because they have disappeared altogether, in others because I have not had access to them. What remains, therefore, is a total of 105 titles; and, of these, almost half (51) engage directly or indirectly with South Africa's migrant-labour system. (The other 'half' comprises such categories as songs of mainly metaphorical resistance or protest; religious songs, including instances where religious imagery is a code for political opposition or emancipation; and songs of 'traditional' provenance.)

My concern here is with those 51 songs that engage in some way with the migrant-labour system. We can divide these into four broad categories: (1) songs focusing directly on migrancy (at 22 titles, this is by far the biggest category – indeed, it is probably the biggest in their entire *oeuvre*); (2) songs of mourned love that reveal the impact of labour migrancy on marriages or partnerships; (3) songs which vilify women; and (4) songs which evoke a generalised social catastrophe. Within each category, moreover, the lyrics revolve around a number of relevant themes, or clusters of themes. For the sake of ease of apprehension, I tabulate these categories below, together with the theme clusters that constitute them. I derived the themes in the following way. First, since the overwhelming majority of the Manhattan Brothers' songs are in Zulu, Xhosa or Sotho (only a few are in English), I asked my research assistants[8] to produce full translations. I then met with each of them to discuss the translations, and to seek jointly to resolve the kinds of problems that inevitably arise during translation. My next step was a necessary expedient. Since it was clearly going to be impractical to publish, in full, the original lyrics and (where applicable) the translations of 51 songs, I set about trying to distil from each song its core issue, or most essential statement, endeavouring as far as possible to do this by using the song's own words. This of course entailed discernment, judgement and decision – a process I sometimes undertook in consultation with individual translators. In what follows, then, I give only this 'distillation' of the lyrics of each song, rather than the complete text. Frequently the songs deal with – and a 'distilled' lyric may therefore suggest – more than one theme. But in the interests of conciseness I have listed each song once only, in what seems to me to be its most appropriate category.

I now present, with minimal further comment, these thematic categories and their 'distilled' lyrics (with, in brackets, the title of each source song). One comment, however, applies to all the songs listed below, and must be made at once. The evidence brought forward in my previous narrative highlighted, in broad terms, the inhumanities of the apartheid migrant-labour system. That evidence had an objective character. In contrast, when the Manhattan Brothers deal with these issues, they give them a subjective character: thus they add important new content, and also make familiar content more precise.

Songs of migrancy

The songs in this first category focus directly on migrancy: they tell us that the pain suffered by migrant workers, as well as by their families and loved ones, was complex, nuanced and severe. It involved not only the trauma of separation, but also the fact that such people would now experience themselves as being at a material distance from those they cared about. Memory, accordingly, came to play an important part in their lives. And there are further tropes here: migrants were wanderers; in the pursuit of work, they had to deal with both the barbarous insecurities of influx control and the alienation of city life; what helped many survive was the hope that, in the end, they would go home.

Examples:[9]

- In search of work, the young brothers left, and nations died: I weep ('Makanise').
- They've disappeared over the valleys into the city – let them come back home ('Andiboni').
- I have abandoned my parents and have been wandering among 'mountains' [a metaphor here for the mine-dumps along the gold reef in the vicinity of Johannesburg] ('Abazali Bam').
- I have left my parents and crossed the mountains ('Pesheya Kweza Ntaba').
- My wandering has brought tears to my mother, and my friends have abandoned me ('Saduva').
- Tears of parting in a dark world – but we'll meet again ('Namhlanje').

Songs of mourned love

Among the most devastating effects of migrancy were, as we have seen, the destruction of family life. While a sense of this reality pervades the entire corpus under consideration here, there is a category of songs in which the Manhattan Brothers vividly indicate some of the subjective dynamics being played out at the level of marriages or partnerships. These are songs of mourned, or unhappy, love; they reveal the impact of labour migrancy on marriages or partnerships. Their lyrics turn on such themes as the loss of a partner, dependency on the lost partner, betrayal, blame and guilt.

Examples:

- I've lost my love at home in Lesotho – my life is over, I'm going home ('Komponi').
- Through my own sin I've abandoned my love, so now I'm alone and in a terrible condition ('Insono-Sami' ['Brazilian Nuts']).
- I think of you when the cattle return; I've been looking for you in the city and mountains – come back home ('Laku Tshoni' Langa').
- Remember me, Lindi, write to me – without you I'm nothing ('Phezulu Emafini').
- Sindiswa, come back home: the children are crying for their mother and I'm desolate ('Sindiswa').

Songs which vilify women

Much of the evidence presented in my second narrative bore upon the particular ways in which migrancy affected women, and women's attitudes to men – and, reciprocally, the consequences of this for what was already a crisis of male gender identity. We also saw that the state and its apparatuses played a fundamental role in helping to re-empower men at the expense of women. This next group of Manhattan Brothers songs is directly symptomatic of the new tendencies in male attitudes to women. In ways that are immediately recognisable from that second narrative – and that also recapitulate some of the themes from the first – these songs vilify women by presenting them as spendthrifts, temptresses and prostitutes, or as fickle, loose and defiled.
Examples:

- The good-time girls are soliciting men and getting paid ('Good Time Baby').
- Our girlfriends are roving from house to house, causing us problems, making our children suffer ('Mama Benkele').
- You're beguiling, you break hearts – you're a devil-woman ('Lovely Lies').
- Hey men, this woman is following me, tempting me ('Lomfazi Yandilandela').

Songs of catastrophe

We saw earlier the calamitous effects of migrancy on the economic infrastructure and socio-cultural fabric of the African population of South Africa. This final category of Manhattan Brothers songs paints a very similar picture. The songs evoke a sense of a general social catastrophe – sometimes represented as a kind of moral dissolution – and they do so primarily in metaphorical terms, through images such as collapse and death. Though the songs in this category do not name migrancy directly, their imagery is utterly consistent with it. (The fact that such imagery is often also consistent with the effects of, say, colonialism or apartheid in general, by no means detracts from this.)

Examples:

- We need more priests to stop our nation's moral decay ('Abefundisi').
- My family must flee from the thunder, rain, fire ('Dipsy Doodle').
- The rain, the flood, is going to ruin the maize ('Tsie').
- People dying as foretold by a witch ('Sangoma').

Thus far in this section, my comments have focused on lyrics only. So how does the music of the Manhattan Brothers complicate this picture? We have seen that the general context of the songs, and the explicit or implicit locus of their lyrics, is that of labour migrancy and influx control in South Africa. What is so striking, then, is that their idiom – based as it is on models such as the Mills Brothers – is so firmly metropolitan and international. Or, to put this differently, one might wonder why it is that this metropolitan, international idiom is asserted despite a context, and a set of textual themes, seemingly at odds with it. This is indeed a paradox. But the point is that the ostensibly incongruous musical idiom in fact plays a centrally important role: it frames the spatial location of the modern metropolis, which is precisely the centre around which and in which the dynamics of labour migrancy are played out, and whose presumed benefits fuel its drama. In so doing, more-over, the musical idiom unfailingly signals that this is a drama of modernity. Though the song lyrics are suffused with memory and commonly speak of return, the music insists without reservation that there can be no real return, because history has moved on. Importantly, the music performs this work even in those instances where the lyrics pull most forcefully in the opposite direction. The lyrics of a song such as 'Zulu Swing', for instance, explicitly evoke a deep notion of 'Zuluness': 'you are a nation of Zulu', the lyrics declare, 'you will need to go around like a Zulu, wandering like thunder, singing the beautiful songs from Zululand'. Yet even here the music remains uncompromisingly fixed upon its American models – even to the use of the ubiquitous harmonic progression from Gershwin's 'I've Got Rhythm', and some generic doo-wop riffs. The song therefore offers nothing less than an attempt to fuse 'Zuluness' and modernity, and to give a new meaning to Zulu identity.

The songs – lyrics and music – of the Manhattan Brothers thus conjoin two domains that one might, from a commonsense perspective, have thought to be quite distinct, with differences that were irreconcilable. The reality, as I have argued, is more complex. In seeking, and achieving, this conjunc-tion, the Manhattan Brothers showed a profound grasp of the identity and consciousness of a majority of their black South African urban contempo-raries: they knew that if they were to appeal to the urbanite or even the urban sophisticate (as they unfailingly did through their music), they would also have to appeal to the migrant still buried within his or her consciousness (as they did through their lyrics).[10]

An insistence upon modernity is, however, only one of the ways the music of the Manhattan Brothers 'complicates' the lyrics of the songs. It does so in other ways, too. The songs make particular use of irony – but it is the music of a song that in the main bears responsibility for this device. Characteristically, a song will signal a situation of pain and distress, but will at the same time point beyond it, in a gesture of transcendence. Though this transcendence may be suggested in the words, the real work of evoking it, of making it 'felt', is done by the music. Among what I have called the 'Songs of catastrophe', 'Hlompa', for example, addresses a context marked by profound alienation, and death:

	Translation:
Otlwela hle sello sammao	Can you hear your mother crying
Olla ka pelo e bo hloko	Crying with a broken heart
Okgathe tsehile ka bobe bahao	Grieved by the evil that you do
Hoba otsamaya obolaya batho	When you go around killing people
Hoba otsamaya obolaya batho	When you go around killing people

Yet when we attend to the music, we will notice that the song's musical simplicity, gentleness and 'choral' character (there are no solos) counterposes a kind of haven in which there is not only warmth and solidarity but also an attitude of social responsibility and respect. In other words, the song points to a fatal alienation not in order musically to illustrate it, but rather to illuminate an alternative to it.

This is typical of the 'Songs of catastrophe' that deal with death. 'Vuka Vuka', one of the Manhattans' most thinly disguised political songs, is a call to arms: 'death is at hand' because 'the kingdoms are coming with power'. But here what is transcended is death itself – surely in part because of the defensive call to arms, but more strikingly because the bright, vibrant music, so much in opposition to death, is a resounding evocation of life itself. 'Tsie' speaks of the political, and of death, only slightly more metaphorically, as the coming rain and flood that will destroy the maize. But musically, only the sudden ('lightning') flashes of the guitar interjections suggest the storm. For the rest, the music seems entirely to evoke an inner calmness from which the flood can be addressed, or else suggests, through its stillness, some state of transcendence beyond it. And in 'Kweminye Imizi', while the text speaks chillingly of children who are starving in houses with 'a lot of furniture', a strong hint of an Nguni drum pattern in the musical background provides both an ironic, framing context, and a 'conscience', for the text's criticism.

The music is vested with these tasks of irony in relation to a range of textual themes. For instance, in my category of 'Songs of migrancy' there are songs dealing with the pain of separation. 'Mvenane' is one: astonishingly, the music has a joyous, up-tempo character that, far from endorsing the child's tears alluded to by the lyrics, instead picks out the hints of consolation – that 'your parents...will come back with smiling faces', will bring 'delicious things', and will 'wipe the tears from your eyes'. 'Amazw' Amnandi' is not dissimilar. Addressed to young migrants, its lyrics refer to what has been lost through migrancy: here father, mother and origins are named. If there remains any 'happiness in your hearts', as the lyrics hint, only the music vouches for it. Unexpectedly bright and gentle, it is the music that makes this song heartbreakingly ironic.

In these ways, words and music in the Manhattan Brothers' songs are in a state of productive contradiction, or at least of creative tension. But of course music does not always play this 'complicating' role in their work. The Manhattans also give music a simpler, more immediate relationship to lyrics: music then performs the age-old task of word-painting, in which it seeks to illustrate the lyrics. When this happens, the subjectivities of the lyrics seem to find an eloquent voice. In the 'Songs of migrancy' category, for instance, where many lyrics speak of the pains of separation, the music aims to find a musical expression of these feelings. Often this happens most strikingly in a solo vocal part, through a musical representation of weeping, or of wailing. Examples include the bluesy, bent-note final solo as a poignant expression of the cries of migrant loneliness in 'Abazali Bam'; Miriam Makeba's solo in 'Tula Ndivile', where one hears both the anguish of homelessness and a plea to the weeping mother to 'stop crying!' (*'O, thula mama, thula, thula ma, thula ma ukulila ma'*); or the blue-note lamentations in 'Pesheya Kwezo Ntaba', in which a migrant regrets having abandoned home. Other subjective manifestations are also represented musically: tearful parting in 'Namhlanje', or the restless agitation of the sleep-deprived migrant in 'Sana Lwam'; or, indeed, the depth of feeling associated with home in 'Izikhalo Zegoduka'. In this song, an unhappy migrant, disappointed by his experience of Johannesburg, sings of going back home and reuniting with the woman he loves. The pervasive, cyclical group vocalisations (*'hewu, hewu, hewu'*), like the repeated drum pattern, are hints of 'traditional' music and suggest something of what, on his return journey, 'crossing the Gqili [river]'[11] will mean to him.

Since music operates in this illustrative manner through each of my four song categories, the kinds of mood or emotion that attain musical representation are remarkably diverse. This diversity includes also a prayerful musical invocation of the 'Holy Spirit' to help save a nation that is disintegrating through moral decay ('Abefundisi'); a moving musical plea for release from the pain of alienation in one's own motherland ('Somandla'); and slow ballads in which prominent, lyrical vocal solos give musical form to a variety of feelings associated with the loss of a partner ('Marie', 'No Goli', 'Khumbula Jane', 'Ungowami' and 'Laku Tshoni' Langa').

Finally, in many songs the music seeks to illustrate not just an emotion, but rather a particular situation or event as seen from the perspective of the text's own subjective standpoint. The music of 'Bayandi Biza', for example, conjures 'home' in a specific way. The lyrics tells us that a migrant 'hears' his parents calling him home: this is represented musically by an insistent, background trumpet 'call', which is then echoed in vocal scatting (*'dudududu'*). Not only is any nativist notion of 'home' problematised by such modernist inflections; 'home' now also means that 'my brothers are dead, my fathers are dead' – a realisation that the music captures through a moment suggestive of hymnody. In 'Manyeo' – to shift perspective – the percussive disruptions in the sung melodic line stand, musically, for what the migrant says to his supposedly fickle woman ('Hey you! Don't behave like that!'); and the song's rhythmic unpredictability – particularly through the counterposition of different orders of triplets – mimics the woman's supposed waywardness. Similarly, in 'Lomfazi Yandilandela', a pervasive, dancing clarinet *obbligato* can be read as a musical image of the temptress mentioned in the lyrics: the woman who is 'waiting for me', 'following me', 'tempting me'.

Conclusion

What I have called my third narrative is subjectively richer than the second, just as the second is objectively richer than the first. But this third narrative also invites comparison with the first, since both of course refer directly to aspects of popular music or its practices in South Africa during the 1940s and 1950s. Nevertheless, these first and third narratives differ utterly. The first describes the masculinisation of popular music performance by the 1950s, a process that had put men into a position of complete dominance. This process had also handicapped women by limiting them to carriers of sexual frisson for men's groups, had reduced them to passive objects of contestation and display, and had restricted them to nurturing roles. The third narrative, by contrast, shows that at least at the level of aesthetic production, the (all-male) leading vocal group of the era speaks to a very different set of relationships with, and concerns about, women: because the songs of the Manhattan Brothers engage deeply with the social and political issues of the time, they are suffused subjectively with pain, dependency and loss. While attitudes that diminish women are not absent from the songs, the proportion these occupy is small in relation to the general concerns of this corpus, and tends to insignificance when placed against all the ways in which the songs actually value women. The first and third narratives, then, largely contradict each other.

In the face of such disparities, it would be tempting to conclude that one of these accounts must be wrong, or that the third narrative – because it has in a small way transposed this contradiction into its own structure – must be incoherent. But such conclusions would miss the point. For once we read the contradiction between the first and third narratives (and within the third) *against* the second narrative, as the socio-political history that grounds these other stories – once we do this, then the contradiction falls away. Or better: the contradiction remains, but we understand both sides of it to be true. Men in South Africa during the 1940s and 1950s reified women, undermined and vilified them, strove aggressively to assert unbridled power over them; and *at the same time* men grieved for their women, agonised over their loss, despaired about what could be done, worried about their children.

If this is a more complete – a more complex – picture of a historical social reality than we would otherwise have had, the reason is that we have resolved an (apparent) contradiction through an understanding of its material foundation. But there is a further reason: we have also taken serious account of popular song, and thus grasped a hidden – subjective – reality. For popular music, in its interiority, can present us with real subjective evidence that may not be available in other discourses. Indeed, this evidence may at times not be available anywhere else at all. Popular music may thus not only be a repository of significant social memory; it may also be a unique social record.

Notes

1.   I presented a preliminary version of this chapter as a paper at the Tenth International Conference of the International Association for the Study of Popular Music, in Sydney, in July 1999. A different version of this chapter appeared in Ballantine (2000). That version is a much more detailed presentation of the argument, and includes a discography. I thank Rob Allingham, the archivist for Gallo Africa (Pty.) Ltd., for his expert assistance with discographical matters, and the University of Natal for its contribution to research funding.

2.   For a history of South African popular music up to the mid-1940s – or a prehistory of the present story – see Ballantine (1993).

3.   The gender dynamics in other male groups that had opted to import a decorative female singer were, typically, identical to these. See Ballantine (2000).

4.   During the 1950s, instances of notable opposition by women themselves to this situation of generalised exploitation were extremely rare; moreover, as efforts at autonomy they were at best problematic. See Ballantine (2000) for examples.

5.   For more information see Hindson (1987: 60–3) and Posel (1991b: 124 and passim).

6.   There was no shortage of immediate occasions for such activism. See Ballantine (2000).

7.   The Manhattan Brothers were Nathan 'Dambuza' Mdledle, Joe Mogotsi, Rufus Khoza and Ronnie Sehume. The group recorded almost entirely on 78 r.p.m. shellac discs: the very first reissue of a selection of their songs was released in South Africa in October 1999. The compilation, on compact disc, is by Rob Allingham and is entitled *The Very Best of the Manhattan Brothers: Their Greatest Hits 1948–59*. Several of the songs discussed in this chapter can be found on the CD. In an earlier study (Ballantine 1999), I dealt with the output of the Manhattan Brothers in relation to a different, but complementary, set of socio-political imperatives.

8.   Temba Mbhele, Prince Kupi, Tobeka Ramncwana and Xoli Nkosi, all at the University of Natal, Durban.

9.   For reasons of space, I give here and below selected examples only. For further examples see Ballantine (2000).

10.   William Beinart's research into the consciousness of South African workers provides convincing independent corroboration of the point at issue here. In work carried out many years after the era of the Manhattans, Beinart investigated the peculiar intersection of worker consciousness, ethnic particularism and nationalism in South African migrants in the three decades before 1960. He showed that there were important continuities in migrant consciousness, notwithstanding the radical changes migrants suffered. See Beinart (1987).

11.   Officially known as the Vaal river.

References

DRIVER, DOROTHY, 1996: ' "*Drum*" Magazine (1951–9) and the Spatial Configurations of Gender', in Kate Darian-Smith, Liz Gunner and Sarah Nuttall (eds), *Text, Theory, Space: Land, Literature and History in South Africa and Australia*. London and New York: Routledge.

GLASER, CLIVE, 1992: 'The Mark of Zorro: Sexuality and Gender Relations in the Tsotsi Subculture on the Witwatersrand'. *African Studies* 51 (1): 47–68.

HINDSON, DOUG, 1987: *Pass Controls and the Urban African Proletariat*. Johannesburg: Ravan Press.

LODGE, TOM, 1983: *Black Politics in South Africa since 1945*. Johannesburg: Ravan Press.

MOODIE, T. DUNBAR, 1997. 'Manliness in Migrants and Colonizers: Vicissitudes of Male Desire'. Paper presented at Colloquium on Masculinities in Southern Africa. University of Natal, Durban.

POSEL, DEBORAH, 1991a: 'Men's Authority: Rethinking Patriarchy'. Paper presented at Conference on Women and Gender in Southern Africa, University of Natal, Durban.

——, 1991b: *The Making of Apartheid 1948–1961*. Oxford: Oxford University Press.

RAMPHELE, MAMPHELE, 1992: 'Social Disintegration in the Black Community', in David Everatt and Elinor Sisulu (eds), *Black Youth in Crisis: Facing the Future*. Johannesburg: Ravan Press.

RAMPHELE, MAMPHELA AND EMILE BOONZAIER, 1988: 'The Position of African Women: Race and Gender in South Africa', in Emile Boonzaier and John Sharp (eds), *South African Keywords*. Cape Town and Johannesburg: David Philip.

WALKER, CHERRYL, 1990: 'Women and Gender in Southern Africa to 1945: An Overview', in Cherryl Walker (ed.), *Women and Gender in Southern Africa to 1945*. Cape Town: David Philip; London: James Currey.

——, 1991 [1982]. *Women and Resistance in South Africa*. Cape Town and Johannesburg: David Philip; New York: Monthly Review Press.

2

Analysing popular songs

Luiz Tatit

Translated by *Lorraine Leu*

In 1965, issue no. 6 of the journal *Communications* published a pioneering article on commercial song written by Edgar Morin. The very title of the piece, 'We Know Nothing about Popular Song', was ahead of its time in criticising academic indifference to this form of artistic expression whose emergence was seen as being contaminated by technological progress and the vices of the culture industry. Its origins were pedestrian and lay outside of accepted aesthetic frameworks. Scholars therefore ignored all of commercial song's merits – even its undeniable popular success – which would have made song a worthy object of analysis, much like cinema, comics or pop art. In other words, for the French scholar, what had been dismissed by the elite required closer examination.

His comments represented only the tip of the iceberg – at that time the worldwide Beatles phenomenon was still incipient – but Morin was already calling attention to the fact that any future study of popular song would have to take as its starting point the 'totality of music and lyrics'. At that time, Morin was still unable to conceive of a descriptive model for constituent elements of the music, maintaining that they were resistant to conceptual analysis. However, he believed that rhythmic movement and instrumental arrangement were sufficient to facilitate classification of the songs into 'genres, styles and modes', which would later serve to orient a sociological approach to the study of song.

The year 1996 saw the publication, once again in France, of a comprehensive dictionary of world song, which has been produced since 1945. The work recognises song as an autonomous artistic form with aesthetic rules of its own, which relies on the voice for communication. This work merits special mention, since it is unusual to find such a wide-ranging work whose selection of entries relies on ideas that are still not universally accepted. For example, its organisers clearly distinguish between song and instrumental music, such as much of jazz music. For them, instrumental music also 'constitutes a discipline in itself, quite different from the form of popular expression that is song' (Plougastel, 1996: 175).

These events are significant precisely because they occurred in France, a country with a long conceptual tradition, but which is not often immediately identified with the world of commercial song. The latter is widely acknowledged to be based on the American continent and to find its greatest expressive forms in England. Perhaps because it maintains a reasonable distance from the whirlwind of the commercial music scene, the French approach has managed to decipher more successfully the basic characteristics of the aesthetics of sound, contributing to a more considered approach to the establishment of analytical parameters.

Song is a composite of melody, lyrics, voice and instrumental arrangement which should not be confused with the way we think of music in the strict sense, or even with popular practices for creating sound and improvisations which dispense with singing. This is a necessary analytical strategy, not an attempt to compartmentalise and stagnate artistic language. Lacking adequate means to describe what the composer – or the performer – has actually produced, the critic tends to devalue song, which does not possess the refinements typical of other areas of the arts.[1] By failing to highlight the characteristics of song in which its greatness lies, such approaches can only serve to marginally widen the concept of music and literature to include songwriters who can be likened to erudite artists. In Brazil, therefore, even when artists deny a link with 'high' culture, songwriters such as Tom Jobim, Chico Buarque and Caetano Veloso are frequently portrayed as professionals deserving respect from critics and fellow songwriters alike, because of the elements of erudite music and literature in their work.

Only when the specific characteristics of the language of popular music are understood and appreciated will the critic be suitably equipped to evaluate the effect of its interaction with other languages, as well as the extent of its interventions into the social, aesthetic and cultural worlds. After all, song is becoming less and less of a pure form. Radio song has increasingly lost ground to televised song, because of the overwhelming presence of music videos. As a result, popular song has been incorporating the image into its basic forms of communication, which has introduced considerable complexity to its analysis.

In this study, although necessarily restricted to the Brazilian music world, I intend to characterise elements of the language that makes commercial song a global object of desire. In fact, any demonstration of the inner workings of a song, regardless of its origin, should also reveal the elements that will be highlighted here.

The role of recording

Consciously or not, the elements which constitute popular song were present in all of the historical moments in which the voice dominated the musical soundscape. Of all musical instruments, the voice is undeniably the manifestation of sound most closely identified with the 'sensitive being' (Rousseau, 1970: 175) which produces it. Additionally, it is impossible to separate the singing voice from the speaking voice, as to do so would result in an artificial distinction, since the singing voice is always saying something, even if the content remains in the background.

All countries learnt to cultivate their songs as a real necessity for the preservation of ethnic and cultural traditions, independently of the progress made in the field of musical or literary creation. At the end of the nineteenth century, however, a particular technological advancement – recording – came to alter the aesthetic conventions of song that had been previously established in the West. Until then, literature had survived in volumes on library shelves and music had endured through written scores, while song, entrusted to memory and oral tradition, was constantly being transformed into different versions. Gradually one version would give way to the next and the singing voice almost always yielded to the ephemeral instability of the speaking voice. Recording was established as the first effective way of registering and preserving these forms, which had a significant effect on their acceptance as an aesthetic type.

The arrival of early recording technology in Brazil coincided with a period of intense musical activity. Slavery had recently been abolished (1888) and the waged labour market was unable to absorb the excess skilled labour. Entry to the liberal professions depended on apprenticeship and training, an option not open to the majority of the black population. Former slaves therefore either continued working in the sugar mills, accepting whatever conditions were laid down by the owners, or migrated to urban centres in search of scarce employment opportunities. During this period, many blacks and mulattos who originated from the state of Bahia settled in the Saúde neighbourhood of Rio de Janeiro, then the country's capital. This group found itself economically and culturally marginalised by the demands of the new urban market, which was gradually dismantling the agrarian structure in favour of an incipient process of modernisation. In the face of this marginalisation, they turned to the houses of the so-called *tias*, Bahian women who practised religious rituals, held social gatherings and ensured that the customs and traditions of the ancestors survived in the new environment. Apart from being renowned for their cooking skills, the *tias* could also sing, improvise verses and dance to the rhythm of the *batucadas*[2] that would eventually give rise to *samba*. Their houses were taken over by musicians, enthusiasts and the jobless, who, while they awaited employment, would be working instead on their rhythmic and melodic skills.

According to Muniz Sodré, in the drawing-rooms of these houses, more refined music was played (polkas or even *lundus*)[3] while the back of the house was given over to *samba de partido alto* (a type of samba performed in a circle which alternates between song and dance). The backyard was the domain of *batucada*, which still maintained some of its original religious functions. In any case, these houses contained a considerably representative sample of Brazilian popular music in the early twentieth century. This characteristic distribution of musical genres into permeable, yet distinct compartments was not just the result of class differences between the musicians. It actually responded to practical concerns: the sambas performed at the back of the house were expressly prohibited by the police in public spaces.

Outside of the protected space of these houses, only Brazilian music after a European fashion was given an airing. The producers of this music, which was always transcribed into scores, showed no interest whatsoever in the new recording equipment, as the preservation of their work was already guaranteed. Additionally, these precarious technical resources were far from capable of faithfully reproducing the minute details of their creations. Neither did the pioneers of the cylinder phonograph consider any application of the new technology to this already consecrated field of erudite expression. Instead they focused on recording the voices of the last representatives of the Empire and the first Republican leaders.[4] Their intention was to turn to music after their successes in the area of speech recording.

At that moment, the search for an ideal song and the pressing need to record were united. On the one hand, the producers discovered a technically viable instrumental form for recording in those backyards, in so far as all the sounds centred on the voice. On the other hand, these improvisers of sung verses needed to register their musical and poetic creations, which were vanishing day by day, like simple manifestations of everyday speech. Some singer-songwriters, like Baiano, Cadete, Nozinho and Eduardo das Neves, were then plucked from the *tias'* houses and professionally contracted by Edison to make Brazil's first records.

Carnival and 'mid-year' songs

The general physiognomy of Brazilian popular music was now configured, centred on the form of vocals and accompaniment. However, it took thirty more years to fully define what we know today as popular song. In addition to recording, which demanded a certain preparation of the song for the available technical resources, two other factors contributed to define the ideal song form, which was already focused by this time on the incipient consumer market. The first was the consolidation of radio as the primary vehicle for the diffusion of popular song creations. The second was the consecration of carnival as the most important festival in the country, towards which a large part of annual song production was channelled. In addition to the question of aesthetics and entertainment, these factors introduced into the developing language of song a utilitarian aspect that would always influence the practice of song composition and performance in Brazilian popular music. From that moment on, apart from being aesthetically pleasing, a good song also had to contain consumer appeal.

Months before carnival, competitions were organised to choose the most representative *marchinhas* (marches) or sambas of the period. The winners were announced on the radio relatively quickly, and this had immediate repercussions on the sales of records, which had been making use of advances in electro-magnetic technology since 1927. It was at this time that the typical form of the genre was confirmed as having two distinct parts, with one of these almost always identified as the refrain. This format was reproduced *mutatis mutandis*, in the songs produced during the rest of the year, but with a clear difference in tempo. If the carnival songs were always accelerated as befitted the atmosphere of the festival, the so-called 'mid-year' songs slowed down the rhythm in order to adequately treat the theme of love which also had its place in the popular imagination.

As a result, the two main forms of creating sound in popular song forms emerged, both based on the meeting of melody and lyrics. The accelerated form tended to reduce vowel sounds to their stresses, which in turn seemed to fuse with the accentuation of the consonants. Precisely because of this dominance of accentuation, the rhythmic motifs were outlined more clearly, projected in the phonic chain as reiterative or contrasting units. The prevalence of reiterative elements was always one of the main resources of fixing the melody in the memory. The slow form was based on the prolonging of the sound of the vowels, foregrounding the full extent of the intonational process. The fixing of the melody was consolidated more by the lingering of the voice on each vowel and by the gradual building up of the melody than by the formation of motifs or themes. Because of this, the oscillations in pitch are always more meaningful in slower songs.

It is worth emphasising that Brazilian popular song has never lost its intonational root. This means that throughout popular song's history the natural relationship between intonation and everyday verbal language has remained intact. The descending intonational phrases indicate affirmation, the ascending or suspended phrases (those which neither rise nor fall) suggest continuity of communication, the melodic emotional inflexions produce emphases here and there in the chain of the linguistic text. Overall, the spontaneous compatibility between speech and its appropriate intonation, as well as other characteristics of speech, are preserved on an artistic plane in popular song. Frequently the popular composer will attempt to disguise them with the rules of musical composition, in order to ennoble the creative gesture. However, it has become increasingly clear that the persuasive power of a song lies precisely in this intonational process (in Barthes' 'grain of the voice') which makes the performance believable, even if the performer does his or her best to camouflage it.

Therefore, this way of *figurativising* songs (creating the impression that the sung phrases would be spontaneously uttered in speech with the same melodic inflexions) underlies all the genres which have developed over the twentieth century. This applies to songs with a slow or a fast pace, and occasionally it even develops into a separate genre. This is the case, for example, with *samba de breque*,[5] which like radio was also consolidated in the 1930s; with *repente*, the traditional regional rhythm of the north-east of Brazil; and with contemporary rap music.

Thematic and *passional* songs

For the moment, let us examine what we have come to call fast and slow song forms. The suitability of the fast form to carnival and the slow form to the rest of the year is more than just a question of physical stimulus. It is more than just a distinction between the so-called 'dance' music produced by the first and the more relaxing effects of the latter. The rapid development of themes in faster songs influences a similar development in the pace of the melody, based on the reiteration and unfolding of these thematic elements. Each theme is integrated into a melodic sequence by means of a simultaneous process of identity and alterity. In the first place, all themes contain traces of preceding and subsequent themes, which confer a chronological identity upon them within a song: they are a little of what has gone before and a little of what is to come (see Lopes, 1989–90: 157). Second, every theme has a certain degree of singularity which distinguishes it and defines it as an 'other' in the sequence. The greater the number of identity markers, the greater the cohesion of the sequence and the slower the progress of the narrative. The melody appears to be going nowhere as it continually reverts to what went before, whether it is to the small units of the song – what we can term *thematisation* – or to the integral parts – what we know as the refrain. The dominance of the identity markers corresponds, therefore, to a process of melodic involution. However, actual songs are rarely restricted to the extreme situation described here. In order for us to recognise the identity markers, the themes must develop into different (or even marginally different) rhythmic or melodic resolutions, in order to produce a certain degree of evolution within the song. Finally, a refrain is only defined as such when the song takes a different direction, thereby creating a profound sense of anticipation of a return to the refrain.

This movement of fast-paced melody is paralleled to a considerable degree in the linguistic component of the song. Within the song's linguistic content, identity is expressed through the encounters between subjects, or in the encounters between subject and object. The subject voice develops out of past and future achievements within the space of the song. Because of the subject's need for completion – that is, for integrating with its equal and with its world – it links itself to the past and the future and is consolidated as a being in transition. However, as this being never attains perfection (completion), the subject is also defined by a continuous absence. It no longer possesses everything it possessed before, and still does not possess everything it would like to possess in the future. If, on the one hand, this feeling of absence fractures the integrity of its identity, on the other, it also restores to it the idea of alterity: the subject needs the 'other' in order to be complete.

It is widely acknowledged that in fast songs identity markers predominate, both in the melody and the lyrics. The musical reiterations resist, as much as possible, the evolving force of the sound, as if the melodic themes were already self-sufficient. Fast songs are concentrated around the refrain and the predominant rhythmic motifs, from which they only depart in order to emphasise their return. This melodic fullness, characterised by little need of the 'other', is clearly reflected in the lyrics. The subjects of fast songs celebrate encounters and successes over misunderstanding and loss experienced in the past, or imagined in the future. These subjects are strengthened by being united with their objects and through links with other subjects. This reinforcing of identity produced both in the melody and the lyrics is what conveys the impression of *compatibility*, and what makes the marches and sambas of the 1930s appropriate to the euphoria of carnival.

In slow songs, alterity prevails. Prolonging the durations of the tones slows down the progress of the melody. This significantly checks the development of the themes, or they are redirected towards other sound spaces more often than not by the tones. These movements develop out of a searching impulse that the other song genre does not possess. At any given point in its trajectory, this type of melody appears to be in transit, needing other elements in order to be complete.

Within the themes elements of identity are configured, in one way or another. However, these identities never satisfy the searching impulse of each segment which maintains the progress of the melody. This constant evolution creates an overall sense of gradual progress, both of the notes (as if following the contours of a scale), as well as of the motifs. The melody moves higher or lower, but frequently the sense of continuity is broken by intervallic leaps, whose main effect is occasionally to quicken the slow evolution of the sound. However these leaps are always followed by a gradual movement which re-establishes continuity in the relatively controlled progress of the song.

This search for completion in the area of melody is evident in the lyrics in the form of lovers' misunderstandings and of separations between subject and object. There is always a subject who needs an 'other' in order to constitute his or her own identity. The subject feels linked to this other on a temporal level (s/he remembers someone or something from the past, or nurtures hope for a future encounter), but acknowledges the spatial distance between them. Subjective conflict and typical *passional* tension is derived from this. However, the dissatisfaction produced by the separation is, generally, the element which influences the movement of the melody. Quite apart from the number of thematic identities (reiterations), the slow melody becomes a quest, which appears to be attempting to recover the lost contact described in the lyrics.

These characteristics of the two types of popular song – *thematic* or *passional* – were consolidated in Brazil with the advent of radio in the 1930s, in the form of carnival and mid-year songs. These characteristics were responsible for what was seen at the time as a welcome triumph of 'stable song' over 'unstable speech'. Much more than a single development without widespread impact, they defined an approach to making melody and lyrics compatible which would be fundamental to songwriting thereafter. While it is possible that these characteristics may appear in commercial song production around the world, in each region the consolidation of these traits has certainly resulted from specific local, cultural and technical conditions and markets.

Case study

To give a practical example of these characteristics, let us turn our attention to 'The Girl from Ipanema' (Tom Jobim and Vinícius de Morais), a Brazilian

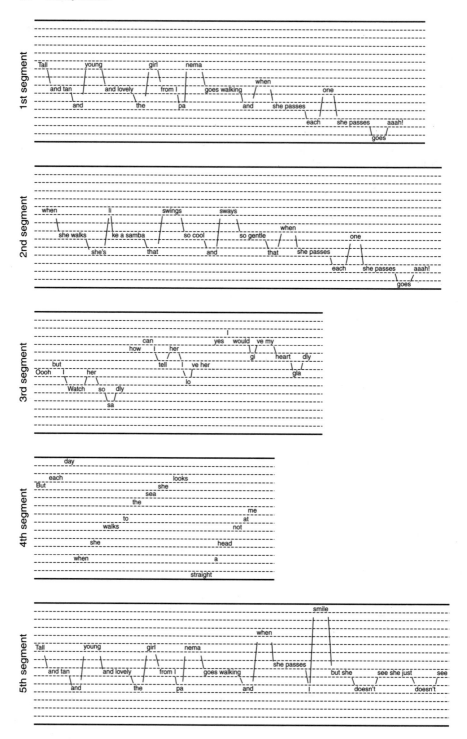

Figure 2.1

song which is very widely known and already exists in an English version (see Figure 2.1):[6]

Tall and tan and young and lovely
The girl from Ipanema goes walking
And when she passes
Each one she passes goes 'aaah!'

When she walks she's like a samba
That swings so cool and sways so gentle
That when she passes
Each one she passes goes 'aaah!'

Oh, but I watch her so sadly
How can I tell her I love her?
Yes, I would give my heart gladly
But each day when she walks to the sea
She looks straight ahead not at me

Tall and tan and young and lovely
The girl from Ipanema goes walking
And when she passes
I smile, but she doesn't see
She just doesn't see,
No, she doesn't see.

The first two segments constitute a kind of melodic refrain which plays an intensifying role within the song, not just because of the basic reiteration (the second segment repeats the first), but chiefly because of the highlighted identity markers of its internal themes:

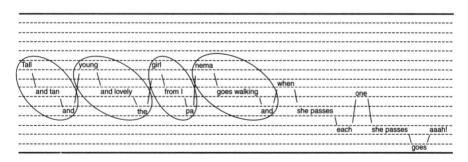

Figure 2.2

Even when the first altered intervals begin to emerge – which, from the fifth thematic unit, directs the movement of the melody towards the lowest pitch – the predominance of identity markers is still felt:

- the design of the melodic motif is basically the same:

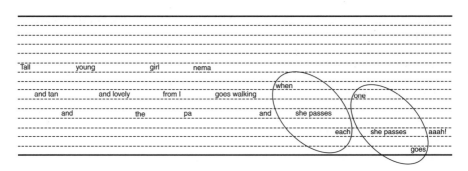

Figure 2.3

- and the descent obeys a tonal gradation which, like all gradation, can be anticipated (in this sense, the descending or ascending gradation reproduces, on the 'vertical' axis, the same amalgamation of musical elements that the reiteration promotes on the 'horizontal' axis):

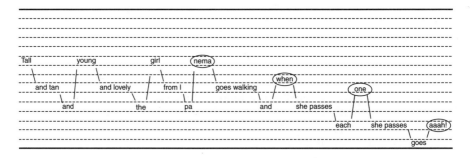

Figure 2.4

On the other hand, one cannot deny that the internal alterations and the resulting change of direction of the melody indicate, even if in a recessive form, an example of musical development directed by the idea of alterity. This alterity does not attenuate the intensifying force of the refrain. However, its small irregularities do point to the presence of the 'other', in this case of the other melodic material whose direction is not restricted to a return to the refrain.

A closer examination of the first segment will clarify the processes that consolidate identity and alterity in the melodic sequences.

The initial thematic units are identical as far as their frequency and rhythmic patterns or contours are concerned. However, with regard to the position they occupy within the syntagmatic chain, there are always differences between them, however minimal. Putting the lyrics aside for the moment, we can confirm that the melodic sequence of 'young and lovely the...' is different from the initial 'Tall and tan and...', at the very least because it follows it in the melodic line. The note for the word 'young', for example, is the starting point of the second thematic unit, but is also heard as a point of arrival of the previous unit; this is sufficient to differentiate it from 'Tall' which only has an inchoative[7] function. A little further on, the note for the word 'girl', apart from absorbing the flow of the preceding themes, is modulated by the change in chord which always produces the effect of a change in direction of the melody. Finally, the note corresponding to the syllables '...nema' retrospectively confirms the process of thematic reiteration (or melodic involution), but previews the new direction of the music (the melodic evolution). In other words, at the same time that it

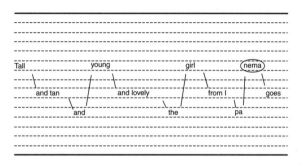

Figure 2.5

introduces the last unit in the process of thematisation, the fragment '...nema' implants the descending movement which unfolds into the notes corresponding to 'when' and 'one', until reaching the sighed 'aaah':

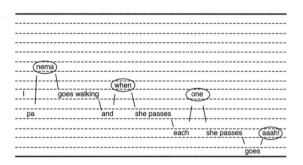

Figure 2.6

These observations demonstrate that the elements that establish identity in a song are also imbued with elements of alterity, which is why the melody always appears to be in progress. Notwithstanding this, the predominance of thematisation, with its numerous resources for the assimilation of one motif by another, maintains the tendency to concentration. The basic repetition of the melody in the second segment further reinforces the emphasis on the involution of the melodic line.

These identity markers are conveyed in the lyrics in different ways. The figure of the 'girl from Ipanema' is composed of a group of attributes which make her unmistakeably female. Apart from what we might call her more 'statistical' qualities ('tall', 'tan', 'young', 'lovely'), the girl is presented as being blessed with bodily movements which are so attractive that merely the way she walks ('goes walking', 'she passes') becomes another aspect of her identity. We therefore have a series of junctions between the protagonist and her attributes which translate lyrically the continuity and repetitions of partially identical melodic motifs and their concentrational force. Additionally, there is the well-known presence of a narrator who not only describes the scene, but also includes himself in it as an emotionally involved eyewitness. In this way, the functions of subject and object are consolidated: the girl exercises her powers of attraction, while the narrator directs full attention to her.

However, it so happens that the full definition of the subjective state (the state of the subject) depends on the relationship that is maintained with the object. A subject in complete communion with the object would have its identity fully defined but would immediately cease to be a subject, since the latter is always produced by a feeling of absence or need of the 'other'. A total (and hypothetical) identification between the subject and object would ensure completion of the subject, but would certainly thwart its sense of purpose. The tensions that propel the subject towards its goals would disappear.

Returning to our example, we can say once again that there is identification and alterity at the same time between the narrator and the character of the girl. The identification is manifested in the attraction and desire that end up creating a kind of 'long-distance union' between them. Alterity is evident in the absence of physical contact that is already suggested in the first verses. In other words, following what was described earlier, this state of contemplation between subject and object is configured as a temporal proximity – based on hope in a possible encounter – which coexists with the spatial distance. The discrete melodic developments that we find in the first segments represent the musical signs of this separation between subject and object. This is the reason why, on abandoning the simple reiteration of the initial thematic unit, the melody outlines a descending trajectory, as if it were searching for something which it still does not possess. Considering, however, that this movement towards the grave relies on the same rhythmic motifs and the same melodic contours that had characterised the thematisation, what remains is a general sense of significant identification. This contributes to emphasising the suggestion of an encounter between subject and object in the first part of the lyrics, to the extent that this emphasis is maintained until the beginning of the second part, represented by the third segment of the diagram:

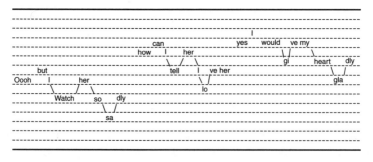

Figure 2.7

We can say that in this passage, the main melody is finally denied in favour of other musical activity: the tones are dilated (the vowels are prolonged), the pattern of the new themes is modified and the direction of the melody becomes ascending.

More than just a simple thematic change, the move to the third segment represents a significant alteration of speed within the musical structure. What was:

Figure 2.8

becomes:

Figure 2.9

The slowing down of the speed itself immediately brings about a change in the melody, in the sense that it attenuates the effects of the vowel accentuation and consonantal attack, and so dilutes the structural formation of the motifs which is typical of faster songs. The deceleration tends to exchange motifs for progression or, in other words, concentration for extension. Unable to enjoy immediate encounters within the motifs – since they lose their clarity – a slow melody generally contains within it the absence of the 'other'. Because of this it seems to evolve as if its objective were to find its own identity (i.e. define its melodic project) at some point in its progression. This project, which is at times materialised in a refrain, for example, can become lost in the irregularities of the melody and end up nowhere. In any case, it never completes its trajectory without leaving a sonorous trace of its intentions (directions taken or simply suggested) to which the harmonic base contributes a great deal. There is, however, a reason why the decelerated melody carries *passional* content: it contains within it both missed encounters and the quest. The melody needs to define a direction which touches on the irregularities and so shows the predominance of the principle of alterity. Each melodic motif is justified as part of a syntagmatic whole that will only be fully evident when the whole melodic project is complete.

The accelerated melody creates a space within the song of almost self-sufficient thematic identities and is therefore appropriate to the celebration of encounters. The *passional* melody, however, is always pointing towards a future moment in its evolution which in reality is only attained at the end of the song. The fast melody makes the musical process its own end, with this process experienced as a conjunctive period in which the subject is permitted to savour its integration with the object.[8] In the slow melody the musical process is simultaneously transient and dependent on what is to come. It compensates for the insufficiencies of its isolated motifs with the construction of rich itineraries. In other words, the *passional* melody needs the effects of insufficiency generated by its musical process in order to be compatible with lyrics that also convey feelings of loss.

The second part of 'The Girl from Ipanema' (third segment) introduces, therefore, some variations which are worth pointing out:

1. structural deceleration of the melodic component;
2. ascending movement of its sonorous elements;
3. the establishment of a melodic 'verticality' which undoes the rigorous 'horizontal' axis on which all of the first (and the last) part rests.

The prolonging of the notes coincides with the suspension of thematic activity that was dominant until then. It is as if the 'other' were showing itself at last in all of its splendour. The decelerated form makes each note important, particularly the longer ones, de-articulating the thematic progression and calling attention to the direction of the song's trajectory. The integration of the motifs is substituted for the quest which is undertaken throughout the range. In this case, the sense of searching is consolidated in the ascending movement, first undertaken in a moderate form (third segment) and then, immediately, in a more sudden way (fourth segment):

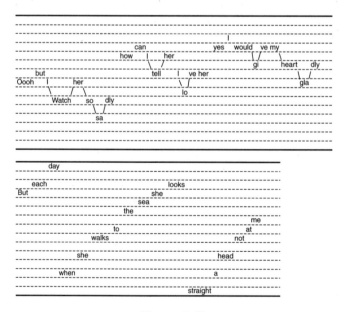

Figure 2.10

Parallel to this new melodic development, the lyrics begin to reveal the suffering of the narrator who fails to find a way of attracting the attention of the 'girl'. What is produced is a *passional* state characterised by compatibility between melody and lyrics:[9]

> Oh, but I watch her so sadly
> How can I tell her I love her?
> Yes, I would give my heart gladly
> But each day when she walks to the sea
> She looks straight ahead not at me.

Although a kind of long-distance connection between subject (narrator) and object (girl) remains – represented melodically in the gradation of the ascending motifs in the third segment – the disjunctive aspect becomes dominant both in the lyrics and in the melodic changes which highlight alterity. Finally, the tendency to 'verticalisation' of the melodic line reaches its peak in the fourth segment, when the motifs unravel into ascending scales (see Figure 2.10).

This is the moment of greatest distance between subject and object, simultaneously conveyed by the verbal and musical language of the song. In the lyrics, the girl walks to the sea without realising the repressed desires of the narrator. In the melody, the themes which guarantee a moment of union give way to the searching movements, whose emphasis on alterity previews the imminent return of the refrain. Ultimately, what we have here is a predominantly thematic song type in which the developments serve to highlight the importance of the return to the centre.

Effectively, the last segment takes up again the initial relationship between the melody and the lyrics which has become contaminated by this point by the *passional* activity of the second part. Note that the tonal gradation from the syllables '...nema' now appears inverted in an ascending movement ('...nema → 'when' → 'smile'), as if it were already imbued with *passional* content or with the feeling of absence mentioned earlier. Such a melodic development inserted into the structure of the refrain, as if it were a state of disjunction articulated within junction, maintains a perfect equivalence with the concessive (or adversative) form expressed by the verse 'I smile, but she doesn't see':

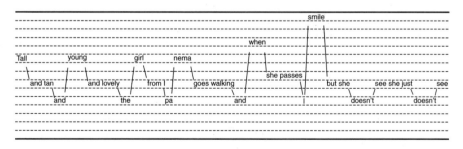

Figure 2.11

Although it is not one of the principal considerations of this work, I cannot help but comment in passing on the parallel *figurative* treatment of the whole melody in its performance by the voice. Together with the processes examined previously, the narrator of 'The Girl from Ipanema' also mobilises the intonational norms which are integral to natural speech. In this sense, the descending movement of the first two melodic segments is a result of the affirmative attitude adopted by the narrator who contemplates the movement of the girl. All of the physical qualities attributed to the character, as well as their effects on her admirers, are incontrovertible facts which require the conclusive form of intonation. The second part (third and fourth segments) introduces an enquiring and hypothetical tone, represented by expressions such as 'How can I tell her I love her?' or 'I would give my heart gladly'. This is compatible with the ascending movements of the melody which indicate at one point the uncertainty and lack of conviction of the narrator, and, at another, the decomposition of the rhythmic cells (especially in the fourth segment) which had characterised the song until then. The decomposition of the melodic motifs is a typical feature of *figurative* performance: the musical rules are broken in favour of intonational spontaneity. The fact that the melodic contours are elevated is also significant from the point of view of intonation: there is a sense of continuity in the narrator's statement. The girl's indifference is always foregrounded, giving her admirer no chance and making some kind of commentary from him imminent, which is signalled by the intonation.

The return to the first part, in the fifth segment, re-establishes the affirmative tendency of the initial segments, but with alterations in the melodic trajectory. The accentuated elevation of the curve over the word 'smile' makes the return to the middle region – in which the 'horizontal' nature of the *thematicisation* is developed – appear as an affirmative descent. From the point of view of the relationship between the singer and the listener, this tendency towards descending movement is one way of showing the persuasive resources manipulated by the former, with the intention of maintaining the attention of the latter. By producing statements akin to those of speech, the narrator is making use of his *figurative* competence or, in other words, his ability to modulate the melodic contours as if they were linguistic intonations, in such a way that the content of the lyrics becomes increasingly 'true to life'.

Final considerations

These creative forces, *thematic*, *passional* and *figurative*, described in 'The Girl from Ipanema', were consolidated in Brazil in the 1930s and their diverse handling by composers has resulted in the styles of composition and interpretation which are evident today. Some specialise in foregrounding *thematicisation*, leaving the *passional* appeals and *figurative* references in the background. Others, the so-called romantic composers, are distinguished by their subordination of *thematic* and *figurative* elements in favour of *passional* strategies for persuading the listener. Others still use song as an arena for exercising their oratorical skills (although not in the solemn ways of the old masters), emphasising the production of characters, the creation of 'modes of speech' in a popular, at times even vulgar, register, and significantly reducing thematic and *passional* performance. In all cases, however, the composers have been operating with these three creative elements, altering them in accordance with the intention of each song.

There were periods in which just one of these creative forces was projected, for example *passionalisation* in the 1950s,[10] which was characterised by a certain stylistic excess. As a result, Brazilian songwriters invented a regulating mechanism which, from time to time, establishes a form of selection in the artistic process, eliminating excess and re-establishing equilibrium between the creative elements. This mechanism came to be known as bossa nova. The most perfect translation of this form of decantation of the essence of Brazilian music is the artistic trajectory of the singer João Gilberto. However, bossa nova must be understood as a gesture of bringing together the fundamental resources of musical creation, through which artists would take up again the vigour of their own styles. Brazilian MTV is currently promoting a project, already hailed as a success, of acoustic recordings by several consecrated names in national song – such as Gilberto Gil, Rita Lee or even rock groups such as Os Titãs – with the intention of reinvigorating their respective careers, and of course increasing record sales. In this project the artists divest themselves of the electronic resources and the volume of sound that usually characterise their work, in order to demonstrate the essential characteristics of their creative style. This is a true example of the bossa nova attitude.

The counterpart of this attitude can be defined as the Tropicalist gesture. Just like bossa nova, Tropicalism had a phase of explicit intervention into the history of Brazilian song.[11] This can be described as a denial of the exclusionist pretensions of politically committed music of the 1960s, but the Tropicalist diction is summoned every time that a 'superior' genre revindicated by a 'popular elite'[12] is ventured. The Tropicalist gesture establishes the mixture of genres and of boundaries. For Tropicalism, Brazilian song is made up of all of the dictions ever practised in the country. Commercial music, regional and folkloric music, and the influence of foreign dictions, all contribute to constituting a national identity in popular music.

Bossa nova and Tropicalism provide enough material for a separate article on Brazilian popular music. However, we cannot avoid mentioning them in order to demonstrate the range of musical achievements evident in just one century of the evolution of musical language in Brazil. Apart from developing the means for creating compatibility between melody and lyrics, configured here as thematic, *passional* and *figurative* projects, Brazil's popular music has also elaborated mechanisms for controlling excess and for aesthetic insufficiencies in the selections and mixtures of bossa nova and Tropicalism.

Notes

1.   Generally, critics tend to describe song within erudite musical parameters merely as instrumental pieces or, alternatively, they apply completely inadequate literary criteria to the object of study.

2.   Translator's note: Circle dance and song type based on heavy percussion, thought to have been brought to Brazil by slaves from the Congo region.

3.   Translator's note: A dance and musical form which preceded samba, brought to Brazil by Bantu slaves. By the second quarter of the nineteenth century, *lundu* had been combined with elements of the Portuguese court aria and transformed into high-society salon music.

4.   Brazil was declared a Republic in 1889.

5.   Translator's note: From English 'break', a type of samba characterised by breaks in the rhythm, to allow for improvised, often humorous, spoken commentary by the performer.

6.   The diagrams used in this piece transcribe melody and words simultaneously. Each line corresponds to a semitone and the double lines at the end define the range (highest and lowest point) occupied by the integral melody.

7.   'Inchoation' indicates the beginning of a process.

8.   This is one more reason why this genre of music stimulates dance as a euphoric expression of the body.

9.   This compatibility does not always come from a temporal conjunction of linguistic and melodic elements as occurs in 'The Girl from Ipanema'. Often a melodic passional element is only confirmed linguistically at another stage of the song, or even in the configuration of the text as a whole.

10.   A period in which mid-year music was consecrated into the genre of *samba-canção* (samba-song) which was strongly influenced by the Argentinian tango, the Paraguayan *guarânia*, and the Cuban bolero disseminated throughout Latin America.

11.   For bossa nova this occurred in the late 1950s, for Tropicalism, the late 1960s.

12.   With the absence of erudite music which could be said to form part of national culture and with the weight attributed to the art of commercial song a popular elite was formed in Brazil which demanded quality in the production of popular music.

References

LOPES, EDWARD, 1989–90: 'Paixões no espelho: sujeito e objeto como investimento passionais primordiais'. *Cruzeiro Semiótico* 11–12.
PLOUGASTEL, YANN (ed.), 1996: *La chanson mondiale – depuis 1945*. Paris: Larousse.
ROUSSEAU, JEAN-JACQUES, 1970: *Essai sur l'origine des langues*. Bordeaux: Guy Ducros.

Bibliography

Lorraine Leu, the translator of this chapter, has provided a short bibliography of some work in English about Brazilian popular music.

CASTRO, RUY, 2000: *Bossa Nova: The Story of the Brazilian Music that Seduced the World*. Chicago: A Capella.
MCGOWAN, CHRIS AND RICARDO PESSANHA, 1998: *The Brazilian Sound: Samba, Bossa Nova, and the Popular Music of Brazil*. Philadelphia: Temple University Press.
PERRONE, CHARLES, 1989: *Masters of Contemporary Brazilian Song*. Austin: University of Texas Press.
PERRONE, CHARLES AND CHRISTOPHER DUNN (eds), 2001: *Brazilian Popular Music and Globalization*. Gainesville, Fla.: University Press of Florida.
TREECE, DAVID, 1997: 'Guns and Roses: Bossa Nova and Brazil's Music of Popular Protest, 1958–68'. *Popular Music* 16 (1): 1–29.

3

Cover versions and the sound of identity in motion

Dai Griffiths

Simon Frith and Jon Savage (1993: 116) have described an ideal pop criticism as consisting of 'anthropology, archetypal psychology, musicology . . . which has a grasp of pop both as an industrial and as an aesthetic form'. Cover versions emerge in industrial conditions, but nevertheless mount dialogues and debates between texts and performers. They help to raise retrospectively for the textual study of popular music useful points of comparison around questions of identity and political power. The examples I shall present[1] will illustrate one facet of cover versions as text-based material and will traverse a wide range of historical periods, although it is possible to observe, as does Weinstein (1998) common practice in covers at particular times. The musicologist's specific task in this complex framework is, it seems to me, to suggest how texts, in this case often consisting of the pair, original and cover, in some way describe or 'call into being' the social within given industrial conditions.

Cover versions look two ways. They invite the sociology or cultural studies class to consider the effect of musical change, and even the extent to which those very terms are informed by our musical experience. For the music class, the exercise is an important pointer to what would happen if subject specificity were to collapse, and the 'arts and humanities' were to become part of the negotiations and demonstrations, critical and creative, of cultural history and cultural studies. However, the topic is rich enough to lead in many directions, and the particular one I wish to follow here is the way in which covers illustrate identity in motion: a record originally sung by a man covered by a woman, and so on. The following should only be seen as an introduction: the examples I have chosen to present involve crossings, movements and comparisons involving gender and sexuality, race, and a shorter final group which brings together place, class and language.

Gender and sexuality

As cross-identity covers, those based on male–female shifts are relatively easy to theorise. One basic change is in the very sound of the cover, with a male voice occupying a relation to the instrumental or sound support which it will share with other male voices, and recognisably different to the female voice. Second, there will be a tendency for the sense of subject position, addresser and addressee, to change, with sexuality introducing a further variable. From here each individual case presents its own sense of relative proximity or distance between the original and cover. For these metaphors of distance, it may be appropriate from a performer's point of view to substitute the terms 'rendition' and 'transformation', rendition being a straightforwardly faithful version of the original, carrying with it some of the connotation of performance in classical music, transformation being a more determined claim on the original – at certain times it would be better even to speak of an 'appropriation' of the original. Finally, it is worth making the point that a rendition, a 'straight' cover with little alteration, can alter meaning simply because the historical or cultural context of the performance or its recording changes. These are variables, however, and a sequence of examples may bring about some basic steps in the progression of the topic.

Three versions of 'Don't Leave Me This Way' – the original by Harold Melvin and the Bluenotes with Teddy Pendergrass's vocal of 1977, Thelma Houston's cover of the same year, and the Communards' 1986 British hit – traverse and illustrate many differences. Between the first and second, we hear the difference between a male vocal, 'inside' or 'under' the sound, and a female voice 'inside' or 'above' the sound. The implied addressee of the song in its performance changes, which is not to deny that it could be heard in many more ways by listeners. The change in production is also immediately perceptible and significant: the original was a Kenny Gamble and Leon Huff production for the Philadelphia label – they also wrote the song with Carry Gilbert – while the second saw Motown trying to capture the disco market: the cover is more immediately a dance-orientated recording. The Communards presented a gay and lesbian duet, as suggested in the promotional video of the time, with Jimmy Somerville addressing a male second person, Sarah Jane Morris, a female. Cleverly in this third version the voices were 'inverted', with Somerville angelically high and Morris gutturally low. Again, what is often interesting with cross-identity covers is how the texts actively change, even on the tiniest level, a listener's response or perception. This effect can be summed up in fragments: the 'you' of 'Don't (you) leave me this way' is the key point of address.

The song 'Just Like a Woman' was written and recorded by Bob Dylan in 1966. In the original, possibly chauvinist words are meliorated somewhat by a soft Nashville production sound and a 'yearning' quality to Dylan's voice. That said, what would a woman do with sentiments such as that of the chorus: 'she aches just like a woman . . . but she breaks just like a little girl'? Well, Roberta Flack in a 1970 recording simply makes herself the subject of the chorus: '*I* ache just like a woman', and so on. Robert Shelton heard her version as an 'answer song' to the original (Shelton, 1987: 323). The 'answer record' could be described as a distinguished relation of the cover version, in which a cover of the original, or a song freshly put together in response to the original, addresses some contentious assertion made or position adopted by the original: these forms of public debate often concern gender politics. Arguably more daring is Judy Collins' 1993 cover, where Collins really does sing the song 'straight'. This allows four possible interpretations: (a) a monologue, that is Collins casting herself both as the 'I' of the opening and as the 'she' of the chorus; (b) a lesbian version, effectively a transfer of the original, including the reference in the lyrics to 'Queen Mary, she's my friend'; (c) a situation where Collins addresses another woman, a friend or even a mother to a daughter; or (d) a strict rendition of the original in the manner of classical music. What is interesting, in teaching this example for many years, is the lengths to which people go to avoid interpretation (b), in some ways, or at least in respect to the original, the most obvious one. Perhaps this has something to do with the musical context of the Collins cover, the production, instrumentation, vocal style and so on. However, it does also seem to me, and I have no idea why, that we bring slightly different expectations to female covers that allow a lesbian interpretation, where with male covers we might leap more swiftly to a gay interpretation. The point about the whole sequence, original and both covers, is that they all have separate historical contexts, and say something back to the power politics of interpersonal relations and the impact of feminism, both with respect to their original time and to how we hear them now. Roberta Flack's version needs to be seen against the background of women's lives in the 1970s, Collins' against the background of the aftermath of feminism.

What we see in the versions so far in this section is the cover acting as a form of public debate, of critique and empowerment, and the cover offering to us, as listeners in the present, forums for debate: how do *you* hear these examples, and why? In the remainder of the section, I am going to supplement further examples with evidence outside the records, from journalism and biographies, in order to show how these issues help inform the discursive world around the pop music text.

The availability of interpretative stances, and their potential for assertions of interpersonal and even legal power, is illustrated by the case of Janet Jackson and her former husband Rene Elizondo. It appears that Elizondo is 'threatening to write a book telling all' about Jackson, and that 'his main claim is that she's a lesbian'. (Needham, 2001: 16). In a magazine account what follows is a form of public debate around a cover version:

> Elizondo's Exhibit A may well be a cover of Rod Stewart's 'Tonight's the Night', which Janet performed on *The Velvet Rope* without changing the gender of the song's subject, making it sound like a lesbian love ballad – although in fact it's meant to depict a *ménage à trois*.

Jackson in interview then adds her own performer's perception:

> 'I've loved that song since I was about ten years old', Janet declares in her high wispy voice, adding that a love song from one woman to another 'is true for a lot of people. There were some people . . . that said, "Well, wait a minute, do you really think you should do this? Are people going to think this or that?" It's like, so what? If people think this they're gonna think it anyway, they've thought it before in the past. This is the song I love and I wanna sing it just as it is'.

In fact, Jackson says at the start of the track that 'this is just between me and you, and you', clearly indicating a three-way affair. At one point too she sings the same chorus line once with 'boy' and once with 'girl', so all of the textual ground is fairly clear. Again, it is interesting to revisit the original in light of the cover: Rod Stewart's song depicts gender relations very much of their time, Rod the lip-smacking ladies' man, with Britt Ekland brought on towards the end of the track as a rather unlikely French virgin. One particularly pointed line in Stewart's original, 'don't say a word, my virgin child' earned the record a ban from daytime airplay in 1976 by the British Broadcasting Corporation, and the line survives into the cover. Jackson's recording, produced by Jimmy Jam and Terry Lewis, takes the song into an R&B, soft-rap setting, which may function similarly to Rod Stewart's use of Tom Dowd as producer and a Hollywood studio for the original.

To move from these examples to Bryan Ferry's cover of 'It's My Party' of 1973, originally recorded by Lesley Gore ten years earlier, is to notice the effect of a named person, in this case the 'Johnny' who walks out on the singer at her (or his) party. Here it is much harder to hear the song as anything other than a gay version, and it turns out that Ferry was aware of this perspective:

> The only tongue-in-cheek thing [on *These Foolish Things*] I can think of was the 'It's My Party' where I didn't change the gender thing, and . . . I had a lot of gay friends in Newcastle and [*mock censoriousness*] the artworld's full of them, you know.

> (As heard on BBC Radio One, 12 May 1996)

Ferry's version belonged to the early 1970s, before the emergence of gay rights. Whether Gracie Fields' recording of 'Sally' in 1931 would have had the same effect depends on historical convention, though Fields' autobiography reveals that she too was aware of the potential problem:

> 'Let's hear the new one in my dressing-room', I suggested, but when they sang it to me I didn't care for it much on first hearing. 'I want another good comic song from you,' I told Bill Haines. 'I think "Sally" is a number for a man to sing, I don't think it'd be much good for me. Now go on, buzz off. I've got to change me skirt for the next scene.'

> · (Fields, 1960: 83)

Fields' recording was popularly known in Britain over a long period of time and, as though to confirm her initial instinct, 'Sally' was eventually covered by a man, Gerry Monroe, and was in the top ten in the UK in the summer of 1970. Finally, when Sandie Shaw came to cover the Smiths' song 'Jeane' in the early 1980s, awareness of gay rights was now clearly at issue, and her autobiography in turn draws attention to the way the political and historical context, especially around awareness of sexism and homophobia, is an important background not only for interpretation but for practice too (Shaw, 1992: 119–21). These three examples – Bryan Ferry, Gracie Fields and Sandie Shaw – are all complicated by the naming of a person in the song but, as with the three versions of 'Just Like a Woman' or the example of Janet Jackson, would need ultimately to be set into a fuller historical context than this brief examination is able to offer. I hope to have suggested, however, that cross-gender cover versions can be seen as instances where the practice of cover can itself be a form of public debate, with always at least an element of empowerment or critique in the chain of interpretation.

Race

Upon this identity crossover can be mapped an entire history of rock and soul, with many cases of cover either as rendition or as transformation serving as key markers of generic history: in fact, it is here that the word 'appropriation' could be used purposefully to evoke the connotation of power and exploitation which needs to be kept under this heading as a possible critical tool. This is an area impossible for formal musical analysis to occupy without an element of cultural theory and where socio-industrial analysis has to factor in questions of history and power. Describing industrial practice in the 1950s, James Miller suggests that:

> Nobody thought twice about black groups knocking off R&B versions of pop hits, just as nobody thought twice about white acts knocking off pop versions of R&B recordings . . . The trick was to pull a 'switch', as record men called it, aiming a new version of an established song at a fresh section of the pop market, for example by having a country artist do a pop hit, or a pop singer do a country song, or a vocal group do a ballad made popular by a crooner.

> (Miller, 2000: 76)

However, as Miller will be aware, leaving it at just this is surely to underestimate the 'asymmetry' of power between black and white in the United States at this time.

Racially based covers raise a series of comparisons which ask us to consider carefully questions of power and exploitation: answers to these questions will vary from case to case and from listener to listener.[2] A group of covers spanning no more than 17 years from 1947 to 1964 will help begin to illustrate the differences: two black originals covered by white singers (Big Mama Thornton's 'Hound Dog' of 1953 covered by Elvis Presley three years later, and Little Richard's 'Long Tall Sally' of 1956 covered in the same year by Pat Boone); a white original covered by a black singer (Hank Williams' 'Your Cheatin' Heart' of 1953 covered ten years later by Ray Charles); and finally another black original covered by a white band (Big Joe Williams' 'Baby Please Don't Go' of 1947 covered by Them in 1964). In chronological order:

1947: 'Baby Please Don't Go', Big Joe Williams

1953: 'Your Cheatin' Heart', Hank Williams

1953: 'Hound Dog', Big Mama Thornton

1956: 'Hound Dog', Elvis Presley

1956: 'Long Tall Sally', Little Richard

1956: 'Long Tall Sally', Pat Boone

1963: 'Your Cheatin' Heart', Ray Charles

1964: 'Baby Please Don't Go', Them

To say that these examples are all cross-race covers only touches the surface, under which lie very many subtleties. With Presley, hearing the cover in-juxtaposition with the original emphasises forcefully the point made by Peter

Guralnick that it was 'a very odd choice for a male performer, since it was written from a female point of view' (Guralnick, 1995: 273). It is fascinating to set this original cover pair next to Little Richard and Pat Boone. Presley is clearly aiming to sound *like somebody like Little Richard*, forming the alliance that we recognise as rock 'n' roll, but Boone takes rock 'n' roll somewhere else altogether. Presley's record seems to be about *expression*, while Boone's is seemingly, and strangely perhaps to us now, about *rectitude*. That said, however, and a very important point, Boone's version is in many ways closer to Richard's original than is Presley's 'Hound Dog' to Thornton's. The observations in Table 3.1 attempt to map these subtleties, where micro-level and macro-level discrepancy becomes crucial.

From these notes it will appear that Boone's is a more faithful rendition of 'Long Tall Sally' than is Presley's of the original 'Hound Dog'; but now the micro-differences start to count, and Richard Middleton has analysed these in comparing the vocal styles of Boone and Presley (Middleton, 1990:

Table 3.1

Big Mama Thornton, 'Hound Dog' (song by Leiber and Stoller)	Opens with voice. Sparse instrumentation, emphasis on rhythm in drums and handclaps. A dialogue between voice and guitar. Blues-style vocal which during guitar solo speaks and produces 'hound dog' effects. Blues-style guitar solo. Medium pace at *c.* 76 beats per minute (b.p.m.) – record lasts 2 minutes 48 seconds. Form: three vocal 12-bar periods (chorus – verse – chorus), two periods of guitar solo with vocal interjection, two more vocal periods (verse – chorus). Ends with 'hound dog' vocal effects.
Elvis Presley, 'Hound Dog'	Opens with voice. 'Block' instrumentation – instruments hammering away together, with famous snare drum punctuation at end of vocal sections. Led largely by voice with occasional guitar licks. Fast and energetic pace at *c.* 90 b.p.m. – record lasts 2 minutes 12 seconds. Form: three vocal 12-bar periods (chorus – verse – chorus), one period guitar solo (blues meets country picking) with male backing vocals, one vocal 'verse', one period guitar solo with backing vocals, two more vocal periods (verse – chorus). Dramatic close: voice alone and instruments ending together.
Little Richard, 'Long Tall Sally' (song by Johnson, Penniman and Blackwell)	Opens with voice. Led by voice with instruments hammering away together in driving rhythm. Fast pace at *c.* 90 b.p.m. – record lasts 2 minutes 8 seconds. Form: three vocal 12-bar periods ('pre-verse' – verse – second verse); sax solo over two 12-bar periods; two vocal periods (verse – second verse, i.e., dropping the 'pre-verse'); vocal coda for one more 12-bar period and end.
Pat Boone, 'Long Tall Sally'	Opens with voice. Led by voice with instruments slightly more separated than original. More pronounced swing beat in drums and backing vocals accompanying voice. Fast pace at *c.* 90 b.p.m. – record lasts 2 minutes 10 seconds. Form: three vocal 12-bar periods ('pre-verse' – verse – second verse); sax solo over two 12-bar periods; two vocal periods (verse – second verse, i.e., dropping the 'pre-verse'); vocal coda for one more 12-bar period and end.

262–3). Boone certainly makes precise but important differences to Richard's vocal: in melody, the actual content of the words and their diction. Even the sax solos are subtly different: the Little Richard example rhythmic and 'honking', the Boone version slightly more melodic. We can also suggest that there is a link between Presley and Richard in vocal style, but we should be careful here too – the slightly syrupy male backing vocals are present in Presley's record as in Boone's. Defending Pat Boone, Roger Dopson points out that:

> The hard facts were that back in those ultra-conservative mid-50s *everyone* benefited from cover versions: the artist, because it exposed their songs to a wider audience (one that their black skin would have excluded them from unless *someone* covered their record); the writer (often the artist, anyway); and (particularly) the music publisher.
>
> (Dopson, 2000)

In fact, a more egregious appropriation may have happened elsewhere. The iconography of Boone's records – cover in the 'album cover' sense – was a quite different story and much closer to a visual appropriation, far more pointedly a matter of racial and class-based exploitation (see Ochs, 1996: 117 and 138). The album covers for Little Richard and Fats Domino (on the Specialty and Imperial labels) were cut-and-paste examples, with black and white photos superimposed on plain backgrounds; Boone's covers (on the Dot label) depict the very essence of 'preppy' aspiration, with the singer pictured outside Columbia University, or a still life of sports blazer, books and college pendant.

Ray Charles's recording of a country original, another fascinating example, is also a significant shift in sound – characteristic of much of the two volumes of *Modern Sounds in Country and Western Music*, the addition of strings, mixed-gender backing vocals and cocktail piano quite transformed Williams' sparse original, if indeed Charles was covering the Williams original, rather than hit versions in 1953 for Frankie Laine and for Joni James. Charles adds nearly a minute to the time of the original and does not even include Williams' second verse. There is no doubt that for the relationship between black singers and country music Charles's covers were crucial interventions, and it is worth noting, with reference to the discussion above, that Charles did not flinch from iconographic engagement: the cover of his third country album, *Country and Western Meets Rhythm and Blues* of 1965, presents Charles in his standard dark tuxedo shaking hands with Charles in a white cowboy outfit (see Ochs, 1996: 342).

Finally, the arrangement by Them, with Van Morrison's vocal, of Big Joe Williams' original is carefully musical. Where Williams begins with Sonny Boy Williamson's harmonica over a sparse bass accompaniment, Them open with two quite separate and charged musical ideas – a 'twanging' guitar lick giving way to a driving guitar and harmonica riff. This conveys a literal sense of distance from the original coming through the artful arrangement. For British Invasion bands such as the Beatles, the Rolling Stones, the Who, Them, and the Animals, covers of black originals seemed to be bound up in issues of British class expression, where the act of cover seemed to have functioned as a gateway to various forms of authentic self-expression.

The examples so far in this section simply present some of the issues involved under this complex heading, and I should beg the reader's patience as we lurch historically forward. During the mid-1980s, sampling introduced a further level of complexity, and in truth the matter of how sampled reference relates to cover is beyond the confines of this essay. It is worth saying even here, however, that the 'songs' of James Brown, for instance, were more performative and thus less likely to be covered as such. Indeed, Keith Negus makes the point that 'rap tracks are routinely compared to conventional songs, and it is asserted that they cannot be "covered" – re-recorded, re-sung, re-performed by other artists. Hence, rap tracks are judged to have a short catalogue shelf life, in terms of their ability to bring in ongoing copyright revenue from their re-use' (Negus, 1999: 93–4). However, the performative elements of the original recordings – drumbeats, vocalisations, bass riffs – seem to have been the very facets that made them the common source for much early sampling. Here, too, as Tricia Rose suggests, hip-hop DJs were often aware of their use of funk originals as 'a means of archival research, a process of musical and cultural archaeology' (Rose, 1994: 80), a phrase which could usefully be transferred to certain cover versions – tribute albums often contain words to that effect.

That said, it could be argued that even sampled reference always contained a tendency towards a return to something closer to cover. One of the earliest examples might be the sampling of Lou Reed's 'A Walk on the Wild Side' by A Tribe Called Quest as 'Can I Kick It?' which, simply by sampling as a loop the two pitches played by double bass in the original, effectively sampled the whole 'song', making it a chorus section separated by freer verse interludes. This was a powerful tendency for the sampled rap, lying behind such tracks as 'I'll Be There For You/You're All I Need To Get By' by Method Man featuring Mary J. Blige, Puff Daddy's 'I'll be Missing You', Coolio's 'Gangsta's Paradise', and Public Enemy's 'He Got Game' – see the discography for sources of the sampled material. Outside the context of rap, Gabrielle's 'Rise' is another case where effectively the whole 'song', as repeated chord sequence, is sampled. In all of these tracks a substantial element of the original is looped as extended sample or performed as cover, but in a context which effects a complete reworking or reinvention. Dislocations familiar in cover versions arise from changes in context: 'Big Yellow Taxi' was an early example of environmental awareness for Joni Mitchell in 1970, where Janet Jackson and Q-Tip make the hook line of the original the basis of a dialogue on personal relationships in the late 1990s.

Finally under this heading, 'Bridge Over Troubled Water' illustrates the way in which covers take part in chains of signification. The source for the title is a line from the 1959 record 'Mary Don't You Weep' by the Swan Silvertones, a gospel quartet which featured the Rev. Claude Jeter (later to appear as a singer on Paul Simon's 'Take Me to the Mardi Gras'). As part of an extended fade, one of the singers enunciates the line 'I'll be your bridge over deep waters if you trust in my name'. Note that the first person, I, is Jesus and the 'you' is Mary Magdalene (the story told at John 20: 11–18). When Paul Simon picked up on this line and worked it into a song for his duo with Art Garfunkel, he was doing two things. First, he made secular the person identification, so that I and you become simply something for the 'me generation', or appropriate to a later generation out of an episode of *Friends*.

Second, however, particularly through Larry Knechtel's piano part, there is an additional evocation of gospel. Garfunkel's voice is key: virtuosic and wide-ranging but characteristically 'pure' and, indeed, quite notably white, with even a connotation perhaps of high-church religion.

Aretha Franklin, at the time she covered 'Bridge Over Troubled Water', could be described as a critical musicologist, covering many songs in which white singer-songwriters appeared to be evoking gospel (see also her versions of John Lennon and Paul McCartney's Beatles song 'Let It Be' and Elton John and Bernie Taupin's 'Border Song'). As well as introducing a change of gender and colour, Franklin, as she would often do, takes the song back to church. So now the song really does carry firmly the additional ambiguity of its 'you' being a friend or lover on the one hand or God on the other, at the same time. 'Was the second person singular you or You?', as Peter Guralnick asks (1991: 26), an ambiguity now beyond the words of the case in point. Dave Marsh draws attention to the formal extension to the original, taking two minutes at the opening where Knechtel took about 20 seconds (Marsh, 1989: 364–5). Her voice stretches and fragments Garfunkel's steady melody, and the words become displaced in a more immediately expressive presentation. The substitution for Knechtel's piano of piano with organ, the addition of call-and-response vocals, these elements are crucial in taking us firmly into a church setting. The circle between the gospel quartet and Franklin seems unbroken, but the journey through Simon's song and Garfunkel's performance says so much to the time and attitudes that these versions traverse – the cover version has become part of, as we shall see, a 'songline'.

Place: class, nation, language

Cover versions often present points of observation or even metaphors for the movement of people under modernity. Randy Newman's 'Louisiana 1927' is an example of a singer-songwriter affecting a character distant in place and time. Newman's own sense of the way that Louisiana was inscribed in his own family history is beautifully detailed in the first two tracks of a later record, *Land of Dreams* (1988). On record, Newman's voice has to my British ears no localised accent specific to this song, and it is particularly moving then to hear it performed by Aaron Neville or by Marcia Ball, since in both cases the singers through their voices 'take the song home' to New Orleans. 'Going home' or 'leaving home' are effects familiar under this heading, and which may affect a listener's response or understanding.

Covers will often bring out in perceptible textual terms some of the arguments about art-school influence in Britain made by Simon Frith and Howard Horne, suggesting a second, class-related dimension to examples such as the one illustrated by the example of Them in the previous section (Frith and Horne, 1987: 88–9). Similarly, Ray Charles's cover of 'Your Cheatin' Heart', mentioned earlier as part of a crucial intervention between country and R&B, can interestingly reappear here too. Under the heading of class it may be appropriate to ask a slightly different set of questions and listen out for different facets of the comparison, now more from the point of view of the Williams original than the Charles cover. Under this heading the questions concern crucially the difference between the small-band recording of the Drifting Cowboys' original, Williams' authorial presence, the steely grit of Williams' vocal performance, and the bigger, more lavish, showbiz sound of Charles's cover, the interventions of Sid Feller as producer and Marty Paich as arranger.

One of the most important given limits on 'coverability' of a song is language, and the traffic in covers across languages enables us to observe some of the power movements involved. English clearly acts as the hegemonic norm in this respect, and there is a tradition of bands re-recording originals in different languages: from David Bowie's version of 'Helden' (inspiringly concerned with the Berlin Wall), through the Wedding Present asking 'Pourquoi es tu devenue si raisonnable?', to Cypress Hill's covers of their greatest hits for the Spanish-speaking market in 1999 as *Los Grandes Éxitos en Español*. Whether these translations are successful is another matter: what I find most grating on Paul Simon's *Graceland* is the mellifluous moment at the end of 'Homeless' when Simon actually joins in the language of Ladysmith Black Mambazo. It smilingly encapsulates the bad faith I hear less precisely elsewhere on the record, like a handshake confirming an exploitative transaction. Translated versions of American or English originals are legion: for instance, in France in 1965 Hugues Aufray issued a whole collection of Dylan translations, including 'N'y pense plus, tout est bien', the same year that Eric Charden took 'Amour limite zero' to the French charts (Tyler, 1998: 49–57). However, what seems not to happen is for originals in a language other than English to be covered as such, a small but important margin in the relation of local and global. Plenty of songs are translated – Dusty Springfield's 'You Don't Have to Say You Love Me' and Frank Sinatra's 'My Way' are two famous English-language records with origins in originals in European languages (Italian and French), but the idea of Bobby Darin actually performing Charles Trenet's 'La Mer' as 'La Mer' not as 'Beyond the Sea' as happened, seemingly does not arise. Indeed, the one-way traffic of language in pop may always introduce the danger with 'world music' that the voice of the other language is simply another exotic instrument, consumption of which serves to reinforce hegemonic control – another charge which could also be levelled at *Graceland*. So, when Fairport Convention performed Bob Dylan's 'If You Gotta Go' as 'Si tu dois partir', was it an unnecessary and purposeless obscurity, or the merest hint that English-speaking people could go beyond the confines of their language's hegemony?

Welsh-language pop music offers a few clues as to how a minority language, emerging from demonstrable conditions of historical oppression, gradually develops a sense of past through cover versions.[3] The majority of covers in Welsh-language pop undoubtedly fit into the pattern of translations which are as covers 'renditions through language'. Thus, the translation of 'One Day at a Time' as 'Un Dydd Ar Y Tro', the signature tune of singing farmer Trebor Edwards, simply claimed the same ground as repetitive performance of the original in English: entertainment and vocal expression for a Welsh-speaking audience with no great transformative intention or effect (although, as with Aretha Franklin, it is arguable that 'sweet Jesus' undergoes a conversion of

religious denomination though language). Next step: rendition can be 'straight'
but context changes meaning. So Dafydd Iwan, a committed Welsh nationalist,
sings Woody Guthrie's 'This Land is Your Land' in Welsh translation, as 'Mae'n
Wlad i Mi', and the reinterpretation of Guthrie's class-based song as patriotic
sentiment is powerfully evident. What did not appear to happen, however, was
for Welsh-language pop music to develop a sense of its own inner dialogue –
covers of Welsh-language originals are few and far between, reflecting perhaps
the fact that industrial conditions disallow the development of 'classic' status.
However, the 1990 tribute album covering in its entirety the seminal record by
Geraint Jarman a'r Cynganeddwyr, *Hen Wlad Fy Nhadau* – an accolade the
album shares with the Beatles' *Sgt Pepper's Lonely Hearts Club Band* (covered
in its entirety on at least two occasions), Hüsker Dü's *Zen Arcade*, and NWA's
Straight Outta Compton – signalled a new and positive awareness specifically
of the Welsh-language pop. past. Super Furry Animals have since covered 'Y
Teimlad' by Datblygu, whose 'Amnesia' is sampled on rap band Tystion's
'Llosgwch y Llosgach'. This latter development would suggest that 'past consciousness' and 'class or identity-group consciousness' seem intertwined, and
why 'past-consciousness' arises when it does is a very interesting question,
important for cover versions in general. It may yet have been – at a guess – that
the technological development of sampling was crucial in putting 'past-refer-
ence' on the agenda, so to speak, which cover version in turn reflected.

Conclusion: songlines

This article is an initial presentation of the way that cover versions can supply case studies for the textual illustration and mounting of discussion
around questions of identity and political power, the latter ultimately the
key lesson which cultural studies offer the wider arts and humanities cur-
riculum. There are some things to add by way of provisional conclusion.
First, the headings are hardly exhaustive – in fact, there are as many headings as there are case studies, with each case bringing a slightly different
set of emphases. There are further headings concerned with age, time and
value which I have considered but not illustrated here. Second, it is worth
stressing that covers are simply a *device* – there is naturally no harm in
mounting a comparison between Otis Redding's 'Mr Pitiful' and Aretha
Franklin's 'Dr Feelgood', simply that seeing the two singers through the
shared ground of 'Respect' offers a handy analytical tool. Finally, this
article raises as many questions as answers, especially in some quite basic
issues about what the 'text' in popular music study really is, as cover
encompasses a wide range of related but subtly different terms or sets of
terms: song, record, track; performance, rendition, transformation, appropriation; allusion, reference, sample. Finally, to evoke again Frith and
Savage's ideal discourse, copyright offers a legal instrument for the separation of these terms. But another version may be the one described by Bruce
Chatwin in *The Songlines* (Chatwin, 1987: 13):

> He went on to explain how each totemic ancestor, while travelling through the
> country, was thought to have scattered a trail of words and musical notes along the

line of his footprints, and how these Dreaming-tracks lay over the land as 'ways' of communication between the most far-flung tribes.

'A song', he said, 'was both map and direction-finder. Providing you knew the song, you could always find your way across country'.

Notes

1. Many of the examples are based on exercises set in teaching popular music at Oxford Brookes University, and I am grateful to the students for their engagement in these issues.

2. One of the basic 'textual' questions which race cover raises is the difference between race 'heard' and 'seen'. On hearing, many people will think 'Play that Funky Music' by Wild Cherry (1976) to be sung by a black funk band, and 'She's My Rock' by Stoney Edwards (1972) to be sung by a white country singer, and being mistaken in both cases underlines not only the importance of generic markers in instrumental support but also that the voice can be an unreliable racial marker. Alongside the immediately perceptible, prior knowledge and visualisation are both important.

3. My thanks to Sarah Hill and Pwyll ap Siôn on this point.

Bibliography

CHATWIN, B., 1987: *The Songlines*. London: Jonathan Cape.

DOPSON, R., 2000: sleevenote to *Pat's 40 Big Ones*. See discography.

FIELDS, G., 1960: *Sing As We Go*. London: Frederick Muller.

FRITH, S., 1996: *Performing Rites: On the Value of Popular Music*. Oxford: Oxford University Press.

FRITH, S. AND HORNE, H. 1987: *Art into Pop*. London: Methuen.

FRITH, S. AND SAVAGE, J. 1993: 'Pearls and Swine: Intellectuals and the Mass Media'. *New Left Review* 198: 116.

GURALNICK, P., 1991: *Sweet Soul Music: Rhythm and Blues and the Southern Dream of Freedom*. Harmondsworth: Penguin.

—— ,1995 *Last Train to Memphis: The Rise of Elvis Presley*. London: Abacus.

MARSH, D., 1989: *The Heart of Rock and Soul: The 1001 Greatest Singles Ever Made*. Harmondsworth: Penguin.

MIDDLETON, R., 1990: *Studying Popular Music*. Buckingham: Open University Press.

MILLER, J., 2000: *Almost Grown: The Rise of Rock and Roll*. London: Arrow.

NEEDHAM, A., 2001: 'Enemas, Piercings, Strap-Ons . . . Welcome to the Frank and Explicit World of Janet Jackson'. *New Musical Express*, 5 May.

NEGUS, K., 1999: *Music Genres and Corporate Cultures*. London: Routledge.

OCHS, M., 1996: *1000 Record Covers*. Cologne: Taschen.

ROSE, T., 1994: *Black Noise: Rap Music and Black Culture in Contemporary America*. Hanover: Wesleyan University Press.

SHAW, S., 1992: *The World at my Feet: A Personal Adventure*. London: Fontana.

SHELTON, R., 1987: *No Direction Home: The Life and Music of Bob Dylan*. Harmondsworth: Penguin.

TYLER, K., 1998: 'C'est Fab! French Pop in the 60s'. *Record Collector*, 230, October.

WEINSTEIN, D., 1998: 'A History of Rock's Pasts through Rock Covers', in A. Herman, J. Sloop and T. Swiss (eds), *Mapping the Beat: Popular Music and Contemporary Theory*. Oxford: Blackwell, 137–51.

Discography

Cover versions

'Baby Please Don't Go'
Big Joe Williams [1947]: *Folk, Gospel and Blues: Will the Circle Be Unbroken?* (Sony, 1999), Them: *Them – Featuring Van Morrison* (Decca, 1964).

'Bridge Over Troubled Water'
Simon and Garfunkel: *Bridge Over Troubled Water* (Columbia, 1970), Aretha Franklin (Atlantic, 1971).

'Don't Leave Me This Way'
Harold Melvin and the Blue Notes (Columbia, 1977), Thelma Houston (Motown, 1977), Communards (London, 1986).

'Hen Wlad fy Nhadau'
Geraint Jarman a'r Cynganeddwyr (Sain, 1978), Amrywiol [Various] (Ankst, 1990).

'Heroes' – 'Helden'
David Bowie: *Heroes* (RCA, 1977), *Rare* (RCA, 1982).

'Hound Dog'
Big Mama Thornton [1953]: *The King's Record Collection,* vol. 1 (Hip-O, 1998), Elvis Presley [1956]: *The King of Rock 'n' Roll: The Complete 50s Masters* (BMG, 1992).

'If You Gotta Go' – 'Si tu dois partir'
Bob Dylan [1965]: *The Bootleg Series,* vols. 1–3 (Columbia, 1991), Fairport Convention: *Unhalfbricking* (Island, 1969).

'It's My Party'
Lesley Gore (Mercury, 1963), Bryan Ferry: *These Foolish Things* (Island, 1973).

'Jeane'
The Smiths (Rough Trade, 1983), Sandie Shaw (Rough Trade, 1984).

'Just Like a Woman'
Bob Dylan: *Blonde on Blonde* (Columbia, 1966), Roberta Flack: *Chapter Two* (Atlantic, 1970), Judy Collins: *Just Like a Woman* (Geffen, 1993).

'Long Tall Sally'
Little Richard [1956]: *22 Classic Cuts* (Ace, 1986), Pat Boone [1956]: *Pat's 40 Big Ones* (Connoisseur, 2000).

'Louisiana 1927'
Randy Newman, *Good Ol' Boys* (Reprise, 1974), Neville Brothers [1991]: *With God on Our Side* (A&M, 1997), Marcia Ball: *Let Me Play with Your Poodle* (Rounder, 1997).

'One Day at a Time' – 'Un Dydd ar y Tro'
Lena Martell [1979]: *One Day at a Time* (Castle, 2000), Trebor Edwards *Un Dydd ar y Tro* (Sain, 1980).

'This Land is Your Land' – 'Mae'n Wlad i Mi'
Woody Guthrie [1940]: *This Land is Your Land: The Asch Recordings,* vol. 1 (Smithsonian Folkways, 1997), Dafydd Iwan [1966]: *Y Dafydd Iwan Cynnar* (Sain, 1998).

'Tonight's the Night'
Rod Stewart: *A Night on the Town* (Riva, 1976), Janet Jackson: *The Velvet Rope* (Virgin, 1977).

'Why Are You Being So Reasonable Now?' – 'Pourquoi est tu devenue si raisonnable?'
Wedding Present: *George Best* (Cooking Vinyl, 1997).

'Your Cheatin' Heart'
   Hank Williams [1952]: *40 Greatest Hits* (Polygram, 1988), Ray Charles [1962]: *The Complete Country and Western Recordings 1959–86* (Rhino, 1998).

'Y Teimlad'
   Datblygu [1995]: *Datblygu 1985–1995* (Ankst, 1999), Super Furry Animals, *Mwng* (Placid Casual, 2000).

Sampled references

'A Walk on the Wild Side' – 'Can I Kick It?'
   Lou Reed: *Transformer* (RCA, 1973), A Tribe Called Quest: *People's Instinctive Travels and The Paths of Rhythm* (Jive, 1990).

'Big Yellow Taxi' – 'Got 'Til It's Gone'
   Joni Mitchell: *Ladies of the Canyon* (Reprise, 1970), Janet Jackson: *The Velvet Rope* (Virgin, 1977).

'Every Breath You Take' – 'I'll Be Missing You'
   Police: *Synchronicity* (A&M, 1983), Puff Daddy and the Family: *No Way Out* (Puff Daddy, 1997).

'For What It's Worth' – 'He Got Game'
   Buffalo Springfield [1967]: *Box Set* (Rhino, 2001), Public Enemy: *He Got Game* (Def Jam, 1998).

'Knocking on Heaven's Door' – 'Rise'
   Bob Dylan: *Pat Garrett and Billy the Kid* (Columbia, 1973), Gabrielle: *Rise* (Go Beat, 1999).

'Pastime Paradise' – 'Gangsta's Paradise'
   Stevie Wonder: *Songs in the Key of Life* (Motown, 1976), Coolio [1995]: *Tommy Boy's Greatest Beats* (Tommy Boy, 1999).

'You're All I Need to Get By' – 'I'll Be There for You/You're All I Need to Get By'
   Marvin Gaye and Tammi Terrell [1967]: *Motown Hits of Gold*, vol. 2 (Motown, 1985), Method Man featuring Mary J. Blige [1995]: *Def Jam 1995–2001* (Def Jam, 2001).

Single tracks

'Homeless'
   Paul Simon: *Graceland* (Warner, 1986).

'Llosgwch y Llosgach'
   Tystion: *Hen Gelwydd Prydain Newydd* (Ankst, 2000).

'Mary Don't You Weep'
   Swan Silvertones [1959]: *Testify! The Gospel Box* (Rhino, 1999).

'Play that Funky Music'
   Wild Cherry [1976]: *Superfunk* (Virgin, 1994).

'Sally'
   Gracie Fields [1931]: *That Old Feeling* (ASV, 1989).

'She's My Rock'
   Stoney Edwards [1972]: *From Where I Stand: The Black Experience in Country Music* (Warner, 1998).

4

(In search of) musical meaning: genres, categories and crossover

David Brackett

Musicology and musical meaning

What does it mean to 'study music' as opposed to studying other forms of symbolic expression? How does music differ from painting, theater, cinema and literature? The way in which we choose to answer these questions by delimiting the social functions and formal processes that mark this difference will determine both how we distinguish music from other forms of communication, and how we differentiate musicology from other scholarly fields. Musicologists have often used the phrase 'the music itself' to refer to this irreducible level of 'music', but the phrase is potentially misleading.[1] Some critics of conventional musicological analysis have even gone so far as to respond to this phrase by saying that 'music has no "self"'.

While obviously a contentious and possibly polarizing retort (though also humorous to those who are sympathetic to the point of view that animates it), this response does indicate some of the difficulties with the uncritical use of the phrase 'the music itself', a phrase implying that music may be understood autonomously, without reference to a social framework. To reply that 'music has no "self"', then, is also to emphasize that humans perceive, describe and analyze music, and that the elements of music which are important or pertinent to a detailed description and analysis are interwoven with the social context in which they occur. At the same time, however, admitting the importance of identifying which musical details may be socially pertinent does not mean negating the importance of describing music's sonic materiality. Rather than use the phrase, 'the music itself', I find the phrase 'the details of musical style' more open-ended. 'Musical style' in this case refers to a bundle of characteristics that may be linked to a particular musician or recording and that participate in a socially recognized musical genre.

Music scholars who specialize in methods of description and analysis learn a technical meta-language for which no real parallel exists in the study of other arts. Fluency in this meta-language is tied to the ability to read Western staff notation, and is an important component in arranging music, in communicating details of music to others, and in learning how to compose Western art music. Unfamiliarity with this meta-language will render most work in music analysis opaque to the uninitiated. Due to these aspects of music analysis, it becomes fair to ask whether a musicologist's specialized training can contribute anything to the study of music to someone who is not a formally trained musician. While such an undertaking may require the musicologist to restrict the use of analytical meta-language, to describe music in terms that will seem relevant to a large portion of the readership who are familiar with the music, and to explain what some analytical terms mean, I believe that it is possible to share the insights that come with the practice of music analysis with non-musicologists. My stance here has parallels in the analysis of other cultural practices: many studies of literature, cinema, television, etc., even by those who are not considered specialists in those fields, still refer to the textual details that mark the specificity of the medium.

In the relatively brief history of popular music studies, it has proven difficult to integrate methods of musical analysis with prevailing approaches based in cultural studies. The resistance to textual description and analysis within popular music studies stems from both the opacity of analytical meta-language and from non-musicologists who feel inhibited in discussing music because they are unfamiliar with its technical terminology, or are intimidated by its 'abstract', 'non-representational' quality, and thus restrict themselves to discussing non-sonic elements such as lyrics or visual imagery (of videos, album covers, advertisements, etc.). Regardless of feelings of resistance, few will dispute that the sonic level is crucial to conveying meaning and that it affects perception of words and images conveyed through song.

Meaning and genre

'Meaning', 'pertinence', 'details of musical style': if the sonic materiality of music does not exist autonomously, how does one decide which details are pertinent? If music is not mimetic, how does one discuss its meaning?[2] I stated earlier that 'musical style' refers to a bundle of characteristics that distinguish a socially recognized musical category or genre; and a good way to start answering these questions is by addressing the notion of genre. Genres, for our purposes here, consist of ways of categorizing popular music so as to create a connection between musical styles, producers, musicians and consumers, and include labels such as 'pop', 'rock', 'R&B', 'country', 'hip-hop', 'alternative', 'techno', etc.[3] By trying to understand individual musical texts (songs, recordings, performances) in the context of genres and their relationships to one another, one places the meaning of an individual song within a larger field of meaning. Genres bring with them connotations about music and identity which may encode specific affective qualities such as 'conformity', 'rebelliousness', 'commercialism', 'selling out', 'art for art's sake'; and they may encode a whole variety of social characteristics including race, class, gender, place, age and sexuality. Genres not only encode such characteristics; the specific musical processes and formal qualities associated with them create modes of encoding that are genre-specific (e.g. 'sincerity' may be conveyed differently in hip-hop and country).[4] In this way, genres may be understood as mediating the discursive web (spun between the media, consumers and industry personnel) in which musical meaning circulates and the objects to which these meanings are attached – the sonic materiality of specific performances and recordings. As should be obvious by now, genres are not defined by characteristics of musical style alone but also by performance rituals, visual appearance, the types of social and ideological connotations associated with them, and their relationships to the material conditions of production (see Fabbri, 1982: 52–63 and Frith, 1996: 91–3).

Genres do not consist of essential, unvarying characteristics, but rather exist as a group of stylistic tendencies, codes, conventions, and expectations that become meaningful in relation to one another at a particular moment in time (cf. Fabbri, 1982: 53; Toynbee, 2000: 103; Neale, 1980: 19). A quick illustration will suffice: during the 1950s in the US, the musical characteristics of rock 'n' roll connoted hedonism and rebelliousness; by the 1980s, these same musical characteristics might be found in the songs of country musicians or oldies groups, and would have connoted nostalgia, or at least a relatively wholesome form of hedonism, ceding 'youthful rebelliousness' to other genres. On the other hand, while 'rhythm and blues' in the 1940s and 1990s maintained many of the same social characteristics (along with many important differences as well), few would confuse the sound of one for the other.

Genres also overlap, and are constituted differently in different contexts: trade publications, radio formats, record stores, critics, musicians and fans may project varying conceptions of genres at the same time (cf. Negus, 1999: 29). Due to this phenomenon, a given musical text may belong to more than one genre simultaneously, either due to the context under consideration, or because the text presents a synthesis that exceeds contemporary comprehension of generic boundaries. While close enough inspection of any text will throw into doubt that it belongs simply to a single genre, so is it also impossible to imagine a genre-less text.[5] Similarly, the more closely one describes a genre in terms of its stylistic components, the fewer examples actually seem to fit (see Toynbee, 2000: 105).

Although the range of sonic possibilities for any given genre may be quite large at a particular moment, it is not infinite: in the US, when tuning in to a country music station, going to a club featuring country music, or going to the country bin in the local music store, one has some idea of what to expect. The particular ability of the musicologist might then be used to analyze what accounts for the sonic tendencies of country music and the relationship between these tendencies and those of other genres; this, in turn, may then create the possibility of describing the relationship (or lack of a relationship) between these particular musical characteristics and the social connotations of country music during a given period.

The sonic differences between categories, then, are intimately related (if not inextricable) from the discourses that circulate about them. In order to explore the interaction of musical elements and social processes in the categorizing of genres, I will look in detail at one historical moment in one particular location: a period of about eight months spanning the years 1982–3 in the United States. Furthermore, I will examine one very specific relationship during this period: that of 'black popular music' to the 'mainstream'. Examining the process of categorization illuminates how black popular music relies on the maintenance of a sense of difference that permeates the circulation of musical sounds and verbal discourse about music.[6] To understand how a distinct black popular music circulates in relation to the mainstream, one must look closely at the *specific* interconnections between institutional policies, discourses of categorization and formal stylistic tendencies within a narrow period of time.

The term 'mainstream', so often a 'blank' term in discussions of popular music genres and aesthetics, merits further discussion. Jason Toynbee discusses several aspects of what he calls 'mainstreaming' in greater depth elsewhere in this volume, and my usage of the term shares much with his. I agree with Toynbee that the term need not be pejorative, and that 'a mainstream is a formation that brings together large numbers of people from diverse social groups and across large geographical areas in common affiliation to a musical style' (Toynbee, Chapter 9 of this volume). Like Toynbee, I make no claim that the 'mainstream' refers to a stylistically consistent or homogeneous genre, or that it addresses 'a coherent social group'. In a sense, however, this raises a larger issue, as I am skeptical whether any genre, if examined closely enough, would prove to be stylistically consistent or address a homogeneous audience (though this also varies, and does not proscribe general stylistic tendencies and dominant factions within the audience).

One of the problems highlighted by attempts to describe the mainstream is that of a confusion between different *levels* of genre. The names for *Billboard* popularity charts – such as 'Hot 100' (mainstream pop), 'rhythm and blues' (black popular music), 'country', 'Latin' and 'dance' – both coincide with and differ from radio formats and consumer genres with similar names.[7] However, as shown in Table 4.1, the 'marketing categories' for R&B and (especially) country tend to have a tighter correspondence with consumer genres bearing the same (or a similar) name than the mainstream, which exists more as a general concept. Nevertheless, the concept of the mainstream retains its currency through its ability to provide a 'center' for other 'marginal' or 'alternative' genres. By admitting the role of marketing strategies in influencing the wider discourse on genre, it becomes possible to understand the names in the 'marketing category' level of Table 4.1 as 'genres'. These categories function as 'supra-genres', and will serve as the focus for the analysis to follow later in this chapter.

For my purposes here, the clearest approach to understanding a popular music mainstream lies in surveying the overlapping of charts such as *Billboard*'s 'Hot 100' with radio formats such as 'Top 40' and playlists for video channels such as MTV and VH-1, as well as in examining how the term functions in mass media discourse about popular music. By surveying many songs in, for example, the top ten in these categories over a fairly limited period of time, one can become aware of an ever-shifting hierarchical assemblage of genres that form the mainstream 'supra-genre' during that period. While the mainstream may be heterogeneous, not all genres have the same status within it: some are excluded, or are never as prominent (or occur as a 'one-hit' novelty).[8] The genres that are most strongly coded as 'African-American',

Table 4.1 The different levels of genre

Marketing category	Rhythm and blues (black popular music)	Pop (the mainstream)	Country
Chart name (as of April 2001)	Hot R&B/hip-hop	Hot 100[b]	Country
Radio format[a]	R&B, urban contemporary, hip-hop, quiet storm, soul	Top 40, mainstream Top 40, adult top 40, adult contemporary, modern rock, mainstream rock, AOR	Country
Media-fan genres	Hip-hop, R&B, funk, disco, rap, new jack swing, neo-soul, quiet storm	Modern rock, mainstream rock, teen pop, adult contemporary	New traditionalists, hat acts, alt-country

[a] Names given in the 'radio format' and 'genre' categories are an amalgamation of names that have been used from the early 1980s up to the present (2001).

[b] Since 1991, with the advent of electronic monitoring of sales and airplay with soundscan and broadcast data systems (BDS), the *Billboard* charts that represent the mainstream have included sales and airplay data from all formats and genres within the range of those monitoring systems. This shift in how the 'Hot 100' is tabulated creates an interesting disjunction between notions of 'the mainstream' in other media and *Billboard*'s 'mainstream' chart.

if included at all, are often 'marginal' (country, on the other hand, is marginal but more often *not* included). The popular forms most strongly associated with black identity thus function rather like a colony, a source from which the mainstream may draw periodically to replenish itself in times of scarcity (see Garofalo, 1993; Brackett, 1994; Toynbee, chapter 9 of this volume).

One of the aims of this chapter is to show how this 'hierarchy of genres' functions. The most interesting situations occur precisely because of the inconsistent valuation of genre within the mainstream supra-genre, for this highlights how the formation of the margins and mainstream is anything but a neutral arrangement of genres based on musical style. The analysis of media discourse provides important clues as to the role of power in establishing genre constellations at a given moment. It is always important to remember the *relational* nature of the mainstream: a concept of the mainstream depends on an equally strong concept of the 'margins' – one cannot exist without the other. In fact, as stated earlier, the identity of a genre depends on its relationship to other genres coexisting with it at any given point in time.

Genres and crossover in the early 1980s

The position of genres within the mainstream can be usefully analyzed through the notion of 'crossover', a term referring to the process by which a song becomes successful on one chart after initial success on a different chart (usually moving from the margins to the mainstream). This chapter discusses a particularly fertile period for crossovers by African-American artists in which increasing numbers of recordings began to enjoy success on the 'pop chart' either simultaneously with success on (what was then called) the 'black chart', or following initial success on the black chart.[9] This period is notable because such crossovers were relatively rare during the five-year period that immediately preceded it. Although songs moved regularly between the R&B chart and the 'Hot 100' or 'mainstream' pop chart from the mid-sixties through the mid-seventies, developments in the late seventies such as Album Oriented Rock radio (also known as 'AOR') – which catered to a suburban, white demographic – revealed a growing rift between the strategies used to market different types of music to black and white audiences and influenced the decline in the number of crossovers between the R&B chart and the 'Hot 100'. Another component of this rift was the 'backlash' in the rock press and among AOR audiences against disco, a style largely associated with African-American, Hispanic and gay audiences. The advent of MTV in 1981 only exacerbated the rift between 'white rock' and black popular forms, owing to that channel's initial refusal to screen videos by African-American artists.

I will analyze the function of genre and crossover during 1982–3 in the United States by looking at the placement of several recordings within the overall context of popular music. This 'context' includes the various pop music genres that were circulating at the time as well as the public discourse of the music industry as conveyed by *Billboard*, the leading publication of the United States' entertainment industry. Although the producers of *Billboard* intend it primarily to deliver facts about the music industry to merchants who make their living from it, it can also be read as a publication devoted to detailing the relationship between race and musical style written in a special code.

Three topics emerge from a close reading of *Billboard* in the period from June 1982 to April 1983 that bear directly on my concern with the relationship between genre and race. The first of these is the subject of radio formats, specifically the content and conflict between 'black' or 'urban contemporary' (UC) formats and AOR. Several articles addressed the relationship between the style of music and the makeup of the audience for stations in those formats. Radio stations in the US surveyed their audiences extensively, resulting in ratings of the stations' market share known as the 'Arbitron ratings'. During this period, the Arbitron ratings were quite high for UC and relatively low for AOR. *Billboard* explained this by observing that UC stations had a looser playlist, while AOR suffered from a decrease in spontaneity in favor of consistency and homogeneity (George and Grein, 1982; Sachs, 1982).

While *Billboard* devoted much space to scrutinizing the presence or absence of white artists on UC, comparatively little attention was spent discussing the absence of black artists on AOR. The way in which these statements appeared in *Billboard* exemplifies how widespread expectations about the racial makeup and 'correct place' of genres are reproduced in the marketing and categorizing of music. It is not so much that record company employees, radio station managers and *Billboard* writers consciously employ racist attitudes as that they bring with them certain ideas about the audience (and its predilections) for a certain type of music (cf. Negus, 1999). The influence of such preconceptions helps explain why the articles do not analyze the contradictions that appear embedded in them: if UC stations have high audience ratings, why do not songs that are played frequently on them appear high on the pop charts if those charts reflect sales and air play in general?

Intertwined with the issue of radio formats is the subject of crossover, the second topic to emerge from a close reading of *Billboard* during this period. Michael Jackson's *Thriller*, which was in many respects a watershed crossover album, figured in several discussions following its release in December 1982. Even at an early stage, writers recognized its genre-busting capabilities, with the song 'Beat It' generating particular interest. One front-page article, which focused on the generally favorable response to the song at AOR stations, nonetheless described listeners as having problems either upon discovering that Michael Jackson was responsible for the recording or with the idea that Eddie Van Halen was 'selling out' by appearing on it. A further problem appeared to be indecision about whether to make 'Beat It' the second single from *Thriller* stemming from the reluctance of Jackson's record company 'to hand black radio two pop-oriented singles in a row [when they] would prefer to follow "The Girl Is Mine" with a more mainstream black track, probably "Billie Jean"' (Grein 1982). It would appear from these statements that 'Beat It' was doubly accursed: simultaneously given the cold shoulder by AOR listeners because of Jackson's image and Van Halen's sellout, and by black radio for-matters as 'too pop'. Yet in the end the song provided a good example of how previously unexplored syntheses of genres can construct new (and very large) audiences: eventually the third single released from *Thriller*, 'Beat It' reached no. 1 on the 'Hot 100' in April 1983, and remained there for three weeks.

At the same time that the racial politics of radio formats were being debated in the pages of *Billboard*, a third recurring topic surfaces in a series of articles by Nelson George describing the deteriorating conditions for African-Americans in the retail end of the business despite the healthy sales of black music relative to pop music (George, 1982a; George, 1982b; George, 1982c). Thus we have counterpoint during this period between, on the one hand, nar-ratives that describe the increasing popularity of black popular music and a few extremely successful 'crossover' acts, and, on the other hand, narratives that describe the increasing difficulty of people in the African-American com-munity to benefit from the success of black artists because of either failing retail businesses or the tendency of black artists to hire white promoters for their concert tours (George, 1982d; George, 1982e; George, 1983).

How did these debates about formats and crossovers work in terms of how the popularity of actual songs was represented in the charts? The crossover process functioned much the same during this period as it had since the inception of separate charts for 'popular', 'country and western', and 'rhythm and blues' during the 1940s. That is, the 'black' chart functioned as a 'testing ground' in relation to the 'Hot 100', revealing extraordinarily popular songs that might have broad enough appeal to cross over to the mainstream. Influencing whether a song would cross over or not were industry-wide expectations based on previous chart performance, initial strength of popu-larity in the R&B charts, and the musical style of the recording.[10] In other words, as indicated earlier, the expectations about genres and audiences that circulate between industry employees, writers, musicians and fans have the power to affect the way in which the chart performance, and hence the 'popularity', of different genres is represented.

A closer look at two sets of two songs that were released and were popular at roughly the same time will enable us to understand a bit better the

Table 4.2 Comparison of crossover success for four songs, November 1982–July 1983

Date	Michael Jackson/Paul McCartney, 'The Girl Is Mine'		Chaka Khan, 'Got to Be There'		Michael Jackson, 'Billie Jean'		George Clinton, 'Atomic Dog'	
	Black	Hot 100	Black	Hot 100	Black	Hot 100	Black	Hot 100
(1982)								
6 Nov	–	45	69	–				
13 Nov	21	36	51	–				
20 Nov	10	14	38	–				
27 Nov	6	9	28	–				
4 Dec	3	8	20	–				
11 Dec	3	5	11	–				
18 Dec	3	4	8	–				
25 Dec	3	3	8	–				
(1983)								
8 Jan	3	2	8					
15 Jan	1	2	8					
22 Jan	1	2	5	82	–	47		
29 Jan	1	5	5	74	31	37	39	–
5 Feb	9	16	5	69	8	27	26	–
12 Feb	13	34	5	67	1	23	15	–
19 Feb	21	82	20	92	1	6	8	–
26 Feb	22	91	21	98	1	4	6	–
5 Mar	25	97	22	98	1	1	5	–
12 Mar	46	–	23	–	1	1	5	–
19 Mar	91	–	33	–	1	1	5	–
26 Mar			57	–	1	1	3	–
2 Apr			91	–	1	1	3	–
9 Apr				–	1	1	3	–
16 Apr				–	2	1	1	–
23 Apr				–	2	5	1	–
30 Apr					3	7	1	101
7 May					3	14	1	–
14 May					11	24	4	–
21 May					12	29	11	–
28 May					23	42	16	–
4 June					40	58	19	–
11 June					66	65	27	–
18 June					77	70	36	–
25 June					84	73	42	–
2 July					91	98	53	–
9 July							70	–
16 July							91	–
23 July							98	–

relationship between politics and musical style at play in the process of 'crossover' (see Table 4.2). From this chart, we can see that 'The Girl Is Mine' was earmarked for dual chart success from the beginning; its ascent and descent on both 'black' and 'Hot 100' charts are roughly parallel. On the other hand, Chaka Khan's 'Got to Be There' (a cover version of a 1971 hit by Michael Jackson) displays a different type of crossover pattern; it 'fights' its way onto the lower reaches of the 'Hot 100' after prolonged success on the black chart. Similar to 'The Girl Is Mine', Michael Jackson's 'Billie Jean' appeared almost immediately on both charts (actually one week earlier on the 'Hot 100'). However, its ascent up the black chart was much faster, landing it at no. 1 a full three weeks before it hit no. 1 on the 'Hot 100'. In contrast to this, George Clinton's 'Atomic Dog' followed a very different pattern, closer to that of 'Got to Be There' but more extreme. Despite prolonged success on the black chart, it didn't even crack the 'Hot 100', instead 'bubbling under' (*Billboard*'s term) at no. 101.[11]

Musical analysis of crossover

For pages now I have been describing the situation of popular music in the United States at this time in order to understand the role of racial politics in the delimitation of popular music genres. The previous discussion has attempted to clarify why the process of categorization is important, but now I want to test a claim made in the introduction to this chapter – that music analysis can help make us aware of sonic differences between genres.

At the historical conjuncture studied in this chapter, several issues involving music analysis seem particularly pressing: how do particular examples of 'crossover' and 'non-crossover' R&B songs from the time resemble or sound different from one another? What role does this sonic difference/similarity play in the way these songs were understood at the time and in representations of their popularity? And what conclusions might be extrapolated from these examples to general tendencies of the time, including stylistic differences and resemblances between crossover and non-crossover songs, and between black popular music and the mainstream?

I will analyze two songs in Table 4.2, 'Atomic Dog' and 'Billie Jean', and move from the most general observations about sonic difference to increasingly specific observations that gradually introduce specialized musical terminology. Basic differences in the two songs can be heard in their introductions: 'Atomic Dog' presents a much denser texture with many more fragmented musical ideas overlapping with one another than 'Billie Jean'. While the beat and 'groove' are very clear in both examples, 'Billie Jean', due to its sparser texture, presents a 'cleaner', 'lighter' groove. The resulting groove in 'Atomic Dog' is 'heavier' and feels more complex. Listeners may experience 'Atomic Dog' as pulling them physically in several directions simultaneously, whereas 'Billie Jean' offers a more unilinear, straightforward pull. In terms of timbre, or the sonic quality of particular instruments and voices, differences between the two songs are also striking: 'Atomic Dog' features wildly varied, overtly synthesized sounds, synthesizer bass and

* = syncopated attack

+ = sounds one octave lower than written

Example 1. 'Billie Jean' (ca. 0: 21-0:24)

* = syncopated accents
** = upbeat accent
x = indiscernible pitches
+ = sounds one octave lower than written

Example 2. 'Atomic Dog' (ca. 0: 05-16)

Example 3. 'Atomic Dog' bass riff (0:31-0:32)

electronic hand claps. On the other hand, 'Billie Jean' features synth keyboard along with drum and bass sounds that are non-synthesized (or sound non-synthesized). Michael Jackson's vocal quality in 'Billie Jean', while recognizably African-American, is also clearly singing (as opposed to speaking) in a somewhat 'cleaner' timbre (including what were to become Jackson's trademark vocal 'hiccups') than that heard in the singing on 'Atomic Dog', which mixes exaggerated gospel-derived mannerisms, sung by solo and group vocalists, with drawling, spoken passages, and even occasional barking dog-type effects.

In technical terms, we could describe the difference in rhythmic texture between the two songs in terms of amount of syncopation or polyrhythm (or, in other words, the number of rhythms that produce tension against the basic background pulse): very ('Atomic Dog') vs. modest ('Billie Jean'). In 'Billie Jean' (Example 1) the bass plays a steady eighth-note pattern (that is, it plays two pitches for every beat that divide the beat evenly in half) against the background of the drums which provide an accent on the snare drum on every other beat (the backbeat) while also subdividing the beat into two on the hi-hat cymbal (a pattern that is reinforced by the maracas, another percussion instrument).[12] The keyboard plays a pattern that produces some tension against the background beat, as every other chord (several pitches played simultaneously) arrives slightly ahead of the beat (see Example 1; arrows indicate beats; asterisks indicate syncopations). In 'Atomic Dog' (Example 2) the drum part is actually sparser than in 'Billie Jean', with the drums playing only on the beat and eschewing any clear subdivision of it (although other percussive sounds perform this function during different passages of the song, including what sounds like a chorus of panting dogs). The drum sound is much heavier, however, with a backbeat thunderously reinforced by electronic hand claps. The bass, in contrast to 'Billie Jean', plays a fragmented, syncopated pattern, and does not play continuously, frequently leaving gaps. Other synthesized instruments and chanting voices form a kind of collage effect of short, overlapping, syncopated musical ideas (Example 2). Example 3 shows a short, three-note bass riff that underlies long sections of 'Atomic Dog'. Its highly syncopated pattern – the first two attacks fall within the beats before the third attack, which is the only note in the pattern to land on the beat – occurs in many funk songs.[13] It is interesting to note that the archetypal riff in Example 3 first appears after Clinton presents a list of the different kinds of dog addressed by the song: 'clapping dogs', 'rhythmic dogs', 'harmonic dogs'. Musicians, too, are conscious of how musical elements function in a technical sense within a larger discourse of genre.

The area of pitch relationships (the way that 'notes' sound) is often the most difficult to explain to non-musicians (though it is the area most emphasized in formal musical study). In terms of melody (the relationship of successively sounding pitches) and harmony (simultaneously sounding pitches), 'Billie Jean' features relationships that are closer to the norms of European art music.[14] In experiential terms, listeners may feel a sense of periodic tension and relaxation, produced by the coordination of many musical elements, and aided by the way in which melody and harmony work together; this sense of tension and release occurs most dramatically in the transition into the chorus (at ca. 1:25), resolving with the words 'Billie Jean is not my girl'. The melody of the song consists of clearly defined phrases which rise and fall, peaking in the chorus in a way that complements the aforementioned tension and release of the harmony. 'Atomic Dog' features no such harmonically based sense of tension and release, relying instead on open-ended sections underpinned by either a single harmony or an alternation of two harmonies. Melodically, 'Atomic Dog' relies on shorter, 'riff-like' phrases; and the succession of phrases does not create the sense of melodic direction found in 'Billie Jean'. While sections of 'Billie Jean' use 'functional harmony' (pitch relationships related to those found in eighteenth- to nineteenth-century European art music) to generate musical interest, 'Atomic Dog' relies more on changes of texture and the constant shifting relationships created by different melodic fragments to create a kind of rhythmic tension and release.[15] Differences in the lyrics also play into distinctions of genre: 'Billie Jean' employs a lyric depicting a domestic narrative focused on the drama of an individual, while 'Atomic Dog' features playful, allusive lyrics lacking a clear narrative ('Why must I feel like that? Why must I chase the cat'?). The playful use of the signifier 'dog', which describes its low-down qualities even as it revels in them, also references a mode of discourse widely understood in the US as African-American.[16]

In addition to the foregoing observations, musical style also plays an important role in how we interpret the lyrics and, hence, the meaning of the song. Jackson's tense vocal performance, and the driving, moderately up-tempo dance feel of 'Billie Jean' are largely responsible for whatever mood of aggression, defiance and angry denunciation the song may convey. If we imagine the same lyrics at a very slow tempo, accompanied by a large orchestra with a much less clear beat, the song, even with the same lyrics, melody and harmony, might come to seem a somber, reflective meditation on the end of a relationship. The lyrics of 'Atomic Dog' are more difficult to disassociate from the music, but the words might lend themselves to a children's song if matched with a simple melody featuring closed phrasing, steady, non-syncopated rhythms, and accompanied by celeste rather than a funk band.

So far I have compared these two songs in terms of their formal features while also commenting on connections between this comparison and the analysis of media discourse presented earlier. What this type of formal analysis does is make assumptions about an ideal type of listening – which details matter most and how a listener would be likely to respond to them. While I would posit that many listeners enculturated in the Western world during the last 50 or so years would be likely to have a similar response to what I described (even if they could not articulate it in the terms I used), other responses are possible – some people may find that I have omitted elements that figure prominently in their response. However, my main goal has been heuristic rather than prescriptive: to delimit differences between the two songs in the areas of rhythm, timbre, pitch and lyrics. Now the challenge is to place these differences within a larger field of musical meaning and relationships.

If we were to try to apply more broadly the meaning uncovered in the songs thus far, we would run the risk of overly facile interpretation and racial stereotyping. The earlier discourse/chart analysis established how 'Billie Jean' was a 'crossover' song that succeeded in both the 'black' and 'mainstream popular' categories while 'Atomic Dog' did not cross over. It would be difficult, however, to extrapolate from these two examples to a general theory about the differences between black and mainstream popular music at this time. A more effective description of such differences necessitates analyzing a much broader cross-section of songs in order to make associations that are not naively simplistic.

The top 40 during 1982–3 was dominated by slick, funk- and soul-influenced pop songs that featured liberal doses of newly developed digital synthesizers along with older analog synths mixed with frequent dollops of heavy-metal-influenced guitar. These were the days of Toto, REO Speedwagon, and Hall & Oates. New Wave lingered on, adding new synthesized timbres and dance rhythms in bands such as Men at Work and the Cars. Aided by the strong and novel visual presence of MTV, many British 'technopop' groups figured prominently, such as A Flock of Seagulls, Soft Cell and Duran Duran. This trend overlapped significantly with the New Romantic genre, which consisted of British-based groups who fused neo-soul singing with modified funk and disco rhythms, used plenty of synthesizers (of course), and sported a fashion sense signifying a revolt against punk. While Culture Club was the most successful exponent of this trend in the US, other bands such as the Fixx and Spandau Ballet achieved chart success during this period. Although heavy metal was not yet fully accepted within the mainstream, several 'lite-metal' bands such as Def Leppard and Quiet Riot had major hits, and, as mentioned above, many non-metal songs featured metal-influenced guitar solos.

The most obvious sonic connection between 'Atomic Dog' and 'Billie Jean' and this 'mainstream' lies in their reliance on synthesizers and funk rhythms. The presence of aspects of funk style in the mainstream illustrates the difficulty (if not impossibility) of making airtight associations between musical style and race, as the mainstream was already saturated with musical style markers that bore strong associations with African-Americans. Understanding the makeup of the mainstream at this time, however, does highlight some important distinctions about which factors were involved in the ability of certain R&B songs to cross over. Songs that were too funky (such as 'Atomic Dog' or the Gap Band's 'You Dropped a Bomb on Me'), or had too much gospel influence ('Got To Be There' or Aretha Franklin's 'Jump To It') had limited mainstream success. The role of race in the construction of the mainstream is revealed by the appearance of funky dance numbers by white artists, such as 'Let's Dance' by David Bowie, in the 'Hot 100' immediately upon their release.[17]

An another important axis of the mainstream during 1982–3 revolved around lyric content and the use of a romantic ballad style; this realm of expression, however, was not open to rhythm and blues songs projecting a straightforward romantic message, very few of which crossed over at this time. By way of contrast, soulful ballads were quite successful in the mainstream, but only when recorded by white singers such as Michael McDonald ('I Keep Forgettin' (Every Time You're Near)'), Joe Cocker and Jennifer Warnes ('Up Where We Belong'), and numerous New Romantics (Lionel Richie stands as an exception to this rule). The inaccessibility of the widest public forum in popular music for the expression of serious emotions – given that crossover songs of the period were prone to be party and dance numbers – might tend to project an image of African-Americans as frivolous, happy-go-lucky, and hedonistic, and therefore unready for the mature, romantic commitments available to white, pop artists. This partial access to the mainstream contributed to a double standard and higher bar for economic success for African-Americans, a phenomenon which becomes more odious when we reflect back to earlier observations about how the economic rewards from black popular music were increasingly being diverted from African-American entrepreneurs during this time.

A comparison of the two other songs tracked in Table 4.2 adds further weight to these observations about crossover. 'The Girl Is Mine' has a mild, funk ballad feel, akin to songs in the 'quiet storm' genre, and thus makes for a good comparison with 'Got to Be There' (an exemplary quiet storm number). Gospel influence in Jackson's singing is present (especially in the bridge) but muted, and more or less absent from McCartney's singing. The degree of gospel influence, in conjunction with timbre, also accounts (at least in part) for why Jackson and McCartney's voices are not as strongly coded as 'black' as Chaka Khan's. 'The Girl Is Mine' is presented as a light-hearted song that might be found in a musical comedy, a quality that undercuts the passages with the most passionate effects (such as Jackson's singing during the bridge) in comparison to the impassioned quality that characterizes Khan's performance throughout. That 'The Girl Is Mine' is played for laughs also accounts for how it was able to cross over at this time despite its ostensible identity as a romantic ballad. The recording also undoubtedly benefited from the fact that Jackson had such a long track record of crossover success that his releases (including ballads) were *expected* to cross over, even during periods when crossovers were rare. Sharing credit for the recording with Paul McCartney also did not impede its progress on the 'Hot 100'.

This survey of the mainstream enables us to make further inferences about the social meaning of these songs. Through their placement in contrasting but overlapping 'genre worlds' (Frith, 1996: 88), we have mainly established differing relationships of the songs to discourses about black and non-black identity. 'Atomic Dog' and 'Got to Be There,' due to their exclusion from mainstream media sources, would have been heard publicly through various radio formats directed towards African-Americans. As noted above, both of these songs contain musical features that were rare within the mainstream of the time (and non-existent when produced by black musicians) and would have therefore projected a more exclusive sense of black identity than the crossover songs of Michael Jackson. The songs therefore provide different points of identification for listeners depending on how they perceive their racial identity.

During this period, the arrangement of genres/marketing categories remained clearly hierarchical, as it had been since the inception of multiple categories for popular music in the US during the 1920s. While musical style – the 'formal and technical rules' observed by Fabbri as a component of genre – plays an important role in defining genre at the level of the 'supra-genre' or marketing category, musical style seems to exist more as a set of general tendencies within supra-genres than to play a determining role. Above all, racial ideology in the US plays an extremely important role in determinations of marketing categories, so much so that it results in occasional contradictions in terms of musical style. At the 'lower levels' of genre, musical style may function more consistently and play a larger role in relation to sociological factors; the relative importance of different factors undoubtedly varies depending on the genre. But merely because musical style cannot be mapped effortlessly onto genre regardless of level does not negate its importance. An analysis that reveals inconsistencies in style–genre relationships may actually become more convincing by highlighting the role of power in the constitution of marketing categories. I would argue further that to deal with the subject of genre is to deal with inconsistency and contradiction, with that simultaneous 'participating' without 'belonging' of texts within genres which lends genre the allure of a possible answer to the question of musical meaning: an answer, however, which hovers constantly beyond the grasp of the questioner.

As the preceding study has demonstrated, understanding the social significance of musical style is not a straightforward task. Meaning cannot be read directly off from the text, and merely analyzing musical relationships by themselves has limited utility. Yet the *sound* of 'Atomic Dog' and 'Billie Jean' is an important part of their story – how one remained in a musical ghetto while the other received an entrée to white, middle-class America (on the symbolic, if not the literal, level). If sound by itself cannot account for the different histories of these recordings, sound forms an undeniable part of listeners' experiences of the differing social placement of the songs. Understanding the role of sonic difference can therefore enhance our appreciation of how sound reinforces representations of social difference.

Several years ago, Richard Middleton suggested some of the ways in which musicologists might 'bridge the gap' that sometimes seems to separate musicology from the rest of popular music studies (Middleton, 1993). While the gap may have decreased a bit since then, many working in the field share a sense that an impressive chasm still remains. In an area of study that involves many disciplines other than musicology, none of which require familiarity with the meta-language of music analysis, musicologists need to be aware of what forms of contextualization render their insights about musical style intelligible to other students and scholars of popular music. Yet the effort that is needed to do this should not obscure the value of such insights. Musicology often seems ignored as a possible resource that might enrich popular music studies by actually addressing the specificity of the medium.[18] Explanations of why music sounds the way that it does are not tangential to aspects of experiencing music that non-musicologist, non-musician listeners find meaningful: sonic patterns have social ramifications.

Perhaps further attempts to use these explanations to answer questions that a broad array of popular music students and scholars find important will open a path whereby the explanatory power of music analysis is better appreciated and understood.

Acknowledgments

I would like to thank Lisa Barg and my editors, Dave Hesmondhalgh and Keith Negus, for their comments on earlier drafts of this chapter. Research for this project was supported by a grant from the National Endowment for the Humanities, and by a research leave from the State University of New York at Binghamton.

Notes

1.   For more on the historical and institutional forces operating on the term 'music', see Brackett (1999).

2.   Middleton (1993) discusses the relationship between music and mimesis in making a strong case for the correlation between gesture and somatic processes.

3.   This description of genre takes as its starting point a statement by Franco Fabbri: 'A musical genre is "a set of musical events (real or possible) whose course is governed by a definite set of socially accepted rules" ' (Fabbri, 1982: 52). Simon Frith clarifies further: a genre label 'integrates an inquiry about the music (what does it sound like) with an inquiry about the market (who will buy it)' (Frith, 1996: 76).

4.   For similar approaches to understanding the function and meaning of genre, see Tagg (1992: 375–6) and Walser (1993: 28–9). Hamm (1995) emphasizes the determinative role of performance in the reception of genre.

5.   I am here paraphrasing Derrida when he hypothesizes that 'a text cannot belong to no genre, it cannot be without or less a genre. Every text participates in one or several genres, there is no genreless text; there is always a genre and genres, yet such participation never amounts to belonging' (Derrida, 1980: 61).

6.   Richard Middleton has also discussed the role of difference between genres in the production of meaning (Middleton, 1990: 241). Expanding on the point made here, Negus (1999) stresses that the decisions made by record company personnel are inseparable from the discursive evaluations they have internalized; therefore, he argues that 'culture produces an industry' at the same time that 'industry produces culture'.

7.   Reebee Garofalo (1993) analyzes the confusion around the concept of black popular music as resulting from the failure to distinguish between marketing category (based on who makes the music and who buys it) and genre (based on a style of music rooted in a particular cultural and historical experience). The distinction is important, and I diverge from Garofalo only in thinking of marketing category as a kind of 'supra-genre'. Of course, the process I am suggesting is potentially infinite: the 'supra-genres' of R&B, pop and country can be absorbed into still higher levels of 'supra-supra genres' (e.g. popular music, classical music), and genres can be further divided into 'sub-genres' known to connoisseurs of a genre (e.g. different types of rap, different forms of techno).

8.   In some eras, though, 'novelties' become so numerous as to dominate the mainstream, as in, for example, the late 1940s to the early 1950s (see Brackett, 1999).

9.   For more on crossover and its attendant debates, see George (1988), Perry (1988), Garofalo (1990, 1993) and Brackett (1994).

10.   I substantiate this point further with regards to mid-sixties soul music in Brackett (1994: 777–8, 792). Garofalo (1993) further corroborates these findings.

11.   According to Rickey Vincent, 'Atomic Dog' even experienced difficulty entering the playlist of R&B stations due to 'Clinton's bad reputation with the industry' at the time, and states that it was only eventually adopted because of 'incredibly heavy sales' (Vincent, 1996: 250).

12.   Even those unable to read music can glean much from the appearance of the examples, particularly in the greater variety of appearance in the musical notation of 'Atomic Dog' compared to 'Billie Jean'.

13.   This pattern also forms a polyrhythmic $3 + 3 + 2$ pattern against the background meter. For more on the use of polyrhythms of this sort in funk and rap, see Wilson (1974), Brackett (1995/2000: 137–9), and Walser (1995).

14.   In this case, I use the word 'closer' advisedly, as the basic ostinato of 'Billie Jean' is, in fact, modal, and therefore not typical of eighteenth- to nineteenth-century European art music (the 'common-practice' period); the same is true of many other pitch-related features, including voice-leading and texture. I hasten to add that, even in the transition to the chorus, the deviation of 'Billie Jean' from 'common-practice' norms is at least as striking as the resemblance.

15.   Allan Moore (1993) has developed a typology that describes these differences as the difference between 'open' and 'closed' phrasing.

16.   Musical phrases from 'Atomic Dog' were later adapted by Snoop Doggy Dogg in his 'What's My Name'. Other lines from this song also found their way into the work of Mr Dogg. Paul Gilroy has written insightfully on the trope of 'the dog' in Afro-diasporic discourse: '[Snoop's] filling the mask of undifferentiated racialized otherness with quizzical canine features reveals something about the operation of white supremacy and the cultures of compensation that answer it. It is a political and, I believe a moral gesture' (Gilroy, 1994: 73). Vincent, somewhat more prosaically, notes the 'hilariously accurate expressions of the doglike nature of horny men (and women)' in 'Atomic Dog', and goes on to note the numerous recordings that have sampled or copied the recording's hook, leading to his designation of 'Atomic Dog' as 'the *jam* of the 1980s' (Vincent, 1996: 250).

17.   For more on the double standard applied to songs such as Bowie's 'Let's Dance', see Nile Rodgers' response (Rodgers, 1983) to a previous article (Sachs, 1983) that discussed how urban contemporary stations were banning songs with 'suggestive' song lyrics, one of which was Rodgers' 'Yum Yum' (in a somewhat paradoxical twist, Rodgers was co-producer of 'Let's Dance').

18.   For example, Grossberg (1999) criticizes popular music studies for not developing a concept that defines it as a field of study distinct from cultural studies due to its failure to address the specificity of the medium. The discipline of musicology, however, is not broached as a possible resource that might remedy this failing.

References

BRACKETT, DAVID, 1994: 'The Politics and Practice of "Crossover" in American Popular Music, 1963–65', *Musical Quarterly* 78 (4) (Winter): 774–97.

——, 1999, 'Music', in Bruce Horner and Thomas Swiss (eds), *Key Terms in Popular Music and Culture*. Oxford and Malden, Mass.: Blackwell, 124–40.

——, 1995/2000: *Interpreting Popular Music*. Berkeley and Los Angeles: University of California Press.

DERRIDA, JACQUES, 1980: 'The Law of Genre', in W. J. T. Mitchell (ed.), *On Narrative*. Chicago and London: University of Chicago Press, 51–77.

FABBRI, FRANCO, 1982: 'A Theory of Musical Genres: Two Applications', in D. Horn and P. Tagg (eds), *Popular Music Perspectives*. Gothenburg and London: IASPM, 52–81.

FRITH, SIMON, 1996: *Performing Rites: On the Value of Popular Music*. Cambridge, Mass.: Harvard University Press.

GAROFALO, REEBEE, 1990: 'Crossing Over: 1939–1989', in Jannette L. Dates and William Barlow (eds), *Split Image: African-Americans in the Mass Media*. Washington, D.C.: Howard University Press, 57–121.

——, 1993: 'Black Popular Music: Crossing Over or Going Under?', in Tony Bennett, Simon Frith, Lawrence Grossberg, John Shepherd and Graeme Turner (eds), *Rock and Popular Music: Politics, Policies, Institutions*. London and New York: Routledge, 231–48.

——, 1994: 'Culture versus Commerce: The Marketing of Black Popular Music'. *Public Culture* 7 (1) (Fall): 275–87.

GEORGE, NELSON, 1982a: 'Little Credit for Hitbreakers: Black Retailers Fight Industry Double Standards'. *Billboard*, 5 June: BM-6, 12.

——, 1982b: 'The Rhythm and the Blues: The View from 125th St., Part II'. *Billboard*, 9 October: 46.

——, 1982c: 'Times Even Tougher for Black Retailers'. *Billboard*, 13 November: 1, 58.

——,1982d: 'The Rhythm and the Blues: The Concert Issue Won't Go Away'. *Billboard*, 4 December: 48, 51.

——, 1982e: 'The Rhythm and the Blues: Dimples Promotes His Opinion'. *Billboard*, 25 December: 48, 50.

——, 1983: 'The Rhythm and the Blues: Griffey Seeks Promoter-Talent Ties'. *Billboard*, 8 January: 65, 66.

——, 1988: *The Death of Rhythm and Blues*. New York: E. P. Dutton.

GEORGE, NELSON AND PAUL GREIN, 1982: 'Black Formats Offer More New Act Airplay', *Billboard*, 5 June: 1, 22.

GILROY, PAUL, 1994: ' "After the Love Has Gone": Bio-Politics and Etho-Poetics in the Black Public Sphere'. *Public Culture* 7 (1) (Fall): 49–76.

GREIN, PAUL, 1982: 'Michael Jackson Cut Breaks AOR Barrier'. *Billboard*, 18 December: 1, 58.

GROSSBERG, LAWRENCE, 1999: 'Same As It Ever Was? Rock Culture. Same As It Ever Was! Rock Theory', in Karen Kelly and Evelyn McDonnell (eds), *Stars Don't Stand Still in the Sky: Music and Myth*. New York: New York University Press, 99–121.

HAMM, CHARLES, 1995: 'Genre, Performance, and the Early Songs of Irving Berlin', in *Putting Popular Music in Its Place*. Cambridge: Cambridge University Press, 370–80.

MIDDLETON, RICHARD, 1990: *Studying Popular Music*. Milton Keynes: Open University Press.

——, 1993: 'Popular Music and Musicology: Bridging the Gap'. *Popular Music* 12 (2) (May): 177–90.

MOORE, ALLAN, 1993: *Rock, The Primary Text: Developing a Musicology of Rock*. Buckingham: Open University Press.

NEALE, STEPHEN, 1980: *Genre*. London: British Film Institute.

NEGUS, KEITH, 1999: *Music Genres and Corporate Cultures*. London and New York: Routledge.

PERRY, STEVE, 1988: 'Ain't No Mountain High Enough: The Politics of Crossover', in Simon Frith (ed.), *Facing the Music*. New York: Pantheon Books, 51–87.

RODGERS, NILE, 1983: 'Commentary: The Black Side of Censorship', *Billboard*, 9 April: 8.

SACHS, LEO, 1982: 'Format Consultants: AOR Boon or Bane?' *Billboard*, 12 June: 1, 45.

——, 1983: 'Urban Programmers Hit "Suggestive" Song Lyrics'. *Billboard*, 5 March: 1, 14.

TAGG, PHILIP, 1992: 'Towards a Sign Typology of Music', in R. Dalmonte and M. Boroni (eds), *Secondo convegno europeo di analisi musicale*. Trento: Università degli studi di Trento.

TOYNBEE, JASON, 2000: *Making Popular Music: Musicians, Creativity and Institutions*. London: Arnold.

VINCENT, RICKEY, 1996: *Funk: The Music, the People, and the Rhythm of the One*. New York: St Martin's/Griffin.

WALSER, ROBERT, 1993: *Running with the Devil: Power, Gender and Madness in Heavy Metal Music*. Hanover and London: Wesleyan University Press.

——, 1995: 'Rhythm, Rhyme, and Rhetoric in the Music of Public Enemy'. *Ethnomusicology* 39: 193–217.

WILSON, OLLY, 1974: 'The Significance of the Relationship between Afro-American Music and West African Music'. *The Black Perspective in Music* 2 (Spring): 3–22.

SECTION II

Audiences, consumption and everyday life

EDITORS' INTRODUCTION

One of the most important shifts in popular music studies in recent years has been an increasing dissatisfaction with the concentration on 'subcultures' in understandings of audiences. Subcultures – which were nearly always assumed to be youth cultures – have been a central component of many course units, whether explicitly (in the form of readings of key writings) or implicitly (in the choice of music associated with the best-known musical practices which have long been viewed as subcultures, such as punk). The reasons for the special attention paid to subcultures go beyond the academic histories outlined in the general introduction. For many people, one of the most exciting features of popular music has been its association with symbolic rebellion and with resistance to authority, and this was often felt to be most vividly encapsulated in the dress, behaviour and musical activities of youth subcultures. Many students of popular music have either been 'members' of youth subcultures themselves, or they have been interested observers of them, and this has added to the popularity of subcultures as a way of approaching popular music audiences.

Subcultural studies was always controversial, and some of the most effective challenges came from within youth subcultural studies, notably Angela McRobbie's influential feminist critique (1990/1980) of the romanticised male-dominated discourse of most of the writing in this area. Dave Laing (1985) and Richard Middleton (1990) criticised subcultural theorists for their neglect of musical sound at the expense of visual style. Other sociological critics of subcultural theory emphasised individual differences rather than social class (preferring the term 'lifestyle' to subculture: e.g. Jenkins, 1983) and argued that young people, rather than reflecting their class background in their choice of music, clothes or argot, were in fact creative shapers of their own identities, an argument apparent in the later work of subculturalist Paul Willis (e.g. 1990). In popular music studies, Andy Bennett has followed this tradition in his study of the way that young people use popular music 'to an emancipatory effect' in resisting 'unequivocally oppressive' (Bennett, 2000: 56) local cultures and traditions. A somewhat less sanguine view of youth culture was provided by Sarah Thornton (1995) who criticised subcultural studies for what she saw as a naive romanticised celebration of youth rebellion. Instead, Thornton treated dance club cultures as taste cultures. Inspired by Pierre Bourdieu's (1984) understanding of taste as a struggle for social prestige, Thornton suggested that youth cultures, rather than rebelling against a mainstream or conformist society, were primarily interested in asserting their superiority over rival youth groups.

In spite of many critiques, subculture remains a central term in work on popular music – and a concern with youth continues to preoccupy researchers. Electronic dance music (often labelled 'rave' in the early 1990s) has been by far the most commented-upon musical aspect of youth culture of recent years, and the subject of an increasing number of book-length academic treatments.

Rupa Huq, in her contribution here, explains why she feels that dance music culture cannot be understood through the lens of subcultural theory. For Huq, this is partly because dance music culture lacks the cohesion implied by the term 'subculture'; dance music culture includes a very broad set of musics, tastes and social groups, and cannot be seen as a single entity. Huq also argues that many writers over-invested rave with political meaning, in the traditional sense of intervention in public policy, and downplayed the politics of its pleasures. Her approach here typifies a swing in studies of popular music away from an emphasis on the political role of popular music.

Ian Maxwell, meanwhile, is also concerned with the assumptions informing writers on youth subcultures and music, in particular the tendency for many researchers to identify too closely with the subcultures they analyse – the 'curse of fandom', as Maxwell labels it. Drawing on critical ethnography and the work of Bourdieu, Maxwell argues that the notions of 'insider' and 'outsider' are inadequate as a means of judging research on musical cultures. Instead, he suggests that good fieldwork involves close attention to 'the living, embodied experience of others' (though it offers no guarantees of unmediated access to that experience) and a commitment to reflexivity on the part of the investigator.

The contributions of Maxwell and Huq are indicative of a reaction against the tendency in earlier studies to read popular music as either resistant, or co-opted (see Abercrombie and Longhurst (1998) for a parallel move in the sociology of culture) and a shift towards a more pragmatic and balanced assessment of the role of music in the lives of people. Over recent years a growing number of writers have been arguing for the necessity of studying 'music in everyday life'. This is informed by two key assumptions. The first, and perhaps the most common, is that music, and particularly popular music, is pervasive as we go about our daily life. It is on the radio, on television, but it is also heard in stations, shops, hotel foyers, airports, restaurants, factories; it follows us from the day nursery to the funeral parlour. It is, in short, part of the soundscape, a term popularised by R. Murray Schafer (e.g. 1977). Some of those who focus on this aspect have been concerned about the way music has become part of the manipulative context of our mediated lives. A large part of the music we hear is not there by chance and it has not been put there for our benefit. Philip Tagg (1990, 1994) has pointed out in a number of his writings how the everyday pervasiveness of music is not necessarily part of a society reaching forms of greater enlightenment, but is being used to limit behaviour, manipulate work and consumption, and to promote certain ideological beliefs. In contrast, Tia DeNora (2000) more benignly suggests that much of this music provides possibilities for people to use music in various ways in the construction of their individual subjectivity and social world, and Joseph Lanza (1994) has argued for the social and aesthetic value of what has generically been condemned as irritating and insidious muzak.

David Hesmondhalgh's chapter examines whether the study of music in 'everyday life' might enable empirical studies of popular music audiences to correct some biases and lacks in existing studies, including some of those indicated above: an excessive focus on youth, and on supposedly typical youth experiences and genres; a focus on spectacular and supposedly rebellious uses of popular music, at the expense of the mundane and the banal; and a lack of attention to specifically musical experience. While he feels that the notion of the everyday helps draw attention to these missing dimensions, Hesmondhalgh detects a danger in certain analytical traditions that 'everyday life' will be used to justify an *evasion* of questions of history, power, meaning and value. Anahid Kassabian is also concerned with the social relations of music in everyday life, and in particular with how we might understand the types of subjectivity (or personhood) associated with ubiquitous music, the sounds we do not usually choose to listen to but which are part of our sonic environment and which cannot be avoided. She suggests that if we pay critical attention to this aspect of contemporary experience, then our study of popular music has much to contribute to a more general understanding of the ways our subjectivities are formed and shaped in modern societies.

References

ABERCROMBIE, NICHOLAS AND BRIAN LONGHURST, 1998: *Audiences*. London: Sage.

BENNETT, ANDY, 2000: *Popular Music and Youth Culture*. Basingstoke and London: Macmillan.

BOURDIEU, PIERRE, 1984: *Distinction*. London: Routledge.

DENORA, TIA, 2000: *Music in Everyday Life*. Cambridge: Cambridge University Press.

JENKINS, RICHARD, 1983: *Lads, Citizens and Ordinary Kids*. London: Routledge and Kegan Paul.

LAING, DAVE, 1985: *One Chord Wonders*. Buckingham: Open University Press.

LANZA, JOSEPH, 1994: *Elevator Music*. New York: St Martin's Press

MCROBBIE, ANGELA, 1990/1980: 'Settling Accounts with Subcultures: A Feminist Critique', in Simon Frith and Andrew Goodwin (eds), 1990: *On Record*. New York: Pantheon; London: Routledge.

MIDDLETON, RICHARD, 1990: *Studying Popular Music*. Buckingham: Open University Press.

SCHAFER, R. MURRAY, 1977: *The Tuning of the World*. New York: Alfred A. Knopf.

TAGG, PHILIP, 1990: 'Music in Mass Media Studies', in K. Roe and V. Carlsson (eds), *Popular Music Research*. Gothenburg: Nordicom.

——, 1994: 'From Refrain to Rave: The Decline of Figure and the Rise of Ground'. *Popular Music* 13 (2): 209–22.

THORNTON, SARAH, 1995: *Club Cultures*. Cambridge: Polity.

WILLIS, PAUL, 1990: *Common Culture*. Buckingham: Open University Press.

5

Raving, not drowning: authenticity, pleasure and politics in the electronic dance music scene

Rupa Huq

The vast and varied set of musical styles usually understood to be encompassed by the umbrella term 'electronic dance music' have now been prominent on the youth cultural landscape since the late 1980s. The intervening years from acid house to third millennium have seen dance music undergo something of an institutionalisation, evidenced in the burgeoning number of published retrospectives and insider accounts from 'survivors' (Anthony, 1998; Benson, 1997; Bussman, 1998; Collin, 1997; Garratt, 1998; Harrison, 1998; Reynolds, 1998) and academic accounts of the phenomenon (Gilbert and Pearson, 1999; Malbon, 1999; Rietveld, 1998; Thornton, 1995) which have flourished over recent years. This chapter focuses on electronic dance music culture – formerly termed 'rave' and before that 'acid house'. It examines the phenomenon in terms of what it means for popular music and youth culture at large. The relationship between dance music, politics and pleasure will also be explored.

As Sarah Thornton (1995: 71) points out, 'what contemporary British youth call "dance music" is more precisely designated as discotheque or club music. Rather than having an exclusive claim on dancing, the many genres and sub-genres coined obsessively under the rubric share this institutional home.' Techno, house, garage, hardcore and drum and bass are some of the best-known variants, while Simon Reynolds (1998: 439–76) comes up with an extensive yet now inevitably dated list including 'ardcore, handbag and brutalist. Internal diversity in the dance music scene makes any generalisations about its elements difficult. Importantly there is not just one dance scene but several, spanning ad hoc illegal free parties and superclubs, not to mention a diverse range of musics. This chapter will highlight some of these differences as well as attempting to discuss common characteristics.

Like many musical styles dance music has contested roots. Rave, as it was known at the time, was initially constructed in relation to previous waves of

No lyrics

youth subculture. Sixties hippiedom provided the most obvious template in the dubbing of 1988 as 'the second summer of love'. Punk parallels also surfaced, stressing rave's marginalisation from the mainstream and emphasising an ethos of amateurism. The *New Statesman*'s (13 October 1989) dubbing of rave as 'Britain's most sustained underground since punk' was one example from many of this comparison with punk. Others have shown its roots in disco (Hesmondhalgh, 1997; Tomlinson, 1998).

A common characterisation of acid house/rave was as inauthentic pop. 'Acid House: How Dare they Call It Music?' demanded the right-wing British national daily newspaper the *Sun* (7 October 1988). The left-liberal weekly the *Observer* (18 November 1990) saw the advent of rave as signalling a 'revival minus the revolution' replete with 'uncomfortable realism, an air of despair ... optimism is just not on the agenda in the new sixties'. The right disapproved of dance music's disregard for traditional musical structure while the left decried it for its lack of message. Such anxieties on the left about the alleged lack of purpose in rave recalled earlier debates in the history of recorded popular music in the same way as anxieties about the rhythms of rave can be linked to previous anxieties about the rhythms of popular music.

Rave/acid house arrived at a time when proclamations of the demise of pop music abounded, and perhaps inevitably it was not long before dance music found itself the recipient of the epithet 'the new rock and roll'. Redhead (1995) quotes an unnamed organiser of the International Dance Music Awards held in London in 1994, who declared 'Rock is dead with youth – dance music has taken over'. Dance music traits of sampling and sequencing sharply contrast with insistence on the principle of authenticity and all that this entails. The importance of live performance, melody, harmony and the human voice has been emphasised in many other late twentieth-century Western musical forms. The technological base of the music – evident in the genre term 'techno' – is one of dance music's most noteworthy features and entirely fitting for a generation who have grown up with computers.

It would be easy enough to see rave as another instalment in the unfolding history of UK subcultures. However, a number of rave chroniclers have been at pains to distance themselves from the 'Birmingham school' subcultural approach. Thornton (1995) declares herself to be 'post-Birmingham' in outlook and Redhead (1993: 23) sees what he calls rave's depthlessness as more in keeping with postmodern popular culture than with the insistence on authenticity in subcultural theory. Dance music culture does not display the traditional characteristics of subcultures. It is not a tightly bonded, fringe delinquent working-class group. Nor is it entirely clear that it is a youth culture. Tomlinson (1998: 199) has commented: 'Rave is largely, if not exclusively a youth phenomenon, and youth is a vital component of the rave culture in general.' Be this as it may, by the beginning of the new millennium there was a generation of dance music fans who had been participating in club culture for a decade: a market segment termed 'middle youth'. As a result the whole continued validity of pop as a metaphor of youth culture is one that needs examination in an age when youth lifestyles are reaching up into this category and compressing downwards into the pre-teen years.

Regulation, repression and activism

For Stanley (1997: 50) the status of rave as a subculture of transgression is reinforced by the stolen sounds employed in the practice of sampling, i.e. using fragments of past recordings in the creation of a new track (Beadle, 1993; Goodwin, 1987), a practice which Reynolds and Stubbs (1990: 167) call 'Fairlight robbery' after the synthesiser of the same name.[1] Copyright law has been an important legal issue in dance music but more significant still was dance music's association with illegal drugs. Controversy surrounded the late 1980s contemporary dance music predecessor 'acid house' for its very name alone. Before long it became clear that it was the amphetamine-based substance MDMA commonly known as ecstasy or E, and not LSD, that was the drug of choice for rave and the musical styles derived from it. Indeed negative stories about ecstasy casualties have long made newspaper headlines in the UK. Subsequent similar cases continued to attract press fascination up until the time of writing.[2] There is evidence to suggest that E seemed to intensify certain features of the music. Pini (1997: 154) asserts that 'being "ecstatic" has in many ways replaced previous youth-cultural "styles of being": being "political", being "angry", being "hard" and even (certainly at the very beginning of rave in London) being "fashionable"'. Other commentators are more explicit about the drug itself and its direct effect on dance culture (Collin, 1997; Reynolds, 1998).

But it was also a matter of time before 'being angry' surfaced in rave culture but this was only when rave itself was under threat from the law. Major legal restrictions on the holding of UK dance events have twice been enacted: by the Entertainments (Increased Penalties) Act 1990 – commonly known as the 'Bright Bill' after its sponsor Graham Bright MP – and the Criminal Justice and Public Order Act 1994 – abbreviated to CJA. The different respective kinds of raver targeted by the Bright Bill and CJA are key in explaining the differing grass-roots responses. In 1990 the object of official fear was the stereotypical ecstasy guzzler that tabloid scare stories had created. The resulting 'freedom to party' campaign enlisted to its cause Thatcherite commercial rave promoters with Conservative party links who argued that rave regulation was an anathema to the prevailing enterprise culture (Osgerby, 1997). In 1994 it was the 'crusty', a highly mythologised technopagan/raver/squatter/traveller stereotype (Press, 1995)[3] with a propensity to frequent (or even throw) free parties. The use of the word 'free' was interpreted by proponents as both denoting 'no entrance charge' and as commensurate with liberty itself, e.g. 'The nature of a free festival is just that: freedom. You can do what you like, it doesn't matter how bizarre, as long as it doesn't impinge upon other people. No moralism. No prohibitions' (Stone, 1996: 185). The two definitions were linked, as seen in the explanation of the movement's own internal moral code proffered by free party newssheet *SchNEWS* (3 November 1995): 'Free parties is [sic] about saying no to crap clubs with rip-off prices with numbskull bouncers.' However, 'crusty' itself transformed from underground to overground. Lowe and Shaw (1993: 161) interviewee Jeremy highlights the contradiction therein: 'People called us crusties and that label's stuck and become a sort of fashion thing which is ridiculous really because it was the opposite of that ... It was anti-fashion, anti-image. It was supposed to be a viable alternative way of life. Although the lineage of crusties can be seen in anarcho punk (Gilbert, 1997; McKay, 1996; Press, 1995), it also takes some of its aesthetic and ethic from the New Age travellers (who are *not* a youth culture).[4]

The CJA started life as the Criminal Justice Bill (CJB). The CJB's attempt to limit rave parties by prohibiting, under certain circumstances, 'music wholly or predominantly characterised by the emission of a succession of repetitive beats' has been widely ridiculed for its illogical premise – virtually all Western music is essentially organised sound, dependent on repetition. As Debby of ravers' pressure group Advance Party remarked at the time: 'I guess that's goodbye to Ravel's Bolero then.' The age-old sense of adults legislating against something that they do not understand – youth having more or less harmless fun – was a common motor of the Bright Bill and CJB campaigns. Just as it was said that the Birmingham subcultural theorists' interest in the class politics of youth culture was out of proportion to the value attached to this dimension by the actual participants themselves, academics have emphasised the CJB's specific impact on the dance movement (Gilbert, 1997; Hutnyk, 1996; Huq, 1999; McKay, 1996; 1998) more than the many music-journalist-penned rave histories (with the exception of Collin, 1998). Similarly CJB politics have interested the non-mainstream press more than Fleet Street (*New Statesman, Red Pepper*, etc.). Even at the height of CJA opposition by the free party scene there was a large section of (legal) clubbers who remained blissfully unaware of the legislation or the campaign mobilised by their free party counterparts. My evidence is from personal involvement in the collection of signatures on anti-CJB petitions in London clubs in 1994. Our efforts were met with interest, but there was widespread ignorance of our cause. As a whole the campaign excited the radical left but went largely unnoticed by wider society.[5]

The politics of pleasure

Frith (1996: 269) observes that 'The academic study of popular music has been limited by the assumption that the sounds somehow represent "a people".' The prospect of political fightback by ravers excited 1960s radicals who had previously written it off as apolitical and apathetic. It seemed to contradict widespread early accounts of rave as having no discernible message. For Gilbert (1997) it is the very immediacy of contemporary dance music which makes it so ideally suited to direct-action politics, whereas rock music corresponds more closely with representational politics. NVDA (non-violent direct action) by-passes parliamentary structures in the same way that dance has a healthy disregard for many accepted musical conventions. On the other hand, NVDA shares much with more conventional politics. Both share a certain pragmatism. Class struggle was largely renounced by anti-CJB protesters as it was by the parliamentary left. It is often pointed out that identity politics has assumed a major significance in the CJB rave protests, while class has been insignificant except in the peripheral politicking of Trotskyist groups. Yet paradoxically the messages of rave music often decentre identity by encouraging the dancer to lose themselves or 'let the music take control'. This is captured in the Primal Scream song title of 1990: 'Don't Fight It, Feel It'.

The intellectual left has generally failed to engage with fun for its own sake. The politics of pleasure is difficult to reconcile with the more worthy aims of the wider Marxist project (Harris, 1992). But in acid house/rave culture, free parties became a highly charged political act/statement in themselves. C. J. Stone (1994) claimed at the height of the anti-CJB activity: 'People don't go on demos these days, they celebrate. They don't protest, they party.' The right to rave, despite the political connotations that it took on, unlike CND (future of the planet) or Vietnam (solidarity with the oppressed in a far-off anti-communist war), could be seen as selfish or parochial. But wider effects of the anti-Criminal Justice Bill campaigns can be seen in connected 'overspill' animal and road protests at the time and in later subsequent anti-capitalist demonstrations.

It is worth focusing on the lack of meaning or content in electronic dance music. Langlois (1992: 237) points out how electronic dance music constructed from samples is 'blatantly artificial ... There is no pretence that the record represents a live performance. To the audience this is of no consequence ... it is sensation rather than false integrity they are after'. Willis (1990: 65) makes the same point, describing house music as 'an uptempo and highly syncopated dance music with lots of over-dubbed cross-rhythms, sampled voices and effects ... the words [aren't] of any real significance ... the "feel" behind the music [is] of more importance'. The long-established popular music studies line of lyric analysis (discussed by Swiss et al., 1998) have little relevance to dance music due to its largely instrumental form. Instead, deconstructing dance music down to its very root, its principal function is the pleasure of the dance. Ward (1993) claims that within rational industrial/post-industrial societies dance will be peripheral to the main forms of activity and social relationships and therefore those for whom dance does play an important role are definitely marginal and almost always suspect. McRobbie (1984: 132) too bemoans the serious academic consideration of dance as 'an important absence in both sociology and cultural studies'. Rave music, devoid of any 'authenticity'-laden musical properties (e.g. untreated vocals, live instruments), is arguably nothing more than a vehicle for dancing.

Frith (1996: 125) distinguishes between two types of music performance: 'serious music', which is cerebral and is judged a success if it elicits still appreciation, and frivolous 'fun music' designed for moving the body to. Electronic dance music belongs in the latter category. The interactive element can be seen in the way people will whoop and cheer at appropriate moments at club events. The natural accompaniment to a music that dispenses with the need to know anything (formal) about music is 'a dance which required "no expertise whatsoever"', (Redhead, 1990: 6). The *New Musical Express* (*NME*) explains acid house's initial popularity (25 April 1998): 'People who'd never dreamed of dancing before were now doing so with a frenetic intensity, arms aloft, as if locked in religious experience.'

As has been commented of attempts to put curbs on the internet and police cyberspace, exercising control over illegal dance gatherings to some extent is an attempt to regulate the unregulatable. In keeping with an 'accelerated culture' (Rojek, 1995: 157), time and space are reconfigured in the illegal free party scene. To dance as if there is no tomorrow is made literal as the days dissolve into one another. The temporal parameters of the traditional rock concert are stretched to potentially infinite duration at an illegal event, as there is no curfew when the licence ends. The illegal event is essentially a non-linear event, with no fixed place (secured venue) or (finish) time (Gilbert, 1997; Schehr, 1995; Stanley, 1997: 52). Both are dependent on the DJs' willingness to carry on playing (supply), the crowd size the next morning (demand) and police intervention. The illegal rave will often take place in the open air or on squatted premises. Parties in derelict dwellings or warehouses in the fractured spaces of industrial decline with initiative and imagination often use electricity supply diverted from elsewhere, a typical attribute of squatter culture. In much the same way as legal clubs have brought about something of a regeneration of city centres in Manchester, London and Bristol (Lovatt, 1996; O'Connor and Wynne, 1996) the free party has spread influence beyond the centre to the margins, rippling out a different type of urban regeneration (Hemment, 1998: 210).

Of the traditional youth cultural triad of sex, drugs and rock and roll, moral panic in the media initially concentrated on ecstasy's role in dance culture (drugs) and its unconventional music form (rock and roll) with much less emphasis on sex. Oddly enough for a music which arguably emerged from US black–gay origins, some commentators saw the rave scene as asexual (and indeed colour-blind). Reynolds (1997: 106) sees a regression to the Deleuze and Guattarian infantile 'body without organs', as opposed to the early rave scene's anti-sex rejection of the Oedipus complex in its utopian leanings. Jordan (1995: 30) too uses the BWO to describe the unity of the rave dancefloor where participants lose subjective belief in self and merge into a collective body encapsulating the physical/mental experience of raving. Perhaps the 1990s dance scene and its music are best understood as something of a contradiction: a sexless (i.e. pre-oedipal) but sometimes sensual soundtrack to a world in which in many arenas (e.g. advertising spurred on by the rest of popular culture) sex is ever-pervasive, e.g. risqué Häagen Dazs and Club 18–30 adverts. The perception by female participants of (ecstasy-fuelled) dance clubs as 'safe' spaces, as opposed to the (alcohol-dictated) sexual meat-markets of the high street disco has been seen as an attractive feature of dance music culture (Pini, 1997). Nonetheless the bar is essential to make high street nightclub 'rave nights' financially viable. Rave has been responsible for the rise of both rave-styled energy-boosting smart drinks and alcopops – developed to woo the young back into pubs.

Of course the politics of pleasure in dance music cannot be considered in isolation from the wider leisure industry. Music cultures are inseparable from the business dimension that they operate in. Some traditional models of youth culture assume that movements begin with a moment of subcultural purity amongst the elite before incorporation into the mainstream follows (Hebdige, 1979). Underground thus inevitably becomes overground. However, as Hesmondhalgh (1997: 175) points out, rave was never underground for long – it began as a commercial form, and then was claimed by an underground: 'dance music has always had a profound ambivalence about being popular, about being a mass form'. This can be evidenced in jungle/drum and bass which operates with its own alternative networks of production, distribution and exchange in parallel with the more public face of the music, i.e. the tunes that will make it into the 'drum and bass' sections of high street record stores.⁶ Mysterious, limited-run, white-DJ-only-label, underground 12-inch single releases with usually no information on the track or artist are not even designed to hit the chain-store record racks, circulating in the fraternity alone, although, as Hesmondhalgh (1998) points out, this medium is now mainly used by major record labels as simply another promotional tool.

It could be argued that the new post-industrial economy of dance culture makes possible alternative career structures for young people. McRobbie (1994: 162) has commented 'Subcultures are often ways of creating jobs as more traditional careers disappear.' The democratising and enabling potential of new technology in reducing the costs of music production have given rise to the birth of the 'bedroom DJ' and the bedroom studio (Langlois, 1992; Hesmondhalgh, 1998). But dance music culture also encompasses various support elements in addition to the music-making itself, including events promotion, the design of flyers, lighting, visuals, etc. Digital media have changed traditional working practices in all of these areas, facilitating the circulation of these cultural goods. To incorporate technology into a leisure-based work environment is a natural step for those employed in the creative industry of dance culture. This new generation of culture industry workers complicates the traditional producer–consumer dichotomy.

Dance culture and subcultural theory

The post-war youth studies paradigm of youth culture as subculture is now well known. A number of primary and secondary sources exist, addressing subcultural theory in much greater detail than space allows here (see the introduction to this section, and contributions to this volume by Hesmondhalgh and Maxwell). The Birmingham approach was to see youth as resisting through ritualistic behaviour, in opposition to the dominant order. However, such readings of youth culture as a symbolic working-class response to their lowly status are inappropriate to describe contemporary dance music cultures. Club culture, like acid house and rave before it, has always been more about having a good time than challenging the dominant order (though the Birmingham approach recognised the importance of pleasure in the youth subcultures they studied). Dance music's dalliance with politics around the CJB-enthused left-liberal commentators from academia and media alike conjured up images of a new version of the subcultural idea of youth as agents of radical social change but this was ultimately short-lived and only applied to a minority of those involved in dance culture.

Perhaps the chief failing of subcultural theory in its failure to explain electronic dance music and club culture is its concern with authenticity, which is difficult to reconcile with a blatantly inauthentic musical form. Redhead (1990: 25) has remarked: 'authentic subcultures were produced by subculturalists not the other way round'. Perhaps the only way to describe multifaceted youth cultures such as dance music culture is with multidimensional models. No single term can capture the complexity of contemporary youth styles.

Another problem with subcultural theory is that it implies long-term commitment, whereas participants are always drifting off into other scenes. For Thornton (1995: 3) club cultures 'are taste cultures. Club crowds generally congregate on the basis of their shared taste in music ... taking part in club cultures builds in turn further affiliations ... Clubs and raves therefore house ad-hoc communities, with fluid boundaries which may come together and dissolve within a single summer or endure for a few years.' Youth cultural affiliations probably always were too ephemeral to be the basis of long-term identities, even in the days of the teddy boys, skinheads, mods, etc. described by Birmingham subculturalists (see Hall and Jefferson, 1976). Dance music culture is dynamic – a process not a fixed entity. This fact underscores dance culture at every level. It can be seen in the way that terms emerge and recede at a dizzying rate. As Hesmondhalgh (1997: 168) remarks, commenting on the rapid generic turnover in dance music, 'the terms ... "rave" and "acid house", now sound as out-of-date as the phrase "beat combo" must have done to the early '70s hippies'.

The line of youth cultures described by the Birmingham school were in large part *spectacular* subcultures which attached great value to visual style, e.g. the mods, teds, punks, etc. In contrast, the electronic dance music scene has often been characterised as faceless. Melechi (1993: 37) calls it 'a scene without stars and spectacle, gaze and identification'. White-label 12-inch singles (see Straw's contribution to this volume) have been seen as epitomising this faceless aspect of dance, in complete contrast to the Roger Dean style sleeve design and expansive liner-notes of the pop record of old. For many years, the layout of the club was such that the DJ was often hidden away from public view in a DJ box, unlike the old stage-presence-oozing rock performer. In early rave it was common practice for DJ names to appear on flyers to attract fans who came for the music often not knowing what their idol looked like. Indeed flyers often sold themselves on the technology of events, e.g. the power of the sound system.[7]

But the DJ – 'simultaneously the performer, marketer and composer of the music' (Langlois 1992: 229) – has increasingly taken centre stage in dance music culture. Magazines such as *Muzik, Mixmag* and *Ministry*, implicitly aimed at men, contain lifestyle articles and personal profiles on 'name' DJs alongside articles of a more technical nature for the aspiring bedroom DJ. Acts such as Fatboy Slim or the Prodigy have crossed over to become household names, selling out stadiums for their performances. Thornton (1995: 29) remarks that in dance culture '"liveness" is displaced from the stage to the dancefloor, from the worship of the performer to a veneration of "atmosphere" and "vibe"'. However, there has been an increasing tendency to rockify dance music events: the Prodigy's live concerts arguably offer most of the elements of the traditional rock spectacle.

Dance music culture departs from traditional notions of youth subcultures as distinct groups: it is more all-embracing. To some extent, it crosses class boundaries. Early rave stressed this inclusiveness (Melechi, 1993: 36; Russell, 1993: 126–7). However, a number of variants of dance music exist with their own internally mediated structures and norms. Davis (1991: 213) describes acid house as 'a new youth culture . . . based entirely on the middle class'. Thornton (1995: 25) meanwhile sees raves (oddly) as 'white, working-class, heterosexual and dominated by the lads', whereas others have seen it rooted in gay disco and black DJ culture (Savage 1990). Julie Burchill has written (*Guardian*, 17 April 1999): [Dance music has given popular music back to the young, the working class, the female; all of those shut out of the debates about Bob Dylan and Keats, and none of them giving a damn'] The main conclusion that can drawn from these contradictory positions is that they all have validity if they are taken to apply to sectional audiences. The point is that dance music culture has a wide appeal across class and ethnic cleavages, but different publics will frequent different nights and venues. In other words, even if working-class youth *are* just as at home dancing in clubs as poor little rich kids, crusties, queers or the category that has been termed 'Sharon and Tracey' (Thornton, 1995), these groupings do not dance at the same club nights. Music is a key factor of this differentiation, as are location, entry price, drink price, etc. At different club nights the same physical space (venue) can take on a totally different atmosphere due to factors such as temporary internal décor – and most importantly music]

The diversity of practice makes it impossible to see dance music culture as 'another subculture'. The fragmentation of 'acid house'/ 'rave' into multiple sub-genres makes the notion of any collective response by dance music adherents to material inequality impossible. This may reflect social and cultural changes. Theorists such as Beck (1995) and Maffesoli (1996) comment on the weakening of older structures and the blurring of older divisions where social positions and identities are increasingly unstable. This has a number of results. Careers are more uncertain, yet men and women, for example, can compete on more equal terms. It is easy to get carried away ascribing excessive agency to dance culture participants in the supposed fluidity and flux that passes for contemporary society when many of the old structures do remain. In theorising youth cultures, there is a need to find a middle way between subcultural positions which place a disproportionate emphasis on structure and the romanticised postmodern and sociological accounts that overemphasise the agency of the individual.

Conclusion

Once upon a time, rave was a verb not a noun. The last decade has seen it take on a new meaning. Just as subcultures are no longer common youth currency, a reassessment of the relationship of youth and popular music is begged by the electronic dance music phenomenon. Rave/acid house could be seen as the last subculture as it is exposes the inadequacies of subcultural theory more clearly than any previous youth culture – though this has not stopped some commentators labelling it as a 'subculture' in the old sense of the term. The post-rave fruits of dance culture can be seen as distinctly post-subcultural in theory and practice. Whilst free parties do continue, they are increasingly rare and penalties are stiff. Post-CJB developments have included the advent of the highly visible, purpose-built superclub, e.g. the Ministry of Sound (London) and Cream (Liverpool). With merchandise spanning clothing, record labels, record bags, etc., these are brand names as opposed to simply clubs. Both rave and the politics of its defence are as much about the essential continuities of oppositional youth culture as they are about any sort of rupture. Dancing all night aided and abetted by chemical stimulants is hardly new. It is easy to get carried away with seeing dance culture as an all-encompassing 'way of life' for its participants but 'living for the weekend' has been a feature of youth culture for generations.

Rave's combination of both punk and hippie elements of sartorial and political style/philosophy to a soundtrack of repetitive beats shows that rave did not kill punk, which in turn did not kill hippie. Present-day youth cultures are cumulative rather than successive, and they are constructed from a panoply of influences. Dance culture has its roots in town (high street club, orbital warehouse party) and country (open-air festival). It displays traits of European influence (Mediterranean holiday dancefloors) and anti-Western values (Goa spiritualism). Dance music culture is far from a homogeneous entity. As Gilbert and Pearson (1999: vii) attest, 'Dance cultures are fluid, multifarious formations which will always exceed any attempt to map them'. Despite the rave nostalgia apparent in some of the recent writing on dance music (Anthony, 1998; Benson, 1997; Bussman, 1998; Collin, 1998; Garratt, 1998; Harrison, 1998; Reynolds, 1998),[8] the changing nature of rave in the past decade contains manifestations unseen before in post-war youth culture, as well as moments of *déjà vu*. Raving, despite attempts to legislate it out of existence, has remained an important point of reference for youth at both underground and overground gatherings. Perhaps a suitable epigram for dance music culture in all its permutations could be (with apologies to Stevie Smith) that the youth who enjoy it are simply 'raving not drowning'.

Acknowledgements

My thanks to Dave Hesmondhalgh for his help with this chapter.

Notes

1. The possibility of downloading music from the internet will doubtless accentuate the importance of musical copyright. For the House of Lords case, *Consumer Products* v. *Amstrad* [1988], concerning the selling of copying equipment and whether this constituted the inchoate criminal offence of theft, see Redhead (1990).

2. For example, the cover headline 'Ecstasy: My Tragic Girl's Wasted Life', *Daily Mail*, 9 May 2001, about the case of teenager Laura Spinks who died after taking tablets at a club in Cambridge.

3. Press (1995: 798) writes 'in the public imagination, squatters, ravers and travellers blur together in the "crusty", a smelly drug-addled parasite ready to take over your house while you're on vacation ... [i]n reality there is no generic squatter or traveller; instead there is multitude of "tribes" ... in search of a less restrictive, more communal way of life'.

4. Hetherington (1998: 329) argues, however, that 'New Age Travellers are a hybrid phenomenon. They remain a youth culture, in the sense that that was how their way of life originated and because most, though by no means all of those who travel and live on the road, have tended to be relatively young – but they are more besides.'

5. There was much more to the CJA than simply rave regulation provisions and in retrospect it looks like some of the more heinous sections concerning stop and search have ended up being enforced more than rave powers, e.g. in detaining asylum seekers.

6. Some dance musicians have achieved wider success (especially some superstar DJs – see later) but despite the efforts of the Mercury Music Prize, electronic dance musicians such as Roni Size and Talvin Singh (recipients of the award in 1997 and 1999, respectively) remain niche artists.

7. The self-parody that this image bred was seen in a t-shirt slogan of the mid-1990s, 'faceless techno bollocks'.

8. The general gist of these book-length insider accounts is 'it's not as good as it used to be', expressed in terms of commercialisation, drug purity and music.

References

ADORNO, T., 1990: 'On Popular Music', in S. Frith and A. Goodwin (eds), *On Record: Rock, Pop and the Written Word*. London: Routledge, 43–57.

ANTHONY, W., 1998: *Class of 88: The True Acid House Experience*. London: Virgin.

BEADLE, J., 1993: *Will Pop Eat Itself? Pop Music in the Soundbite Era*. London: Faber and Faber.

BECK, U., 1995: *Risk Society: Towards a New Modernity*. London: Sage.

BENSON, R., 1997: *Nightfever: Club Writing in the Face 1980–1997*. London: Boxtree.

BOURDIEU, P., 1979: *La distinction: critique sociale du jugement*. Paris: Les Editions de Minuit.

——, 1986: *Distinction: A Social Critique of the Judgement of Taste*. London: Routledge.

BUSSMANN, J., 1998: *Once in a Lifetime: The Crazy Days of Acid House and Afterwards*. London: Virgin.

COLLIN, M., 1998: *Altered State: The Story of Ecstasy Culture and Acid House*. London: Serpents Tail.

DAVIS, J., 1991: *Youth and the Condition of Britain: Images of Adolescent Conflict*. London: Athlone.

FRITH, S., 1992: 'From the Beatles to Bros: Twenty-Five Years of British Pop', in N. Abercrombie and A. Warde, 1992: *Social Change in Contemporary Britain*. Cambridge: Polity Press.

——, 1996: *Performing Rites: On the Value of Popular Music*. Oxford: Oxford University Press.

GARRATT, S., 1998: *Adventures in Wonderland: A Decade of Club Culture*. London: Headline.

GELDER, K. and THORNTON, S. (eds), 1997: *The Subcultures Reader*. London: Routledge.

GILBERT, J., 1997: 'Soundtrack to an Uncivil Society: Rave Culture, the Criminal Justice Act and the Politics of Modernity'. *New Formations* 31: 5–24.

GILBERT, J. and PEARSON, E., 1999: *Discographies: Dance Music, Culture and the Politics of Sound*. London: Routledge.

GOODWIN, A., 1987: 'Sample and Hold: Pop Music in the Age of Digital Reproduction', in S. Frith and A. Goodwin (eds), *On Record: Rock, Pop and the Written Word*. London: Routledge, 258–73.

HALL, S. and JEFFERSON, T., 1976: *Resistance through Rituals: Youth Subcultures in Post-War Britain*. London: Hutchinson.

HARRIS, D., 1992: *From Class Struggle to the Politics of Pleasure: The Effects of Gramscianism on Cultural Studies*. London: Routledge.

HARRISON, M., 1998: *High Society: The Real Voices of Club Culture*. London: Piatkus.

HEBDIGE, D., 1979: *Subculture: The Meaning of Style*. London: Methuen.

HEMMENT, D., 1998: 'Dangerous Dancing and Disco Riots: The Northern Warehouse Parties', in MCKAY, G.

HESMONDHALGH, D., 1997: 'The Cultural Politics of Dance Music'. *Soundings* 5: 167–78.

——, 1998: 'The British Dance Music Industry: A Case Study in Independent Cultural Production'. *British Journal of Sociology* 49 (2): 234–61.

HETHERINGTON, K., 1998: 'Vanloads of Uproarious Harmony: New Age Travellers and the Utopics of the Countryside', in T. Skelton and G. Valentine (eds), *Cool Places: Geographies of Youth Cultures*. London: Routledge, 328–42.

HUQ, R., 1999: 'The Right to Rave: Opposition to the Criminal Justice and Public Order Act 1994', in T. Jordan and A. Lent, *Storming the Millennium: The New Politics of Change*. London: Lawrence and Wishart, 15–33.

HUTNYK, J., 1996: 'Repetitive Beatings or Criminal Justice?' in S. Sharma, J. Hutnyk and A. Sharma (eds), *Dis-Orienting Rhythms*. London and Atlantic Heights, N.J.: Zed Press, 156–89.

JAMES, M., 1997: *State of Bass: Jungle the Story So Far*. London: Boxtree.

JORDAN, T., 1995: 'Collective Bodies: Raving and the Politics of Gilles Deleuze and Feliz Guattari'. *Body and Society* 1 (1): 125–44.

LANGLOIS, TONY, 1992: 'Can You Feel It? DJs and House Culture in the UK'. *Popular Music* 11(12).

LOVATT, A., 1996: 'The Ecstasy of Urban Regeneration: Regulation of the Night-time Economy in the Transition to a Post-Fordist City', in O'CONNOR AND WYNNE.

LOWE, R. AND SHAW, W., 1993: *Travellers: Voices from the New Age Nomads*. London: Fourth Estate.

MAFFESOLI, M., 1996: *The Times of the Tribes: The Decline of Individualism in Mass Society*, trans. Don Smith. London: Sage.

MALBON, B., 1999: *Clubbing: Dancing Ecstasy and Vitality*. London: Routledge.

MCKAY, G., 1996: *Senseless Acts of Beauty: Cultures of Resistance Since the Sixties*. London: Verso.

——, 1998: *DIY Culture: Party and Protest in Nineties Britain*. London: Verso.

MCROBBIE, A., 1984: 'Dance and Social Fantasy', in MCROBBIE AND NAVA.

——, 1991: *Feminism and Youth Culture: From Jackie to Just Seventeen*. London: Macmillan.

——, 1993: 'Shut Up and Dance: Youth Culture and Changing Modes of Femininity'. *Young: The Nordic Journal of Youth Research* 1 (2).

——, 1994: *Postmodernism and Popular Culture*. London: Routledge.

——, 1997: '*More!* New Sexualities in Girls' and Womens' Magazines', in A. McRobbie (ed.), *Back to Reality? Social Experience and Cultural Studies*. Manchester: Manchester University Press, 190–209.

MCROBBIE, A. AND NAVA, M., 1984: *Gender and Generation*. London: Macmillan.

MELECHI, A., 1993: 'The Ecstasy of Disappearance', in REDHEAD (1993: 183–9).

O'CONNOR, J. AND WYNNE, D., 1996: *From the Margins to the Centre: Cultural Production and Consumption in the Post Industrial City*. Aldershot: Avebury/Arena.

OSGERBY, B., 1997: *Youth in Britain Since 1945*. Oxford: Blackwell.

PEARSON, G., 1983: *Hooligan: A History of Respectable Fears*. London: Macmillan.

PINI, M., 1997: 'Women and the Early British Rave-Scene', in MCROBBIE.

PRESS, J., 1995: 'The Killing of Crusty', in J. Savage and H. Kureishi, *The Faber Book of Pop*. London: Faber and Faber, 797–806.

REDHEAD, S., 1990: *The End of the Century Party: Youth and Pop Towards 2000*. Manchester: Manchester University Press.

—— (ed.), 1993: *Rave Off: Politics and Deviance in Contemporary Youth Culture*. Aldershot: Avebury/Arena.

——, 1995: Review of *Microphone Fiends* in *Popular Music* 14 (2).

——, 1997: *From Subculture to Clubcultures*. Oxford: Blackwell.

REDHEAD, S., O'CONNOR, J. AND WYNNE, D. (eds), 1997: *The Clubcultures Reader: Readings in Popular Cultural Studies*. Oxford: Blackwell.

REYNOLDS, S., 1990: *Blissed Out: The Raptures of Rock*. London: Serpent's Tail.

——, 1997: 'Rave Culture: Living Dream or Living Death?', in REDHEAD, O'CONNOR AND WYNNE.

——, 1998: *Energy Flash: A Journey Through Rave Music and Dance Culture*. London: Picador.

REYNOLDS, S. AND STUBBS, D., 1990: 'Acid Over', in REYNOLDS (1990).

RICHARD, B. AND KRUGER, H., 1998: 'Raver's Paradise?', in SKELTON AND VALENTINE (1998).

RIETVELD, H., 1998: *This is Our House*. Aldershot: Avebury/Arena.

ROJEK, C., 1995: *Decentring Leisure: Rethinking Leisure Theory*. London: Sage.

RUSSELL, K., 1993: 'Lysergia Suburbia', in S. Redhead (ed.), *Rave Off: Politics and Deviance in Contemporary Youth Culture*. Aldershot: Avebury/Arena, 91–174.

SAVAGE, J., 1990: 'Tainted Love: The Influence of Male Homosexuality and Sexual Difference on Pop Music and Culture Since the War', in A. Tomlinson (ed.), *Consumption, Identity and Style: Marketing, Meanings and the Packaging of Pleasure*. London: Routledge, 153–70.

SCHEHR, S., 1995: 'L'errance comme bulletin de vote'. *Futur Antérieur*, no. 25.

SEFTON-GREEN, J. (ed.), 1998: *Digital Diversions: Youth Culture in the Age of Multimedia*, London: UCL Press.

SKELTON, T. and VALENTINE, G., 1998: *Cool Places: Geographies of Youth Cultures*. London: Routledge.

STANLEY, C., 1997: 'Urban Narratives of Dissent in the Wild Zone', in REDHEAD ET AL.

STONE, C. J., 1994: 'Let's Have a Revolution for Fun'. *New Statesman and Society*, 29 July 1994.

——, 1996: *Fierce Dancing: Adventures in the Underground*. London: Faber and Faber.

SWISS, T., SLOOP, J. AND HERMAN, A. (eds), 1998: *Mapping the Beat: Popular Music and Contemporary Theory*, Maine and Oxford: Blackwell.

TOMLINSON, L., 1998: ' "This Ain't No Disco": Or Is It? Youth Culture and the Rave Phenomenon', in J. Epstein (ed.), *Youth Culture: Identity in a Postmodern World*. New York and Oxford: Blackwell, 195–211.

THORNTON, S., 1995: *Club Cultures: Music, Media and Subcultural Capital*. Cambridge: Polity Press.

WARD, A., 1993: 'Dancing in the Dark', in H. Thomas (ed.), *Dance, Gender and Culture*. Basingstoke: Macmillan.

WILLIS, P., 1990: *Common Culture: Symbolic Work at Play in the Everyday Lives of Young People*. Milton Keynes: Open University Press.

6

The curse of fandom: insiders, outsiders and ethnography

Ian Maxwell

> While much recent work in musicology has at least acknowledged some of the
> complex extra-textual elements of contemporary music . . . there is still a strong
> tendency . . . for musicological analyses to reduce vibrant musics to lifeless corpses
> fit for autopsy.
>
> Chan (1998: 93)

I feel a little bit stuffy opening an article with a series of rhetorical questions.
However, what am I to do? Try these for starters. What is the study of popular music about? Why do we do it, and what do we expect it to achieve?
Or: how can we, as researchers or students of popular music, respond to
Sebastian Chan's colourful metaphor: how can our analyses avoid reducing
the objects of those analyses to desiccated cadavers on a slab? How can we
not be dissectors or, worse, vivisectors? And (which will bring me to the heart
of this chapter's concerns): what kinds of relationships can (or should?)
investigators have to the objects of their investigations? Or, avoiding the ugly
imperative lurking between my parentheses, turn that question around: how
does our relationship to the object of our investigations affect the kinds of
knowledges we generate through those investigations?

I use the phrase 'object of our investigations' advisedly, if only to foreground the question of this relationship. In one sense, I want to offer an expli-
cation of the thesis inherent in Chan's invocation of post-McClary popular
music studies: that the 'object' of such studies is not 'simply' the music itself,
as (relatively) pure form, isolated from living, breathing ('vibrant' says Chan)
social worlds, but, to paraphrase Richard Middleton (1990), the articulation
of meaningfulness to particular musics. In another, expanded sense, however,
I want to explore what is at stake in the attempt to move away from an
epistemology of popular music grounded in objectification, insofar as that
journey leads us towards a radical subjectification. Or, to stay with Chan's
metaphor, what do we risk doing when the breathing of life into the corpses
of music locates the researcher's own living, breathing body, with its desires,
passions, beliefs, commitments, investments and knowledges, as the privileged site of knowing?

Three cameos

How I came to study popular music

Between August 1992 and October 1994, I conducted research for my doctoral thesis – investigating the development of hip-hop culture in suburban Sydney, Australia – through a Department of Performance Studies, supervised by an anthropologist.

Here's *why* I went about doing that research. Public Enemy toured Australia in the winter of 1992, supported by Ice T. A friend and I attended and, later, argued about what we had just experienced: misogynistic cultural imperialism, or something more interesting? (see Maxwell and Bambrick, 1994). My feeling was that the question of what this music was doing was an empirical, rather than a formal one; the question of whether the experience of seeing PE and Ice T had a positive or a deleterious effect on the young teenage audience could only be answered by finding out about the lives of those people, not by simply analysing what the performers did, said or rapped, or the formal properties of their music (granted, these are not mutually exclusive: finding out about those lives involves understanding how the experience of particular forms of music comes to have meanings and effect on those lives).

Here's how I went about *doing* that research: first, by reading everything I could about hip-hop – something I, aged 27, knew next to nothing about – and listening to a lot of music. I was a complete outsider when it came to hip-hop. The (then sketchy) literature on hip-hop flowed into African-American studies, and the questions of identity and politics circulating there (see, e.g. Gates, 1988; Rose, 1994). Then I read everything I could about the way in which popular music and groups of people interested in popular music had been studied: first Hebdige and Willis, steeping myself in the Birmingham literature – that seminal body of work developed at the Birmingham Centre for Contemporary Cultural Studies from the late 1960s, into the 1970s (see the introduction to the present section of this volume). There I found an engrossing, exciting world of political engagement. From there, I moved to musicology: the revelatory writings of Susan McClary and Robert Walser and the methodological rigour of John Shepherd, Allan Moore and Richard Middleton. (For references to these writers and to the work of the Birmingham CCCS, see elsewhere in this volume.) Tipped off about the local Australia and New Zealand chapter of the International Association for the Study of Popular Music, I read the work of Philip Hayward (e.g. 1998) and Tony Mitchell (e.g. 1996). My advisor showed me Steven Feld's ethnomusicology (Keil and Feld, 1994) and Arjun Appadurai's seminal work on globalisation (1990); Pierre Bourdieu's sociology, Michael Jackson's phenomenology (1996) and various post-colonial writers (e.g. Gilroy, 1987, 1993; Bhabha, 1994).

Third, I accosted anyone I stumbled across wearing a Public Enemy baseball cap. In no time at all, I found myself 'doing fieldwork': hanging around with the self-proclaimed Hip-hop Community of western Sydney, attending performances, watching graffiti-writers, sharing sounds and music, learning about the music and how those people were making sense of that music. The research resulted in conference papers, seminar and media appearances, a thesis, book chapters and, not incidentally, a lectureship.

And now, when invited to (say) talk about Eminem on local radio, I will, without fail, be asked whether I am a rapper myself. When I turn up to present a paper, three times out of four I am greeted with (often, slightly disappointed) surprise: 'But you don't *look* like a rapper'. If I present material about popular music and youth culture as part of a course, invariably the students who choose to present material on hip-hop, or rave culture, or Goths, are those students who themselves participate, or are engaged in those practices.

That's one dimension of the 'curse of fandom'. Here's another.

Legitimation strategies

In April 2001, I was invited to participate in a panel discussion at a day seminar convened by the Rutgers University Student Community of Hip-Hop (RUSCH), New Jersey. A student-organised event/celebration, the day featured open-mic sessions, breaking competitions and discussions, resembling less an academic conference than a trade fair: crews paraded their work, passed out promotional CDs, and generally strutted their stuff. The day was framed within the paradigm of an academic event: a 'seminar', held on a highly regarded campus, with a timetable of panels:

> 2.30–3.30 pm: Psychology of Hip-Hop Panel (includes issues on gender, sexuality and race in hip-hop and how some of these issues make play in how hip-hop is looked at in the US).
> 3.45–4.45 pm: Hip-Hop Political Panel
> 6.00–7.00 pm: Professionals in Hip-Hop Panel
> 7.15–8.15 pm: Hip-Hop: Past, Present and Future Panel[1]

I was to speak on the final panel, looking forward to a discussion about global cultural flows, and offering a perspective from Australia, where hip-hop has been taken up in distinct, decidedly non-African-American ways. The seminar organiser greeted me enthusiastically, delighted, she said, to have found 'a doctor of hip-hop'.

When the panel convened, I found myself at the end of a long chain of desks, behind which sat a dozen people. A moderator introduced us, and proceeded to ask a number of questions. Very quickly it became apparent that the panel was not intended to engage with an academic analysis of hip-hop as a global cultural phenomenon, but was to address the realpolitik problem confronting participants 'within' hip-hop: how was hip-hop (understood as 'their' – the *insiders'* – thing) going to preserve its authenticity, its truth, its essence, in the face of those (by now) traditional threats to cultural purity – globalisation, commercialisation, appropriation? No-one was remotely interested in analysing or theorising hip-hop as, already, a global cultural phenomenon, and my contribution was met with little, if any, response. Instead, conversation settled upon the question of whether KRS 1's new album was going to successfully return hip-hop to its authentic roots.

Let me be clear: I am not challenging the 'right' (however such a term may be construed) of the organisers to conduct this event as they did. What interests me is how the event was legitimised through being framed as a 'seminar', thereby arrogating to itself the (disinterested?) authority of academe.[2] In a real sense, such a positioning is only possible because of the burgeoning success of the field of popular music studies.

Identifying (with) the subject

Log onto http://www.cia.com.au/peril/youth/#blurb. The site – 'Youth-Sound-Space' – is billed as 'a resource and mailing list for researchers and interested parties'. The introductory blurb is as follows:

> The Youth, Sound And Space page is mainly designed as a 'crossroads' for young academics and researchers who have common interests in youth cultures that involve musical practices and the construction of social space.
> The group of people involved is diverse . . . working in research arenas such as sociology, musicology, media and communications studies, performance studies and human geography – but also DJs and musicians involved within music scenes in Australia.
> The group, and this site, primarily serve as a forum for debate and discussion about youth cultures in an informal, but academically rigorous manner.
> If you are researching or working in this area and would be interested in being involved . . . email with a short, informal bio on your musical and/or academic interests. Participation is open to and welcome from all people, academics or not.[3]

Note the attempt to build a bridge between practitioners of popular music and academics writing about those practices, framed within a doubled space, at once 'informal' and 'academically rigorous'.

More interesting, however, is the identification of researchers with those being researched: '*young* academics and researchers who have *common* interests in *youth* cultures' (my emphases). Given, too, the development of spatial tropes for understanding popular culture – driven largely by the growth of human geography – note the use of a cartographic metaphor to describe the site – a *crossroads*, where a constituency of young researchers – 'we' – can meet to understand how people – (implicitly) *like us* – 'construct social space'.

Again, a caveat: none of this is wrong. It is, in fact, admirable and productive. The 'Youth-Sound-Space' site hosts essays, bibliographies and reports, and is a useful resource for those wanting to get a feel for a community of investigators and the kinds of issues they are interested in. On the other hand, it is also reveals expectations and assumptions often made about studying popular music and youth culture: the subtle sense of the mapping of theory and practice onto each other, so that those engaged with each of these practices (theorisation is, after all, a distinct practice in and of itself, the distinction redundant) are positioned as sharing a struggle – that of 'youth' to find 'a space'. It is this idea that I want to explore.

pause

Why explore all this? Well, in addition to my observation, above, that I was an 'outsider' to hip-hop, these reflections help us to consider just what the study of popular music is doing, in the most general sense, and, specifically, to interrogate our motives for embarking on particular research projects. My aim is not to debunk or rule out certain ways of doing such research; instead, I want to offer a broad overview of the field and some constructive contributions along the way.

New directions or on the precipice?

In his introduction to the January 2001 issue of *Perfect Beat* ('The Pacific Journal of Research into Contemporary Music and Popular Culture'), Philip Hayward noted that two contributions:

> offer analyses that typify a new direction in sub-cultural research that avoids the fixation of Birmingham School studies around (the supposedly innate) oppositionality of sub-cultural deviants and [instead] examines the internal institutions and negotiations of these movements

(Hayward, 2001: 1)

Before considering the significance of Hayward's observation of a 'new direction' here, I should defend my own slippage from 'popular music studies' to 'sub-cultural research'. Many meetings of the International Association for the Study of Popular Music (IASPM) have, in recent years, had to negotiate a divide between those advocating a musicologically informed and those advocating ethnographic approaches to popular music studies. Included among the themes for the 2000 meeting of the Canadian Branch (apocalyptically breathlessly titled '(Pre)Millennial Tensions: Pop Music at the Precipice'), was this: 'Ethnography and the study of popular music: If it's the answer, what was the question?'[4]

The simplest response to this question is that provided by the title to Chan's short piece quoted at the head of this chapter: 'Music(ology) Needs a Context'. In short, ethnography is that discipline (or set of practices) which can help us flesh out that context.

Chan is responding to an article on Goa Trance in an earlier issue of *Perfect Beat*, an article, writes Chan, exemplifying a 'tendency' towards:

> analyses which are, at best, partial and often significantly skewed (and thereby misleading) . . . [the authors'] study. . .illustrates precisely these limitations [i.e. the 'strong tendency . . . to reduce often vibrant musics to lifeless corpses'] with regards to its notional subject of analysis, the phenomenon of Goa Trance music, its associated subcultural milieu, its habitues and its myths of origin.

(Chan, 1998: 93)

Chan offers a confused statement of the issues I want to think about. I am sympathetic to the desire to recognise and thematise the life in and of popular music – his text is at the head of this chapter in good faith. However, Chan's enthusiasm for an engagement with his chosen field perhaps goes too far.[5] Specifically, Chan's use of the idea of ethnography itself is emblematic of a confusion about that idea. At the heart of this is a confusion about the status of the researcher him or herself, a confusion which a more careful attention to the idea of ethnography might help us to avoid. The original article's authors, Chan claims,

> neglect the contexts in which the music they dissect is produced, circulated, consumed and given meaning to [sic] . . . they fail to critically analyse their primary sources and tend to take the words of local Djs, musicians, Internet sources . . . at face value.

Indeed; the article is not particularly strong. Chan, however, seems to be even more appalled by this:

> their musicological dissection of 'Goa Trance'. . . . draws solely on mass market compilations – which are unrepresentative of the music culture as a whole – for source material.

Initially, then, the critique reads as a claim that the authors of the Goa piece have not been *ethnographic enough*: they are guilty of 'neglecting the context' and thereby distorting the truth. The remedy offered is familiar: a superior insider knowledge framed through an access to less 'mass market' and (therefore?) more authentic recordings, of which the authors have failed to take cognisance. This authority is developed through the implicit claim of access to the truth of that which represents 'the music culture as a whole'. This is really a very big claim: Chan establishes himself as a gate-keeper to the whole field. Already, too, a familiar dyad is in place: insider versus outsiders; authentic versus mass-market.

Towards the end of the piece another binary logic – in fact, an extension of the same binary logic – pushes us to the opposite position vis-à-vis the authors' ethnographic practice:

> By choosing to focus on local Australian artists as source material, Cole and Hannan miss the crucial global contexts which local artists tend to feel they exist outside of . . . The parties on the north coast of the Australian state of New South Wales that Cole and Hannan draw upon as source material for their analysis of DJ sets are themselves a local fusion of traveller mythologies and more urban, specifically Sydney and Melbourne scene fallout [sic] . . . further highlighting the futility of academically 'cordoning off' niche styles for analysis (95–6).

Apparently they have been *too ethnographic*, concentrating on a (mere?) local, missing the (real?) big picture: presumably a truth that exists somewhere else, somewhere in the abstract realm of 'the global', to which (only) some are privy. (And of course, the problem with 'the global' is that it is extraordinarily hard to do ethnographic work about.) And the argument changes again:

> For audiences too, it is more the combination of venue, music and people that creates the meanings of the musical structures rather than the musical structure itself (96).

The argument reverts to the idea that the 'meaning' of a music is given by its context – just not, apparently, the context of a backwater state of Australia.[6] 'To conclude', Chan writes,

> it seems important to see [this] article as an example of how musicology and *overly enthusiastic ethnography* produce skewed results. Rather than bringing to the fore the issues of communality amongst dancers, or philosophies of liberation through dance, the musicological approach ignores these positives by neglecting the social contexts of consumption (96, emphasis added).

The approach condemned as 'overly enthusiastic ethnography' is rebadged as 'musicological'. More significantly, however, Chan reveals his own hand (his own investment?) with his entreaty that the correct approach – although by now it is by no means clear just what that approach would be – should accentuate the 'positives' of the scene. Aside from the serious problem of the limited regard paid to social contexts of consumption, there is something more difficult going on here: rearing its head is the spectre of the fan, or of a kind of fandom: the commitment of (adherence to? advocacy of?) the scholar to 'values' (apparently) inhering in that of which they are writing. The intellectual alibi is that of 'ethnography', putatively as attention to context, but, in practice, as a methodological legitimation of the writer's own authority.

In turn, this leads to a set of questions about the motivations each of us, as researchers or students in this area – or any area – has for our work. In such fields, the absence of a rigorous methodology (or the rejection of the merits of any such methodology) for the conduct of such work creates real problems. We can never hope to eradicate such problems, nor would it be desirable to do so; rather, we need to read the kinds of claims we are advancing in our work carefully against our own aspirations and beliefs. We need to be as clear as we possibly can about these things, lest the field reduce to a simple exchange of opinion, in a kind of show-and-tell meets my-insiderness-is-better-than-your-insiderness. The extreme end of this tendency might well be the kind of radical identity politics alluded to in the opening paragraphs of this chapter: an intellectual practice in which only those who are 'of' the cultural world being analysed are granted leave to speak of/analyse that world: hip-hoppers on hip-hop, DJs on deejaying and so on. Often, of course, such practices are sustained through the selective adduction of a theoretical position: various manifestations of, for example, feminism, 'subaltern studies', 'post-colonialism' and so on have all affirmed the right of those hitherto denied the wherewithal to speak to do so, often to the exclusion of other voices; and I started this chapter with a series of cameos suggestive of this kind of tendency within the field of popular music studies.

In 1992, David Harris critiqued the tendentiousness of subcultural and cultural studies, arguing that the commitment of scholars in the area to a politics of resistance produced flawed theoretical models, the influence of which continues to be felt. Specifically, the repeated attempts to integrate or reconcile successive waves of theory (semiotics, structuralism, psychoanalysis, structuralist psychoanalysis, post-structuralism, feminism(s), post-colonialism) with a relatively unsophisticated received/post-Marxism (i.e. Gramscianism – dismissed as a lightweight, bourgeois fantasy), produced an unwieldy, unrigorous, self-serving monster, the legacy of which haunts cultural studies to this day: as a discipline without a centre, marked by well-meaning but naive scholars who overstate the political import and significance not only of the cultural phenomena they study, but that of their work itself.

The shift in thinking about popular music cultures identified by Hayward is against the Birmingham oppositionality paradigm: that is, away from a desire to base analyses in tendentious claims for the political value of particular cultural forms. The papers to which Hayward refers negotiate these tendencies: the first, for example, an examination of 'Reclaim the Street' activity in Sydney, offers a pre-emptive caveat:

> this paper is not trying to find or magically uncover resistance where it may well not exist. . . rather, it sets out to examine actions that have been positioned by their participants as explicitly oppositional.
>
> (Luckman, 2001: 49)

Luckman's critique is well made, and reflects, as she notes, a growing sophistication in the field. However, the problem does not seem to go away.

At stake in such work, however, and only barely hinted at, is a politics of pleasure: a phenomenology of embodied engagement with music. I now want to take up this idea, arguing for a more rigorous understanding of what an ethnographically informed approach might offer the study of popular music, nuancing that approach through Bourdieu's reflexive criticality. My limited contention is that a critically reflexive ethnographic practice has much to offer to the study of popular musics and those people who enjoy, participate in and commit themselves to them. Not only does outsiderness itself offer insight and knowledges not available to insiders (although I would rather problematise such a dichotomy altogether); ethnography offers a model for engaging, critically and analytically, with embodied, phenomenological modes of participation in popular music, modes of participation of great explanatory significance in our attempts to understand how popular music and peoples' lives are intertwined.

A case for ethnography[7]

So, just what is ethnography? Among the first claims that I would want to make is that ethnography is a mode of engaging with cultural practices which, as a priority, takes cognisance of 'issues of communality . . . contexts of consumption', and if not engaging with 'philosophies of liberation through dance' as a mode of analysis or ontological category, certainly seeks to understand how agents in specific cultural worlds might use such ideas to explain their participation.

There is something more to ethnography other than this attention to context. Although it is notoriously difficult to argue that ethnography constitutes an absolutely coherent methodology, it is possible to talk about what constitutes an ethnographic *practice*. The problem is, as Stephen Nugent has pointed out, that 'ethnography has become generic in a fairly desultory fashion' (Nugent, 1997: 4).[8] This is part of the problem we see in Chan's confusion, above. He is not alone; much work pays lip service to an idea about ethnography, while limiting its analysis to, for example, internet mailing lists or newspaper articles (see, for example, Taylor, 1997). Such work is more correctly a form of discourse analysis and, as such, less attuned to embodied practices than to representations.[9]

At the centre of ethnographic work is *fieldwork*: a sustained temporal and em-placed engagement with a set of cultural practices and social agents. Certainly, fieldwork often figures as an 'ad hoc accommodation', or even a 'fetish' (Nugent, 1997: 6). Nonetheless, its attention to lived, embodied experience, and, specifically, the lived, embodied experience of others – of those who are not like us – is its most powerful feature. In Signe Howell's formulation, ethnography involves the figuring out of 'how people, who in many ways are so very different from ourselves, make sense of themselves and the world in which they live' (1997: 103). An orientation to others need not entail making absolutist (colonialist) epistemological claims: an ethnographer need not claim to access, to *know* the experience of others in an absolute sense. Indeed, one of the tenets of recent ethnographic theory is a recognition of the primacy of relations between subjects, rather than of an ontology of 'inside' and 'outside', a shift away from an attempt to capture subjectivities, or to make claims for identification (the kind of epistemology sustaining the researcher-as-participant paradigm).[10]

Further, the ethnographic, fieldwork-based approach privileges, as Howell suggests, *people*, rather than representations; experience, rather than abstractions (1997: 107–8).[11] Through an involvement with difference, the ethnographer decentres their own understandings and assumptions, in order to bring the experiences of others into our attention; through a direct involvement with the bodies of others, the ethnographer privileges those bodies as sites of knowledge. It is these kinds of knowledges that are lost when the analysis turns to abstract generalisations: 'the' people, 'space', rather than *these* people, *this place*. And it is there that we are likely to uncover the politics of enjoyment: the kinds of ludic, affective engagements with music likely to breathe life into our accounts.

However, arguably the most valuable insight to be gained from ethnography is this: Michael Jackson's assertion that 'the knowledge whereby one lives is not necessarily identical with the knowledge whereby one explains life' (1996: 2). Georgina Born, in her analysis of IRCAM,[12] makes a similar point: an ethnographic approach, through its attention to the micropractices of everyday life, provides a means of discerning between a conscious discourse *about* a field and a less conscious discourse *within* a field. The claim here is a simple one: as an 'outsider', Born was able to move 'beyond' (the metaphor is Born's) the discourse of those in the field in order to trace its embeddedness in certain historical and contemporary social and cultural formations, and by moving 'behind' and 'across' their discourse in order to elucidate its gaps and contradictions, I have attempted to analyse forces *that are not readily perceivable by those subjects* (1995: 10).

Herein lies the fundamental flaw in the dismissal of the outsider: the assumption that cultural worlds are transparent to those who live within them.

Reflexivity

Among the powerful aspects of the embodied encounter is the capacity of that encounter to effect change upon the investigator. In the most simple of terms, this might be described as the potential of things as they are – as we find them in the world – to fail to conform to the analytical categories we take to them. Or worse: the capacity of our assumptions and agendas to do violence to the world as we find it.

The postmodern moment in anthropology reflected long and hard on the politics and poetics of the encounter with difference; James Clifford (1988; with Marcus, 1986), in particular, under the sway of deconstruction, drew attention to the very active role of the ethnographer in constructing the object they might, at one time, have claimed to be simply describing. Difference is never encountered as pure difference; the ethnographer distorts by their very presence in the field, and again in writing up that experience. For Clifford, this necessitated an urgent attention to the poetics of writing under the rubric of 'reflexivity'. Ethnography, accordingly, turned its attention to its own practice: a self-fascinated return of a hitherto outwardly directed, imperial, gaze. A corrective to the objectivism implicit in structuralist anthropology, Clifford's advocacy of a reflexive ethnographic practice marks a highly significant moment in the discipline's development; since Clifford, there is no sense in which fieldwork is considered an unreconstructed, unmediated encounter with difference.

Back across the Atlantic, however, a more nuanced model of reflexivity affords a more thorough, productive model for thinking through the questions raised by this complex of ideas. Rather than simply becoming (self-) 'infatuated with the hermeneutic process of cultural interpretation in the field and the (re)making of reality through ethnographic inscription', Bourdieu advocates a reflexive practice in which it is not the 'individual consciousness of the researcher but the epistemological unconscious of his [sic] discipline that must be unearthed' (Wacquant, 1992: 41). Rather than seeking an epistemological foundation in 'a spurious primitivist participation', Bourdieu demands that the sociologist/anthropologist turns their gaze upon the collective unconscious embedded in a given discipline, to guard against the production objects of analysis 'in which the relation of the analyst to the object is not unwittingly projected' (ibid.).

For Bourdieu, three types of bias 'blur the sociological gaze'. First, that created by the researcher's own 'social origins and co-ordinates (class, gender, ethnicity, etc.)' (Wacquant, 1992: 39). This is the obvious problem first confronting the ethnographer entering an alien cultural field: that of not projecting one's own frames – values, beliefs, desires – onto a different context. (It is also the problem most pressing for Clifford et al.) The history of the development of anthropology in the latter half of the twentieth century is a history of critical reflection on such biases, and the concomitant shift away from the universalising project of anthropology (understood as the attempt to ground all possible humans within a common humanity) to that of ethnography, with its recognition of the active role of the researcher in constructing (a) narrative(s) about (a) culture. Interestingly, such biases are far more easily identified the further away from one's usual context one travels: the closer to home the culture being researched, the easier it is to overlook significant differences.

The second 'much less often discerned and pondered' bias is that 'linked to the position that the analyst occupies, not in the broader social structure, but in the microcosm of the *academic* field' (ibid.). Under this rubric, researchers of popular music may be led to reflect upon where, institutionally, popular music is researched, and what methodological and theoretical resources are used. In Bourdieu's terms, given the specific gravity of the field of academic work (in the global, as well as in local terms), how do individual researchers of popular music position their work? How do they create distinctions – of methodology, or epistemological differences – in order to compete in the academic economy: getting conference abstracts accepted, manuscripts read and published, finding a job? How do these aspects of the practice of being an academic come to affect the nature of the research work itself?

Finally, Bourdieu notes the 'intellectualist' bias which 'entices us to construe the world as a spectacle, as a set of significations to be interpreted' (ibid.). This bias, Wacquant notes, is 'more profound and disturbing than those rooted in the social origins or location of the analyst in the academic field . . . risk[ing] collapsing practical logic into theoretical logic' (39–40). Bourdieu's target is, explicitly, the theorist who withdraws from the field of practice into that of theory; here, however, I have argued that an analogous situation may be discerned under the rubric of the 'curse of fandom': the fallacious adduction of a theoretical paradigm to sustain and justify both a mode of engagement with particular practices, and the construction of a discipline in which an identity politics or, perhaps, a 'spurious primitivism', becomes part of the collective theoretical unconscious.

Back to/from the field

Implicit in the idea of fieldwork, too, is the *return* from the field; disengagement and reflection upon experience from a distance. What might this mean for the practice of popular music studies?

Think back to the beginning of this chapter: the archaeology of my own practice which, now, hopefully, might be understood to have been undertaken less in the spirit of what Geertz has called 'the diary disease' (Wacquant, 1992: 41, citing Geertz, 1987) than in the name of Bourdieu. Armed with Gramsci via Birmingham, with the literature of hip-hop as politics, I found, in the 'field', resistance, hegemonies, homologies, subversion, politics.[13] The folk I met talked the talk: 'we are the oppressed, fighting the power, resisting, finding our voice'. More startlingly, the discipline in which I understood myself as working had *preceded* me: I was introduced – and introduced myself – as a researcher doing 'subculture' research, and thereby became complicit in the construction of a particular (sub)cultural capital. My reports to my fellow students and academic colleagues-to-be brought me the kind of career upward mobility and (admittedly limited) celebrity attending the selection of a 'happening' doctoral topic. It all made sense: people – those who could give me work and publish what I had to say – seemed to want to hear; those I was researching had their practice affirmed as important, and I was finding my voice: a win–win–win situation.

Yet, as the work progressed and, significantly, as I effected a withdrawal from the field, I was able to rethink what I had experienced – precisely because I was no longer part of it. At a distance, I was able to discern the terms of my engagement: my own desire to find a politics of resistance, my own corporeal *involvement* – at the level of the beats, of the thrall of the crowd, of the glimpse into belongingness I was afforded, and the institutional drive to finding something *significant* in all this stuff. I was able to reflect upon what, exactly, was at stake for me in producing particular narratives about those experiences, and about that cultural world. And the results – the arguments I produced about popular musics and the ways in which people engage with them – took me by surprise (Maxwell, 1997a; 1997b; 2001; forthcoming).

Acknowledgement

Thanks to Mark Evans for the title, first used in a paper at the Australian and New Zealand IASPM conference, University of Technology, Sydney, July 1997.

Notes

1. Press Release: RUSCH Hip-Hop Seminar: 21 April 2001.
2. *Knowledge* has figured as a key organising concept in hip-hop. Cf. Public Enemy's 'Don't Believe the Hype':

Rock the hard jams – treat it like a seminar
Teach the bourgeois, and rock the boulevard.

('It Takes a Nation of Millions to Hold Us Back', 1988)

3. http://www.cia.com.au/peril/youth/#blurb (20 May 2001).
4. Admittedly, this kind of hyperbole was exacerbated by the Y2K millennial thing. It is worth remarking, however, that the invocation of crisis has become, by now (independently of any calendrical happenstance), a generic marker of conference-making. Yawn. Note, too, that 'taking stock' need not imply the apprehension of a crisis: that is certainly not the implication of my writing. Nor necessarily is crisis unproductive. It just behoves us not to be too credulous.
5. Having said that, however, I would also want to point out the dearth of ethnographic writing on popular music – something that makes the construction of the argument I want to make a bit difficult. Chan's position is a (problematic, as I suggest) response to this dearth.
6. Perhaps the original authors might have been more circumspect in the claims they were making for their research: 'The Embodiment of Goa Trance in Northern New South Wales' might have been a better title for their paper than the rather all-encompassing 'Goa Trance'.
7. Thanks to my colleagues at the Department of Performance Studies at the University of Sydney – Lowell Lewis, Kate Rossmanith and Paul Dwyer – for their sustained attention towards and debates around these questions.
8. A quick word on the slippage between the terms 'anthropology' and 'ethnography'; perhaps a truncated etymology might illuminate things: *anthropos* – 'man' and *logos* – 'word/knowledge'; *ethnos* – 'people' and *graphos* – 'writing'. Ethnography is the practice of writing about people in their lived worlds, a decidedly localised project, as distinct from the universalising, somewhat abstract, 'knowledge of man' implicit in the anthropological project. The objectivity towards which ethnography might aspire is given, as Marshall Sahlins argues, through a process of ongoing comparison with a body of ethnographies (in Nugent, 1997: 4).
9. Howell uses the example of Ang's 1992 study of *Dallas*-watching, suggesting that an ethnographic approach would involve not only an analysis of (written) responses to an advertisement placed by Ang soliciting viewers' attitudes, but 'some participant-observation in people's homes while they are actually watching the series' (Howell, 1997: 108).
10. And of course, the question of just how close the ethnographer gets is often, itself, disputed (see Chan, 1998: 70). What I am resisting, however, is a binary logic of 'insider' v. 'outsider': some insiders are more inside than others.
11. Howell's critique is levelled primarily at cultural-studies-based writing about globalisation. Nugent paraphrases George Marcus's defence of the subsumption of

anthropology by cultural studies: 'as the conventional anthropological project (outward – other – oriented, empirically driven, comparativist) exhausts itself, and as globalisation continues to homogenise cultural difference, anthropology will be superseded' (Nugent, 1997: 4–5). This seems an overstatement of the state of the world: unsustainable, and, unfortunately, typical of much recent writing about globalisation (namely, Taylor, 1997; Hannerz, 1996; as well as those cited by Howell, 1997).

12. Institut de Recherche et de Coordination Acoustique/Musique in Paris.

13. Another caveat: I am not denying the political import of hip-hop. Elsewhere (Maxwell, forthcoming) I argue that, in the context of the phenomenon I was investigating, the discourse of politics circulating around and within the hip-hop scene did not constitute sufficient explicatory grounds for the level of engagement and participation I witnessed.

References

APPADURAI, ARJUN, 1990: 'Disjuncture and Difference in the Global Cultural Economy'. *Public Culture* 2 (2): 1–24.

BHABHA, HOMI K., 1994: *The Location of Culture*. London and New York: Routledge.

BORN, GEORGINA, 1995: *Rationalizing Culture: IRCAM, Boulez, and the Institutionalization of the Musical Avant-Garde*. Berkeley: University of California Press.

BOURDIEU, PIERRE, 1984: *Distinction: A Social Critique of the Judgement of Taste*. Cambridge, Mass.: Harvard University Press.

——, 1977: *Outline of a Theory of Practice*. Cambridge and New York: Cambridge University Press.

CHAN, SEBASTIAN, 1998: 'Music(ology) Needs a Context – Re-interpreting Goa Trance'. *Perfect Beat* 3 (4): 93–7.

CLIFFORD, JAMES, 1988: *The Predicament of Culture: Twentieth-Century Ethnography, Literature, and Art*. Cambridge, Mass.: Harvard University Press.

CLIFFORD, JAMES AND MARCUS, GEORGE E., 1986: *Writing Culture: The Poetics and Politics of Ethnography*. Berkeley: University of California Press.

GATES, HENRY LOUIS JR, 1988: *The Signifying Monkey: A Theory of Afro-American Literary Criticism*. New York: Oxford University Press.

GEERTZ, CLIFFORD, 1987: *Works and Lives: The Anthropologist as Author*. Stanford: Stanford University Press.

GILROY, PAUL, 1987: *There Ain't No Black in the Union Jack*. London: Hutchinson.

——, 1993: *The Black Atlantic: Modernity and Double Consciousness*. London and New York: Verso.

HANNERZ, ULF, 1996: *Transnational Connections: Culture, People*. New York: Routledge.

HARRIS, DAVID, 1992: *From Class Struggle to the Politics of Pleasure: The Effects of Gramscianism on Cultural Studies*. London and New York: Routledge.

HAYWARD, PHILIP, 2001: 'Introduction'. *Perfect Beat* 5 (2): 1–2.

——, 1998: *Music at the Borders: Not Drowning, Waving and their Engagement with Papua New Guinean Culture (1986–96)*. Sydney and London: John Libbey.

HOWELL, SIGNE, 1997: 'Cultural Studies and Social Anthropology: Contesting or Complementary Discourses?', in S. Nugent and C. Shore (eds), *Anthropology and Cultural Studies*. London and Chicago: Pluto Press, 103–25.

KEIL, CHARLES AND STEVEN FELD, 1994: *Music Grooves*. Chicago: University of Chicago Press.

JACKSON, MICHAEL, 1996: 'Introduction: Phenomenology, Radical Empiricism, and Anthropological Critique', in M. Jackson (ed.), *Things As They Are: New Directions in Phenomenological Anthropology*. Bloomington: Indiana University Press.

LUCKMAN, SUSAN, 2001: 'What are They Raving on About? Temporary Autonomous Zones and "Reclaim the Streets"'. *Perfect Beat* 3 (4): 49–68.

MAXWELL, IAN, 1997a: 'Hip Hop Aesthetics and the Will to Culture'. *Australian Journal of Anthropology* 8 (1): 50–70.

——, 1997b: 'On the Flow – Dancefloor Grooves, Rapping "Freestylee" and the Real Thing'. *Perfect Beat* 3 (3): 15–27.

——, 2001: '*Sydney Stylee*: Hip Hop Down Under Comin' Up', in Tony Mitchell (ed.), *Rapping the Globe: The Universal Language of Hip Hop*. Hanover: Wesleyan University Press.

——, forthcoming: *Phat Beats, Dope Rhymes*. Hanover: Wesleyan University Press.

MAXWELL, IAN AND NIKKI BAMBRICK, 1994: 'Discourses of Culture and Nationalism in Sydney Hip Hop'. *Perfect Beat* 2 (1): 1–19.

MIDDLETON, RICHARD, 1990: *Studying Popular Music*. Buckingham: Open University Press.

MITCHELL, TONY, 1996: *Popular Music and Local Identity: Rock, Pop, and Rap in Europe and Oceania*. London and New York: Leicester University Press.

MOORE, ALLAN, 1993: *Rock: The Primary Text*. Buckingham: Open University Press.

NUGENT, STEVE, 1997: 'Introduction: Brother Can You Spare a Paradigm?', in S. Nugent and C. Shore (eds), *Anthropology and Cultural Studies*. London and Chicago: Pluto Press: 1–10.

ROSE, TRICIA, 1994: *Black Noise: Rap Music and Black Culture in Contemporary America*. Hanover: Wesleyan University Press.

ROSS, ANDREW and TRICIA ROSE, 1994: *Microphone Fiends: Youth Music and Youth Culture*. New York and London: Routledge.

TAYLOR, TIMOTHY D., 1997: *Global Pop: World Music, World Markets*. New York: Routledge.

TURNER, VICTOR, 1969: *The Ritual Process: Structure and Antistructure*. Chicago: Aldine Press.

WACQUANT, LOÏC J. D., 1992: 'Toward a Social Praxeology: The Structure and Logic of Bourdieu's Sociology', in P. Bourdieu and L. J. D. Wacquant, *An Invitation to Reflexive Sociology*. Chicago: University of Chicago Press: 1–60.

7

Popular music audiences and everyday life

David Hesmondhalgh

Two fallacies underlie most discussions of studies of popular music audiences. The first fallacy is that studies of youth subcultures are an important and/or useful way of understanding popular music audiences. Surveys of, and course units in, popular music have tended to devote considerable attention to discussing subcultural theory and ethnography, both the 'Birmingham' version and its many critiques. In fact, as Richard Middleton (1990: 158) has observed, most of the best-known accounts of youth subcultures have very little to say about music at all. There are more than enough critical accounts of work on subcultures and to add yet another would only reinforce the very view that I think is fallacious. Instead, I want to flag an important effect of this first fallacy: many teachers and students assume that the study of popular music is the study of music mostly made by and for young people. In my view, this assumption has unfortunate consequences. Of course, I have no objection whatsoever to the study of the way that young people use music. Young people are as important a category as any other – and no more important than any other. The problem is that, because many books, articles and courses have treated popular music as a phenomenon almost entirely associated with 'youth', the musical experiences of other people, of different ages, and of young people who do not necessarily conform to prevailing conceptions of 'youth', have been marginalised.

The excessive focus on youth culture within popular music studies derives not only from this misplaced obsession with the sociology of youth culture. It also reflects changing relationships between young people and music in 'advanced' industrial countries from the 1950s to the 1970s, economically (young people became the biggest market for music), culturally (music came to be seen as an expression of youth) and politically (youth music was read negatively, as decadence, and positively, as rebellion). Rock and roll, rock and rock-influenced pop were the musical forms at the centre of these developments (see the contributions by Toynbee and Regev to this book). But by the 1980s, rock was losing its economic, political and cultural significance, and its association with youth: the aging baby-boomers were now the biggest spenders. However, academic and non-academic thinking about popular music has continued to be heavily influenced by the rock era's way of conceiving the significance of popular music: as a rebellious expression of what it is to be young. This conception of popular music helped to bring about the excessive focus on subcultures and on youth in popular music stud- ies. It has kept a youth-centred view of popular music on the shelves, but while this approach was always flawed, it was best before 1980. The youth/pop association is also sustained by the contexts in which popular music studies courses are taught. Most university undergraduates taking popular music course units are aged between 18 and 25, and many teachers want, it seems, to provide courses that will supposedly allow students to make sense of their 'own' experience of music. But I believe that privileging youth experiences of popular music is likely to deter, rather than encourage, students to reflect on their own musical experience. The distinctive nature of youth experiences and genres of music – if indeed they are distinctive – would be much better understood if they were set alongside the study of musical experiences and genres that are not so much associated with young people. The use by young people of music to express difference, maintain self-identity and question abuses of political and economic power are impor- tant; but we might have a richer understanding of the politics and aesthetics of music if we were to consider its emotional and social significance, not just for youth subcultures, or for young people as a whole, but for everyone. This means considering a range of experiences, from the transgressive to the banal, without privileging the search for the rebellious, and without assum- ing that youth experience is the most likely site for transgression.[1]

The second common fallacy in discussion of studies of popular music audiences is that there are many empirical studies of these audiences. I sus- pect that this fallacy derives from the way that the story of cultural studies is often told: that in the 1980s, there was a shift in cultural studies, away from textual analysis and studies of the media and cultural industries, towards the study of audiences for popular culture. There is no doubt that the study of audiences became much more fashionable in cultural studies in the 1980s; and it is easy to assume that this carried over into popular music studies. But in fact there are surprisingly few substantial empirical studies of popular music audiences: that is, studies which involved fieldwork with audiences, whether based on interviews or substantial participant observation (rather than just 'hanging out' in the same spaces as certain audiences). The most widely used textbooks on popular music studies courses may appear to con- tain considerable amounts of work on audiences. But a closer examination of such texts suggests otherwise. The main reader in the field (Frith and Goodwin, 1990) has only seven essays which deal with popular music audi- ences much at all (out of 35), and only two of these are based on substantial empirical fieldwork (David Riesman from 1950 and the Vermorels' 1980s interviews with fans). Horner and Swiss's *Key Terms in Popular Music and Culture* has 18 entries, but there is no entry directly related to audiences, and the only entries that discuss audiences more than in passing are those on gen- der (by Holly Kruse) and business (by Mark Fenster and Thomas Swiss). Longhurst (1995) and Negus (1996) devote entire chapters to work on audiences. Yet many of the key studies they refer to consist mainly of specula- tive interpretive work, such as Hebdige's semiotic reading of punk, or Will Straw's article about 'scenes'.[2] In very few – in fact, hardly any – of the studies discussed do we actually get to hear the voices of members of the popular music audience. This problem does not reflect lacks in these particular chapters – indeed some of the arguments below echo some made by Negus in his chapter – but rather it derives from the lack in popular music studies of substantial empirical studies of audiences.

Of course, there have been some important empirical studies of popular music audiences and of 'ordinary' music-related experience. They include:

- A slender but significant body of work on musical taste, including, for example, work on taste in relation to age (Roe, 1985), social class (Peterson and Simkus, 1992) and gender (Shepherd, 1986)
- Sarah Thornton's often-cited study of dance club crowds (1995)
- Andy Bennett's study of the way that young people use and constitute a sense of place in their consumption and production of music (Bennett, 2000)
- Work on fandom (e.g. Cavicchi, 1999), especially in relation to gender (see some of the studies in Lewis, 1992)
- Crafts et al.'s study of 'music in daily life' (1993).

There is some fine work here, but even within these audience studies, there are some curious absences. Even while they reject the subculturalist approach, they are concerned almost entirely with youth experience of music. And these studies only very rarely attempt to deal with *specifically musical experience*. By this I mean: what it is about the role of music in people's lives that distinguishes it from the role of other experiences as a means of gaining pleasure, of coping with life, and of marking, passing or understanding time and space? How does the role of music compare with the role of television, or sport, or sex, for example? This means addressing the nature of musical sound much more seriously than has been the case up to now: certainly more seriously than in work on youth subcultures, where music was largely ignored.

The aim of this chapter is to explore whether studying the role of music in everyday life might help popular music studies move beyond the limitations in work on audiences noted above. I begin by introducing three approaches to the concept of the everyday, briefly assessing their different assumptions and methods. I then assess the strengths and limitations of some recent studies of music in everyday life, focusing on their ability to combine empirical material with a satisfactory theoretical approach to everyday life. I also discuss the importance of questions of meaning and value in these studies. Finally, I offer some more speculative comments on the importance of the concepts of time and space in understanding everyday musical experience.

The concept of everyday life

But first, what is this concept of everyday life? And, as someone once remarked to a friend, 'why would anyone want to study anything so boring as everyday life?' In an overview of the concept of the everyday, Rita Felski shows the good sense not to offer too tight or concise a definition of everyday life, but tentatively offers the following framing: 'the essential, taken-for-granted continuum of mundane activities that frames our forays into more esoteric or exotic worlds'. While everyday life is 'synonymous with the habitual, the ordinary and the mundane . . . it is also strangely elusive, that which resists our understanding and escapes our grasp' (both quotations are from Felski, 1999–2000: 15). This elusiveness is compounded by the long and complex history of uses of the term in social and cultural theory. Building on the comments of Michael E. Gardiner (2000), we can identify three principal strands of work on the subject (though he is concerned only with the second).[3]

Empirical sociology

The everyday is a concept that is intended to draw our attention to the most grounded, concrete practices of human beings. This makes it attractive to various types of sociology, especially those characterised by deep commitment to empiricism, to the view that the most valid forms of social knowledge can be gained from observation, and in particular the interpretivist and interactionist sociologies that developed in the 1960s and 1970s as a reaction against macro theories (see, for example: Douglas, 1970; Karp and Yoels, 1993). But sometimes such sociology runs the risk of merely describing and cataloguing the everyday, without reflecting on what such everydayness involves. The 'everyday' is a taken-for-granted category in such sociology, hardly ever discussed or defined, even in books which carry the term in its title. 'Everyday' in such sociology comes to mean something like 'ordinary human experience', and it is sometimes crudely opposed to systemic, structural processes, which are implicitly understood as unknowable, unanalysable, unthinkable. Those theorists who focus on these more systemic processes are accused merely of offering their own interpretation, because they have not undertaken any empirical work. According to this variant of sociology, understandings of these larger processes can only be undertaken by building up from observation of the micro-interactions of everyday life; and yet such a project of building up from the everyday always seems to be deferred to some later date.

Neo-Marxian philosophy/social theory

On the other hand, there is a long-standing tradition of theoretical, often Marxist-influenced, work which does attempt to understand the very concept of the everyday, rather than assume its meaning. Such work strives to see everyday life historically, as the product of specific social and cultural conditions. For an important strand of this tradition (e.g. Lefebvre, 1971) the everyday is fundamentally ambivalent: it is degraded under conditions of capitalism (or modernity) but it is also full of utopian potential, because of its (unintentional) 'resistance' to bureaucratisation, domination, control. The situationists (e.g. Vaneigem, 1983) emphasised the degraded aspects while others (e.g. Certeau, 1984) emphasised the potential for resistance. Methodologically, the writers in this tradition could hardly be further removed from the sociologists. The attempt to theorise the everyday is a route into understanding the 'totality' of social relations. Empirical detail, and actually talking to people about their everyday lives, would be considered relatively unimportant, even trivial. More recently, a range of academic social theorists have developed this tradition of concern with the everyday (e.g. Maffesoli, 1989; Melucci, 1996), including feminists, most notably Dorothy E. Smith (1987).

Media and cultural studies

A third current of work on everyday life can be found in cultural studies, an interdisciplinary field founded on a concern with 'culture as ordinary'. This was initially a reaction against understandings of culture as 'high culture' or as an expression of civilisation. For many years, many cultural studies saw themselves as dealing with popular culture, but as the term 'popular' has fallen from fashion and favour, the concept of everyday life has become increasingly common as a way of invoking ordinary engagement with symbolic artefacts (see, amongst many other examples, Silverstone, 1994 and Hermes, 1995). The increasing interest in the concept also reflects a shift in media and cultural studies away from a concern with meaning and interpretation ('reception') and towards a greater interest in how media fit into, and help to constitute, the rhythms and routines of people's lives. Instead of assuming that people watch and listen to films, television, etc. intensely, there has been an increasing recognition of other modes of engagement with media texts, such as distracted and casual viewing. As with sociological treatments of everyday life, definitions and historical contexts are rarely provided, and the methods are empirical. But there is generally less hostility to integration with broader social and psychological theory (at least in some cases, most notably Silverstone, 1994).

Music in everyday life

For all the limitations of these different approaches, the everyday retains its power as a way of invoking those dimensions of human experience not captured by much social thought. It is striking how few of the writers who regularly invoke the concept of everyday life in the traditions discussed above show any interest in music (one brief exception is Lefebvre, 1971: 19–20).

Conversely, few writers on music showed much interest in the concept of everyday life, with the exception of some opaque reflections by Lawrence Grossberg (e.g. 1990/1986). Crafts et al's wonderfully entertaining book *My Music* (1993) was a groundbreaking effort to address the role of music in people's lives via fieldwork interviews. But in merely providing transcripts of interviews, with only fragments of commentary, the book left the task of connecting everyday life to music barely started. The question of music's integration into the routines of life is left untouched. And the emphasis on 'letting the interviewees speak for themselves', as if no further comment were necessary, seems to be based on the assumption that the value of music also speaks for itself, that music must be *a good thing*. But this begs the question: why should we celebrate music? Or, perhaps more precisely, what is it about music that we should celebrate? Some reflection on this issue in relation to the interview material would potentially help fill the gap identified earlier, the absence in popular music studies of consideration of the specifically musical nature of musical experience.[4]

Tia DeNora's recent book, *Music in Everyday Life*, is an important intervention, for it not only attempts to address ordinary, mundane uses of music, it also makes a serious effort to theorise such uses of music in a way which is attentive to the specificity of music. The book is based mainly on interviews, most of them with women about the role of music in their lives, and on observations of various musical events, such as aerobics classes and the playing of music in shops. DeNora's approach is based on the underlying view that music has tremendous influence in everyday life; and her book builds a substantial case against anyone who might see music – or even aesthetic experience in general – as a minor or inconsequential supplement to the 'real' business of day-to-day living. She analyses, for example, a number of ways in which women use music to affect their own moods and their own sense of self (DeNora, 2000: 46–74), and to influence the environment in which they interact with other people (109–31).

DeNora mistrusts attempts to extrapolate understandings of the social significance of music from individual interpretations of particular music texts, whether in semiotics or in critical theory. For DeNora, this social significance can only be appraised empirically, through interviews and other fieldwork methods. She is clearly working in the tradition of empirical sociology's approach to everyday life, discussed above, but her concern for the specificity of music allows her to pursue these ideas in a way that goes beyond merely saying that people act on the basis of how they interpret the world around them (the central tenet of interpretivist sociology). In fact, the most interesting discussion in *Music and Everyday Life* is of 'embodied', subconscious relationships to music. In her chapter on 'Music and the body', for example, DeNora argues that, through its patterning of the sonic environment, music can provide us with a sense of bodily 'security', an attunement or fitting in with the world around us. This patterning is achieved through 'regularized relationships between tensions and resolutions, sounds and silences ... and rhythmic arrangements over time that afford expectancy' (85). DeNora's book is not lacking in theoretical weight, then, but it is striking that in a book called *Music in Everyday Life*, DeNora offers no definition or discussion of what she means by the term 'everyday life'. Echoing empirical sociology, DeNora uses the term to invoke a generalised sense of the ordinary and the mundane, without examining the historical and highly uneven development of particular types of everyday life. In fact, the term comes to operate as a means of evading such questions through its loose connotations as something beyond mere socio-political, structural or 'macro' analysis. This means that historical and political questions, potentially raised by work that DeNora criticises as 'grand theory', are never confronted. How might everyday life in the late twentieth century differ from everyday life in other periods? Related to this, how might everyday life in 'advanced' industrial societies differ from that in other societies? These are not questions which a study of music and everyday life might necessarily answer, but any study of the subject would in my view be invigorated by at least some addressing of these questions.

There is also little sense in DeNora's book of how music comes to music users. The women she interviews may be active in their response to, and use of, music but the fact that nearly all the music that they use takes the form of technologically mediated commodities barely enters into the analysis at all. To take account of this fact would raise questions about how the ways in which 'agents' act on their environment through music might at least partly be structured in advance for them, by histories of the ways that technologies are employed, and by ways of thinking about particular musical sounds. These 'agents', in other words, might be seen as making active use of music, but not entirely under conditions of their own making. DeNora is too dismissive of those 'grand theorists' who might draw attention to these issues in ways that are not necessarily apparent to us in our ordinary, mundane practices. The problem here is one of consciousness, of how far we can be reflexively aware, in interviews, of what happens to us as we experience music. Good theory and good criticism can complement empirical work, as writers think carefully about aspects of experience which are not always apparent without considerable thought.

These questions, concerning the historical and technological dimensions of everyday life, are raised by Michael Bull in his book on personal stereos (or Walkmans). Bull is mainly concerned with theorising the nature of *sound* in everyday urban life, and he treats the different categories of aural experience as a distraction from his main goal of understanding the personal stereo's effects, as a technology, on the sensory experience of living in the city (see Bull, 2000: 14–15). The specificity of *musical* experience is, then, elided in his work; and, like DeNora, he is unconcerned with the content and form of music. Nevertheless, Bull's work offers some stimulating directions for thinking about music in everyday life. In particular, his approach is unusual in combining empirical work (interviews with personal stereo users) with a theoretical repertoire that draws heavily on critical theory (principally Adorno, Benjamin and Kracauer) as well as the neo-Marxian social theory of everyday life (e.g. Lefebvre) discussed earlier. This allows Bull to be attentive to the use by individuals of (often musical) sound in their everyday lives, to the fact that they are using sound, as opposed to visual media (thus raising questions about specificity), and to the wider historical forces that help provide context for, and shape, that use.

Bull offers a less optimistic account of everyday life than DeNora. He quotes one of his interviewees:

> But when I'm out looking for things that I see – in the world, human interaction – beautiful things that I think can touch my soul – you know that certain sound at a certain time and it will just move me to tears – and it is filmic . . . That woman in the street. She's really there. She doesn't have anywhere to sleep, but it's because I'm listening to music that's really tender that it moves me even more.

(Bull, 2000: 172)

Bull sees this as an *aestheticisation* of urban experience, as a way of making the city into an object of appreciation or distaste. He uses such statements to criticise recent social theory that would see the aestheticisation of everyday life in generally positive terms. The implication, he feels, is that 'if the music is not right, then somehow the woman in the street, who is really there, will not have the same presence'. The woman in the street observed by this interviewee 'merely constitutes an aestheticised fragment contributing to the user's sense of urban narrative' (Bull, 2000: 172). Bull's point is not ethical condemnation of the personal stereo user here. Rather, he sees such uses as symptomatic of more general social and historical developments including, amongst other aspects, the increasing fragmentation of social life and the increasing mediation of experience. For Bull, personal stereo use seems to be ambivalent and contradictory: such aestheticisation is a retreat from direct social relations with other people, but it is also a way of 'managing' everyday life. All this is linked to a theory, derived from Adorno, of how sound functions in contemporary societies. Because Adorno is one of the few theorists to engage fully with the idea of the specificity of musical experience, this allows for interesting speculations. In particular, Bull pulls out from Adorno's work some pointed comments about music's (and, for Bull, sound's) special relationship to collectivity, and how that relationship has been affected by historical developments, and fetishised in certain forms of music. Music contains a strong utopian impulse, a sense of what life would be like if we were to live 'as one', but has come to pervert that impulse, by offering a false vision of unmediated collectivity, in a time when our relationships with other people are mediated in all kinds of complex ways (see Bull, 2000: 123–5). The personal stereo, then, is an attempt to break the boundaries of social fragmentation, if in an illusory way.

Yet, for all the suggestiveness of the work that Bull draws on, it is not clear that Adornian critical theory offers an adequate understanding of social change, or of the individual, or even of music. There is no space here for an assessment of critical theory, but to raise one point amongst many, Adornian critical theory clearly overstates the degree to which aesthetic experience has been commodified in modern life.[5] In fact, Bull constantly pulls back from a full endorsement of Adorno's view of the degraded nature of contemporary cultural experience. Insights are raised, and are then partially withdrawn. Bull shows that we need a historical conception of everyday life and a fuller historical account of the subject/individual, but can only offer these in very partial, very abstract terms – partly because he is only drawing on a theoretical account of such historical change. It seems that, for Bull, empirical evidence is important for contemporary life, but theoretical-historical assumptions do not need such back-up. There is still a need, then, for work which draws on a satisfactory historical and theoretical framework for understanding contemporary everyday life, and adequately combines it with empirical studies of uses of music.

Value and meaning in everyday experience of music

DeNora and Bull have provided some useful pointers in this direction, but perhaps the most striking lack in their work is their peculiar lack of engagement with issues of value, meaning and taste in music. While DeNora's concern with those aspects of 'embodied' musical experience which are 'beyond' questions of interpretation and evaluation is welcome, the lack of treatment of meaning is debilitating. While some versions of media and cultural studies have only been interested in audience interpretations of media texts, to the exclusion of other important questions about the role of music in everyday life, DeNora does not seem to be interested in such hermeneutic questions at all. The result is that music comes to seem strangely hollow, without content. There is very little reference in *Music in Everyday Life* to people's evaluations of particular musical texts and genres, other than in personal terms, such as when one piece of music reminds one interviewee of her father (DeNora, 2000: 16). Now it may well be that popular music studies has overestimated conflicts over meaning and value in popular music. This may in turn derive from the excessive focus on youth audiences; perhaps young people – especially middle-class youth – are more prone to assert and recreate their personal identity through music than other age groups (see Frith, 1981: 205–24).

This question of meaning is difficult. Academics tend, by the very nature of their work, to be very concerned with interpretation, and they may as a result have overestimated the amount of active interpretation that people carry out in their everyday responses to music. Isn't most contemporary everyday experience of music too casual and distracted to involve interpretation? Much of our everyday experience of music is as 'background' music, and one encouraging development in recent years in writing about music has been a much more careful attention to the role of music in the soundscape, to music as background, whether as muzak, piped music or ubiquitous music, as Annahid Kassabian puts it elsewhere in this volume.[6] Nevertheless, a closer, less distracted engagement with music is an everyday experience for millions of people, for example when dancing, or when listening to personal stereos. Even if popular music studies has overestimated the amount of interpretation that goes on amongst 'ordinary' audiences, it is hard to believe that the everyday experience of music is so devoid of passionate advocacy over value and meaning as DeNora's book suggests. The answer, surely, is to carry out empirical studies that address the full range of musical experience, from passion, absorption and 'attachment' (Gomart and Hennion, 1999) to distracted, almost subliminal hearing. And such an interview project might usefully expand our knowledge of questions concerning 'everyday' evaluation. What kinds of people search hard for meaning in music, and why? Why do people value the texts and genres that they do? This might help to link up the sociology of musical taste, with its correlations and statistical data, with a social theory of musical value. And one route towards making such connections might be a recognition of the importance of time in music and in everyday life.

Music, time and space

Both music and the everyday are intimately connected to time. The everyday is, after all, a word that refers to things that happen in time, every day, or at least most days; as Felski (1999–2000: 18) puts it, in drawing attention to the importance of routine and repetition in understanding everyday life, 'the everyday is, above all, a temporal concept'. In fact, the concept of the everyday needs to be expanded to cover the notion of routine more adequately: events that happen every night or every week, even every month and every year, are part of mundane, ordinary living, and might serve to remind us of lived experience 'beyond' structures of power. (Interest in this 'beyond' is, after all, what unites the approaches to the everyday outlined earlier, even if they read this zone differently.)

There are many ways in which writers have sought to understand the relationship between music and time. This is a vast topic, and I could scarcely do it justice in the space I have here. Ethnomusicologists and other cultural analysts of music have had important things to say about how different cultures produce differently nuanced understandings of time in their distinctive musical traditions (see, for example, Chernoff, 1979) and about the sense of time implied by different forms and styles of music (see Keil, 1994; Toynbee, 2000: 144–50). But how might we think about what the ordinary experience of music does to our sense of time? Simon Frith discusses some relevant thinking about this issue in *Performing Rites*. Echoing other writers, Frith argues that music has a particularly strong ability to shift, freeze or alter our experience of time, and in some way to intensify it; in particular, he suggests that a sense of 'now' is particularly important in music. For philosopher of music Jonathan Kramer (1988) music, which arranges time in a linear fashion, creates through this (paradoxically) a sense of moment time, an experience of, as Frith puts it, the *'continuous present'*. Frith builds on this in seeing music as offering an experience of 'ideal time', in providing a bridge between aspects of life that are

> routinely kept separate . . . the individual and the social, the mind and the body, change and stillness, the different and the same, the already past and the still to come, desire and fulfillment. Music is in this respect like sex, and rhythm is crucial to this – rhythm not as 'releasing' physical urges but as expanding the time in which we can, as it were, *live in the present tense*.
>
> (Frith, 1996: 157, original emphasis)

The 'routinely' here is significant, especially given our concern with music in everyday life. There is a strong sense of music's ability to break the boundaries set up as part of our everyday experience of time, and to transcend 'clock time'. Music provides ordinary access to an escape from ordinariness.

Yet paradoxically it may be that the concept of the everyday invokes too limited a concept of time, concerned as it is with questions of routine, repetition and daily habit. It is worth returning to Crafts et al.'s *My Music* here. The book derives from a project investigating 'music in daily life', but in fact only some of the interviewees discuss their everyday life. A more appropriate title would be 'music in people's lives': there is, in many interviews, a much greater emphasis on the interviewees' life histories. Daily life and everyday life tend to sideline this longer aspect of time, as the remembered experiences and retrospective construction of a life, and of a self (see Finnegan, 1997).

Sara Cohen (1997) provides a case study of the role of music in one man's memories and, in so doing, suggests some further possibilities for combining fieldwork on 'ordinary' experience of music with a theoretical appreciation of the specificity of musical sound. Cohen analyses the crucial part played by music in the life of an 88-year-old Jewish widower, Jack Levy, as he uses music to reconstruct his own personal past, and the past of the Jewish community of Liverpool. In doing so, she makes important connections between questions of time and the emphasis on local place in much of popular music studies (see the introduction to Section IV of this book). Cohen describes how, as he recalls dancing, Jack sways his torso and arms, his eyes closed 'in an expression of blissful engrossment' (Cohen, 1997: 275). For Cohen, the physicality of Jack's memories 'emphasize the intensity of experience evoked by music and its effectiveness in producing a sense of identity and belonging' (277). Cohen echoes here the arguments of Martin Stokes and others, that 'place, for many migrant communities is something constructed through music with an intensity not found elsewhere in their social lives' (Stokes, 1994: 114). She shows that Jack's memories are not only of belonging to a place, and to a particular ethnic group, they are also memories of fantasies of elsewhere.

There are problems in Cohen's approach. Negative, ideological uses of music are associated with wider, social forces, whereas individual uses of music are implicitly portrayed only in positive terms. Although there is plenty of historical detail, this is not historically informed analysis in the sense of understanding how wider social forces are shaped by historical developments (which is Bull's concern, even if he does not adequately address it). There is a tendency towards individualism which echoes that in *My Music* and in DeNora's *Music in Everyday Life*. Nevertheless, this is a valuable study of the special and intense role of music in one individual's everyday life, and in the way that music is used to negotiate his experience of time. How does music come to play this special role in personal and social memory? Cohen usefully collates a number of sources. For Philip Tagg, for example, music's special relationship to identity derives from its 'concerted simultaneity of nonverbal sound events or movements' (quoted by Cohen, 1997: 286). But Cohen also suggests that the *spatial* dynamics of music-as-sound have an important role in constituting music's powers:

> Music fills and structures space within us and around us, inside and outside. Hence, much like our concept of place, music can appear to envelop us, but it can also appear to express our innermost feelings/beings.

> (Cohen, 1997: 286)

Perhaps, then, what we need to focus on in providing a more adequate conception of ordinary experience of music than in existing audience studies is not merely the idea of the everyday, but time and space.

There has been too much focus within popular music studies on the concept of 'youth' and supposedly typical youth genres and experiences of music, at the expense of other age groups, and other types of experience; and there has been too much attention to spectacular and supposedly rebellious uses of popular music, at the expense of the mundane and the banal. The concept of the everyday has, in some recent work, been a useful one for grounding our conceptions of the role of music in people's lives. But when the concept is applied in a loose way, derived from its uses in empirical sociology, it can lead to a de-historicised and de-politicised conception of the context for this role. The study of youth subcultures may have overly politicised the study of music audiences, and the most urgent task may be to fill the void in studies of ordinary, banal musical experience; but if we lose sight of the historical circumstances in which we experience music, and in which we live our every-day lives, then there is a risk of evading questions concerning history, power and meaning (as I think Crafts et al. and DeNora do). While, for some listeners, discussion of the meanings and respective values of different kinds of music is relatively unimportant, my hunch is that for many others (not just bourgeois intellectuals either) such questions are extremely important. We need more research on what people value in particular texts and genres and why, and any future research project concerned with music in everyday life might usefully address this issue.

The most important feature of recent work on music in everyday life might be that it provides some pointers towards understanding what is musical about musical experience. DeNora and Cohen's work reinforces an understanding of this experience as aesthetic and physical. Future research might look at this experience in relation to other forms of aesthetic and physical activity, both in its specificity, and in terms of what it shares with other ways of passing time, and of coping with everyday life.

Notes

This survey of existing studies (in English) of music in everyday life was written as preparation for a research project, Music and Dance in Everyday Culture, currently under way as part of the Open University's National Everyday Cultures Programme.

1. This echoes points made many years ago by Birmingham critics of Birmingham subcultural theory, including those by Angela McRobbie (1980) and by Gary Clarke (1990/1981). And in media and cultural studies, a number of writers have argued for a shift away from an emphasis on transgression and resistance amongst audiences towards a study of the way that media relate to the practices and routines of everyday life (e.g. Hermes, 1995). Negus (1996: 28) has made a similar point in relation to the study of popular music audiences.
2. Sara Cohen's book on Liverpool rock culture (1991) and Barry Shank's book on Austin, Texas (1994) are often cited as studies of scenes, but they deal not with audiences, but with musicians. Work on scenes has been useful, then, in encouraging more thinking about the relationship between audiences and musicians (see especially Harris, 2000) and especially about the spatial dynamics of music. But the concept of 'scene' is not fundamentally concerned with audiences, and is unlikely to inspire empirical studies of them.
3. Needless to say, this is not a definitive categorisation: it excludes important contributions from cognitive psychology, for example. And the categories are not watertight: Certeau's work (1984) belongs to the second category, but exerted a profound influence on the third. Cohen and Taylor (1975) come from the first category, but prefigure some of the concerns of the third.
4. Charles Keil himself has devoted close and valuable attention to such questions in other places – see Keil and Feld (1994) for a sample of his essays – but not in relation to interview material.
5. See, for example, Bernard Miège's criticisms of Adorno's concept of the culture industry (Miège 1989), a concept invoked frequently by Bull. I discuss Adorno and Miège in Hesmondhalgh (2002).

6. Much of this work prefigured, or at least paralleled, the move in cultural studies away from audience studies which focused on uncovering the 'real' meaning of texts. The lack of reference in media and cultural studies to this work on 'background music' reflects the unfortunate lack of dialogue between media and cultural studies, and popular music studies.

References

BENNETT, ANDY, 2000: *Popular Music and Youth Culture*. Basingstoke: Macmillan.

BULL, MICHAEL, 2000: *Sounding Out the City*. Oxford: Berg.

CAVICCHI, DANIEL, 1999: *Tramps Like Us*. New York: Oxford University Press.

CERTEAU, MICHEL DE, 1984: *The Practice of Everyday Life*, trans S. Rendell. Berkeley: University of California Press.

CHERNOFF, JOHN MILLER, 1979: *African Rhythm and African Sensibility*. Chicago and London: University of Chicago Press.

CLARKE, GARY, 1990/1981: 'Defending Ski-Jumpers: A Critique of Theories of Youth Subcultures', in FRITH AND GOODWIN (1990).

COHEN, SARA, 1991: *Rock Culture in Liverpool*. Oxford: Clarendon Press.

——, 1997: 'Sounding Out the City: Music and the Sensuous Production of Place', in Andrew Leyshon, David Matless and George Revill (eds), *The Place of Music*. New York and London: The Guilford Press.

COHEN, STAN AND LAURIE TAYLOR, 1975: *Escape Attempts*. Harmondsworth: Penguin.

COULDRY, NICK, 2000: *Inside Culture*. London: Sage.

CRAFTS, SUSAN D., DANIEL CAVICCHI, CHARLES KEIL AND THE MUSIC IN DAILY LIFE PROJECT, 1993: *My Music*. Hanover and London: Wesleyan University Press.

DENORA, TIA, 2000: *Music in Everyday Life*. Cambridge: Cambridge University Press.

DOUGLAS, JACK D. (ed.), 1970: *Understanding Everyday Life*. Chicago: Aldine.

FELSKI, RITA, 1999–2000: 'The Invention of Everyday Life'. *New Formations* 39: 15–31.

FINNEGAN, RUTH, 1997: ' "Storying the Self": Personal Narratives and Identity', in Hugh Mackay (ed.), *Consumption and Everyday Life*. London, Thousand Oaks and New Delhi: Sage/The Open University.

FRITH, SIMON, 1981: *Sound Effects*. New York: Pantheon.

——, 1987: 'Towards an Aesthetic of Popular Music', in Richard Leppert and Susan McClary (eds), *Music and Society*. Cambridge: Cambridge University Press.

——, 1996: *Performing Rites*. Oxford: Oxford University Press.

FRITH, SIMON AND ANDREW GOODWIN, 1990: *On Record*. London: Routledge; New York: Pantheon.

GARDINER, MICHAEL E., 2000: *Critiques of Everyday Life*. London and New York: Routledge.

GOMART, EMILIE AND ANTOINE HENNION, 1999: 'A Sociology of Attachment: Music Amateurs, Drug Users', in John Law and John Hassard (eds), *Actor Network Theory and After*. Oxford and Malden: Blackwell/The Sociological Review.

GROSSBERG, LAWRENCE, 1990/1986: 'Is There Rock After Punk?', in FRITH AND GOODWIN (1990).

HALL, STUART AND TONY JEFFERSON (eds), 1976: *Resistance Through Rituals*. London: Hutchinson.

HARRIS, KEITH, 2000: 'Transgression and Mundanity: The Global Extreme Metal Music Scene'. Ph.D. thesis, Goldsmiths College, University of London.

HEBDIGE, DICK, 1979: *Subculture*. London: Methuen.

HERMES, JOKE, 1995: *Reading Women's Magazines*. Cambridge: Polity Press.

HESMONDHALGH, DAVID, 2002: *The Cultural Industries*. London and Thousand Oaks: Sage.

HORNER, BRUCE AND THOMAS SWISS (eds), 1999: *Key Terms in Popular Music and Culture*. Oxford and Malden: Blackwell.

KARP, DAVID A. AND WILLIAM C. YOELS, 1993: *Sociology in Everyday Life*, second edition. Itasca, Ill.: F. E. Peacock.

KEIL, CHARLES, 1994: 'Participatory Discrepancies and the Power of Music', in KEIL AND FELD (1994).

KEIL, CHARLES AND STEVEN FELD, 1994: *Music Grooves*. Chicago: University of Chicago Press.

KRAMER, JONATHAN, 1988: *The Time of Music*. New York: Schirmer.

LEFEBVRE, HENRI, 1971: *Everyday Life in the Modern World*, trans. S. Rabinovich. New York: Harper & Row.

LEWIS, LISA (ed.), 1992: *The Adoring Audience*. New York and London: Routledge.

LONGHURST, BRIAN, 1995: *Popular Music and Society*. Cambridge: Polity Press.

MAFFESOLI, MICHEL, 1989: 'The Sociology of Everyday Life (Epistemological Elements)'. *Current Sociology* 37,1: 1–16.

MCROBBIE, ANGELA, 1990/1980: 'Settling Accounts with Subcultures: A Feminist Critique', in FRITH AND GOODWIN (1990).

MELUCCI, ALBERTO, 1996: *The Playing Self*. Cambridge: Cambridge University Press.

MIDDLETON, RICHARD, 1990: *Studying Popular Music*. Buckingham: Open University Press.

MIÈGE, BERNARD, 1989: *The Capitalization of Cultural Production*. New York: International General.

NEGUS, KEITH, 1996: *Popular Music in Theory*. Cambridge: Polity Press.

PETERSON, RICHARD A. AND ALBERT SIMKUS, 1992: 'How Musical Tastes Mark Occupational Status Groups', in Michèle Lamont (ed.), *Cultivating Differences*. Chicago and London: University of Chicago Press.

ROE, KEITH, 1985: 'Swedish Youth and Music: Listening Patterns and Motivations'. *Communication Research* 12 (3): 353–62.

SHANK, BARRY, 1994: *Dissonant Identities*. Hanover: Wesleyan University Press.

SHEPHERD, JOHN, 1986: 'Music Consumption and Self-Identities: Some Theoretical and Methodological Reflections'. *Media, Culture and Society* 8 (3): 305–30.

SILVERSTONE, ROGER, 1994: *Television and Everyday Life*. London and New York: Routledge.

SMITH, DOROTHY E. 1987: *The Everyday World as Problematic*. Buckingham: Open University Press.

STOKES, MARTIN, 1994: 'Place, Exchange and Meaning: Black Sea Musicians in the West of Ireland', in Martin Stokes (ed.), *Ethnicity, Identity and Music*. Oxford: Berg.

STRAW, WILL, 1991: 'Systems of Articulation and Logics of Change: Communities and Scenes in Popular Music'. *Cultural Studies* 5 (3): 368–88.

THORNTON, SARAH, 1995: *Club Cultures*. Cambridge: Polity Press.

TOYNBEE, JASON, 2000: *Making Popular Music*. London and New York: Arnold/Oxford University Press.

VANEIGEM, RAOUL, 1983: *The Revolution of Everyday Life*, trans. D. Nicholson-Smith. No Place: Left Bank Books.

8

Ubiquitous listening

Anahid Kassabian

Music not chosen

I have always been drawn to studying the engagements of music and subject-ivities. I find that intersection of text, psyches and social relations particularly intriguing when the texts in question are sequences of music neither chosen by their listeners nor actively listened to in any recognizable sense. This body of music includes, of course, film and television music, but also music on phones, music in stores, music in video games, music for audio books, music in parking garages, and so on. A quotation in Jonathan Sterne's 'Sounds Like the Mall of America' confirmed my suspicion about the music: we hear more of it per capita than any other music.

The 21 October 2000 issue of *The Economist* had a graph showing annual world production of data, expressed in terabytes. According to researchers at UC Berkeley's School of Information Systems and Management, about 2.5 billion CDs were shipped in 1999. Music CD production far outstrips news-papers, periodicals, books and cinema. And most of the music is being heard often, if not most often, as a secondary activity.

Music to follow you from room to room

By most reckonings, this is a trend that will continue to increase for some time to come. One mark of that might be Bill Gates' ideas for the 'house of the future'. All residents would have unique microelectronic beacons that would identify their wearers to the house. Based on your stored profile, then,

> Lights would automatically come on when you came home . . . Portable touch pads would control everything from the TV sets to the temperature and the lights, which would brighten or dim to fit the occasion or to match the outdoor light . . . Speakers would be hidden beneath the wallpaper to allow music to follow you from room to room.

> (cnn.com, 2000)

The Cisco Internet Home Briefing Center imagines a similar musical envi-ronment:

> Music also seems to have no boundaries with access to any collection, available in virtually any room of the house through streaming audio. A Digital Jukebox or Internet Radio eliminates the limitations of local radio, and can output music, sports and news from around the world.
>
> (Cisco Internet Home Briefing Center, 'Entertainment')

These ideas are among the most basic and least radical in the field known as ubiquitous computing, or ubicomp. First articulated in the late 1980s by Mark Weiser of Xerox PARC (Weiser, 1991; Gibbs, 2000), ubicomp has become a very active field of research. It is concerned with 'smart rooms' and 'smart clothes', with the seamless integration of information and entertainment computing into everyday environments. This would be akin to the penetration of words, or reading, in everyday life. Texts were first centrally located in, for example, monasteries and libraries; next, books and periodicals were distributed to individual owners; now, words are almost always in our field of vision, on labels, bookshelves, files, etc. Written language is ubiquitous, seamlessly integrated into our environments.

From the perspective, for example, of the Broadband Residential Laboratory built by Georgia Tech last year, these 'stereo-piping tricks of "smart" homes . . . [are] just a starting point' (as quoted in Gibbs, 2000). Their Aware Home has several audio and video input and output devices in each room, and several outlets and jacks in each wall. The MIT Media Lab, as Sandy Pentland has said, has gone in a different direction. They have 'moved from a focus on smart rooms to an emphasis on smart clothes' (Pentland, 2000: 821) because smart clothes offer possibilities that smart rooms do not, such as mobility and individuality. For example, the Affective Computing Research Group 'has built a wearable "DJ" that tries to select music based on a feature of the user's mood' as indicated by skin conductivity data collected by the wearable computer (Picard, 2000: 716).

What do we know about most of the music we hear?

Music scholarship across the disciplines is utterly unprepared to think about such practices. As it stands, there are few studies of the music that follows us from room to room, variously called programmed music, background music, environmental music, business music, functional music (Gifford, 1995; Bottum, 2000). One landmark study is Joseph Lanza's book *Elevator Music* (1995) which is first of all a history of music in public space, and, second, a defense of the intramusical features that were part of elevator music in its prime: lush strings, absence of brass and percussion, consonant harmonic language, etc. The book is an invaluable resource, and it makes some fascinating arguments; for example, Lanza suggests that elevator music became the quintessential twentieth-century music because it focused, as did much of the century's technologies, on environmental control.

Sterne takes another tack. Commoditized music, Sterne argues, has become 'a form of architecture – a way of organizing space in commercial settings' (Sterne, 1997: 23). Not only does the soundscape of the mall predict and depend on barely audible, anonymous background music of the 'Muzak' type, but it also shapes the very space itself. The boundaries between store and hall-way are acoustically defined by the different music played in each space:

> To get anywhere in the Mall of America, one must pass through music and through changes in musical sound. As it territorializes, music gives the subdivided acoustical space a contour, offering an opportunity for its listeners to experience space in a particular way (31).

For Sterne, the issue is one of reification – music has become a commodity relation that supplants relations between people and that presupposes listener response.

In 'Adequate Modes of Listening', Ola Stockfelt (1997) argues that modes of listening develop in relation to particular genres – he calls these 'genre-normative modes of listening' – and the style itself develops in relation to its listening situation. He says:

> Each style of music . . . is shaped in close relation to a few environments. In each genre, a few environments, a few situations of listening, make up the constitutive elements in this genre . . . The opera house and the concert hall as environments are as much integral and fundamental parts of the musical *genres* 'opera' and 'symphony' as are the purely intramusical means of style (136).

In Stockfelt's argument, modes of listening, listening situation, and musical style co-produce each other. In terms of background music, this helps explain the musical parameters we all know. What Stockfelt calls 'dishearkening' has produced a particular set of practices for arranging background music. There is a focus on moments of pleasant 'snapshot listening' rather than development over time, and a focus on comforting timbres (legato strings) over vivid ones (brass).

None of these studies, however, can cope with the ubicomp world proposed by Xerox PARC and the MIT Media Lab, nor even with some already existing soundscapes. Prevailing scholarly notions of listening subjectivity and agency, even in the most innovative works, will not account for the music we wake up to.

Where did this music come from?

I lead a happy life. Every day I wake in the best of all possible moods and dance my way around the room as I get dressed. Then, while I prepare a pleasant breakfast in my tiny kitchen, several happy bluebirds land on my windowsill and twitter cheerfully. Outside, a tall man in coat-and-tails tips his hat and bids me good-day. A half-dozen scruffy children chase a hoop down the street, shouting gleefully. One of them cries out, 'Mornin' mister!'

Ah yes, life is wonderful when you live in a musical from the fifties. Now, perhaps you're wondering, 'How could this possibly be true?' Well, I have the unspeakable good fortune to live directly behind my local supermarket and each morning I wake up to a careful selection of merry tunes which easily penetrate my thin walls to rouse me from my slumber.

(Schafer, website, 'The Sound of Muzak')

Thus does Tokyo resident Own Schafer begin his eloquent, elegant think-piece about Muzak. Sedimented here is a trace of one of functional music's siblings, i.e. film music and musical theater. To tell functional music's history, one might begin with music hall, or even earlier. Another trace could be followed to radio, and from there to music in salons and gazebos. Or from workplace music to work music and chants. Strangely, these remain untold histories of the omnipresence of music in contemporary life in industrialized settings.

Two histories *are* told – an industrial one and a critical one. The former begins with General George Owen Squier, chief of the US Army Signal Corps and creator of Wired Radio, the company now called Muzak. This history, best represented by Joseph Lanza's book (1995) and Bill Gifford's (1995) *FEED* feature 'They're Playing Our Songs', continues through shifts in technologies and markets, to Muzak's 'stimulus progression' patents, to the 1988 merger with small foreground music provider Yesco (Gifford, 1995: 3, 2) and the rise of competitors AEI and 3M.

The other documented history is a counter-history, a story of how a music came into being that could be confused with functional music, but is of course nothing like it – ambient music. That history begins with Erik Satie's experiments in the teens and twenties with *musique d'ameublement* (furniture music), soars through John Cage's emphases on environmental sound and on process, and leads inevitably to Brian Eno, from whose mind all contemporary ambient music has sprung. (For versions of this story, see any of the scores of ambient websites.)

This history goes to great pains to distinguish ambient from background music on the grounds of its available modes of listening. As musician/fan Malcolm Humes put it in a 1995 on-line essay:

> Eno . . . tried to create music that could be actively or passively listened to. Something that could shift imperceptibly between a background texture to something triggering a sudden zoom into the music to reflect on a repetition, a subtle variation, perhaps a slight shift in color or mood.
>
> http://music.hyperreal.org/epsilon/info/humes_notes.html

What is important to defenders of the ambient faith is its availability to both foreground and background listening. But since the mid to late 1980s, background music *has become* foreground music. In the language of the industry, background music is what we call 'elevator music', and foreground music is work by original artists. While background music has all but disappeared, you can now hear everyone from Miriam Makeba to the Moody Blues to Madonna to Moby in some public setting or other and quite possibly all of them at your local Starbucks.

Foreground music seems to make talking about music in public spaces impossible – and perhaps it should be. Certainly there is a several-decades-long history of debate about the dissolution of public space and the public sphere. As Japanese cultural critic Mihoko Tamaoki has argued in her work on coffee houses, Starbucks transforms customers into not a public, but an audience. Moreover, she argues (Tamaoki, unpublished manuscript):

> Starbucks now constitutes a 'meta-media' operation. It stands at once in the traditional media role, as an outlet for both content and advertising. At the same time, it

is actually selling the products therein advertised. And these, in turn, are themselves media products: music for Starbucks listeners.

This is Starbucks' genius as a music label; it is a meta-media operation that produces its own market for its own product all at once, in what once might have been public space. But if we focus too closely on the distribution of recordings, we will not fully address the problems foreground music poses to contemporary listening.

How do we listen to foreground music?

If one attends to discourse about music in business environments, it has hardly registered the change from background to foreground. By and large, most people talk about music in business environments as annoying and bad, and it is rare indeed to hear anyone talk about music in these settings as music they listen to intentionally elsewhere, even though that seems an obvious connection to make. The reason, I want to argue, is that they are not discussing music, but rather a mode of listening about which most of us are at best ambivalent, thanks in no small part to the disciplining of music in the western academy.

In the wake of Foucault, critiques of music's disciplinary practices have been well argued. We have discussed canon formations, architecture and training; we have argued about analysis and we have talked about transcription. We have talked at length about the expert listening held in such high regard by Adorno and so carefully cultivated by Western art music institutions such as the academy and symphony orchestras. It is perhaps primary among the forces that produce and reproduce the canonical European and North American repertoire. But in all these discussions we have not taken our own collective insights quite seriously enough. Logically, if expert, concentrated, structural listening produces the canon, do not other modes of listening produce and reproduce other repertoires?

This is, I believe, Stockfelt's most important point. Through changes in the arrangement of Mozart's G-minor 40th symphony, he argues, different settings, different sets of musical features, and different modes of listening are co-productive. Text, context and reception create each other in mutual, simultaneous and historically grounded processes. But as foreground music programming has increased, this combination or mutual dependence seems less and less consistent or predictable. When *anything* can be foreground music, does it still make sense to talk about a mode of listening? And if so, what is its relationship to questions of genre?

Do we hear or listen?

One possibility is to think of this most disdained activity as hearing rather than listening. This idea appears repeatedly, including in the sales literature of programmed music companies. But the distinction poses some interesting problems. In Webster's, each term is defined by the other:

hear vt

to perceive (sounds) by the ear; to receive an impression of through the auditory nerves of the ear; as, to *hear* a voice; to *hear* words.

O friends! I *hear* the tread of nimble feet. – Milton.

to listen to and consider; specifically, (a) to take notice of ; pay attention to; as, *hear* this piece of news; (b) to listen to officially; give a formal hearing to; as, he will *hear* your lessons now; (c) to conduct an examination or hearing of (a law case, etc.); try; (d) to consent to; grant; as, he *heard* my entreaty; (e) to be a member of the audience at or of (an opera, radio broadcast, lecture, etc.) ; (f) to permit to speak; as I cannot *hear* you now. To be informed of; to be told; to learn.

(1983: 836)

hear vi

to be able to perceive sound; as, he is deaf, he cannot *hear*.

to listen; to attend; as, he *hears* with solicitude. To be told; to receive by report; as, so I *hear*.

(1983: 836)

listen vi

to make a conscious effort to hear; to attend closely so as to hear.

to give heed; take advice; as, to *listen* to warning.

(1983: 1055)

One obvious problem with the distinction is the circularity of the definitions, but that is, as we know, in the nature of language. That notwithstanding, we could probably agree that hearing is somehow more passive than listening, and that consuming background music is passive. Certainly everyone – from Adorno to Muzak – seem to think so.

The connotation of passivity in the term 'hearing' is precisely why I prefer 'listening'. To the extent that 'hearing' is understood as passive, it implies the conversion of sound waves into electrochemical stimuli (that is, transmission along nerves to the brain) by a discretely embodied unified subject (that is, a human individual). Yet our engagements with programmed music surely extend beyond mere sense perception and, as I will suggest below, mark us as participants in a new form of subjectivity.

Is there, then, a programmed music mode of listening? Here I want to offer an anecdote as a beginning of an answer. Recently, I asked the students in my popular music class to write an essay on a half-hour of radio broadcasting. Ryan Kelly, a member of the New York City Ballet corps de ballet, began his essay by identifying himself as a non-radio listener. He described sitting down to listen to the tape to begin his essay, and ten minutes later finding himself at the kitchen sink washing dishes. This is, of course, only one story, but an eminently recognizable one.

Jay Larkin of Viacom described to me a proto-ubicomp kind of system he had set up – he has speakers under his pillow, so that he can sleep listening to music without disturbing his wife and without the intrusion of headphones. (He also listens to music constantly at work.) Larkin is profoundly articulate about this matter – he thinks of music as an 'anchor', keeping his mind from spinning off in various directions. Parents of children with attention deficit disorder are often advised to put on music while the kids are working for just such purposes.

From its inception, Gifford says, musak was about focusing attention in this sense. Workers' minds 'were prone to wandering. Muzak sopped up these non-productive thoughts and kept workers focussed on the drudgery at hand' (Gifford, 1995: 2, 2). My babysitter Anett and many of my students leave the radio or MTV on in different rooms, so that they are never without music. They say it fills the house, makes the emptiness less frightening. Muzak's own literature says 'Muzak fills the deadly silence.'

These have always been background music's functions. We learned them from Muzak, and now they are a part of our everyday lives. As Muzak programming manager Steve Ward says:

> It's supposed to fill the air with sort of a warm familiarity, I suppose . . . If you were pushing a cart through a grocery store and all you hear is wheels creaking and crying babies – it would be like a mausoleum.

> (as quoted in Gifford, 1995: 3, 2)

All these listeners and music programmers and writers share a sense of listening as a constant, grounding, secondary activity, regardless of the specific musical features.

A ubiquitous mode of listening?

Those of us living in industrialized settings (at least) have developed, from the omnipresence of music in our daily lives, a mode of listening dissociated from specific generic characteristics of the music. In this mode, we listen 'alongside' or simultaneously with other activities. It is one vigorous example of the non-linearity of contemporary life. This listening is a new and noteworthy phenomenon, one that has the potential to demand a radical rethinking of our various fields.

I want to propose that we call this mode of listening 'ubiquitous listening' for two reasons. First, it is the ubiquity of listening that has taught us this mode. It is precisely because music is everywhere that Ryan forgot he was doing an assignment and got up to wash the dishes.

Second, it relies on a kind of 'sourcelessness'. Whereas we are accustomed to thinking of most music, like most cultural products, in terms of authorship and location, this music comes from the plants and the walls and, potentially, our clothes. It comes from everywhere and nowhere. Its projection looks to erase its production as much as possible, posing instead as a quality of the environment.

For these reasons, the term 'ubiquitous listening' best describes the phenomenon I am discussing. As has been widely remarked, the development of recording technologies in the twentieth century disarticulated performance space and listening space. You can listen to opera in your bathtub and arena rock while riding the bus. And it is precisely this disarticulation that has made ubiquitous listening possible. Like ubiquitous computing, ubiquitous listening blends into the environment, taking place without calling conscious attention to itself as an activity in itself. It is, rather, ubiquitous and conditional, following us from room to room, building to building, and activity to activity.

However, the idea of ubiquitous listening as perhaps the dominant mode of listening in contemporary life raises another problem: does this mode of listening produce and accede to a set of genre norms?

A ubiquitous genre?

Genre comes from Aristotle and is a term from literary theory for the classification of types of text. 'Members of a genre have common characteristics of style and organization and are found in similar cultural settings' (Bothamley, 1993: 228). By those common characteristics, then, members of a genre can be recognized. Across the media, genre has, of course, become a central organizing principle of both production and consumption; as John Hartley puts it: 'genres are agents of ideological closure – they limit the meaning potential of a given text, and they limit the commercial risk of the producer corporations' (Hartley, 1994: 128). In this sense, genres might be understood to discipline reception.

The most widely cited definition of genre in popular music studies, Franco Fabbri's 1982 essay 'A Theory of Musical Genres', sees it as a complex of style or musical features, performance space and performance and fan/listener behavior – less a discipline than a field of activity. Rob Walser's discussion in *Running with the Devil* expands in this direction, combining Jameson's text-based discussion with Bakhtin's 'horizon of expectations': 'Genres are never sui generis; they are developed, sustained, and re-formed by people, who bring a variety of histories and interests to their encounters with generic texts' (Walser, 1993: 27). In this way, a popular music genre is understood to include both shared musical features and audience expectations and practices. In Stockfelt's terms, style, listening and situation are all part of genre-making processes.

In all these discussions of genre, musical features are conceived expansively, reaching beyond pitch, melody, harmony and rhythm to include timbre, vocal inflections and recording techniques. Taken together, a ubiquitous mode of listening and a careful, socially grounded understanding of genre might make the case for a genre called 'ubiquitous music'. It has, as I have argued, a specific mode of listening. It shares certain features of performance space – simultaneity with other activities and a sense of sourcelessness. While including an extraordinarily wide range of musical features, it is generally shaped by mono playback, absence of very high and very low frequencies, absence of vocals, and particular attention to volume as a condition of the other simultaneous activities.

The problem is, of course, that ubiquitous music does not depend on texts belonging only to its own genre, but rather welcomes all texts in a pluralist leveling of difference and specificity (which might explain its partiality for adopting world music forms). Perhaps it is a new kind of genre, what we might, tongue firmly in cheek, call a postmodern pastiche para-genre. But more likely, I think, it signals the death knell of genre as a primary organizing axis for popular music activities.

A ubiquitous subjectivity?

Unabashedly polemical, this argument is the necessary precursor to a rethinking of how we approach both the study of music and the idea of subjectivity. As more and more kinds of music are played in more and more settings alongside more and more activities, it becomes crucial to develop ways of approaching this phenomenon. As Gifford (1995: 6, 3) puts it:

> Muzak anticipated the way we live our lives today, accompanied by a constant soundtrack of radio, television, video and film . . . Muzak's real significance is that it paved the way for a new ambient culture, a culture that Sensurrounds us with digitized music and pixelated images, endlessly looping screen savers and point-of-purchase interactive displays, occupying all areas of our multitasking minds.

But many analysts insist on continuing to see the music industry in very traditional terms. According to the phenomenal foresight of experts in an *Economist* special supplement on E-entertainment (7 October 2000), for example:

> If the music industry manages to sort out the piracy problem, the internet will become a hugely important source of revenue. The record companies sold their music all over again when the CD came out, and they can now sell it all over again over the internet, again. What is more, they can sell it in more flexible packages to make it more attractive to different kinds of consumers (32).

What the *Economist*'s writers do not say, and apparently do not even think about, are the vast social changes attendant on these new technologies. The same music will be sold yet a third time, in more flexible packages, precisely because it makes it easier to use the music as an environmental technology, conditioning and conditioned by a new kind of subjectivity.

This third selling is a performance of the ubicomp world in the making. Its attendant subjectivity is not individual, not defined by Oedipus or agency or any discrete unity. The listener of this third selling is no mere subject, but rather a part of an always moving ever-present web. S/he is not a listener of a genre first and foremost, but rather a listener *tout court*. Ubiquitous music is cable that networks all of us together, not in some dystopian energy-producing array à la *Matrix*, but in a lumpy deployment of dense nodes of knowledge/power figured by, for example, the SETI@home project. SETI@home uses home computers when they are otherwise idle as a resource for ramping up computer processing power for the Search for Extra-Terrestrial Intelligence project. In this extreme model of distributed computing, each home computer is a little lump or node in an enormous array of computing activity. Likewise, we are each nodes in an enormous array of listening.

There are numerous attempts to describe what I am getting at here, from many different directions – from Xerox PARC to Donna Haraway to Gilles Deleuze. In *Autoaffections: Unconscious Thought in the Age of*

Teletechnology, Patricia Clough proposes, as she puts it, 'a new ontological perspective and an unconscious other than the one organized by an oedipal narrative' (Clough, 2000: 20). Throughout, *Autoaffections* works in two genres – academic prose and prose poetry. Not only the chapters, but also the genre shifts themselves are performances of the book's work.

It opens with a prose poem, 'Television: A Sacred Machine'. It is a work of remarkable power, both more beautiful and more clear than what we usually call theory. Clough says:

> My machine has more parts; it has more action,
> Like the action of fingertips attached to ivory keys,
> Playing in between the beats of a metronome's patterning (22).

The node we usually call 'self' is attached through keys that make hammers hit wires that make sound that attaches to another node, sound disciplined by the metronome machine to attach the nodes in particular ways.

> Still, I was destined by that piano,
> Destined to find myself in attachment to machines (25).

This attachment is, as I have suggested, the stuff of contemporary science fiction. Cyborgs, matrices, webs, nets – all these dystopias threaten us with the dissolution of the boundaries of our very selves. But they fail to see what Clough hears: that dissolution is already well under way.

What I am proposing is a theory of subjectivity based on ubiquitous music. I think we should call it ubiquitous subjectivity. Like ubiquitous music, parts phase in and out of participation in ubiquitous subjectivity, but it never leaves us – and we never leave it. If that sounds ominous, it is not meant to. It is simply a habit of mind from an earlier notion about our discreteness, and it is time to notice that ubiquitous music and ubiquitous listening have been forging a different subjectivity for quite some time now. Like *Star Trek*'s Borg, we are uncomfortable being unhooked from the background sound of ubiquitous subjectivity, so we turn radios on in empty rooms and put speakers under our pillows. We hang up when a telephone connection is not kept open by sound. We prefer to be connected, need to listen to our connections, cannot breathe without them. We already live a network we insist on thinking of as a dystopian future.

This networked-through-music subjectivity could seem similar to ideas about music and collectivity. As Eisler and Adorno argue in *Composing for the Films* (1947), many anthropologists and writers about music suggest that music operates differently from the oculocentric individual of contemporary Western culture. They say that music listening:

> preserves comparably more traits of long bygone, preindividualistic collectivities . . . This direct relationship to a collectivity, intrinsic in the phenomenon itself, is probably connected with sensations of spatial depth, inclusiveness, and absorption of individuality, which are common to all music (21).

Other writers do not attribute this collective quality to music per se, but do – quite rightly – note that music is a part of many social formations and practices in different historical and cultural settings.

I am not suggesting that ubiquitous music has reintroduced such a collective identity through music to modern or postmodern societies. Far from it. What I am arguing, rather, is that ubiquitous music has become a form of phatic communication for late capitalism – its purpose is to keep the lines of communication open for that lumpy deployment of dense nodes of knowledge/power we call selves. We are Borg because isolated consciousness – silence – is unpleasurable in the extreme.

As we continue through the second century of the disarticulation of performance and listening, new relations are developing that demand new models and approaches. It is easy to see that the industry is changing. It is perhaps harder to hear the changes in music, in listening and in subjectivity that all of this portends. Yet musics, technologies, science fiction, social relations and subjectivities have been fermenting these changes throughout the twentieth century. At least in the industrialized world, listening to music is ubiquitous, and it forms the network backbone of a new, ubiquitous subjectivity.

Acknowledgments

Earlier versions of this essay were presented at UCLA Department of Musicology in March 2001 and at Carnegie Mellon's Center for Cultural Analysis in April 2001. My deep thanks to the graduate students and faculty who invited me and engaged in wonderful, provocative discussions of this material, and to the Ames Fund at Fordham University for supporting this research.

References

BOTHAMLEY, JENNIFER, 1993: *Dictionary of Theories*. London, Detroit and Washington, D.C.: Gale Research Intl. Ltd.

BOTTUM, J., 2000: 'The Soundtracking of America'. *Atlantic Monthly*, March. http://www.theatlantic.com/issues/2000/03/bottum.htm

CISCO INTERNET HOME BRIEFING CENTER: 'Entertainment'. http://www.cisco.com/warp/public/779/consumer/internet_home/

CLOUGH, PATRICIA TICINETO, 2000: *Autoaffections: Unconscious Thought in the Age of Teletechnology*. Minneapolis: University of Minnesota Press.

CNN.COM, 2000: 'The House of the Future is Here Today.' http://www.cnn.com/2000/TECH/ptech/01/03/future.homes/

CUBITT, SEAN, 1984: 'Maybellene: Meaning and the Listening Subject'. *Popular Music* 4: 207–24.

THE ECONOMIST, 2000a: 'A Survey of E-Entertainment' (special supplement), 7 October.

THE ECONOMIST, 2000b: 'Byte Counters: Quantifying Information', 21 October.

EISLER, HANNS AND THEODOR ADORNO, 1947: *Composing for the Films*. New York: Oxford University Press (reprinted 1994, Athlone Press).

FABBRI, FRANCO, 1982: 'A Theory of Musical Genres: Two Applications', in David Horn and Philip Tagg (eds), *Popular Music Perspectives*. Götheborg and Exeter: International Association for the Study of Popular Music, 52–81.

FINK, ROBERT, 'Orchestral Corporate', *ECHO* 2 (1). http://www.humnet.ucla.edu/humnet/musicology/echo/Volume2-Issue1/fink/fink-article.html

GIBBS, W. WAYT, 2000: 'As We May Live'. *Scientific American*, November.
http://www.sciam.com/2000/1100issue/1100techbus1.html

GIFFORD, BILL, 1995: 'They're Playing Our Song', *FEED*.
http://www.feedmag.com/95.10gifford/95.10gifford1.html

HARTLEY, JOHN, 1994: 'Genre', in TIM O'SULLIVAN ET AL.

KASSABIAN, ANAHID, 2001: *Hearing Film: Tracking Identifications in Contemporary Hollywood Film Music*. New York and London: Routledge.

KRAMER, LAWRENCE, 1994: *Music As Cultural Practice, 1800–1900*. Berkeley: University of California Press.

LANZA, JOSEPH, 1995: *Elevator Music: A Surreal History of Muzak, Easy-Listening, and Other Moodsong*. New York: Picador USA.

MCCLARY, SUSAN, 1986: 'A Musical Dialectic from the Enlightenment: Mozart's Piano Concerto in G Major, K. 453, Movement 2'. *Cultural Critique* 4: 129–70.

O'SULLIVAN, TIM, ET AL., 1994: *Key Concepts in Communication and Cultural Studies*, second edition. London and New York: Routledge.

PENTLAND, A., 2000: 'It's Alive!'. *IBM Systems Journal* 39 (3/4): 821–2.

PICARD, R. W., 2000: 'Toward Computers that Recognized and Respond to User Emotion'. *IBM Systems Journal* 39 (3/4): 705–19.

SCHAFER, O.: 'The Sound of Muzak'. *Tokyo Classified Rant 'n' Rave*.
http://www.tokyoclassified.com/tokyorantsravesarchive299/265/tokyorantsravesinc.htm

SCHWARZ, DAVID, 1997: *Listening Subjects: Music, Psychoanalysis, Culture*. Durham, N.C.: Duke University Press.

STEPHENSON, NEAL, 1992: *Snowcrash*. New York: Bantam Spectra.

STERNE, JONATHAN, 1997: 'Sounds Like the Mall of America: Programmed Music and the Architectonics of Commercial Space'. *Ethnomusicology* 41 (1): 22–50.

STOCKFELT, OLA, 1997: 'Adequate Modes of Listening', trans. A. Kassabian and L. G. Svendsen, in D. Schwarz and A Kassabian (eds), *Keeping Score: Music, Disciplinarity, Culture*. Charlottesville, VA.: University Press of Virginia.

SUBOTNIK, ROSE ROSENGARD, 1991: *Developing Variations: Style and Ideology in Western Music*. Minneapolis: University of Minnesota Press.

TOMLINSON, GARY, 1994: *Music in Renaissance Magic: Toward a Historiography of Others*. Chicago: University of Chicago Press.

WALSER, ROBERT, 1993: *Running with the Devil: Power, Gender, and Madness in Heavy Metal Music*. Hanover and London: Wesleyan University Press (University Press of New England).

WEISER, MARK, 1991: 'The Computer for the Twenty-First Century', *Scientific American*, September. http://www.ubiq.com/hypertext/weiser/SciAmDraft3.html

SECTION III

Production, institutions and creativity

EDITORS' INTRODUCTION

For many years the study of popular music, and the study of culture more generally, has been riven by a division between those focusing on and emphasising questions of industry and production, and those concerned to stress consumption and the reception of cultural forms. During the 1990s these separate points of scholarly focus sometimes resulted in writers adopting unhelpful rhetorical polemics, with various attempts to position 'cultural studies' against 'political economy' (see, for example, Ferguson and Golding, 1997). Yet while these skirmishes preoccupied certain individuals, and occasionally grabbed the intellectual headlines, a number of writers were more quietly attempting to draw insights from both traditions of enquiry and to think about the interconnections *between* consumption and production.

An awareness of these connections had been growing over a 25-year period during which various writers had been conducting studies of musical production. Political economy provided an initial impetus and inspiration for many researchers, as it enabled insights into the ways that corporate ownership impinges upon musical production, drew attention to how production occurs within a series of unequal power relations, and showed how the control of production by a few corporations can contribute to broader social divisions and inequalities, not only within nations but across the world. Steve Chapple and Reebee Garofalo (1977) raised such points in their historical study of the growth of the recording industry in the United States, arguing that the control of musical production by a few major labels led to the erosion of oppositional or 'anti-materialist' performances and the co-optation of musicians into an entertainment business which had become 'firmly part of the American corporate structure' (1977: 300). Garofalo (1986: 83) was later to re-assess the scale and certainty of their critique by acknowledging that 'there is no point-to-point correlation between controlling the marketplace economically and controlling the form, content and meaning of music'. The industry cannot simply set up structures of control and operate these in such an instrumental manner. Those who focus on ownership and control often forget the less orderly organisational life within the companies: the human beings who inhabit the corporate structures, not to mention the range of activities engaged in by consumers.

For many years the activities of these workers within music business organisations were explained through analogies with an 'assembly line' or 'production line'. The production of hit songs was observed to resemble industrial manufacturing and critics presented images of bureaucratic 'song factories' engaged in the habitual bolting together of standardised and interchangeable melodies, lyrics and rhythms. Some of Adorno's less sophisticated and more tendentious musing about 'pseudo-individuality' and the 'part-interchangeability' of musical elements implies such a scenario (see Adorno, 1990; Gendron, 1986). Organisational sociologists proposed a synonymous systems model of anonymous administrators mechanically shifting products sequentially from artists to the public (Hirsch, 1972).

In contrast, Richard Peterson (1976) sought to challenge such parallels with bureaucratic manufacturing industries, stressing how culture is 'fabricated' by a range of occupational groups and within specific social milieux and illustrating this with a series of detailed studies of the 'organisational structures' and 'production systems' within which country music has been manufactured (Peterson, 1997). Whilst Peterson was writing in the United States, Antoine Hennion (1982, 1983, 1989) was researching musical production in France and reaching similar conclusions about 'collective creation', and arguing that music industry personnel act as 'intermediaries', continually connecting together artists and audiences.

These ideas were pursued further by Keith Negus (1992) in a study of the acquisition, development and promotion of artists in Britain. Negus showed how the major record companies are disunited entities characterised by considerable interdepartmental conflict and rivalry – particularly when it comes to taking credit for success and apportioning blame for commercial failure. Emphasising how production is connected to the broader contexts of consumption outside the institutional environment, Negus sought to highlight how company cultures and the prioritising of repertoires are informed by a series of gender, class and ethnic divisions which influence aesthetic judgements and commercial decisions. In further work (1999) he researched the broader cultural and economic processes through which rap, salsa and country are constituted as both musical categories and forms of social identity. Through in-depth case studies he illustrated how the formal separation of genres within music organisations is uneasily connected to a broader series of social divisions and tensions.

Research by David Hesmondhalgh has both challenged and complemented the emphasis that Negus has placed on the centrality of the major recording corporations. Arguing for the need to understand independent and alternative patterns of musical production, Hesmondhalgh has highlighted how musicians and record companies can play an active role in attempting to change the conditions under which music is produced and distributed. Yet because of the nature of music as a cultural industry (where high levels of risk are offset by various strategies, including the star system, and strict control of circulation), this active role can become complicated and compromised by the very same discourses of independence which motivate musicians and record company staff in the first place (Hesmondhalgh, 1998, 1999).

A key theme in the work just outlined has been an increasing recognition that production and consumption are interrelated. However, while this has been acknowledged, it has not been so easy to theorise and research this issue. Although it is perhaps desirable, it is far too early to locate an emergent perspective which is capable of fully theorising the complex processes which link those practices condensed into the terms 'production' and 'consumption'. Equally, we should not underestimate the very practical difficulties of attempting to research production and consumption simultaneously. However, these caveats noted, we are witnessing writers using a variety of approaches in an attempt to grapple with the way that the production of music can no longer be solely equated with a study of the corporate institutions and the organisational routines of the recording industry. There is a discernible tendency for researchers to proceed with an awareness that a consideration of production inevitably entails thinking about a broader range of social, political, cultural and economic dynamics.

The contributions in this section, whilst still inspired by conventional questions about production, are attempting to think outwards from a strictly institutional focus. Via discussion of technology, performance, creativity, genre and various intermediary activities, the contributors here share a concern with asking questions about the relationships between musical interactions and social interactions, and the processes which link musical organisation to social organisation.

This is apparent in the chapter by Jason Toynbee. Taking issue with those who are suspicious of, or who dismiss the notion of the mainstream, he focuses on the processes through which mainstreams are formed. In doing this, he places the institutional production of music in a broader historical and geographical context. Using the Gramscian concept of hegemony, he points to the specific times when particular styles and institutions became dominant to make an argument about how mainstreams are formed. He then considers a moment during the 1980s when rock ceased to be the dominant mainstream and highlights the movement towards more dispersed, less exclusive and less hegemonic networks of mainstreams clustered around a range of genres.

Will Straw, meanwhile, pays attention to what often falls 'between the cracks' of music-industry analysis by focusing on technological change and the circulation of music commodities. His study of the 12-inch single draws attention to a neglected dimension in popular music studies: the material culture of music – the actual records, CDs, tapes, etc. that constitute the world of popular music objects. Straw highlights how one particular popular music artefact was intended by record companies as a marketing device but did not completely 'fit' with prevailing industry practices. Instead, it assumed a far more significant position as a material artefact and became the stimulus to, and centre of, an international underground dance culture.

Keith Negus and Michael Pickering argue that a critical interrogation of creativity should be central to any understanding of musical production. They review a range of approaches to creativity, highlight the plethora of meanings that have become clustered around and attached to the term, and suggest that we should not seek an easy resolution of any apparent contradictions (such as those between the mundane and exceptional, for example). Drawing insights from Raymond Williams and Norbert Elias, they suggest one way of exploring the link between production and consumption by approaching creativity in terms of the communication of experience – the tangible social aesthetic which connects performer with public.

Jocelyne Guilbault stresses the need to address the specificity of music industries in particular places and, refreshingly, in a field rarely characterised by political pragmatism, draws out some of the ways in which cultural policy might encourage the growth of the local industry, and create better conditions for musicians. In doing this her study echoes the important work of Roger Wallis and Krister Malm (1984) on the music industry in 'small countries'. Through a detailed survey of the particularities of the calypso business, Guilbault argues that the music industry involves a lot more than the recordings and routines of the major companies. It entails thinking about a world of music industries (in the plural). In our technology and media-dominated age, she also makes us aware that the history of the business of musical production should lead us much further back in time than to the introduction of recording technology.

References

ADORNO, THEODOR, 1990: 'On Popular Music', in Simon Frith and Andrew Goodwin (eds), *On Record*. London: Routledge.

——, 1991: *The Culture Industry, Selected Essays on Mass Culture*, ed. J. Bernstein. London: Routledge.

BOURDIEU, PIERRE, 1986: *Distinction. A Social Critique of the Judgement of Taste*. London: Routledge.

CHAPPLE, STEVE AND REEBEE GAROFALO, 1977: *Rock'n'Roll is Here to Pay*. Chicago: Nelson-Hall.

FERGUSON, MARJORIE AND PETER GOLDING (eds), 1997: *Cultural Studies in Question*. London and Thousand Oaks: Sage.

GAROFALO, REEBEE, 1986: 'How Autonomous is Relative: Popular Music, the Social Formation and Cultural Struggle'. *Popular Music* 6 (1): 77–92.

GENDRON, BERNARD, 1986: 'Theodor Adorno Meets the Cadillacs', in Tania Modeleski (ed.), *Studies in Entertainment*. Bloomington and Indianapolis: Indiana University Press.

HEBDIGE, DICK, 1979: *Subculture, The Meaning of Style*. London: Methuen.

HENNION, ANTOINE, 1982: 'Popular Music as Social Production', in D. Horn and P. Tagg (eds), *Popular Music Perspectives*, vol. 1. Exeter: Association for the Study of Popular Music, 32–40.

——, 1983: 'The Production of Success: An Anti-Musicology of The Pop Song'. *Popular Music* 3: 158–93.

——, 1989: 'An Intermediary Between Production and Consumption; The Producer of Popular Music'. *Science, Technology and Human Values* 14 (4): 400–24.

HESMONDHALGH, DAVID, 1998: 'The British Dance Music Industry: A Case Study of Independent Cultural Production'. *British Journal of Sociology* 49 (2): 234–51.

——, 1999: 'Indie: The Institutional Politics and Aesthetics of a Popular Music Genre'. *Cultural Studies* 13 (1): 34–61.

HIRSCH, PAUL, 1972: 'Processing Fads and Fashions: An Organizational Set Analysis of Cultural Industry Systems'. *American Journal of Sociology* 77 (4): 639–59.

NEGUS, KEITH, 1992: *Producing Pop: Culture and Conflict in the Popular Music Industry*. London: Edward Arnold.

——, 1999: *Music Genres and Corporate Cultures*. London: Routledge.

PETERSON, RICHARD, 1976: 'The Production of Culture. A Prolegomenon', in R. Peterson (ed.), *The Production of Culture*. London and Thousand Oaks: Sage, 7–22.

——, 1997: *Creating Country Music, Fabricating Authenticity*. Chicago: University of Chicago Press.

TAGG, PHILIP, 1987: 'Musicology and the Semiotics of Popular Music'. *Semiotica* 66 (1–3): 279–98.

——, 1993: '"Universal Music" Music and the Case of Death'. *Critical Quarterly* 35 (2): 54–98.

——, 1994: 'Subjectivity and Soundscape, Motorbike and Music', in H. Järviluoma (ed.), *Soundscapes: Essays on Vroom and Moo*. Tampere, Department of Folk Tradition.

THORNTON, SARAH, 1995: *Club Cultures*. Cambridge: Polity Press.

WALLIS, ROGER AND KRISTER MALM, 1984: *Big Sounds from Small Peoples*. London: Constable.

WILLIS, PAUL, 1990: *Common Culture*. Milton Keynes: Open University Press.

9

Mainstreaming, from hegemonic centre to global networks

Jason Toynbee

Whether spoken or on the page there is usually a dismissive ring to the word 'mainstream'. It suggests a type of music which is standardized, popular and easy to listen to. It also hints at why such a style might exist. Like junk food the mainstream has been produced as a commercial product, and foisted on undiscriminating consumers by an industry concerned only with making a profit. Significantly, people who talk about the mainstream this way contrast their own taste with it. What they like is 'real music', produced by independent artists and encapsulating authentic values of expression.

For Sarah Thornton (1995: 92–115) that is the whole point about 'mainstream'. Its function is ideological, serving to distinguish the taste of those who use the term – in her case study, the fashionable members of London dance subculture. In practice, though, there is no evidence that the mainstream exists as a substantive category. The singles chart, for instance, far from being homogeneous, 'is mostly a pastiche of niche sounds'. What is more, even 'buyers of the same records do not necessarily form a coherent social group' (1995: 100). For Thornton, then, the mainstream is just a myth.

This chapter takes a contrary position. For while 'mainstream' is often deployed in an ideological way, behind the myth there is, as we shall see, a concrete social and musical phenomenon. The trouble is one has to start almost from scratch in making such a case because academic accounts which *do* refer to the mainstream as a real social formation tend to echo the pejorative discourse used by fans and musicians. Dick Hebdige (1979), for example, treats mainstream popular culture as the antithesis of subculture. Not only is the former 'normalised' and 'naturalised' (100–2), it invariably latches on to, and then incorporates, subcultural style in an ideological process of 'defusion' (90–9).

One way out of this relentlessly negative approach might be to go back to an earlier usage of the term. In the mid-1950s the jazz critic Stanley Dance suggested that certain older musicians belonged to the mainstream, people like Coleman Hawkins who had been influenced by modern jazz but whose playing was still rooted in the older, swing style (Carr et al., 1988: 318–19). For Dance mainstream was both a descriptive and an evaluative term. It pointed up continuities in the jazz tradition, and lent them a certain weight. It also emphasized the inclusiveness of jazz, implying that despite the recent rebellion of bebop this music was really a tolerant and open form. In the end Dance's conception is too parochial to be applied to popular music at large. Also it does not allow for the conflict and contradiction which constantly threaten consensus in the big mainstream formations I am going to delineate. However, aspects of Dance's approach can certainly be borrowed, particularly the importance of affiliation.

So, here is a redefinition which brings this out. *A mainstream is a formation that brings together large numbers of people from diverse social groups and across large geographical areas in common affiliation to a musical style.* Looked at in this way it is best conceived as a process rather than a category, hence the 'mainstream*ing*' of the chapter title. I want to suggest that three currents have kept the popular music mainstream flowing along its rocky course historically. The first is hegemony. According to Antonio Gramsci (1971), leading social groups attempt to make their world view legitimate across the divided terrain of capitalist society. Crucially, such a hegemonic project depends on negotiation and alliance with subordinate groups rather than simple domination. As we shall see, the popular music mainstream encapsulates just this sort of dynamic. Second, mainstreaming includes a popular urge to find an aesthetic of the centre, or stylistic middle ground. This also involves negotiation with 'low-other' musics (Middleton, 2000) which are, putatively, beneath it. Third, there is an economic current. The music industry always tries to map a market on to hegemonic, mainstream taste. Yet this can never be fully achieved. For mainstreams are inherently contradictory.

These currents then combine in different ways over three, overlapping periods. Actually, they are distinct enough to suggest we should talk about mainstream*s* in the plural. The first runs from the early 1920s to the turn of the 1950s. In Tin Pan Alley–Hollywood (or TiPAH) industrially manufactured music gains mass distribution for the first time through the media of records, radio and film. The production centre and main market are in America, but the music is also heard across Europe, and in the colonial world wherever there are appropriate media. Rock then constitutes a second mainstream, beginning in the 1950s and reaching its height in terms of scale and influence in the 1970s. Rock is Anglo-American in origin, although it too traverses the world, and becomes indigenized in important ways. Since the 1980s we have been living in a third moment of plural, international networks. Rap and reggae, for example, circulate at a global level, yet are also produced in local, hybrid forms. A key question, which we shall come back to at the end of the chapter, is whether the term 'mainstream' can still be applied to these 'glocal' (Thornton, 2000) phenomena. But let us start by looking, historically, at the three currents of the mainstream.

Hegemony – at the Alley and on the Rock

As Tony Bennett suggests, Gramsci's theory of hegemony enables popular culture to be 'viewed as a force field of relations shaped, precisely, by . . .

contradictory pressures and tendencies' (Bennett, 1986: xiii). It thus avoids the pitfalls both of all-out enthusiasm and its opposite, mass cultural scepticism. Instead, popular culture is seen to be ambivalent, encapsulating dominant class interests while also, and necessarily, taking on board oppositional values. This flexible approach to the relation between politics and cultural expression also enables investigation into how race, ethnicity and gender intersect with class.

In the period since Bennett's essay was written the concept of hegemony has fallen out of favour in cultural studies. In part this is because class-based analysis, even in the relatively supple form of hegemony theory, has been replaced by work with a much stronger emphasis on *cultural* difference, especially ethnic, gender and sexual difference. These terms have tended to supplant rather than complement class analysis. There has also been an increasing interest amongst researchers in *local* forms or instances of popular culture, a tendency which has been particularly important in popular music studies. The result is that the theory of hegemony, with its aspiration to explain the totality of social and cultural relations, has become redundant.

However, I want to hang on to it for a little longer. Quite simply, it can help to explain how large-scale cultural formations, like the popular music mainstreams we are dealing with here, have coalesced and then sustained themselves over decades. Much academic writing (not to mention talk among fans) assumes that mainstreams are the inevitable cultural outcome of the development of modern capitalist societies and mass media technologies. I would suggest this is far from being the case, and that popular taste has always needed to be *assembled*, often under difficult conditions.

In the TiPAH period, for example, the formation of mainstream taste and style took place in the context of intense social dislocation in the United States. Immigration, chiefly from Europe, reached its peak in the first two decades of the twentieth century, with the result that in 1920 across much of the USA more than half the population was foreign-born (Burchell and Homberger, 1989: 160). True, mass immigration helped to mitigate against acute social conflict of the sort experienced in Europe because ethnic difference occluded class identity. But ethnic difference also represented a barrier to the formation of an integrated national culture of the sort required in America's emerging mass consumption economy. What is more, with the deepening of the Depression in the 1930s, class struggle *was* much more strongly in evidence. Now, though, it was superimposed on demographic diversity and regional distinctiveness (Davis, 1980).

It is against this background of ethnic fragmentation and social conflict that we need to see the emergence of a mass mediated, musical mainstream in America. The first thing to note is the sheer coherence of TiPAH style. As Charles Hamm (1979) points out, most popular songs in this period were in four sections, usually of eight bars each (361). The sections were then arranged in set patterns – AABA (as in 'Somewhere Over the Rainbow') was the most common. In effect the 32-bar, 'standard' song form represented a hegemonic first base. It enabled significant variation between songs in the areas of harmonic development, melody and phrasing. Yet it also provided consistent structure and therefore easy recognition for a diverse audience, many of whose members did not speak English as a first language.

A second hegemonic tendency can be identified in the themes of song lyrics. A study done towards the end of the TiPAH period shows that hopeless love or the breaking up of relationships predominated over fulfilment (Horton, 1957/1990: 23). The world of the popular song was thus one of desire, of longing to belong to another. What is more, many songs used the first and second person form giving a strong sense of the singer as subject (the 'I'), and audience member as the one being sung to (the adored 'you' of the song).[1] In this way an ideal relationship was set up between the persona of the singer and the listener. Most of all, the bond depended on sincerity, the belief on the part of the audience that the singer/lover really meant what he or she was singing.

What were the political implications of the TiPAH mainstream? In an obvious sense this was a hegemonic style which, in hailing subjects from diverse social groups, actually reflected middle-class interests and capitalist order. Standard songs provided the soundtrack for an emerging consumer society, and if they offered a utopian dream of romance this was also domestic and quiescent in character. On the other hand, during the 1930s TiPAH brought Americans together in cinemas and around radios which were broadcasting the liberal agenda of the New Deal. More generally, we can note a certain cosmopolitan urbanity in the standard song itself – however sentimental it might appear. Mostly produced in New York by Jewish composers who were immigrants or the sons of immigrants, it was not easily assimilated to the atavism of the radical right (Melnick, 1999).

Of course the liberalism of the TiPAH mainstream looks mild enough in contrast to the oppositional stance of rock. In fact the association of rock and rebellion is so strong that it might seem perverse to consider rock a mainstream at all. To show that this was indeed the case I want to examine rock music in terms of the same three factors, discussed above, which underpinned the hegemony of the standard song.

On the question of form, unlike standards rock songs were relatively heterogeneous. In the British scene alone there was a 'a profusion of styles' during the 1970s (Moore, 1993: 104–53). Yet it seems in retrospect that rock's star system eclipsed its formal heterogeneity. As Will Straw (1990) has argued, rock in all shapes tended to rely on a cluster of durable stars. During the 1970s this musician elite dominated album charts and the big stadia, releasing new records at large intervals. There are clear parallels here with the stable (if longer lasting) reign of the standard song.

What *is* significantly different about rock is that musical form was actually less salient as a marker of style than textural quality. From the start the timbric range of its standard ensemble defined rock: electric guitar, bass and drums, sometimes augmented by organ or piano. Moreover, through the combination and modification of voices in recording, a new sense of three-dimensional space was created, something we can hear right at the beginning of the period in Elvis Presley's recordings at Sun Records with their use of echo effect and sound balancing. 'Virtual textural space', as Allan Moore calls it (1993: 106), was then extended via stereo and multi-track recording from the mid-1960s onwards. Thus, when we enlarge musical form to include timbre and gestured space, rock appears, if not homogenous, then extremely coherent – and markedly different from TiPAH music. It is this phenomenological shift, I want to suggest, which enabled rock to become the focus for a new hegemonic alliance.

Crucially, where TiPAH had relied on a core middle-class constituency (Hamm, 1979), and offered an idealized image of bourgeois life which subordinate social groups might aspire to, rock involved the construction of a new 'youth culture'. As Simon Frith puts it, this was a 'culture which was apparently classless and rebellious, but which rested on the gradual middle-class adoption of the trappings of working-class teenage life' (1978: 22) – a hegemonic move for the times. We can hear the shift most clearly in mode of address. Where, 'I' and 'you' were lovers or putative lovers in TiPAH, this set-up was replaced by a more aggressive tone and new *dramatis personae* in rock. The subject of 'My Generation' by The Who (1965), for example, was a representative of Youth, while the second person 'you' (of 'Why don't you all fade away?') became a despised other – nothing less than the whole older generation. As for theme, love songs did continue to be written. But whatever they were about songs frequently employed a lofty and self-consciously poetic register in which spirituality supplanted the Tin Pan Alley heart. This too was a hegemonic move, but in the opposite direction, 'upwards' towards a cerebral realm of purity.

Aesthetics of the centre and the margins

Consistency and inertia are the truistic qualities of mainstreams. Yet mainstreams also pass through periods of intense turbulence. Thus, while TiPAH hegemony involved keeping 'jazz' on the outside up to the mid-1930s, jazz (in the form of swing) almost swallowed up US popular music at the end of the decade. Later, in the transitional period of the late 1950s and early 1960s, there was a struggle for hegemony as rock'n'roll competed with the established TiPAH mainstream. Actually, it is now clear that rock as a whole was premised on a cycle of 'revolutions': first rock'n'roll, then beat music and rock, then punk.

At a general level we can explain such turbulence in terms of the 'moveable' nature of hegemony (Bennett, 1986: xvi), and its propensity to crisis (Hall, 1996: 422–3). More specifically, however, we need to examine the relationship between African-American musical culture on the one hand, and on the other a mainstream which denied ethnic difference while remaining predominantly white. This relationship was rarely manifest or the subject of reflection. Yet it was absolutely crucial to the historical development of the mainstream, and particularly the oscillation between inertia and upheaval. How are we to understand it?

All styles have a centripetal tendency. The desire for pleasure leads to repetition (Middleton, 1987), and an obsessive return to key features which are heard as being in the middle. However, the gravitational pull of the centre – exemplified by those consistencies in the mainstream we examined in the previous section – inevitably wanes over time (Toynbee, 2000: 104–7). This may be through exhaustion, when aesthetic possibilities of a given genre run out, but it may also have to do with the attraction of *other* musical voices on the margins of a style. It is this latter process we are concerned with here.

The mainstream has always depended on the importation of musical authenticity, a primordial source of energy from without. Richard Middleton (2000) calls this source the 'low-other'. The need for it derives from a pervasive sense of lack in Western music which Middleton traces back to the elevation of bourgeois art music to an autonomous realm during the eighteenth and nineteenth centuries. In effect this shift effaced the sensuousness and immediacy of music that had been the spur to autonomization in the first place. The response of composers was to turn to the popular (gesturally 'below') as a source of material to ground their refined musical structures.[2] Middleton identifies two strategies here: assimilation, which involves incorporation of the low-other into high musical form, and projection, 'where the other . . . is externalized in a sphere of apparent social difference' – for example in the through-composed 'folk' songs of Vaughan Williams or Bartók (62). Significantly, both these strategies are used in popular music as a way of translating and controlling African-American music, the mainstream's chief source of otherness.

There is some argument about how much of the Tin Pan Alley idiom is African in origin (see Van Der Merwe, 1989; and Negus, 1996: 143–5 for a discussion). However, it is certainly the case that TiPAH composers and performers were using identifiably African-American voices right at the beginning of the period. As Charles Hamm shows, during the early 1910s Irving Berlin adopted the generic code of the 'coon song', with '[h]ints of "black" dialect in the text . . . and passing suggestions of syncopation in the music' (1994: 146). A key factor in this projection of African-American style was the mediating role played by Jewish-American writers and performers. As Jeffrey Melnick has it, Jews were sanctioned 'to act as public representatives of Black music' (1999: 26). The best-known case was that of Al Jolson whose black face routine in *The Jazz Singer* effectively launched the Hollywood screen musical. But many of the most successful TiPAH song writers, like Berlin and George Gershwin, were Jewish mediators of black style too.

In rock, on the other hand, musicians used the blues as a root stock for the new style in a more direct way. In the 1950s white rock and rollers covered contemporary rhythm and blues tunes. For a short period it even became possible for black performers like Little Richard and Chuck Berry to address a generic, rock and roll audience. In the second phase, during the 1960s, British groups explicitly paid homage to the blues, including the archaic country form, from a spatial and cultural distance. The blues was 'projected', in Middleton's terms, by the Rolling Stones, Cream and so on in a new kind of electric folklorism. Finally, in the 1970s the fabric of the blues guitar sound continued to be developed in rock music (Palmer, 1992), but its status as a locatable voice was effaced; a strongly assimilative move.

So, both historic mainstreams positioned black music in two places at once: in the centre, where it was used as a source of vital energy; and on the outside, where it was low, other and the exemplar of everything the mainstream was not. Such a contradictory form of interaction was of course premised on racialized power in which the terms and conditions of movement between margin and centre were not determined by black musicians and audiences. However, this was never a fixed principle. As we have seen, the theory of hegemony explains how leadership, in this case the setting of a cultural agenda, always involves concession, the negotiation of crisis and the *possibility* of radical change.

In the late 1960s the case of the black American guitarist Jimi Hendrix shows this very well. Hendrix played a key role in the development of rock sonority, but in a geographically marginalized theatre of production – Britain. Here, although still cast as a racialized other (Henderson, 1990: 66–7), he was able to deploy such otherness much more on his own terms than in America. As Perry Meisel puts it: 'In Hendrix, cowboy and dandy, black and white, English and American, electric and voice – all these familiar differences or oppositions – are trampled, reconstituted, blurred, crossed over' (1999: 118). Yet ultimately Hendrix must be seen as an exceptional figure. If his work signalled the possibility of a major shift towards hybridity within the mainstream, then it was a promise denied. By the early 1970s Hendrix was dead and rock hegemony had reorganized itself. Now a colour-blind universality was proclaimed. In all branches, though, musicians were white, and, with very few exceptions, turned their backs on contemporary black music.

Mainstreams and markets

The development of musical genres is thoroughly entwined with the discursive process of naming and defining. 'Death metal', 'rockabilly' and 'swing', for example, represent their respective styles positively because the titles are epithetic, and negatively because they signify difference from other genres, other tastes. This double signification gives genres great potential in marketing. The mainstream represents almost the opposite case though. For here is a formation whose identity must be (precisely) nebulous and all-encompassing if it is to include difference. To put it another way, we might say that hegemony depends on ambiguity rather than precise naming.

Despite this inherent flaw in the mainstream as a marketing category, the music industry has always had a strong interest in addressing a large market which traverses geographical and social space and can be sustained over time; in other words a mainstream. Clearly, conventional economies of scale obtain here. But there is an added factor. As in other cultural industries, production costs (those incurred up to the moment of the 'first copy') are high relative to the costs of reproduction (pressing, distribution and so on). As a result 'the marginal returns from each extra sale tend to grow, leading in turn to a powerful thrust towards audience maximization' (Garnham, 1990: 160). Thus, while the marketing logic of the music industry mitigates in favour of the particular and the nameable, the logic of production prefers the general – the largest possible category. The industry has responded to this situation with two strategies, for segmented and mainstream markets.

The first, and still most significant, segmented market was African-American. Here the industry adopted the category of race music in the 1920s (Kennedy, 1994). Then in the late 1940s, when 'race' smacked too much of overt segregation, the term 'rhythm and blues' was coined (Wexler and Ritz, 1993). This strategy represented what I have elsewhere called 'racialized marketing' (Toynbee, 2000: 118–19), that is the superimposition of a market on to a music culture which had already been 'subjected to a racial epidermal schema' (Fanon, 1992: 221) and marked out as subordinate in the field of the social. Such an approach was therefore *anti*-hegemonic, in that it worked against alliance. Yet it was, paradoxically enough, also well-targeted marketing. And it strongly contributed to a thriving music culture which endured on its own terms until at least the 1980s (George, 1988). Finally, race music and rhythm and blues served as a low-other to the mainstream in the sorts of ways we have already examined. In terms of market it enabled 'crossover', the selling of notionally black music to white, mainstream audiences (see Brackett, this volume).

This strong demarcation of black music can be contrasted with the music industry's marketing of the mainstream where, instead of *categorizing*, we find a strategy of *invitation to acclaim*. The popular music chart has been a key means for this. Generic Top 40 or Top 10 charts not only display the popularity of songs and artists, but also put choice-making on show. They represent, as Martin Parker puts it, 'a democracy of taste' (1991: 210): actually a serial plebiscite because they are published weekly. The charts are thus very much oriented towards process rather than topic. Of course it matters which records appear, which go up or down. Yet precisely because of the chart's universal nature, quality is produced in relation to quantitative value. Record buyers celebrate or commiserate in response to how the chart ranks the records they like, dislike or are indifferent about.[3]

A second means of marketing the mainstream is through stardom and canonization. In part stars are produced through the charts. Their records achieve high rankings, and stay popular for a relatively long time. But they also have a public presence, or what Richard Dyer (1979) calls 'star image', which persists between chart appearances, record releases and concert tours. Stars thus embody the continuity of the mainstream, its temporal flow. One explanation for stardom is psychoanalytical. The star is an object of desire, a present-absent figure, 'tantalisingly close and similar, yet at the same time remote and dissimilar' (Ellis, 1992: 618). But stardom can also be understood in terms of an economic model. It is a response to consumer preference for the sharing of knowledge about artists. Fans choose a limited range of (successful) artists because this makes learning and sharing more economic. The same factor also produces addiction: consumers tend to want more of the same artist (Adler, 1985). In the case of TiPAH, but even more so in rock, knowledge about music was institutionalized in journalism, biography and the construction of canons (Toynbee, 1993). In effect each mainstream produced its own 'selective tradition' (Williams, 1965) which gave weight and continuity to an otherwise ephemeral form.

Global *and* mainstream?

Tensions in the music industry between the construction of an inclusive mainstream built around charts and stars, and a separate racialized market and repertoire source demonstrate, yet again, hegemonic process. The question for the final section is whether such an analysis still applies in a period when popular music, the cultural industries and indeed whole societies are becoming globalized.

Will Straw (1993) has suggested that in the early 1980s a new 'pop mainstream' emerged in North America. Actually, it now seems that the phenomenon he describes is better conceived as the death knell of the mainstream. It was characterized first by increasing speed of innovation (records cycled much more quickly through the charts), as Top 40 radio revived and the new format of MTV took off. Increasingly, however, diversification became the key factor. By the end of the decade more than 20 per cent of US record sales were in the categories rap/hip-hop and R&B/urban – or music of black origin.[4] 'Crossover' into the white, mainstream market was now an important market phenomenon. Meanwhile an older generation raised on rock was left stranded by these developments, and began to buy once again the canonical rock albums of its youth, but on the new, 'yuppie' format of the compact disc. As Keith Negus points out, the changing taste of this cohort also helps to explain the extraordinary rise of country music over the same period (Negus, 1999: 118–19). In effect, then, fragmentation of the popular music market in Anglo-African-America during the 1980s ended the hegemony of the rock mainstream.

Yet what I want to argue now is that it also heralded the emergence of *global* networks and forms of affiliation whose geographical reach and complex connectivity have come to transcend the preceding organization of mainstream hegemony. To begin with, a brief 'story board' account of globalization. Shot one shows the declining significance of nation states and economies, and the growth of global networks and flows over the last quarter-century (Castells, 1994; Held et al., 1999). In the second shot we cut to the social consequences of such change: greater differentiation and inequality, but also more individualization as each actor is extracted from her/his embeddedness in traditional social structures (Giddens, 1990; Lash and Urry, 1994). Shot three is still being filmed. It tracks emerging global symbolic forms as they define new routes and regions (Appadurai, 1996; Tomlinson, 1999).

In fact music has been a precociously global form. As Pekka Gronow points out, 'the leading companies set their goals internationally from the very beginning', and by 1910 had built pressing plants and created distribution networks throughout the world (1983: 56). The ubiquity of recorded music in the period since then can be explained in terms both of the nature of production – recording is relatively cheap – and of dissemination – flexible duplication, cheap sound carriers and even cheaper access through broadcasting all contribute here. A further consideration is popular music's translatability, the fact that it travels across cultures and can be hybridized more easily than language-based narrative forms like film and television fiction. If these factors have enabled local music making to thrive alongside international repertoire (Laing, 1986), in practice the two historic mainstreams (US and then Anglo-American) have served as the major source of music globally. As in other forms of communication (see Hamelink, 1995) one-way flow, from core to periphery, has predominated.

In what sense, then, might it be possible to talk about new kinds of connectivity which transcend the uni-directional model? I want to propose three types of emergent network. They are like mainstreams in that they involve affiliation across social, cultural and geographical space, and produce much larger communities of taste than the merely local. They are also similar to mainstreams because they incorporate those tensions between stability and change, inclusivity and exclusivity, centre and margin which we examined earlier. But they are quite different from the historic Anglo-American mainstreams in their geographical and cultural range and complexity.

The first type is 'world music'. This consists of music made in peripheral countries which is then sold to a middle-class audience in the core. Simon Frith (2000) argues that world music represents nothing less than the continuation of the rock aesthetic – a quest for authenticity and roots, but in another, exotic place. Indeed, as Steven Feld (2000) points out, world music is invariably packaged as primitive music. In terms of mode of address, world music offers a version of classical mainstream rhetoric but with a twist. Because the words of songs are incomprehensible to the metropolitan audience, lyrics may be heard as universal statements of spiritual truth.[5] This is a 'talking in tongues' which speaks directly to the listener's soul.

World music has a completely different role at the level of its production and primary reception though. Here it is a domestic, often a hegemonic, style. Take the case of North African rai. Tony Langlois (1996) suggests the music serves as a transmission belt between local tradition and modern, cosmopolitan identity. On the one hand it embodies 'creative conservatism', or reference via electronically synthesized voices to traditional forms and sounds of the Maghreb (264). On the other it signifies modernity: disco beats on backing tracks and whisky bottles on the covers of cassettes (268). There is a *direct* link to global modernity too, in that the world market for rai brings these sounds to the core. Jocelyne Guilbault (1993) describes zouk from the Antilles in a similar way. Zouk is creolized music which builds on local traditions, but through its simultaneous address to a metropolitan and diasporic audience across the Francophone world, and in its embrace of technology, it promotes a hybridizing, glocal identity. World music thus constitutes a dialogical network: core and periphery, modern and traditional gesture towards one another, albeit on grotesquely unequal terms.

The second type of global network is dialogical too, but in rather a different way. Rap and reggae were originally site-specific. They emerged in Africa–America and Jamaica respectively. Crucially, however, global marketing of these styles has been followed by the development of local scenes in certain parts of the world. Examples include rap in France, Germany, Italy, Brazil and New Zealand/Aotearoa (see Fjeld, 1996; Mitchell, 1996; Bennett, 1999; Wright, 2000); and reggae in Zimbabwe, Australia, South Africa (Mitchell, 1996; Kwaramba, 2001). Here musicians have inflected the genre archetypes with an indigenous sonority, using local language in lyrics and raps.

How and why has this happened? One factor is that rap and reggae were deeply (and manifestly) hybrid in their original contexts. Both represented the 'versioning' aesthetic of the black Atlantic; both crystallized out of African diasporic cultures of resistance *and* adaptation (Gilroy, 1993). This blueprint has proved to be immensely adaptable by ethnic minorities and diasporic communities around the world. Amongst *gastarbeiter* youth in

Frankfurt-am-Main, for example, Turkish-language rap has become a means of articulating identity through the translation of voices from the parent culture into hip-hop idiom (Bennett, 1999). Such doubling of marginal identity (for Frankfurt, African-American 'times' Turkish) involves a complex exchange, whereby hip-hop functions as a universal low-other form, simultaneously local *and* south central L.A.

Glocal rap and reggae are pretty marginal in economic terms. The contrast here is with a third kind of global formation, the regional market/genre. Dave Laing (1997) suggests that three 'regional blocs' now constitute a real alternative to the Anglo-American international music market. They are Mandarin and Cantonese pop in East Asia, Spanish-language music in the Americas, and pan-European repertoire, especially dance music. Laing's argument depends on a careful analysis of charts and music industry data. But it also includes a normative assessment: these networks incorporate a more diffuse and fluid distribution of power than the hierarchical 'platinum triangle' of the rock era, still based in North America, Britain and Australasia.

Conclusion

In this chapter I have argued for the importance of mainstreaming as a social and musical process. Much more than a subcultural myth (Thornton, 1995), or simple manifestation of cultural dominance (Hebdige, 1979), the mainstream brings together large numbers of people from diverse social groups in common affiliation to a musical style. Historically, we can identify two overlapping periods of the mainstream, TiPAH and rock. Hegemony offers a cogent way of understanding both. On the one hand, people congregate in the mainstream, which tends towards the universal in its inclusivity and synthesis of difference. On the other hand, the drive towards universality is always partisan, in that leading social groups and economic interests attempt to coordinate the mainstreaming process. This often involves the appropriation, and then exclusion, of 'low-other' musics and identities (Middleton, 2000), particularly African-American music.

Mainstream hegemony supposes an 'imagined community' (Anderson, 1991), a unitary culture which provides an aesthetic centre and core constituency. It thus fits the bill very well in the case of TiPAH and rock, and their respective national contexts of the United States and Anglo-America.[6] However, by the 1980s the rock community had already begun to break up. Popular music was increasingly organized around distinct generational cohorts and diverse tastes and identities. Emerging trends towards globalization then compounded this fragmentation. As a result, in the contemporary period successive singular mainstreams have been replaced by parallel multiple networks. I have identified three, namely world music, glocal scenes and regional blocs. But these are likely to mutate and others may well take their place.

Clearly, the plurality of the networks and their transnational ambit represent a major change in the nature of the popular music mainstream. So should we still use the term? Is there enough continuity between the periods before and after rock to make this a worthwhile move? I would say yes. Most importantly, the desire to affiliate, to produce large congregations which span social and geographical space, persists, often in a strong form. World music, for instance, expresses a hegemonic urge to 'join up' in both its constituencies, that is local music scenes in developing nations, and a coterie of middle-class connoisseurs in the richer ones. Moreover, the music industries are eager to turn these forms of affiliation into markets when economic conditions appear favourable. World music sales are small right now, but they represent a significant niche market, one which can be readily enlarged when conditions are right. And regional blocs are already important market-repertoire systems in their own right.

If mainstreaming has carried over into the new era of increasingly globalized social and cultural relations, then perhaps the final issue to address is how to evaluate this phenomenon. Operationally, one might say, mainstreams produce others: self-conscious others like Thornton's (1995) elite club goers who use the mainstream as a means of distinction, but also, and more importantly, marginalized musics and identities – low-others. Ultimately, mainstreaming is an ambivalent social process in that it alternates between building mutuality for all and regulating difference according to unequal relations of power. However in a world where economic inequality and social differentiation are spiralling, new mainstreams do provide means of *hearing through* difference. In this process we should expect exclusion and the selective appropriation of otherness to continue. But we should also expect, and actively seek out, new routes towards a cosmopolitan musical culture where other also means equal.

Acknowledgement

Thanks to Keith Negus for extremely helpful critique of earlier versions of this chapter.

Notes

1. In relation to 'I/You' songs, 18 of Charles Hamm's 'twenty-three representative Tin Pan Alley songs' (1979: 360) fall into this category.

2. Middleton is *not* suggesting here that low and high are absolute categories. Rather his point is that they are historical, being produced by relations of power, and especially the rise of the middle classes.

3. Clearly, specialist charts like R&B or country *are* named, but this only serves to reinforce the non-specific, hegemonic nature of the 'Top Forty'.

4. Source: Record Industry Association of America (*Music and Copyright* 185, 5 July 2000: 6). On the beginnings of the new era of crossover in the early 1980s, and its discursive as well as musical terms and conditions, see David Brackett's chapter in this volume.

5. Thanks to Kevin Buckley for this observation.

6. Anglo-America represents a rather odd case. In the period of the rock mainstream it constitutes a temporary dual-national community. For a satirical vision of this, see the film *This is Spinal Tap*.

References

ADLER, M., 1985: 'Stardom and Talent'. *American Economic Review* 75 (1): 208–12.

ANDERSON, B., 1991: *Imagined Communities: Reflections on the Origin and Spread of Nationalism*, second edition. London: Verso.

APPADURAI, A., 1996: *Modernity at Large: Cultural Dimensions of Globalization*. Minneapolis: University of Minnesota Press.

BENNETT, A., 1999: 'Hip hop am Main: The Localization of Rap Music and Hip Hop Culture'. *Media, Culture and Society* 21 (1): 77–91.

BENNETT, T., 1986: 'Introduction: Popular Culture and "the Turn to Gramsci" ', in T. Bennett, C. Mercer and J. Woollacot (eds), *Popular Culture and Social Relations*. Milton Keynes: Open University Press.

BORN, G. AND D. HESMONDHALGH (eds), 2000: *Western Music and Its Others: Difference, Representation and Appropriation in Music*. Berkeley: University of California Press.

BURCHELL, R. AND E. KOMBERGER, 1989: 'The Immigrant Experience', in M. Bradbury and H. Temperly (eds.), *Introduction to American Studies*, second edition. London: Longman.

CARR, I., D. FAIRWEATHER AND B. PRIESTLEY (eds.), 1988: *Jazz: The Essential Companion*. London: Paladin.

CASTELLS, M., 1994: *The Rise of the Network Society*. Oxford: Blackwell.

DAVIS, M., 1980: 'The Barren Marriage of American Labour and the Democratic Party'. *New Left Review* 124: 43–84.

DYER, R., 1979: *Stars*. London: British Film Institute.

ELLIS, J., 1992: 'Stars as a Cinematic Phenomenon', in G. Mast, M. Cohen and L. Braudy (eds), *Film Theory and Criticism: Introductory Readings*, fourth edition. New York: Oxford University Press.

FANON, F., 1992: 'The Fact of Blackness', in J. Donald, and A. Rattansi (eds), *'Race', Culture and Difference*. London: Sage/Open University.

FELD, S., 2000: 'A Sweet Lullaby for World Music'. *Public Culture* 21 (1): 145–71.

FJELD, J., 1996: 'Boyz from Brazil'. *Artforum* 34 (8): 38 and 118.

FRITH, S., 1978: *The Sociology of Rock*. London: Constable.

——, 2000: 'The Discourse of World Music', in BORN AND HESMONDHALGH (2000).

GARNHAM, N., 1990: 'Public Policy and the Cultural Industries', in *Capitalism and Communication: Global Culture and the Economics of Communication*. London: Sage.

GEORGE, N., 1988: *The Death of Rhythm and Blues*. New York: Pantheon.

GIDDENS, A., 1990: *The Consequences of Modernity*. Cambridge: Polity Press.

GILROY, P., 1993: *The Black Atlantic: Modernity and Double Consciousness*. London: Verso.

GRAMSCI, A., 1971: *Selections from the Prison Notebooks*, trans. and ed. Q. Hoare and G. Nowell Smith. London: Lawrence and Wishart.

GRONOW, P., 1983: 'The Record Industry: The Growth of a Medium'. *Popular Music* 3: 53–75.

GUILBAULT, J., 1993: *Zouk: World Music in the West Indies*. Chicago: Chicago University Press.

HALL, S., 1996: 'Gramsci's Relevance for the Study of Race and Ethnicity', in D. Morley and K.-H. Chen (eds.), *Stuart Hall: Critical Dialogues in Cultural Studies*. London: Routledge.

HAMELINK, C., 1995: 'Information Imbalance across the Globe', in J. Downing, A. Mohammadi and A. Sreberny-Mohammadi (eds), *Questioning the Media: A Critical Introduction*. Thousand Oaks: Sage.

HAMM, C., 1979: *Yesterdays: Popular Song in America*. New York: Norton.

——, 1994: 'Genre, Performance and Ideology in the Early Songs of Irving Berlin'. *Popular Music* 13 (2): 143–50.

HEBDIGE, D., 1979: *Subculture: The Meaning of Style*. London: Methuen.

HELD, D., A. MCGREW, D. GOLDBLATT AND J. PERRATON, 1999: *Global Transformations: Politics, Economics and Culture*. Cambridge: Polity Press.

HENDERSON, D., 1990: *'Scuse Me While I Kiss the Sky: The Life of Jimi Hendrix*. London: Omnibus.

HORTON, D., 1990/1957: 'The Dialogue of Courtship in Popular Song', in S. Frith and A. Goodwin (eds.), 1990: *On Record: Rock, Pop and the Written Word*. London: Routledge.

KENNEDY, R., 1994: *Jelly Roll, Bix and Hoagy: Gennet Studios and the Birth of Recorded Jazz*. Bloomington: Indiana University Press.

KWARAMBA, A., 2001: 'Chimurenga Music in Zimbabwe', *The Literature and Culture of Zimbabwe* (http://landow.stg.brown.edu/post/zimbabwe/music/chimurenga.html) (accessed 03 June 2001).

LAING, D., 1986: 'The Music Industry and the "Cultural Imperialism" Thesis'. *Media, Culture and Society* 8: 331–41.

—— 1997: 'Rock Anxieties and New Music Networks', in *Back to Reality: Social Experience and Cultural Studies*. Manchester: Manchester University Press.

LANGLOIS, T., 1996: 'The Local and Global in North African Popular Music'. *Popular Music* 15 (3): 259–73.

LASH, S. AND J. URRY, 1994: *Economies of Signs and Space*. London: Sage.

MEISEL, P., 1999: *The Cowboy and the Dandy: Crossing Over from Romanticism to Rock and Roll*. New York: Oxford University Press.

MELNICK, J., 1999: *A Right to Sing the Blues: African Americans, Jews, and American Popular Song*. Cambridge, Mass.: Harvard University Press.

MIDDLETON, R., 1987: 'In the Groove, or Blowing your Mind? The Pleasures of Musical Repetition', in T. Bennett, C. Mercer and J. Woollacot (eds), *Popular Culture and Social Relations*. Milton Keynes: Open University Press.

——, 2000: 'Musical Belongings: Western Music and its Low-Other', in BORN AND HESMONDHALGH (2000).

MITCHELL, T., 1996: *Popular Music and Local Identity: Rock, Pop and Rap in Europe and Oceania*. Leicester: Leicester University Press.

MOORE, A., 1993: *Rock: The Primary Text, Developing a Musicology of Rock*. Buckingham: Open University Press.

Music and Copyright 185 (5 July 2000): 6.

NEGUS, K., 1996: *Popular Music in Theory*. Cambridge: Polity Press.

——, 1999: *Music Genres and Corporate Cultures*. London: Routledge.

PALMER, R., 1992: 'The Church of the Sonic Guitar', in A. DeCurtis (ed.), *Present Tense: Rock & Roll and Culture*. Durham, N.C.: Duke University Press.

PARKER, M., 1991: 'Reading the Charts – Making Sense with the Hit Parade'. *Popular Music*, 10 (2).

ROBERTSON, R., 1992: *Globalization: Social Theory and Global Culture*. London: Sage.

STRAW, W., 1990/1983: 'Characterizing Rock Music Culture: The Case of Heavy Metal', in S. Frith and A. Goodwin (eds), *On Record: Rock, Pop and the Written Word*. London: Routledge.

——, 1993: 'Popular Music and Postmodernism in the 1980s', in S. Frith, A. Goodwin and L. Grossberg (eds), *Sound and Vision: The Music Video Reader*. London: Routledge.

THORNTON, S., 1995: *Club Cultures: Music, Media and Subcultural Capital*. London: Routledge.

THORNTON, W., 2000: 'Mapping the "Glocal" Village: The Political Limits of "Glocalization" '. *Continuum: Journal of Media and Cultural Studies* 14 (1): 79–89.

TOMLINSON, J., 1999: *Globalization and Culture*. Cambridge: Polity Press.

TOYNBEE, J., 1993: 'Policing Bohemia, Pinning up Grunge: The Music Press and Generic Change in British Pop and Rock'. *Popular Music*, 12 (3): 289–300.

——, 2000: *Making Popular Music: Musicians, Creativity and Institutions*. London: Arnold.

VAN DER MERWE, P., 1989: *Origins of the Popular Style: The Antecedents of Twentieth Century Popular Music*. Oxford: Oxford University Press.

WEXLER, J. AND D. RITZ, 1993: *Rhythm and the Blues*. London: St Martins.

WILLIAMS, R., 1965: *The Long Revolution*. Harmondsworth: Pelican.

WRIGHT, S., 2000: ' "A Love Born of Hate": Autonomous Rap in Italy'. *Theory, Culture and Society* 17 (3): 117–35.

10

Value and velocity: the 12-inch single as medium and artifact

Will Straw

At the end of 1999, Elton John's single 'Candle in the Wind' still remained near the top of Canada's Top 10 singles chart. Released in 1997, the single had long since disappeared from sales charts elsewhere in the world. By late 1999, it sold only 600 copies per week in Canada, but in a country where few singles are domestically released and very few are bought, 600 was sufficient to keep 'Candle in the Wind' near the top of popularity charts (*Billboard*, 1999). While the singles charts in other countries might still convey a sense of turbulent excitement, Canada's has been marked, for many years, by a sense of stagnation and meaninglessness. Exchange rates, free trade agreements, and a relatively small market have stopped the domestic production of singles, and made those which are imported seem unappealingly expensive. Those which show any movement whatsoever in the national market thus come to play a distorted role within measures of popularity and change. Their immobility within music retail stores, where they accumulate in obscure corners, is striking.

This example is a trivial one, but it is full of lessons about the ways in which commodities, and their circulation, shape the character of national cultural life. The movement of musical recordings gives national musical cultures their distinct sense of speed and change. It may turn regions within such cultures into dead ends, filled with artifacts which arrive too late, or with too little promotional push. Alternately, it may make national cultural markets effective conduits within the international movement of objects and influences.

In arguments which continue to inspire me, the folklorist Orvar Lofgren suggests two lines of development for the cultural study of artifacts (Lofgren, 1997). The first requires commitment to the study of objects as *things*, postponing a consideration of them as texts, meanings and messages (the common fate of artifacts within cultural analysis). We must pursue an analysis of materiality, but not because this is somehow more 'materialist'. In the movement of objects across and between cultures we may map those lines of movement and processes of sedimentation which anchor and constrain other cultural processes. The sense that consumption is only ever a struggle over meaning has long been central to the study of popular music, and to cultural studies more generally. By privileging (and circumscribing) the encounter between consuming subject and cultural artifact, this sense of things has blocked attention to the ways in which cultural resources move, accumulate and are unevenly distributed across the world.

In any given cultural space, the provenance of punk singles, price of American alternative rock CDs, availability of 12-inch vinyl dance singles and access to information surrounding new musical commodities will shape the contours of regional/national musical cultures. Objects arrive at destinations bearing meanings which the distance of their travel and the manner of their acquisition have inscribed upon them. The second of Lofgren's directions for analysis takes us towards what he calls 'the everyday workings, the cultural thickenings of . . . belonging'. We need, he suggests, an analysis of 'the nationalization of trivialities, the ways in which national differences become embedded in the materialities of everyday life, found not only in the rhetoric of flag-waving and public rituals, but also in the national trajectories of commodities' (Lofgren, 1997: 106).

The 12-inch single as artifact

This essay is concerned with one such 'triviality', the 12-inch vinyl single, and with the circumstances of its emergence within one national culture (that of the United States) during the years 1975–77. We will treat the 12-inch single as one example of the material culture of music – as a tool, artifact, commodity and medium. Musical styles and movements take shape across a multitude of practices and locations, and there is more to the histories of hip-hop or house music than the recording configurations in which these histories are embedded. Nevertheless, we will limit ourselves here to an analysis of the 12-inch single as a particular kind of object. As objects, 12-inch singles moved across music markets and cultural spaces at speeds distinct from those of other recording configurations. In doing so, they produced lines of fracture within musical culture, as parts of that culture came to change at rates which challenged the ability of other parts to profit from that change. As an object which was characterized, much of the time, by its scarcity, the 12-inch single highlighted inequities of access between center and periphery, and, more broadly, between the US market and national musical markets elsewhere. As the focus of highly speculative investment, the 12-inch single's value, to consumers and fans, moved between two extremes. At one, it was a precious, hoarded insider's tool; at another, it stood for wasteful over-production and the miscalculation of demand. Virtually all these features of the 12-inch single became quickly evident in the three years which followed its introduction.

Origins

Long cuts with complex Latin-style percussion underpinning seem particularly effective with the discotheque market.

(*Billboard*, 1974b)

In 2000, the 12-inch vinyl single, used by disc jockeys in dance clubs throughout the world, marked a quarter-century as an legitimate 'configuration' within the music industries. This anniversary was rarely noted, though the 12-inch single itself is venerated within the recent wave of books on club culture, DJ practice and raves. Confusion over the 12-inch single's date of birth is compounded by its slippery status in the mind of consumers of recorded music. For North American consumers in particular, the 12-inch was, for many years, one more option amidst the messy array of EPs, remix albums, medleys and other textual forms which have served as carriers for dance music culture since the 1960s. The history of disc jockey practice, elaborated across these recent books, has focused more on the mixing of fragments from vinyl albums or other raw materials than on the development of the 12-inch single itself. This has made histories of dance club music more heroic, but it has pushed to the side the more mundane ways in which the 12-inch single entered into the lives and labors of night club disc jockeys and music consumers in the mid-1970s.

Recent histories of dance club culture have reached only partial agreement about the sequence of events through which the 12-inch single was introduced. Controversy surrounds the three moments presumed to mark this introduction: (1) the production of the first 45 r.p.m. record on which a single song was extended across a 12-inch vinyl disc; (2) the first official release of a 12-inch single as a promotional device distributed to dance club disc jockeys exclusively; and (3) the first release of a 12-inch single intended for the commercial retail market. These events, which mark the movement of the 12-inch single from underground to public musical culture, unfolded in the United States between 1974 and 1976.

Brewster and Broughton claim that New York DJ Tom Moulton produced the first 12-inch single, a remix of 'So Much for Love' by Moment of Truth (2000: 178). The date of this single seems to be unknown, but one can assume it was released in the very early months of 1975. (No one has claimed that 12-inch singles were released before 1975.) 'So Much for Love' was distributed informally, as a test pressing, to a small group of club DJs; for that reason, it is not considered an official release. There are competing claims as to the first 'official' 12-inch single released for promotional purposes by a record label. The long-held belief that this was RCA's 'Dance, Dance, Dance', by Calhoon (sent as a promotional tool to disc jockeys in the spring of 1975) has been challenged in recent years, as a wave of oral histories, internet-based disco chronologies and on-line record markets have produced new candidates.[1] A 1975 *Billboard* article claimed that Doug Riddick, head of Atlantic Records' disco division, had 'introduced the first 12-inch, $33\frac{1}{3}$ disco disc', though the article provided no title for this release, and may simply have been referring to the first 12-inch single to use the $33\frac{1}{3}$ speed. (Calhoon's 'Dance Dance Dance' was released at 45 r.p.m.) Tom Moulton himself, in an on-line interview, claimed that 'Free Man' by the Southshore Commission (on Scepter/Wand Records) was the first promotional 12-inch single; a website devoted to disco history lists 'Call Me Your Anything Man' by Bobby Moore on Scepter Records as the first ('Tom Moulton Tribute' website; 'Disco Music History' website). There is general agreement that 'Ten Percent' by Double Exposure (Salsoul

Records, June 1976) was the first 12-inch single released to the general retail market.

Disagreement about these various events is unsurprising, given the compressed time period in which they occurred. This uncertainty is symptomatic, as well, of the hazy distinction between limited-run 'test pressings', produced for local disc jockeys, and fully fledged promotional copies produced as part of the larger release strategy for a disco single. Histories of the 12-inch single have been troubled by the overlapping of experimental prototypes and official releases, something common in the case of those industries (like that producing computer software) for whom professional insiders constitute an important market. The claim, by Brewster and Broughton (2000: 180), that 'the 12-inch is the only format of recorded music introduced as a result of consumer demand rather than record company marketing guile' risks confusing the promotional activism of small labels with the consumer demand of disc jockeys during this period.

Like other media histories, that of the 12-inch has spawned one set of narratives fixated on a moment of punctual discovery and others which recount minor mutations from within a set of possibilities. In an oft-repeated account of the 12-inch's birth, Tom Moulton described his collaboration with an engineer on the mastering of a 7-inch dance single which Moulton had remixed. The engineer had run out of 7-inch blanks for cutting the master disc, and proposed using the 12-inch masters which remained on site. Against Moulton's skepticism, the engineer suggested spreading the grooves, which were intended for a 7-inch record, across the span of the 12-inch. '[W]hen I heard it I almost died', Moulton remembered, in an interview with Brewster and Broughton (2000: 178). The wider grooves made possible in the 12-inch format lent themselves strikingly to the demands of superior dance club sound systems, and low-end frequencies could be heard with greater clarity.

On a website devoted to the 12-inch single, this birth narrative is extended across two stages, from the contingent use of 10-inch masters through the deliberate choice, in a later mastering exercise, to embrace the 12-inch form. Here, Tom Moulton recounts the process of discovery as follows:

> So, the thing is – one day I went in there to José – [mastering engineer] José Rodriguez – and I had 'I'll be holding on' by Al Downing and I said; 'José, I could really need some acetates.' And he said; 'Just Tom, I don't have any more 7-inch blanks. All I have is like the 10-inch.' And I said; 'Well, if that's the only thing – we're gonna do it, what difference does it make?' So he cut one, I said; 'It looks so ridiculous, this little tiny band on this huge thing. What happens if we just like . . . can we just like, you know, make it bigger?' He goes; 'You mean, like spread the grooves?' and I said; 'Yeah!' He goes; 'Then I've got to rise the level.' I said; 'Well, go ahead – rise the level.' And so he cut it like at +6. Oh, when I heard it I almost died. I said; 'Oh my God, It's so much louder and listen to it. Oh! I like that – why don't we cut a few more?' So it was by accident, that's how it was created.
>
> But for the next song we cut, we went for the 12-inch format instead of the 10 inch and the song was 'So much for love' by Moment of Truth. That was the birth of the 12-inch single.
>
> ('Tom Moulton Tribute' website)

By this point, in fact, record companies had already experimented with albums featuring songs extended across an entire side, 7-inch singles recorded at $33\frac{1}{3}$ r.p.m. to expand their length and sound frequencies, two-sided 45 r.p.m. singles (with distinct, club-oriented versions of songs on one side), album-length, segued medleys of dance music, and most other imaginable variations of playback speed, song format and disc size. If the 12-inch single was discovered in a stereotypical instance of accidental invention, it was clearly, as well, the result of ongoing experimentation with a variety of options. Sarah Thornton's *Club Cultures* (1995) discusses many of these options in her detailed historical account of the use of records in dance clubs over several decades. (Further detail on developments in the 1970s may be found in Brewster and Broughton (2000) and Fikentscher (2000).) The 12 inch single assumed importance as an efficient resolution of technical problems facing dance club disc jockeys. Just as importantly, however, it became the object of an inter-institutional consensus which lasted several years, and which compelled disc jockeys, record companies, record retail outlets and other players in the dance music industries to confront the problems caused by their shared commitment to its fate.

Displaced practices

Prior to 1974, disc jockeys drew on a variety of musical forms in their practice. Reggae, afro-funk, old and new soul and other forms were pulled into the repertory of dance clubs; the constant difficulty of finding these recordings was bemoaned in various press accounts of disc jockey work. The few retail outlets which serviced disc jockeys in the early 1970s assembled repertories of club music out of African or Jamaican imports, old records bought on the second-hand market, bootleg pressings of out-of-print titles and contemporary releases judged suitable. Record companies like Motown and Mercury regularly reissued old titles as demand for them on the part of disco jockeys promised a renewal of their commercial value. Many of the early tools of disc jockey practice moved in and out of legality, as cherished singles were bootlegged or tapes circulated between clubs and individuals (see *Billboard*, 1974f, 1975a).

Two aspects of disc jockey practice during this period would wither with the widespread dissemination of the 12-inch single, after 1975. One was the regular recourse to rediscovered records from the past, and the sense of an available repertory whose origins spanned several years but whose suitability for dance club play remained relatively stable. The other was the extent to which disc jockey practice, before 1975, presumed the existence of autonomous fields of musical production (such as that of soul music) as the primary source for records to be played in clubs. The original sense of disco records, as those which 'crossed over' from other musical fields, would diminish as the process of crossing over became inscribed in the texts of records predestined for the disco market, like the disco versions of soul, pop, rock, Broadway and classical pieces which continued through the late 1970s. Records from the past, or from previously distinct musical fields, would persist in DJ practice primarily as the source of beats, breaks or idiosyncratic effects.

Over time, the 12-inch single took part in the displacement of older modes of listening, in the home and in clubs. In its early years, the lack of a standardized speed for 12-inch singles (which were released in either $33\frac{1}{3}$ and 45 r.p.m. versions) was seen as causing problems for those who listened to records by stacking them on their record players at home. For a musical form associated with parties, and with an unbroken stream of rhythmic music, this seemed a genuine problem, though stackable turntables were already disappearing in an age of component home stereo systems. In Japan, the extended duration of the 12-inch single, and its invitation to segue from one track to another, seemed incompatible with national traditions of deejaying, in which DJs typically spoke between songs and derived much of their popularity from this patter. More generally, around the 12-inch single, minor but controversial modifications of listening practice took shape. The 12-inch single helped make listeners accustomed to the idea that a record might contain much more than would typically be heard. It also nourished that ongoing search for variant versions which is central to present-day record collecting (*Billboard*, 1977c, 1977d).

Aligning the disco industries

In its October 1977 issue, the *Journal of Marketing* published the article 'Disco: Birth of a New Marketing System' (Stibal, 1977). There is no reason to assume this article was read widely within the music industries, but the system for marketing disco music which it described had become entrenched within those industries over the previous two years. The model outlined an efficient sequence in the promotion of new recordings, from dance club to album sales. Under this system, record companies would deliver 12-inch single versions of new singles to dance club disc jockeys. Disc jockeys, in turn, would report back to record companies on the apparent success or failure of these records with dance club audiences; a favorable response by club-goers would lead to purchases of the 7-inch, commercial single in music retail outlets. These sales, in turn, would stimulate the addition of records to radio playlists, leading to further sales of the single and, ultimately, success of the album from which it was taken. At each sign of momentum, promotional resources could be marshaled to extend a record's commercial lifecycle, taking a song from the 12-inch promotional single on which it first appeared through success as a 7-inch single and, ultimately, high sales in album form.

Trade press accounts of the disco industry in 1974 show signs of a move towards this sort of integration of that industry's various components. *Billboard*'s disco columnist, Tom Moulton, mediated between the New York City-based underground components of that culture and a variety of activities transpiring across the nation. As a remixer who reported on the introduction of new recording formats, and whose column recounted the efforts of record companies to service disc jockeys with promotional product, Moulton (and *Billboard* magazine more generally) magnified local developments into national events within a rapidly expanding industrial dynamic.[2] In 1974, record labels such as Mercury and London began to systematize their relationship with nightclubs, drawing up lists of clubs and disc jockeys, and providing free copies of records for play in discotheques. Other labels would follow suit over the next 18 months (*Billboard*, 1974a, 1974c).

Since the 1960s, it had been common for record labels to supply promotional copies of dance records to discotheques. Through the 1970s, it became established practice to distribute them to disc jockeys themselves (see, for example, *Billboard*, 1974a). Nightclubs were notoriously short-lived, and the residencies of disc jockeys unstable – both these factors led record companies to see the dance club industries as chaotic fields resistant to the effective coordination of promotional activity. The choice of disc jockeys themselves as the appropriate recipients of free records sprung in part from ongoing lobbying by disc jockeys. It was rooted, as well, in the recognition that disc jockeys were important sources of feedback to record companies and thus more useful points of contact. In the years 1974–75, two sorts of organization would emerge or evolve to play mediating roles in the process of disseminating promotional 12-inch singles. One was the independent promotion company, which could compile lists of disc jockeys and discotheques and undertake the complicated labor of reaching each of these with promotional copies of new records. Firms such as Provocative Promotions offered record companies their ability to produce credible lists of disc jockeys and interact with them in an effective manner. The second and more novel organizational form was the DJ pool, a locally based organization of disc jockeys formed for the purpose of facilitating a smoother flow of recordings from record companies. Disc jockeys in New York City formed a pool in June of 1975, and other cities or regions followed (Los Angeles in December 1975; Florida in July 1976; Chicago in February 1977, and so on).

Very quickly, the barriers between various institutions within the disco industries would be blurred and roles condensed, as the fact of occupying a strategic role within the flow of information and recordings encouraged a variety of other activities. While disco pools seemed, in part, to displace independent promotion firms in 1975, many managers of pools had turned their pools into promotion and distribution centers by 1977. Many pool managers owned specialty record stores, or the 'one-stop' distribution outlets which served independent stores. With time, it might be argued, this looseness of roles would contribute to the unraveling of the industry structure on which the commercial success of disco seemed to depend. The integration of disc jockeys within the promotion, distribution and (eventually) remixing and production of disco records ensured a smooth flow of technical expertise and information throughout the whole system. Increasingly, however, this integration removed any lingering advantages held by large-scale labels in the production or distribution of disco music. New networks of DJ mixers, small labels and clubs could easily produce and disseminate much of the music which these networks required. By the 1980s, the infrastructure of DJ pools, newsletters, specialty record stores and distribution networks, which major labels had viewed as one level within a broader industry system, would serve to support the musical styles and commodities of a smaller, much more insular musical subculture.

As a token of exchange, the history of the 12-inch single is bound up with the sorts of institutions and practices which, at various points in its history, it has served to interconnect. In 1974–77, this interconnection seemed at its most efficient and expansive. The unfolding lifecycle of a 12-inch single traced lines of passage from the locally based realm of the nightclub through the institutions of music retail, broadcasting and mainstream commercial success. Already, by 1977, however, blockages and shortcuts in this sequence had become apparent. As large numbers of consumers began to buy 12-inch singles and neglect the albums on which their songs appeared, the translation of a 12-inch's success into that of the more mainstream album format slowed. Successful 12-inch singles pre-empted the sales of albums, and those which failed (and which had little value as 'cut-outs') were seen to litter the marketplace with worthless commodities. The life cycles of 12-inch singles were either too long (12-inches lingered after they were intended to retreat, to give way to albums) or too short (12-inches disappeared from the playlists of status-conscious disc jockeys before audiences had grown attached to them). By 1977, as well, the rise and temporary success of disco radio formats in the United States had weakened the role of nightclub DJs in launching new records. Disc jockeys were meant to play pivotal roles in that process of selection by which, from among the hundreds of records released each year, several dozen would be chosen for exposure in nightclubs and the most successful of those adopted by radio stations. When record companies began servicing radio stations directly, as they did in the late 1970s, this sequence would unravel. (See, for accounts of these problems, among many other articles, *Billboard*, 1979a, 1979b.)

Brian Winston has argued that one crucial dynamic in technological development leads to the suppression of innovation's radical potential (e.g. Winston (1998), usefully discussed in Schaap (2001)). The fate of the 12-inch single is a useful parable in evaluating this claim. Very quickly, in the year which followed its introduction, it served to focus industrial processes of 'crossover' – processes designed to pull marginal musical forms into the commercial mainstream. Each 12-inch single carried musical information through which the stylistic development of disco was communicated; most 12-inches, in the years 1975–77, initiated industrial processes meant to result in the sale of long-playing albums. This brought dance records above ground, rendering them one artifact in a promotional sequence. Almost as quickly, however, the 12-inch set in place a logic of differentiation, whereby the institutions of dance music, intimately interconnected as they had become, began to diverge from those of the larger music industries. As an artifact which spawned new formats for making music and new circuits for its dissemination, the 12-inch single ultimately served to transform the underground club culture of the early 1970s into an internationally interconnected set of dance music undergrounds which persist to the present. The major label's involvement in disco music, in the mid-1970s, served principally to mold the dispersed elements of dance music culture (DJs, 12-inch singles, remixes, pools and so on) into a relatively efficient professional subculture.

Secrecy and identification

For record companies, the effectiveness of disc jockeys and discotheques as promotional channels for new recordings presumed that the patrons of nightclubs could learn the titles and artists of the music they heard. As Gitelman notes, the question of how sound recordings might be identified to their listeners goes back as far as 1891, when it was common to speak a record's title into the recording apparatus as the process of recording began (Gitelman, 1999: 156). The principle at work here – that the medium of identification (in this case, sound) should be the same as that of the principal text itself – would later be realized in the radio announcer's identification of songs and in the practice of those club DJs who still spoke between bits of music. By the mid-1970s, however, as DJs almost invariably segued from one record to another, there was no obvious means to convey the identification of a song to those who had just heard it. Articles in *Billboard* addressed this problem regularly, as in the following:

> [Izzy, Atlantic disco promotion director] Sanchez feels that a deejay's need for concentration, and the rigors of the job, or rules of his club which prevent him from speaking over his record, is a retardant to efforts to enlist his aid in promotions.
> 'However, we do encourage him to display the jacket of the disk he is playing as a means of informing his audience what's on the turntable,' he states.

> *(Billboard, 1979a)*

This silence of concentration, of course, would be received in dance club culture as the sign of cool diffidence, such that disc jockey patter would be consigned to the denigrated realm of mobile disc jockeys (those who played weddings and private parties) or absorbed within the textuality of hip-hop DJ practice. One result of the disco DJ's silence was a proliferation of forms of written, public identification designed to compensate for the identificatory silence of the record itself. Casablanca Records, in 1977, introduced a 'disco awareness program' involving 'cocktail napkins designed with artists' names, coasters with label information, posters, T-shirts, album jacket display holders and other in-club displays' (*Billboard*, 1977f). The Record Depot, a store in Los Angeles, distributed copies of its business card to disc jockeys in the area. When customers at discotheques asked for the title of a record being played, they would be handed back one such card, with the title handwritten on its back, and encouraged to purchase the recording from The Record Depot. Similar arrangements were worked out between the 'Dogs of War' disc jockey pool in Chicago and local disco record retailers (*Billboard*, 1976b, 1977e).

The gimmickry of these modes of identification ensured their failure. The sense that records went by too fast for their titles to be noted would come to seem symptomatic of broader divergences between the velocities of disco culture and those of the consumers and institutions disco records were meant to win over. The problem of identifying records heard in clubs was, for large numbers of consumers, compounded by the difficulty of finding them in retail stores. Many companies releasing 12-inch singles issued these in standard jackets which contained only the name of the recording firm. These jackets were manufactured in large quantities, and used for a wide range of different titles (*Billboard*, 1976a). By 1978, in response to the problems of identification discussed here, many companies had turned to the use of distinctive 'picture sleeves' (similar to those in which albums were packaged) for each 12-inch single released (*Billboard*, 1978). The difficulties of marketing 12-inch singles to the broad record-buying public were the regular focus of discussions at industry trade conferences:

> Panelists reviewed a number of problems involved in merchandising disco 12-inch singles at the retail level: that simple sleeves are not conductive [sic] to display; that many retailers still don't have separate disco sections, if they stock the product at all, and that disco 12-inchers are most often purchased by singles buyers, who are just learning the business.

(Billboard, 1977g)

In 1977, the Long Island DJ Association announced publication of the Long Island Disco Timetable, which would make available to the general public the schedule of forthcoming disco record releases *(Billboard,* 1977a). Here, as in other attempts to broaden public familiarity with disco recordings, the challenge was seen as that of making record releases seem punctual, public events, rather than secret processes unfolding according to obscure logics. Problems of secrecy and identification intensified as disco became more popular after 1977 (and following the success of the movie *Saturday Night Fever*). As the number of new releases grew significantly, the distinctive identify of each was harder to convey.

In turn, competition among disc jockeys had led to a growing use of imported 12-inch singles, from such places as Montreal or Munich. The provenance and identity of these were often jealously guarded by disc jockeys; their status as imports, in any case, made them even harder for club patrons to find in retail stores. At the same time, because imported records were unlikely to receive radio airplay, they did not figure on the radio playlists which retail stores typically used in determining their buying inventory. In countries like Canada, where imports had always been a primary source of material for disco DJs, these problems were compounded. Local subsidiaries of record companies could not usually supply promotional copies of imported singles fast enough to meet disc jockey demand, and stores typically lagged behind disc jockeys in their access to new, imported releases. As disco music became more regionalized in the late 1970s, with important innovations coming from Europe and Canada, the sense that the records played in clubs were of obscure origin and unavailable to ordinary patrons increased *(Billboard,* 1977b; 1977h; 1975b).

By the late 1970s, with discotheques popular throughout much of the world, disco records would appear in most countries as imports, typically played in clubs before local recording industries had moved to release them domestically. In small markets, like that of Canada, a semblance of equity between domestic supply and public demand lasted only a couple of years, between 1975 and 1977. Thereafter, as in many countries outside the US–UK axis, disco records would veer between the extremes of rarity and over-production, as the industry's basic difficulty in calculating release times was compounded by the difficulty of international rights negotiation and competition from import sales. The continued (and increased) reliance of disc jockeys in most countries on imported titles has compounded the obscurity and secrecy which surround dance records for most consumers. Since the mid-1970s, as well, this dependence on imports has weakened the links between disc jockeys in most countries and their domestic recording or radio industries.

Space, time and the 12-inch single

Their time will not be the time of enduring tradition but rather that of technique

(Stamp, 1999: 62)

As a technology, the 12-inch single represented the accommodation of dance music recording to the new demands of super club sound systems and enlarged club spaces that were often converted from industrial use. As a medium, the 12-inch single became the central form through which innovation within dance music was communicated between the various components of dance music culture. While each 12-inch single typically carried relatively minor instances of transformation on its own, the rapid accumulation of these marks of change, across an ongoing series of 12-inch releases, produced the sense of dynamism which has marked dance music culture over the past quarter-century. As a commodity, the 12-inch single regularly perplexed industry personnel, who were compelled to calculate the desirable ratios of free promotional copies to expected sales, to anticipate the fading of a single's value and convert its appeal into that of albums.

As a cultural form, the 12-inch single is light, in the sense that it travels quickly and its commercial and cultural lifecycles are typically brief. With few exceptions, individual 12-inch singles are influential less for the significant marking of historical change provided by any single title than because their ongoing succession serves to maintain relationships across space. This succession holds in place (or slowly transforms) relations between a set of institutions and practices which are internationally dispersed and, typically, small-scale but numerous.

The compact disc reissue draws its authority from slowly elaborated processes of canonical judgment; it enters the marketplace accompanied by the presumption that its lifecycle will endure. The 12-inch single, like other single formats before it, poses much more obviously the problem of technique: of how to efficiently coordinate the fragile set of interconnecting events which will ensure its popularity across a broadly dispersed musical culture. These are, arguably, time-biased and space-biased media, in the sense given these terms by the Canadian historian Harold Innis (see, for a discussion, Innis (1995: 317) and Stamp (1999: 61)). When the events of the 12-inch single's life are not effectively coordinated, the material artifactuality of the 12-inch is foregrounded. It will become unavailable and, thus, precious, or remain in the marketplace as cultural waste (sold off, as they were in Montreal in the late 1970s, at the rate of five for a dollar).

Conclusions

The history of the 12-inch dance single is rich with evidence about the role played by secrecy, scarcity and uneven access in the dissemination of musical forms and styles. By the early 1990s, the absence of any vinyl pressing facility in Canada meant that all 12-inch vinyl singles for the club market were imported.[3] Until major Canadian labels began releasing single-artist or

DJ-remixed dance CDs in significant numbers in the late 1990s, dance music culture in Canada was shaped by an economy which operated at two extremes: between the connoisseurist culture of imported 12-inch singles and independent record stores, at one end, and the market for domestically pressed CD compilations of pop-house, at the other. There were few of the mediating institutions and little of the artifactual production which would sustain fine gradations of taste and connoisseurship between these two extremes: no locally pressed vinyl 12-inch singles anymore, no dance singles to be found in major record stores and a market for CD singles which continued to be weak and underdeveloped. This gulf exaggerated the fetishistically connoisseurist character of underground dance music just as it nourished the perception of the rest as abject and degraded. When all 12-inches are imported, however, and thus equally expensive, their prices do not vary with their distance from a musical and industrial mainstream. In these circumstances, the styles and genres of dance club music will multiply and their audiences fragment, as each such style or place of origin comes to seem equally exotic or precious.

More broadly, the 12-inch vinyl single sits, in the year 2002, in a contradictory relationship to scarcity and abundance. On the one hand, the production of masters has become increasingly artisanal, more and more undertaken with inexpensive, desktop equipment which is widely available. On the other hand, manufacture of the 12-inch single requires a material basis (that of vinyl pressing) which is slowly disappearing from the world. Reproduction of 12-inch singles is centralized within a few national economies, such as those of the US and UK – countries which remain at the center of influence and innovation within the dance music field. At a time when new global structures within the mainstream recording industry have evened out differences in the availability of most popular musical titles, the availability of vinyl has become one of the important ways in which national musical cultures remain differentiated.

Acknowledgement

This essay draws on research initially undertaken for my doctoral thesis, then supplemented over the past decade by ongoing research in trade magazines and other sources. Many thanks to Jessica Wurster, Aleksandra Tomic and others who have assisted with this research along the way. This is part of a larger project on the material culture of popular music over the past 25 years.

Notes

1. The claim that the first 'official' 12-inch was probably 'Dance Dance Dance' by Calhoon can be found in Brewster and Broughton (2000: 179) and Harvey and Bates (1993). Researching of these claims is made difficult by the fact that the group's name is sometimes (as in Brewster and Broughton) spelled 'Calhoun' and, at other times, 'Calhoon'. 'Calhoon' is the proper spelling.

2. Histories of disco rely heavily on *Billboard* magazine from this period. The magazine's role in pulling the various elements of disco's unfolding history into a relatively unitary chronology cannot be overestimated. *Billboard* announced the formation of disc jockey pools (and the meetings to organize them) in different cities, organized symposia for disco industry personnel and, perhaps most importantly, published the charts which – until the fragmentation of dance music culture in the late 1970s – held some authority.

3. By 1994, the last vinyl pressing plants had closed in Canada. In that year, Stickman Records, a small, club-oriented label, bought a small vinyl pressing apparatus in the US and imported it to Canada. See *Tribe* (1994).

References

BILLBOARD, 1974a: 'Discotheques Keyed in Mercury Service', 18 May: 33.
——, 1974b: 'Firm to Service Discotheques With New Disks', 15 June: 50.
——, 1974c: 'Labels Eye Discos as Hot Spots To Break R&B Product', 6 July: 1.
——, 1974d: 'Discotheque Culture in England Makes Soul Pirates Flourish', 28 September: 64.
——, 1974e: ''Illegit' Disco Tapes Peddled by Jockeys', 12 October: 1.
——, 1974f: 'Discotheque Wave Spreads to Campus, Dealers' Bins', 19 October: 1, 10.
——, 1975a: '"Disco Tech" Drive Launched by Motown', 8 March: 3.
——, 1975b: 'Canadian Labels Miss Disco Boat', 29 November: 1.
——, 1976a: 'A New 12-Inch 45 Salsoul Disco Label', 15 May: 3.
——, 1976b: 'Disco Disks Hypo Store Gross 50%', 14 August: 4.
——, 1977a: 'Long Island DJs Swing With Retailers & Consumers', 23 April: 50.
——, 1977b: 'Imported Disco Disks Spur License Rivalry', 16 July: 1.
——, 1977c: 'N.Y. Retailer Relies on Specialization', 19 July: 8.
——, 1977d: 'Rocky Road For 12-Inch Singles in Japan; Future Dim', 30 July: 42.
——, 1977e: 'Chi Patrons "Talk" Direct to Labels', 6 August: 52.
——, 1977f: 'Disco III Reaffirms Industry's Maturity', 10 September: 1.
——, 1977g: '12-Inchers Pose Problem in Club, Retail Exposure', 1 October: 68.
——, 1977h: 'Disco Disks Go Regional', 26 November: 4.
——, 1978: '45s Victims Of Production Jam', 30 September: 1.
——, 1979a: 'Disco Radio Challenges Clubs As Hitmaker', 10 February: 1.
——, 1979b: 'Disco Rules, But Where Are the Big Disk Sales?', 19 May: 3.
——, 1999: '"Candle" Still Burning on Canada's Chart', 17 April: 60.
'BMC – Black Culture – The First 12-Inch'. Website: http://laurent.thiebaut.free.fr/bmc/folders/framed/33_small_spinal_list_framed.htm. No date, but accessed August 2001.
BREWSTER, BILL AND FRANK BROUGHTON, 2000. *Last Night a DJ Saved My Life: The History of the Disc Jockey*. New York: Grove Press.
'Disco Music History' Website, 2000: http://www.discostepbystep.com/disco_history.htm
FIKENTSCHER, KAI, 2000: *You Better Work! Underground Dance Music in New York City*. Hanover and London: Wesleyan University Press.
GITELMAN, LISA, 1999: *Scripts, Grooves, and Writing Machines: Representing Technology in the Edison Era*. Stanford, Calif.: Stanford University Press.
HARVEY, STEVEN AND PATRICIA BATES, 1993: 'Behind the Groove.' *DJ* 84 (11–24 March): 4–9 of 'Disco Supplement'.
INNIS, HAROLD, 1995: *Staples, Markets and Cultural Change: Selected Essays*, ed. Daniel Drache. Montreal and Kingston: McGill-Queen's University Press.
MARVIN, CAROLYN, 1998: *When Old Technologies Were New: Thinking about Electric Communication in the Late Nineteenth Century*. New York and Oxford: Oxford University Press.

LOFGREN, ORBAR, 1997: 'Scenes from a Troubled Marriage: Swedish Ethnology and Material Culture Studies'. *Journal of Material Culture* 2 (1): 95–113.

SCHAAP, JESSICA, 2001: 'Electronic Shoeboxes? The Database for Historical Research'. Master's thesis, Montreal: Department of Art History and Communications Studies, McGill University.

SHANNON, DOUG, 1985: *Off the Record: The Handbook to Knowledge, Money and Success.* Cleveland: PaceSetter Publishing House.

STAMP, JUDITH, 1999: 'Innis the Canadian Dialectical Tradition', in Charles R. Acland and William J. Buxton (eds), *Harold Innis in the New Century: Reflections and Refractions.* Montreal: McGill-Queen's Press, 46–66.

STIBAL, MARY E., 1977: 'Disco: Birth of a New Marketing System'. *Journal of Marketing* (October): 82–8.

THORNTON, SARAH, 1995: *Club Cultures: Music, Media and Subcultural Capital.* London: Verso.

'Tom Moulton Tribute' Website, 1999–2000: http:/ /www.disco-disco.com/tributes/tom.html

TRIBE (1994): 'Wait! Wait! Wait!' (February): 10.

'West End Records' Website: http://www.westendrecords.com/newsite/artists/larry_time-line.php3. No date, but accessed August 2001.

WINSTON, BRIAN, 1998: *Media Technology and Society: A History from the Telegraph to the Internet.* London and New York: Routledge.

11

Creativity and musical experience

Keith Negus and Michael Pickering

Creativity is one of the most important yet unexplored issues in the study of popular music. Its significance is routinely noted, usually in passing, and its value often taken for granted. Its conceptual status in music studies is that of an unquestioned commonplace. Most of all, it is raised in reference to what is taken to be in opposition to it, to what is held as restricting or obstructing its realisation and potential. This may be the obtuseness of executive managers, the interference of moral guardians, the financial imperatives driving the global entertainment industry, or any number of other factors or forces. Creativity is then invoked as a lucky talisman in a critical argument about something else. What it involves in its own right or what meanings it is made to carry are seldom subject to any critical attention. This neglect may be due, at least in part, to the difficulties associated with the term, for as soon as we start to look at all closely at the idea of creativity, we quickly become aware of a plethora of contradictory images and associations, assertions and judgements. If these are part of the problem, they cannot be negotiated simply by turning away and passing on to what are deemed to be more pressing concerns. In this chapter we want to begin grappling with all that is caught up in the concept of musical creativity, however difficult this may be.

One way to begin doing this is to start unravelling the tangled web of meanings and associations which have become woven around the term. Among other things, these link together conceptions of the elevated and mundane, the exceptional and ordinary. We follow this initial step by outlining what seems to us a potentially fertile approach to creativity. This is to conceive of it in terms of the communication of experience. How this is achieved and how the quality of the communication is evaluated provides us with a useful way of thinking about creativity, not least because these processes are integral to the politics of culture. Such an approach also enables us to retain a sense of the phenomenological experience of creativity as an act connecting producer with listener. This is an important counter to sociologically reductive forms of analysis which tell us everything about the politics of culture but nothing about the practice of creativity and how it is experienced.

Innovation and novelty

In his brief analysis of the semantics of the term 'creative', Raymond Williams (1976) revealed how the contemporary Western concept of creativity can be traced back through a Judaeo-Christian tradition of thought to ideas about the divine creation of the physical and human world. The strength of this tradition made the emergence of its secularised meanings a slow and protracted process. The term changed only gradually from its earlier, exclusively cosmological reference, as in divine creation, bringing the world itself and the creatures within it into being, with the ancillary term 'creature' deriving from the same etymological stem. Expansion of the sense of the term began in the sixteenth century, particularly in relation to processes of making by people. Its modern meanings emerge from this new humanist emphasis, the earliest tendency to which can be traced in Renaissance theory. Nevertheless, the prior cosmological reference remained powerful enough for human artistic creation to be at times unfavourably compared with nature as the external manifestation of divine creation, or for the word to be used pejoratively to indicate falseness and contrivance.

From the later seventeenth century onwards, the modern sense of the word gained in significance through its consciously validating association with art. By the time of the Romantics, the term's positive value was assured, though threads of its earliest meanings were retained, with artistic activity carrying with it associations of something magical or metaphysical, and with creativity being exclusively manifest in the poet as, in some guises, a sort of messenger from God or, in others, an intensely perceptive spirit able to elevate our seeing to a superior reality. It is through ideas of poetic inspiration that these older meanings of the word 'creative' have proved resilient, even as the terms 'creation' and 'creativity' have themselves been more radically changed. The earliest example (1728) cited by Williams of an explicit connection of imaginative human creation with a noumenal source, in the mythological personification of an artistically inspiring goddess, has a specifically modern emphasis: 'companion of the Muse, Creative Power, Imagination'.

The idea of a Muse has for a long time seemed decidedly dated, with all the resonance of a mannered Romantic conceit, yet the conception of divine inspiration in the act of writing poetry remained a remarkably strong, even if less than central element in modernism. The characteristic effect has been to play down the act of making itself, as a deliberately learned and practised craft. This can, for example, be detected in Yeats's description of the act of poetic creation – 'I made it out of a mouthful of air' – as if his own shaping mind had been absent from the activity of composition. It would be wrong to suppose that this way of accounting for the act of poetic creation is merely an enchanting legacy of the Celtic Twilight. Throughout the twentieth century, when the term 'creativity' became established as denoting the faculty to which the verb 'create' relates as a process, these earlier associations continued to be invoked as an active, and certainly more than residual sense of the term. So, for example, John Lennon distinguished between the songs that he composed simply because a new album had to be produced, and the 'real music ... the music of the spheres, the music that surpasses understanding . . . I'm just a channel . . . I transcribe it like a medium' (quoted in Waters, 1988). John Taverner uses the same metaphor, and refers to 'auditory visions' when he feels that music is being dictated to him (Barber, 1999).

It is this continuing conjunction of the mystical and metaphysical with the material and mundane, the elevated with the profane, which seems to confound any attempt to develop a sociologically informed understanding of musical creativity. In the face of this difficulty, we want to argue that we should attempt to retain a sense of both the exceptional and pervasive meanings of the term. Three sets of issues accompany this attempt. Each of them follow, in different ways, from the inherited meanings and associations of the term which derive from its historical development.

First, any effort to articulate the experience of the creative process pushes us to the edge of what words can say. It inevitably involves having to bridge the gap between the sensational experience of creating – whether a song, a symphony or an improvised saxophone solo – and the necessity of translating an understanding of that experience into language that can be communicated to others. The endurance of this gap is perhaps unavoidable, since those acts of creativity in which someone is immersed and at one with the act itself are quite distinct from subsequent, relatively self-conscious efforts to describe what the creative process involves. This is why we often look to metaphorical forms of expression in referring to the phenomenological experience of creating and it is why certain creative experiences are rendered in a pseudo-religious or non-rational manner. Yet because creativity is always achieved within quite specific social, historical and political circumstances, we should at least be cautious about making or accepting any grand generalisations about the creative process.

A second issue concerns the opposition between that which is felt to be merely produced and that which is experienced as truly inspired and how this informs the valuation of the creative product itself. For example, some compositions, recordings and popular songs have enjoyed considerable critical and commercial success that has subsequently proved ephemeral, whilst others, often less recognised initially, have endured and become 'classics'. The recordings of Robert Johnson, the compositions of Ruth Crawford Seeger, and the soundtracks to 1970s blaxploitation movies are cases in point, where their methods of production have retrospectively been re-assessed as more 'creative' and 'inspired' than recognised in contemporary judgements of the time, or where an earlier local recognition of their creative character has subsequently become more universally acknowledged. Regardless of the processes through which this shift occurs, the reasons for its occurrence and the evaluative principles applied are what generally go uninspected. The emphasis has been far more on certain kinds of art which possess a transcendental quality, any reference to which is generally the point at which analysis itself begins to evaporate.

A third and related point is the way that the idea of creative activity has retained an integral distinction between a type of inspired, 'real' or 'authentic' creativity and a more routine, self-conscious, manipulative and false sense of the term. This dichotomy is apparent in the appeal to the spontaneity of creativity in Lennon's reflections on his 'transcription' of 'real music', and its contrast with material produced as a result of the contractual obligations to deliver new recordings of 'original' songs. This duality can be found formulated in different ways throughout the history of the concept and the gradual process of secularisation, or quasi-secularisation, leading to the shift of emphasis onto human capacity, with its accompanying transfer of originality, of bringing into existence, from God to the human imagination. This was a decisive break, though it would only be realised as such in retrospect. The vital need of imagination in creative practices is often cited as necessary for originality or innovation to occur, and the serious nature of the claim is partly established by the distinction between innovation and novelty. The negative equation of pleasure and novelty has remained powerful, particularly in association with light entertainment and specific types of popular music. For example, in the early twentieth century certain songs were referred to as novelty songs or numbers, usually delivering a short, comic narrative which a mid-century jazz historian described, in pejorative, put-down terms, as depending on 'some obvious contrivance for its appeal, such as a reorganised nursery rhyme or an infectious sort of gibberish' (Ulanov, 1952: 352).

It is probably impossible to get away from contrasts between novelty and innovation in developing any understanding of both the phenomenology of musical creativity and its use as a descriptive term. Yet we do need to be wary of how they have been mapped onto a distinction between exclusive and inclusive approaches, which in turn have been harnessed to ongoing debates about elitism and populism. From an exclusive perspective, human creativity is firmly associated with 'originality' while 'innovation' requires unique, insightful and inspired musicians, singers, writers and composers. In contrast, a more inclusive approach uses the term to refer to a task executed with considerable skill, a problem solved with imagination and panache, an act performed with grace, vivacity or élan, or even an interpretation of a particular artefact such as a song or film score which is judged to be particularly insightful, or at least ingenious. These widened applications of the term, where the reference is to whatever is positively commended, now seem to be potentially without limit. There is, nevertheless, a sharp descent in the conventional value of the term when it is used to designate such commercial practices as 'creative advertising copy' or 'creative accounting'. Although such designations are at times deliberately ironic, the expanded conception of creativity they are part of imbues the most banal of habitual working practices with an aura of artistic inspiration, human worth and social good, as with the commonplace use of 'creative' to distinguish product designers from executives in the advertising industry. Whilst the expanded conception is, at least for some people, motivated by a democratic impulse against forms of elitism, it slips too easily into populist trivialisation, embracing and celebrating as creative all manner of routine everyday discursive practices, postmodern ironic strategies, appropriations, decodings, re-writings and 'symbolic' resistance.

Such a divergence of meaning and value leads to various problems. Stress on the rarity of originality retains traces of an elitist approach to culture and social life, whereby certain gifted or mystically inspired individuals have creative abilities, and the rest do not, being able to do efficiently only that which they have been socialised into, or acquired through formal training. An exclusivist emphasis then denies the possibility of a reflexive, critical or analytical perspective to a process whose wellsprings are held to lie at a psychically deeper level than the one at which rational thinking and analysis operates. The appeal is then to metaphysical, religious or unconscious sources of the creative faculties. Strong retentions of mystical or metaphysical explanations of creativity are found when, for example, singers, performers or dancers explain their creative acts as inspired by, and derived from, the experience of some divine or transcendental entity. Similar continuities apply when all manner of musical artists speak of not being in control of their own body or thought process when composing, writing or improvising.

We can neither accept nor dismiss these as metaphorical conceits or misguided delusions. They are actually integral to the issue we are concerned with. Although we live in an apparently cynical and knowing postmodern age, we have still to engage with religious and metaphysical explanations of creative inspiration because of the ways in which they distil important spiritual and aesthetic concerns for many people.

The distinctions we have been referring to are common enough, but we must always be careful to avoid polarising them into absolute differences, as for example when an opposition is set up between artistic vision and humdrum, mechanical life. This can only diminish our understanding of the range and scope of the creative process. Its diverse realisations in particular cultural and historical circumstances cannot be reduced to this stark opposition. Furthermore, these tensions, dichotomies and contrasting perspectives cannot simply be resolved at a theoretical or conceptual level, for they have their source in the tangible, sensory experiences that coincide with the creative act. Yet when confronted with these divergent meanings, there is a tendency for many writers to attempt to resolve them by prioritising one or the other. This may, for example, be done either by claiming that only a select few – Plato, Dante, Hegel – are truly creative (Steiner, 2001), or by arguing that all everyday actions are potentially creative and adopting a dismissive or sceptical stance towards any notion of exceptionality (Joas, 1996; Willis, 1990).

Instead, we wish to argue for a need to reconceptualise creativity as at once ordinary *and* exceptional. Clearly, the category of genius emerges from a very particular historical epoch and geographical region, associated with European Romanticism, and has been adopted in a manner which lends support to a restrictive and socially divisive canon and rationalises the existence of educational institutions and practices privileging a small minority. But the fact that the great praise and attention accorded to various individuals, and the artworks or products associated with them, may have served certain ideological interests in the past, does not mean that they or their achievements are utterly subsumed by these interests.

Failure to provide a satisfactory answer to the question of exceptionality is a major shortcoming of the sociology of art. In exploring the dynamics of art, creativity and cultural production, we may look to such sociologists as Janet Wolff, Howard Becker and Pierre Bourdieu, but what we find is that exceptionality is evaded or avoided. It tends to be sociologised away. For understandable reasons, it is rejected as ideological, concealed within an analysis of the consensual codes and conventions of art worlds, or barely acknowledged amidst struggles for position and recognition across different fields of production (see, e.g. Wolff, 1981; Becker, 1976 and 1982; Bourdieu, 1983 and 1993).

One sociologist who has attempted to grapple directly with the question of exceptionality and explicitly with the notion of 'genius' is Norbert Elias (1993) in his unfinished work on Mozart, edited and published post-humously. Like Bourdieu (and others) Elias considered social context to be crucial to any understanding of 'a "genius", an exceptionally gifted creative human being' who, in this particular case, was 'born into a society which did not yet know the Romantic concept of genius, and whose social canon had no legitimate place for the highly individualised artist of genius in their midst' (1993: 19). For Elias, the changing social relations between the producers and consumers of art works are of central importance. For Mozart this involved composing during the breakdown of aristocratic patronage and the emergence of freelance artists facing an anonymous and atomised public as their market. Unlike the emphasis Bourdieu places on the 'objective' relations of fields, and the external contexts within which artists are formed, Elias argues for a need to bring together such an external 'he-perspective' with that of 'an I-perspective. . . the standpoint of his own feelings' (7). Whether or not Elias manages to achieve this in an admittedly fragmentary work is debatable, but he does offer pointers to the importance of experience via the social-psychological emphasis he places on a process of sublimation – by which he means the ability of an individual to self-reflexively monitor and control the spontaneous and free-flowing fantasy and dreams of their autonomous mental play and to harmonise these with aesthetic conventions and the social canon without losing their spontaneity. It is to this aspect of the creative experience that we now turn in more detail, attending in particular to how such a process of sublimation must, at some point, communicate to a public body.

Creative expression and the communication of experience

In this section we wish to place the communication of experience as central to the understanding of creativity for three reasons. First, experience only acquires meaning and resonance once it has been creatively worked on, shared and distributed. Second, songs and music (and artworks more generally) are regularly valued for what they say to people about experience and for the creative quality with which they say it. Third, an emphasis on experience can help counter the tendencies to relegate artistic practices to the status of industrial manufacture, to equate aesthetic value and political worth, and to abstract the affective dimension of creativity into 'objective' sociological structures.

Experience does not arise out of an empty box. Industrial production, political context and social conditions are of critical importance for how we understand cultural creativity. But they do not tell us the whole story of the relations between creativity and the communication of experience. If we are to move beyond formula-driven approaches to thinking about creativity, we need to tackle the relations between experience and its communicative forms.

It is of course a mistake to think that an artwork or cultural product is the expression of certain feelings, ideas or values which exist independently of the creative product and which simply result from the intention to communicate them. They only exist as objectively realised in an expressive medium. Expression in this sense presses experience into meaningful shape through the words, images and sounds given to it. In referring to expression we are not suggesting that a musician, songwriter or performer is engaged in directly relaying either a pre-given psychological state or social experience. Instead, it is within their art and practice that they give a voice to or convey a potent sense of such states and experiences as combinations of sounds, words and imagery. Musicians or songwriters are not simply aware of the prior meaning of what they feel in their hearts and then duly find the words and melodic structure to express this feeling. That is a romantic fallacy. What is felt is mediated by the lyrics, rhythm or beat as a form of creative expression. It is realised in sounds, words and gestures, for psychological states of experience like love or anger are given form by the language and music in which they achieve expression even though they do not consist entirely of this expression. The expression itself partly forms them, in dynamic interaction with known or intuitively sensed inter-emotional states or feelings.

So we do not have a fully formed, reflexively comprehended experience which we then reproduce in verbal or sonic form. What this experience means to us, and how we may value it, is usually only discovered in the form of utterance or figuration that is given to it. The expression not only forms the experience but also transforms it, makes it into something whose meaning changes our understanding of it. The relationship between experience and its expression is one of mutual constitution. Without its representation in words or sounds an experience often does not signify for us at all, for a feeling or an idea associated with it is made manifest through the combination of materials that characterise any particular cultural representation. It is because of this that songwriters, composers and musicians are often surprised at what they create and often only retrospectively comprehend what they were attempting to articulate.

Cultural creativity is realised within specific regimes of representation, according to quite obvious stylistic and generic codes and conventions. Yet what occurs when creative expression connects with these regimes and conventions does not entail an endless reproduction of their antecedent patterns and meanings. If that was the case the cultural world would simply stand still. The moment of creativity occurs when we wrestle with existing cultural materials in order to realise what they do not in themselves give to us. A number of writers, as diverse as Edward De Bono (1996), Arthur Koestler (1964), Ulf Hannerz (1996) and Salman Rushdie (1991), have stressed how the creative act involves recombining existing materials in such a way as to bring them into new relations with each other. This involves working both within and against aesthetic genres and social canons. It means going beyond the already signified. As this occurs we can locate tiny steps and big strides, along with multiple gradations in between. In focusing on electronic forms of dance music, Jason Toynbee gives examples of small shifts which cumulatively lead to changes within a field-like 'radius' of creativity. He stresses the little changes, which are both cumulative and collective. But is it necessarily the case that 'the unit of creativity is a small one' (Toynbee, 2000: 35)?

There may be occasions when the new combinations are more radical, disruptive and profound. Charlie Parker's realisation (seemingly obvious only in retrospect) that he could 'fly' away from the root notes of a chord yet still return to them, opened up new possibilities and changed the course which jazz would take. In the mid-sixties, Bob Dylan's almost accidental apprehension that the long rambling rage-driven poem that he had 'vomited' out could be condensed and brought together with a driving 4:4 rock beat is a key instance of the sublimation process, in Elias's sense of it. It led to 'Like a Rolling Stone', a six-minute single that profoundly changed the way that people perceived the possibilities offered by the pop song (Heylin, 2000). These exceptional instants are often dramatic in the short term, and in many ways the epithet 'genius' is not unfair for such moments – 'moments of genius' moving us much nearer the mark than notions of a permanent or in-built condition or state. In the longer term they may, in combination with further recombinations and extensions, result in the generation of new forms or practices.

Achieving communicative value

Like a number of other subsequent writers, we follow Williams in seeing creativity as an inclusive rather than exclusive ability. To see creativity as socially inclusive means that the 'true importance of our new understanding of perception and communication is that it verifies the creative activity of art in terms of a general human creativity' (1961: 41). Whilst this statement may have harboured intimations of the subsequent drift towards cultural populism, Williams was quick to stress that the resulting art *can* be valued: 'we find not only great art but bad art' and infinite gradations between. The critical disparity is not one which can be sought in attempting to grade 'different practice and intention' since it arises as a consequence of the quality of the relationship between experience and communication. In other words, creativity should be judged in terms of its ability to communicate 'the description of an experience' and its potential for this to be shared: art is the 'organisation of experience, especially in its effect on a spectator or an audience' (ibid.: 47). To succeed art must 'convey an experience to others in such a form that the experience is actively re-created – not contemplated, not examined, not passively received, but by response to the means, actually lived through, by those to whom it is offered. At this stage, a number of artworks already fail' (Williams 1961: 51).

We revisit this line of thinking in the early work of Williams, partly because, unlike his extended discussion of the idea of culture, it has been relatively neglected, and also because it does at least suggest an alternative route away from idealist and reductionist conceptions of creativity focused solely on practices rather than the consequences of their reception. There are, we acknowledge, various problems raised by Williams' approach to cultural creativity. One is the transmission model of communication which seems to underpin it, and here we stress that in arguing for a communicative approach to creativity we are not endorsing a transmission or an encoding/decoding model. Instead, our emphasis is more on the experiential and phenomeno-logical aspects through which musical forms acquire value and connect with others. This is not necessarily semiotic and may frequently be non-represen-tational in narrowly semantic terms. In addition, we do not follow Williams in assuming a homological relation between art and experience. This has been a key theme in much writing about popular music. It can be detected in the subcultural sociological tradition of explaining the connection between musical style and social location through notions of structural homologies (notably Willis, 1990; Hebdige, 1979).

A further problem which should be acknowledged is that Williams, among other writers, places a central emphasis on a 'sharing' of (and willingness to 'share') the artistically realised expression of experience as it is 'actually lived through'. This presupposes a prior consensus as the basis of which such culturally shared activities can occur. Musical creativity is often realised despite such a consensus and within conditions of social and aesthetic con-flict. That is why we stress that communication does not mean the study of a pre-sealed 'message' which is simply 'transmitted'. A related difficulty with Williams is that what is actually entailed in judgements of value about this process – the process of creatively turning 'unique experience into common experience' – remains underdeveloped in his thought where he writes of cre-ativity being 'at once ordinary and extraordinary' and 'known and unknown' (1977: 211–12). Nonetheless, Williams was grappling with how the creative process inclines towards the universal and how, although culture is ordinary, the ordinary can become transformed into the extraordinary. The ways in which what is historically specific and locally known moves across and between place and period, to be recognised by later generations in quite different locations, are features of the very process of communication that we wish to foreground. As Elias noted, this 'open question' is too often 'disguised as an eternal mystery' (1993: 54).

It is not surprising that neither Williams nor Elias resolved these issues and that both thinkers left us with an unfinished body of work that 'concludes' in a tentative and open manner. But it is significant that they did not seek to close these questions down. Williams' own contribution facilitated the turn from the 'text in itself'. The whole point of trying to understand creativity in terms of the quality of communicated experience and the forms in which such experience is actively re-created is that it refuses the reification of the musical work, the recording or the performance. Reification in this sense occurs when the artwork or performance is conceived in abstract isolation, as a text or practice removed from the social contexts of which it is or was a component part.

Reification in musical analysis relates to the still prevalent view that music, particularly that selectively identified and canonised as 'great', has an intrinsic autonomy that raises it above the social and political world. This autonomy guarantees its greatness. Reified musical aesthetics have been applied not only to art music but also to forms of popular music. For example, Carl Engel, in an organicist metaphor adopted without acknowledgement by Cecil Sharp, described what have become known as folk songs as akin to the 'wild flowers indigenous to a country, which thrive unaided by art' (Engel, 1866: 23; Sharp, 1907: 1). In England, during the later nineteenth and early twentieth century, this notion informed and supported the co-option of 'folk' music in the nationalist mission of its musical renaissance (Hughes and Stradling, 2001). But the aesthetics of 'music in itself' have had a much broader influence, acting, for instance, as a central tenet of professional musicology's maintenance of boundaries and enclosures and providing appropriate collateral for a 'life and works' paradigm of intellectual scholarship which fails to connect musical composition and structure to 'ideology, or social space, or power, or to the formation of an individual (and by no means sovereign) ego' (Said, 1991: xii–xiii).

Our emphasis on achieving communicative value through experience is intended to connect music not only with these large-scale sociological issues, but also with the realisation of creative possibilities in everyday life. An example of what this involves, bringing 'art' and 'popular' music together and confounding their artificial separation, is the way in which Mahler drew on his childhood experience of apparently unrelated sounds coming from different directions, as for instance in his Third Symphony. Natalie Bauer-Lechner recalled a trip to a country fair with the composer:

> Not only were innumerable barrel-organs blaring out from merry-go-rounds, see-saws, shooting galleries and puppet shows, but a military band and a men's choral society had established themselves there as well. All these groups, in the same forest clearing, were creating an incredible musical pandemonium without paying the slightest attention to each other. Mahler exclaimed: 'You hear? That's polyphony, and that's where I get it from!'

> (cited by Mitchell, 1975: 342)

If a specific experience being communicated is not part of a broader configuration of practices and human relations, its meanings or sentiments will not register. Its communicative possibilities will be unrealised. What is communicated as interpreted experience enters into a series of encounters between old and new cultural forms and practices, traditional and emergent ways of seeing, listening and thinking about the world, as suggested in the above reference to Mahler. Williams referred to this process as the testing of new observations, comparisons and meanings in experience, occurring in any cultural formation in ways that are 'always both traditional and creative' and that involve 'both the most ordinary common meanings and the finest individual meanings'. It is then the conjunction of creative effort and common meanings which is significant, within the networks of relationship in which people find value in and through each other (Williams, 1989: 4 and 283).

This insight is important because it is only in and through the continuities and changes that potential participation becomes possible. The evaluative or emotional response to experience we are focusing on operates in the space between general purposes and individual meanings, between coming together in experience and exploring experience for what it means for us in our own understanding and self-knowledge. It involves us in going beyond the local whilst also recognising the value of localised experience and practice as we try to relate the particular to the general, the abstract to the concrete, the unit to the universal. These negotiations can also involve an open recognition of the contrasts between different cultural traditions and ideals, and generate the impetus to move beyond them towards more open forms of social and cultural relations which can never be fully settled or fixed. In contemporary life, ever more mediated by electronic technologies and the mass media, they have now to be forged in the face of the widespread discontinuity, rupture and displacement that is increasingly defining a common human experience for large numbers of people. Although the meanings and values which we find in music operate in relation to their specific fields of production and performance and their specific genre codes and social conventions, the achievement of communicative value always has the potential to exceed its local and immediate conditions of production: 'cultures and traditions survive and flourish not by enforcing an endless and exact reproduction but by developing and enriching themselves and by remaining relevant to new generations' (Warnke, 1995: 139–40). Enrichment and a sense of remaining relevance therefore depend on a dialogue with difference as much as a connection with changing times.

We make this point to argue that creativity arises not from a cultural context which exists in monolithic isolation, but in their borrowings from each other. Mozart's exposure, on tours as a young child, to significant contemporary compositions in Germany, France, Italy and England, and his understanding and love of the musically frivolous as much as the profound (during an epoch prior to the high/popular cultural split) meant that his aesthetic sensibility was formed from a sense of movement across cultural boundaries. Likewise, many years later, Duke Ellington's boundary-less musical journey, always pushing up against the social walls of racism, formed his self-conscious desire to be 'beyond category' (Hasse, 1995; Lees, 1988: 55). As Edward Said observed, culture 'is never just a matter of ownership, of borrowing and lending with absolute debtors and creditors, but rather of appropriations, common experiences, and interdependencies of all kinds among different cultures' (1994: 261–2).

The permeability of cultures, languages and aesthetic codes is a condition of their ongoing change and a source of creative movement and vitality, yet this is inevitably realised locally by particular embodied people in particular conditions and through quite specific experiences. Interpreted experience as we encounter it in a song or musical performance is always re-interpreted in relation to what we ourselves bring to it and what we attempt to take from it. We do not engage with it in some pristine or insular mode of apprehension, nor does our encounter with it result in some abstract act of transparent understanding. Our understanding of it is based on the degree to which we realise and exceed the finite illusion of the mutual separation of cultures and histories. This is where our imaginative grasp of the possibilities posed by different cultures, traditions and languages becomes a locus of creative extension of our own temporally and spatially specific cultural experience. It is the creation of an enduring relationship between the 'near' and the 'far' which becomes a key dynamic of cultural change and creative renewal.

Moving with the music

Beginning this chapter by untangling some of the meanings of creativity enabled us to point to the endurance of a spiritual dimension within the term even as its semantic range has widened and become secularised. The development of the term demands that we move away from elitist conceptions of creative exclusivity and consider creativity in its more mundane forms. At the same time, this does not require the relinquishment of some conception of exceptionality. We have argued that it is now this fuller range of meanings and associations which must be engaged with, rather than some preferred version which simply swings to the polar opposite of elitist notions. That is why we have adopted an approach which conceives of creativity in terms of the communication of experience. We have suggested that this provides one route into a consideration of the mutually constitutive relation between the ordinariness and exceptionality of creativity, for it is only through this relation, conceived in this way, that music can move between specifically local moments of production and initial recognition and patterns of reception and assimilation which are broader both geographically and historically. If communication is about going outwards from self to other, we are still searching for adequate ways of explaining how everyday localised creativity is able, in certain ways and at certain times, to achieve connections across different cultural and historical formations, and in so doing to connect with and give expression to common experiences.

This is not a search for some universal principle. It is about trying to engage with the dynamic movement which connects cultural practices together to form meta-cultural frameworks of comprehension, meaning and communication. The genius – for want of a better word – of Mozart, Miles Davis or Bob Marley is not that they created universal, trans-historical works of art which we share simply because we are 'human'. Yet we still need to recognise that many people, across divergences of time and space, *do* engage with their music. It is not because they project a shared sense of identity, or because a common meaning is shared between creator and listener. It is because their particular modes of expression – the harmonic order of Mozart's work, the sensitive human voice of Davis's trumpet, the elegant lyricism of Marley's songs – allow all sorts of people a point of entry which enables participation in the work, and activates some connection between what is performed and what is lived. These connections are something to be celebrated, but not mystified. Musical talent is always in part the result of hard work, experimentation and continual effort spent in perfecting a craft – all three of the musicians we have just mentioned produced their share of mediocre work. Their achievements were also the result of a passionate will to push against existing forms and conventions, and an equally passionate desire to communicate beyond immediate temporal and spatial boundaries. As this occurred, they were indeed ordinary and exceptional and we can appreciate their creativity as both an ordinary and exceptional experience. It is this which leads us to argue that musical creativity should be thought of as the communication of experience which always involves gradations of movement between the mundane and exceptional, between novelty and innovation, and between the immediate and the distant. This movement is what we celebrate, and understanding it may give us even more to celebrate.

References

BARBER, L., 1999: 'Simply Divine'. *Observer*, 28 February.

BECKER, H., 1976: 'Art Worlds and Social Types'. *American Behavioural Scientist* 19: 703–18.

——, 1982: *Art Worlds*. Berkeley and Los Angeles: University of California Press.

BOURDIEU, P., 1983: 'The Field of Cultural Production, or: The Economic World Reversed'. *Poetics* 12: 311–56.

——, 1993: *The Field of Cultural Production*. Cambridge: Polity Press.

——, 1996: *The Rules of Art*. Cambridge: Polity Press.

DE BONO, E., 1996: *Serious Creativity*. London: HarperCollins.

ELIAS, N., 1993: *Mozart: Portrait of a Genius*. Cambridge: Polity.

ENGEL, C., 1866: *An Introduction to the Study of National Music*. London: Longman.

HANNERZ, U., 1996: *Transnational Connections*, Routledge: London.

HASSE, J., 1995: *Beyond Category: The Life and Genius of Duke Ellington*. New York: Da Capo.

HEBDIGE, D., 1979: *Subculture: The Meaning of Style*. London: Methuen.

HEYLIN, C., 2000: *Bob Dylan: Behind the Shades, Take Two*. Harmondsworth: Penguin.

HUGHES, M. AND R. STRADLING, 2001: *The English Musical Renaissance, 1840–1940*. Manchester and New York: Manchester University Press.

JOAS, H., 1996: *The Creativity of Action*. Cambridge: Polity Press.

KOESTLER, A., 1964: *The Act of Creation*. London: Hutchinson.

LEES, G., 1988: *Meet Me at Jim and Andy's: Jazz Musicians and their World*. New York and Oxford: Oxford University Press.

MITCHELL, D., 1975: *Gustav Mahler: The Wunderhorn Years*. London: Faber and Faber.

RUSHDIE, S., 1991: *Imaginary Homelands*. London: Granta.

SAID, E., 1991: *Musical Elaborations*. London: Chatto and Windus.

——, 1994: *Culture and Imperialism*. London: Vintage.

SHARP, C., 1907: *English Folk-Song: Some Conclusions*. London: Simpkin.

STEINER, G., 2001: *Grammars of Creation*. London: Faber and Faber.

TOYNBEE, J., 2000: *Making Popular Music*. London: Arnold.

ULANOV, B., 1952: *A History of Jazz in America*. New York: Viking Press.

WARNKE, G., 1995: 'Communicative Rationality and Cultural Values', in S. K. White (ed.), *The Cambridge Companion to Habermas*. Cambridge and New York: Cambridge University Press.

WATERS, J., 1988: 'Deus ex Machina: The Band Who Grew to Earth', in E. Dunphy (ed.), *The Unforgettable Fire: The Story of U2*. Harmondsworth: Penguin.

WILLIAMS, R., 1961: *The Long Revolution*. Harmondsworth: Penguin.

——, 1976: *Keywords*. London: Fontana.

——, 1977: *Marxism and Literature*. Oxford: Oxford University Press.

——, 1989: *Resources of Hope*. London and New York: Verso.

WILLIS, P., 1990: *Common Culture*. Milton Keynes: Open University Press.

WOLFF, J., 1981: *The Social Production of Art*. London and Basingstoke: Macmillan.

12

The politics of calypso in a world of music industries

Jocelyne Guilbault

Calypso music is not a newcomer to the world music market. Its presence on the international scene dates back to 1914 when it was first released by Victor and Columbia recording companies and distributed throughout North America and Europe (Cowley, 1996; Hill, 1993; Liverpool, 1986). And yet even after being well known as a label for over 80 years, the specific character of its music industry has been given scant scholarly attention (with a few exceptions, notably, Hill (1993) and Nurse (1996, 1997)). One of the reasons could be found in calypso's own history. Emerging from slavery, Emancipation, and the post-colonial period, the role of calypso has been described by Caribbean and non-Caribbean writers as a means to rebel, condemn, resist, attract, divide, unite and also deeply enjoy. In all cases, calypso's socio-political commentaries and humorous songs have been interpreted as resulting from the artists' focus on critical consciousness, honor, reputation, and prestige – values nurtured by the colonial and post-colonial regimes and conveniently placed above economic interests and gains in the name of culture. Thus constructed as separate from business practices, calypso has been addressed almost exclusively in terms of the meanings and quality of its lyrics.

Another reason for the lack of coverage on the calypso music industry has to do with the fact that the expression 'music industry' in most publications on popular music has traditionally referred to the workings of the music business as defined, controlled and experienced by particular groups of people living in northwestern European and North American countries (Peterson and Berger, 1975; Hennion, 1981; Frith, 1988: 88–130; Robinson, Buck and Cuthbert, 1991: 32–56; Negus, 1992, 1996; Laing, 1998). Writings on the music industry have been based on notions specific to these experiences, but the insights generated in these regions have been used as if they were universals to describe the music business worldwide. In that business, recordings and videos are considered the prime elements, and strategies for producing, marketing and distributing them represent the central preoccupation. The conventional vocabulary used to discuss such matters includes artist and repertoire (A&R) staff, 'plugging' records, chart positions and growth or decline of 'units' sold. It invokes a star system elaborated through specific rituals of valorization – including fan magazines, award ceremonies, and special programs on star personalities for television and radio broadcast, to name only a few – all designed to further, but at the same time to reify the record companies' goals: commercial appeal and economic success. The conventional scholarship and its vocabulary both circumscribe and promote the conceptual framework from which mainstream music operates, and the infrastructure that characterizes this particular music industry is geared to maximize the earnings from its products and the markets it aims to develop.

The economic power of the mainstream music industry has stimulated the attention of writers on the subject, but in the process it has rendered most other kinds of music industries, such as the calypso music industry, marginal to the point of being generally unknown. When they are discussed, these industries are usually addressed in terms of what they lack vis-à-vis the mainstream music industry, instead of what actually characterizes their specific dynamics.

In this chapter, I want to introduce the music industry of calypso, not to contrast it with the northwestern European and North American mainstream music industry, but to address it in terms of its own framework.[1] The term 'calypso' is used here in the generic sense, and includes all its related musical genres: soca, chutney soca, rapso, ringbang and ragga soca. My thesis is that the music industry of calypso that developed initially in Trinidad and spread throughout the English-speaking Caribbean has evolved from the particular musical activities, conceptual framework and infrastructure specific to competitions, and that it is based more on performance than on recordings. From this perspective, I want to show how such an orientation has contributed to calypso's unique character and also to examine the implications this orientation has had on its positioning – politically, economically and socially – in today's world market.

The orientation of a music industry cannot be presented as a matter of pure choice (aesthetic or otherwise), but must be recognized as embodied in power relations, historical contingencies and ad hoc circumstances. In this vein, I begin by situating the music industry of calypso historically to highlight how the colonial powers were deeply involved in the process of its formation, orientation and marginalization. I then present how competitions have informed the discourses and practices of the calypso music industry. In the last section, I examine some of the main problems and challenges of the calypso music industry. As this study argues, the music industry of calypso should not be seen merely in light of the mainstream music industry. To do so would only obscure its uniqueness. To appreciate fully the complexities and relative positioning of the music industry of calypso within the *world* of music industries (plural), we must pay attention to its specific features and its interactions with the constantly changing dynamics of the world order in which it has evolved.

Out of competitions: historical formation of the calypso music industry

Situating the emergence of the music business of calypso is crucial to our understanding of the dynamics that have shaped it and contributed to its current forms. The history of calypso itself, marked by 'urbanization, immigration, and Black reconstruction in post-Emancipation Trinidad' (Rohlehr 1990: 1) tells us much about the conditions of possibility in which its business practices have evolved. Indeed the history of calypso cannot be dissociated from that of the descendants of enslaved Africans in the Caribbean and their very particular experience: emancipation, colonial regime, governmental censorship, Christian religious sanctions, discrimination, post-colonial economic dependency, little schooling and unemployment.

Calypso as a music business began in the second half of the nineteenth century among the recently freed slaves. At this stage, it encompassed two main activities: competitions and betting, which may be considered part of the 'music business' because it involves money transactions about music. As Rohlehr reports, the 'deeply ingrained spirit of competition' believed to be characteristic of the black population was displayed in the calypso war in a man-to-man contest of improvisation – emulating traditional stickfighting but using only words. The struggle was usually not to defend against an enemy but to raise and safeguard one's own reputation (Rohlehr 1990: 74).

The calypso music business became more organized by the 1890s through the use of calypsos in advertising. The colonial bourgeoisie and colored elite began exploiting the 'ingrained spirit of competition' by sponsoring calypso contests that also served to advertise their own products. In the process, calypso became a source of income, but not a commodity in and of itself. Rather, it was part of a 'service' performed by calypsonians to sell another commodity.

Calypso as entertainment and profitable commodity in its own right was institutionalized with the creation of the calypso tents at the turn of the century. Initially built of bamboo with coconut palms for a roof, the tents provided shelter under which the Carnival bands could practice, learn songs and discuss the affairs of the band (Cowley, 1996: 136–7). As they became major attractions, the tents were turned into more formal spaces in which invited guests and passersby eventually had to pay an entrance fee for their enjoyment (Hill, 1993: 65). Here, too, competitions helped draw business for the tent. Throughout the Carnival season, songsters would visit other bands and compete against one another in song. Interestingly, this focus on competitions eventually led the tents to adopt a very particular presentation format in their shows. Calypso war competitions required the participation of several singers and even if it was reserved for the end of the show, they were the tent audiences' favorite attractions (Rohlehr, 1990: 112). This may be one of the reasons why calypso tents have traditionally featured a large line-up of singers. Whereas in the 1920s such a line-up usually included five or six singers, in the 1990s it regularly featured as many as 20 and at times up to 28 singers in one calypso show. This philosophy, 'the more artists, the better', promoted by the elite through its involvement in coordinating calypso competitions during Carnival to increase their control of both the artists' behavior and the content of their songs has been followed up to the present day.

From the time the freed slaves invaded the streets during Carnival in the late nineteenth century, the colonial powers (including both government and church) and the colored elite attempted to regulate their behavior in an attempt to 'cleanse Carnival of its vulgarity and obscenity'. In relation to calypso, the playing of big keg drums was banned, and only the clean, sharp sound of smaller bamboo pieces from the 'tamboo bamboo' bands was allowed. In an attempt to get rid of French Creole (which was perceived as a primitive language), business people required the use of English in their advertisements, and judges in competitions clearly favored those calypsonians who used English lyrics (Rohlehr, 1990; Liverpool, 1993). Through the institution of various laws, police surveillance and also the creation of Carnival Improvement Committees beginning in the late 1920s, women – who had until then been in the forefront as *chantwèl* (song-leaders) – were discouraged from singing their bawdy songs and performing explicit sexual behavior in public. This obsession with respectability (as defined by the members of the ruling elite and imposed by them on the black population) eventually led women nearly to disappear from the calypso scene for several decades.

Competitions became seen as the means to coordinate calypso's activities in order to further eradicate its 'vulgar' and 'improper' side. In 1939, the Carnival Improvement Committee of Port-of-Spain, Trinidad and Tobago's capital – composed of the mayor, a few city counselors and a representative of the police force – not only sought to hold competitions in each tent, but announced its intention of controlling all the city's competitions (Rohlehr, 1990: 407). Its goal was explicit: to further its control over both the participants' behavior and the song contents. After countless battles against this attempt to develop a centralized organization of the major Carnival features (the parade of bands, Dimanche Gras Queen Competition, and the selection of a Calypso King), the Carnival Committee eventually won over all its opponents by making the Dimanche Gras a showcase of the most creative talent in the country and, significantly, by outdoing any competitive organization in the number of artists it brought to the stage.[2] In 1953, the first true national Calypso King Competition took place, and the tradition of holding national calypso competitions yearly was established. The National Calypso King Competition was renamed 'National Calypso Monarch Competition' after Calypso Rose, one of the few female calypsonians to perform in the calypso arena, won the competition in 1978.

By 1953, most of the elements that give the music industry of calypso its unique configuration had been set forth. Competitions represent *the* privileged way of promoting calypso songs and singers, and national competitions are *the* way of conferring prestige and publicity on the participants. They constitute the organizing principle according to which the musical scene of calypso operates at nearly all levels of participation, whether among professionals or amateurs. For the winners in particular, the national competitions represent a major source of income; however, this is not necessarily from the prizes given on such occasions but, as will be discussed below, because they serve as a passport for regional and international tours.

Implications of the competition framework: discourses and practices of the music industry of calypso

The fact that competitions have formed the basis of calypso's music industry has had profound and manifold implications. As will be shown, such a framework has fostered not only a particular terminology and particular kinds of discourses, but also specific activities, institutions, knowledges, alliances, histories, sensibilities, hopes and frustrations.

Competitions' infrastructure and agencies

From 1953 onward, the organization of the national competitions of so-called 'traditional calypso' has by definition been associated with the government.[3] In practical terms, the government has not been responsible merely for appointing the committee overseeing the calendar of Carnival celebrations. It has also provided the financial support for most of the major traditional competitions during Carnival, including that of traditional calypso. This raises two important points. Overt government involvement with calypso makes it clear that calypso is articulated in the Caribbean not only as an aesthetic object, but also as part of a political project. At the same time, the government's role in the calypso music business cannot be seen simply in terms of coercion, but rather as deeply involved in setting the institutional structures, norms and procedures through which value is formed, transmitted and regulated.[4] Whereas the colonial government (beginning in the 1920s) had worked in concert with the bourgeoisie to temper Carnival activities, after Independence in 1962, the new government took over the organization of the festivities as part of the nation-building project. It promoted and continues to promote Carnival as a symbol of Trinidad and Tobago's patrimony and culture, and also as a main source of revenue for the tourist industry. While still controlling the content of the songs through censorship, the Independent government also continues to view calypso as an articulation point between the people and the government and, perhaps for that reason, it remains deeply involved in calypso competitions (Allor and Gagnon 2000: 3).

In this context and within the framework of tents and competitions, performance has been given the greatest importance in the music industry of calypso. It should be remembered that calypso competitions are judged exclusively on the basis of the artists' performances on the night of the competition. Omitting a line of text because of a memory slip, entering on the wrong beat, or failing to make contact with the public would prevent an artist from winning – regardless of his or her success outside the event.

Even though not the focus of the calypso music industry, recordings have been part of its technologies and have played an important role in relation to calypso competitions. However, recordings have been instrumental to the competition process, not a goal in and of itself. Correspondingly, they have not received financial or institutional support from either the private sector or the government that the performance of calypso has received via the tents and competitions.

Apart from institutionalizing competitions and, by so doing, making them the official agency that grants or denies prestige to calypso artists, the colonial and post-colonial regimes have left other legacies that continue to influence the ways the calypso music industry operates today in terms of both time and space. For example, calypso competitions and tent shows continue to be central to, but also restricted to, the Carnival season. The church's prohibition on singing or humming calypsos during the Lent season[5] or on any Sunday of the year for nearly a hundred years has without a doubt affected the ways in which calypso has been experienced, and has solidified its reputation as a seasonal activity. In the views of most calypso fans, artists and organizers interviewed, such a legacy has made it difficult for many people in the Caribbean to overcome the perception that calypso is a seasonal phenomenon.

As a result of church and government influence, calypsos can be heard only occasionally outside the Carnival period or in contexts other than competitions and tents (for instance, in dancehalls by calypsonians invited for a guest appearance or in special shows organized for a seated audience). In the media, calypso recordings by the most successful calypsonians may also be heard, but most observers contend that this happens only too rarely outside the Carnival season. In any event, it should be remembered that the calypsonians who are invited to perform (regardless of the occasion) or who are sponsored to make a recording are almost exclusively the ones who have made their names and reputations in the tents or in the calypso competitions.

Competitions as regulation

As the main framework from which the music industry of calypso evolved, competitions have constituted a control mechanism that sanctions who can participate and who can be selected in the finals. Until the 1990s, when several new national competitions featuring various musical offshoots of calypso were created (events discussed further below), the National Calypso Monarch Competitions featured – in practice if not officially – artists almost exclusively of African descent to whom the calypso tradition is attributed. Moreover, to be a legitimate participant, it did not suffice to be born in the country, one had to reside there.

The implications of such a tightly controlled admittance to calypso competitions have been manifold. At the local level, calypso competitions have encouraged and been used to articulate a particular politics of representation not only within the music industry of calypso, but also within the national politics of Trinidad and Tobago. Calypso competitions have been the best-known and most visible of all musical competitions held in Trinidad, not only because of calypso's artistic merit, but also because the political will and the financial support of governments made them so – in the hope of gentrifying the black population under the colonial regime, and as a means of promoting a national culture and identity under the new Independent government (particularly from 1962 to 1986 under the People's National Movement). The result has been greater exposure for calypso as an art form than for any other musical practice (through documentation, official promotion and media attention), and greater acknowledgement of the black population than of any other population group in the country. The price calypsonians have had to pay for such attention, however, has been high. Not only are they prey to censorship and criticism by other population groups, but they have remained, to a great extent, under the control of government through its sponsorship.

At an international level, the calypso competition framework has severely limited calypsonians' opportunity to develop an artistic following. Restricted to nationals living in their country of origin, calypso competitions have embodied protectionist measures, promoting local artists on the one hand but, on the other, confining their participation to a tightly controlled artistic milieu defined not only by national citizenship, but also by residence in the nation states where the competitions take place.

In terms of musical aesthetics, calypso competitions have given rise to pre-scriptive discourses of value by establishing particular ways of speaking and forming opinions about calypsos and calypsonians. The criteria used to run the various competitions within the calypso arena have been used not only to describe, but also to evaluate compositions and artists in each style or genre. To give an example: whereas traditional calypso is judged according to melody (30 points), lyrics (30 points), rendition (20 points), presentation (10 points), and originality (10 points), soca is judged according to lyrics (15 points), music (40 points), performance (20 points), and crowd response (25 points) (Jacob, 1998). Correspondingly, traditional calypsos are usually described first and foremost through their melody and lyrics – the elements to which most points are allocated (30 points each) – whereas soca songs are acknowledged instead in terms of their music and the crowd response. While the songs and artists associated with each of these genres are not promoted exclusively on the basis of these criteria, such categories have unquestionably influenced the ways calypso artists' reputations have been built, criticized and promoted.

The selection of judges and their selection of winners are as much polit-ical acts as artistic ones. The public and the contestants are well aware that the judges' qualifications (musical training and competence, knowledge and experience of the given art forms) cannot be totally dissociated from issues of class, race, political agenda and propaganda. For this reason – sometimes before a given competition takes place, but usually after the results are known – there are usually questions about whether the judges' decisions were based on fairness or fraud, or whether censorship played a role in unanticipated defeats. In an attempt to make the process of competition more 'democratic', some steps have been taken to give more voice to the public in the selection of the winners. One strategy has been to make the public's reactions one of the criteria in the evaluation process (as in the case of the Soca Monarch Competition); another method has involved allowing audiences to select their own winner, either by playing his or her song repeatedly (as in the case of the Road March Competition) or by writing the name of the song and its performer/composer in a ballot (as in the case of the competition of the Top 20). However, even in such cases, the selection of winners is still a controversial affair.

Calypso's economic practices

Calypso competitions have not only informed the ways in which calypsos and calypsonians have been defined, valued and positioned (artistically, polit-ically and socially), they have also shaped the economic aspect of the calypso music industry. The prizes given at calypso competitions have constituted a source of revenue in and of themselves – but only for the very few artists selected as winners. Initially, the prizes for calypso competitions were ridicu-lously small compared to those received by the winners of other Carnival competitions, based on the notion promoted by the organizers that the prestige of winning should outweigh monetary considerations (Rohlehr, 1990: 331). Gradually these prizes were adjusted, and today they represent a substantial sum of money. For example, in 1998, the top prizes in the Calypso Monarch Competition in Trinidad included a Honda Civic car, $100 000 cash (Trinidad and Tobago money),[6] a trophy and other prizes (Assang, 1998).

However, calypso artists generally earn most of their income from performance (Henry and Nurse, 1996: 15). The high value traditionally placed on performance among members of the black population, and the fact that piracy, sampling, bootlegging and counterfeiting have dramatically prevented artists and publishers from getting their fair share of royalties from recordings, have made competitions and performance central to the economy of the calypso music industry. For all the contestants who rank high, but especially for the winners, calypso competitions have represented the springboard to local show contracts, overseas performances and tours, and Carnival appearances.

The institutionalization of calypso competitions has given a particular rhythm to the economy of the calypso music industry as a whole. In relation to the yearly calendar, calypso artists speak of a high and a low season, determined by the periods during which Carnival, calypso competitions and related calypso shows and parties take place in Trinidad and Tobago and elsewhere around the world.[7] It should be noted, however, that for the best-known artists, the low season has become quite short, since Carnival is now celebrated in different countries at different times of the year, from the month before Lent to the month of October.[8]

Most calypso shows during and outside Carnival are organized according to the tent tradition. They feature a big line-up of calypsonians following the philosophy of 'the more artists, the better', usually including from 12 to 20 performers who are limited to singing only one or two songs each night. As in the tents, one band supplies the musical accompaniment and the back-up vocals for all the singers. Although the manager works as part of the organizing team of the show, other artists' managers are rarely involved. While the salary for the musicians in the band is usually fixed in advance, the fee for the calypsonians may vary relative to the profits made during each show or series of shows during a given time. The honor and prestige gained by appearing in some of the shows remain profoundly meaningful for performers; for some, this prestige is sufficient incentive to perform in a show, even when pay is poor.

Calypso competitions have also greatly influenced the economic activities generated by calypso recordings. In the past, when recordings were still expensive to produce, they came as a 'reward' – a form of sponsorship for those artists who had developed a reputation through winning calypso competitions. Since the 1980s, as making recordings has become much cheaper, they have become a prerequisite to introducing one's songs in other venues and a promotional tool to gain public support before competitions.

The resulting pressure experienced by calypso artists to release a recording every year before competition has without question influenced the budget they can allot to each production. The amount of time between recordings is usually not sufficient for the artists to raise large sums of money to cover such expenses. As a result, most calypso recordings are produced with a low budget and in very small quantities, ranging most often between 200 and 1000 units. If the first series has sold rapidly, a recording may be reproduced however, to include only up to three or five thousand units in all. To limit the costs of studio time, many recordings are made rapidly, often resulting in low sound quality – which, one could argue, makes it harder for calypso artists to negotiate deals with major distribution companies. Furthermore, if one takes into account the role racial discrimination may potentially play in the music business (as in any other business), the possibility for calypso artists to be distributed by major corporations becomes all the more remote. Regardless of whether sound quality or racial discrimination could be at issue, the fact remains that large distribution companies do not easily cater to small music industries. As the owner of Island Records, Chris Blackwell explained in an interview, 'they're geared up for moving hundreds of thousands ... They can't be expected initially to get that excited about sending two hundred records somewhere' (quoted in Fox,1986: 292).

In summary, calypso activities have been regulated by the Carnival season and, until recently, generated almost exclusively from and around calypso competitions. Calypso recordings have suffered from low production budgets and from being released in very small quantities. Because they are released in such small quantities, the sales potential of calypso records has been further undermined by lack of access to the major distribution channels which – and this is part of the vicious circle – are designed to distribute products only in large quantities. In such conditions, calypso artists and organizers have thus had to function for the most part in parallel, as it were, with the conventions of the so-called mainstream music industry. In the process, they have acted in relation to different market rules, different economic vectors and different sets of priorities.

The calypso music economy is largely dependent on extended informal practices and networks. For example, calypso performance contracts are often signed not before, but after, the show and in relation to the ticket revenues made at the door. Distribution agreements sometimes take the form of formal contracts between a calypso producer and the non-Caribbean owners of big record stores such as HMV. However, given that distribution agreements are usually made between the calypso artists/producers and their friends or family members, no formal documents are signed, and only verbal deals are negotiated. A number of recordings are usually placed in consignment at these friends' or family members' own record shops, or left with them to be distributed by hand to specific record stores in their own cities or neighborhoods (in London, New York, Toronto and so on). Most of those small calypso traders do not pay taxes or keep records. While disc jockeys and special fête organizers as well as the illegal dubbing and sales of cassettes at makeshift street stalls may help promote an artist's songs by giving them greater exposure, this does not entail direct payments to the artists (for example, through copyright royalties). From another perspective, however, it could be argued that the informal economic networks formed around calypso have undoubtedly allowed a wide range of people otherwise excluded from the formal music industries to participate in and to be empowered by the calypso music business.

Calypso competitions as star and anti-star system

From the organizing principle of the calypso competitions emerges what could be described both as a star system and as an anti-star system. In line with a star system, winning a competition means that the calypso artist will be in the limelight on all the local media – even though it may only be for a few days. Winning a competition also means that the artist will be asked to perform locally on special occasions and, in addition, to take part in international tours throughout the rest of the year.[9] In other words, winning a competition becomes synonymous not only with prestige and recognition in the calypso milieu, but also with opportunities to perform and earn an income.

Yet, from a music industry point of view, the organizing principle of calypso competitions could also be seen to foster an anti-star system on several counts. While it is clear that winning a calypso competition gives an artist pride of place, such a coveted place and the opportunities it provides only last for a year, until the next competition. It is important to note that, even though the former winners of one or several titles enjoy great respect in the calypso milieu, they receive few, if any, invitations to perform outside the Carnival season if they have not participated and ranked high in the competitions in that year. It could thus be argued that calypso competitions are less about 'pushing' an artist's career, than nurturing a community process that is itself linked to an exercise of control effected through both the selection of criteria and the selection of judges used to pick a winner.

In the same vein, calypso competitions and calypso tents could be seen as contributing to an anti-star system by helping to perpetuate the tradition of featuring a big line-up of artists in each presentation. Based on the philosophy 'the more artists, the better' promoted under the colonial regime, calypso competition finals continue to include from 12 to 20 performers, and calypso shows during and outside Carnival feature as many as six or even ten performers each night. Given that they can sing only one or two songs at most shows, calypso artists are not only paid less than their counterparts involved in other music genres (such as reggae artists), but their attempts to make further inroads on the regional and international markets – for example, by hiring a manager – are all the more limited due to the lack of financial resources. Thus, it could be argued that, as in the case of competitions (albeit for different reasons), the aim of the producers organizing calypso shows has been less about promoting an artist than about selling a show.

Challenges of the calypso music industry

This chapter has drafted a sketch of the calypso music industry as emerging from the national calypso competitions held throughout the English-speaking Caribbean, with a view to analyzing the legacies of the colonial and post-colonial regimes and better understanding the power relations at play. In so doing, the analysis has shed some light on the ways in which, from its inception, the calypso music industry has been regulated and positioned within singular configurations of complex political, racial, economic, linguistic and aesthetic forces foregrounded by the discourses and practices through which calypso songs and artists have been granted official recognition. It has also shown how the tightly controlled participation and strategies of valorization of calypso songs and artists in the national calypso competitions have left little if any room for the circulation of calypso songs and artists that have not been part of the calypso competition framework.

In fact, the power of the competition framework in the calypso arena has been such that, in order to acquire their legitimacy, the new musical offshoots of traditional calypso (including soca, chutney soca, rapso, ringbang and ragga soca) have each had to develop their own yearly competitions during the Carnival period. Even though these new competitions are held by private entrepreneurs instead of the government – and even though many of them now include the participation of Caribbean artists who are not nationals of the country where the competitions are held – these competitions have nonetheless adopted the same discursive and non-discursive practices of the traditional Calypso Monarch Competition and have inherited the same kinds of problems. Performers still face adverse circumstances: no written contracts before an appearance and therefore no legal option to recuperate any money lost; absence of adequate performance space and facilities; and lack of managers and of managerial skills. Recordings still suffer from the problems of poor-quality manufacturing, weak marketing, limited distribution and retailing, and the lack of enforcement of the law on copyright protection.

These problems, I argue, should not be looked at without taking into account the particular kind of music industry that is in question. They must be addressed in relation to the fact that the music industry of calypso has been articulated through competitions, conceived as a seasonal activity, associated with a particular event (Carnival), and still subject to colonial and post-colonial legacies. From this perspective, the problems this music industry faces cannot be formulated as purely economic issues, but must be viewed as political, social, religious, linguistic and historical issues as well.

To address the problems listed above in ways that are congruent with the calypso music industry would entail prioritizing them according to how this industry is articulated. For instance, what types of initiatives would be developed if performance, as opposed to recording, was viewed as *the* central activity and main source of income in the calypso music industry? What types of measures could be taken to protect it and make it generate more income? One immediately thinks, for instance, about the neighboring rights – 'the rights conferred by law to performers and their performances and to record producers and their productions' – that are often disregarded in many islands of the region and in many industrialized countries which are not members of the Rome convention.[10] What kinds of steps could be taken to ensure the reinforcement and redistribution of the royalties collected under such rights? If one considers the number of Carnivals proliferating around the world, including the best-known ones such as the Notting Hill Carnival in London, Caribana in Toronto and the Labor Day Festival in New York, and the fact that for at least one week in each of these locations calypso music is played almost non-stop, what kinds of income for the artistic community would the reinforcement of neighboring rights generate?

Addressing this issue of neighboring rights would be crucial to an industry such as calypso, which is based on performance. It would entail setting up educational programs to teach calypso artists how to document their musical works and secure their rights; as Keith Nurse remarked, 'A large percentage of musical works by local [Caribbean] artists and publishers are not properly documented and so royalty payments go unidentified, particularly in overseas markets' (Nurse, 2000). It would also entail lobbying the main collection societies, including those in the United States (ASCAP, BMI and SESAC) and in Britain (PRS), whose business practices and royalty distribution underreport live performances based on the methodologies they currently employ, according to Nurse's recent study on Trinidad and Tobago's music industry (Nurse, 2000).

In line with the calypso music industry's distinctive articulation, if recording was considered part of the promotional package designed to boost performance, calypsonians could be encouraged to produce recordings and employ marketing devices tailored to this goal. For example, the recordings produced every year would not have to include ten or more tracks (as is often the case), but rather to present only the two new songs that are to be featured in the competitions that year. (In fact, there has been a trend toward recordings with fewer tracks over the past five years.) A whole compact disc with ten or more songs would then become an event in and of itself, not something expected to happen every year.

What I am suggesting is that thinking in terms that are specific to the unique orientation of the calypso music industry would have profound implications on the ways the problems above would be viewed and the kind of priority they would be given. To recognize the unique orientation of such an industry and to promote it accordingly is crucial for at least two reasons. It would not only help to recontextualize the dictates of so-called mainstream music industry and to approach them more critically. It would also encourage calypsonians to explore and to protect their own artistic sensibility, cultural capital and socio-economic interests.

At both theoretical and methodological levels, we could conclude, the study of any music industry requires addressing its own history and transformations. Rather than asking what it lacks to operate like the 'mainstream' music industry, it is a matter of looking at the music industry in question in positive terms. The focus should be on what sustains it, what gives it its energy, and what makes it important – culturally, socially, economically and politically – for whom and why (Foucault, 1980: 135–7). To insist on the specificity of the music industry under study would not only help us to avoid all sorts of reductionisms (theoretical, methodological, historicist, to name only a few), it would also allow us to show how such an industry within its own conjuncture has contributed to the continuous legitimation and valorization of particular affinities, alliances and affiliations in the contemporary global cultural economy.

Notes

1. As Michel Foucault has advocated, the phenomena we examine should be 'posed in positive terms', that is, in relation to their own technologies of power. See Foucault in Gordon (1980: 136).

2. In 1949, for example, the *Guardian* Carnival Committee (headed by the daily newspaper the *Guardian*, but otherwise formed along the same lines as the Carnival

Improvement Committee) brought on stage steelbands in competition, singing groups and the Police Band, as well as a dance company to complement the Carnival Queen show, and leading calypsonians to participate in the calypso competition (Rohlehr, 1990: 407).

3. In 1998 the major Carnival organizations (steelbands, calypso, mas' bands) were allowed to be in charge of their own competitions for the first time, even though they continued to receive governmental subsidies. Could this recent decision of the government be seen as an attempt to privatize a sector of activities that has become too financially important for the government to assume alone? And could it be that such a decision has been influenced by the commercial success of private enterprises holding new competitions during Carnival since the 1990s?

4. For further information on regimes of value, see John Frow's illuminating writing on the subject (1995: 131–69).

5. The only exception to this rule was on St Joseph's day during which calypso could be sung. As Father Christian Perrera explained, St Joseph's day is a festive day in the Catholic calendar in recognition of St Joseph as the universal patron of the church and the guardian of Jesus Christ's body. As a result, the usual rules and observances are lifted on that exceptional day during the Lent season (Perrera in personal interview, 4 January 2001). I thank Monty Dolly for sharing this information with me.

6. In September 1998 the exchange rate of Trinidadian money was approximately TT\$6.2 for US\$1.

7. Over the past 15 years, the greater ease of mass communication has made it possible for artists to travel more often to perform at special fêtes organized by several Caribbean diasporic populations around the world.

8. For example, while Trinidad celebrates its Carnival in February just before the Lent season, Jamaica celebrates Carnival in April, St Vincent in June, Antigua and Barbados at the beginning of August. And with increasing Caribbean population groups in diaspora, Toronto also celebrates its carnival at the beginning of August, Notting Hill in London in late August, New York in September, and Miami in October, to name only the best known.

9. There are sometimes exceptions to this rule. On a few occasions, some winners have not been invited to take part in tours because their lyrical focus has been deemed too parochial to be understood or appreciated outside Trinidad. Other winners have not performed much outside Trinidad because their daily jobs did not permit them to take extended leave.

10. Citation from an interview with Sach Moore, the Chairman and the Chief Executive Officer of BAMCI (the Barbados Agency for Musical Culture Incorporated), 7 March 1997. For more discussion of neighboring laws, see Wallis and Malm (1984: 177–9); Garofalo (1997: 30–2); Theberge (1997: 235–41).

References

ALLOR, MARTIN AND MICHELLE GAGNON, 2000: 'The Cultural Field'. Working paper of the Center for Research on Citizenship and Social Transformation at Concordia University, Montreal.

ASSANG, SHARON LEE, 1998: 'T&T's Mystic Monarch Reflects on His Victory'. *Internet Express*, 2 March.

COWLEY, JOHN, 1996: *Carnival, Canboulay and Calypso: Traditions in the Making*. Cambridge: Cambridge University Press.

FOUCAULT, MICHEL, 1980: 'Power and Strategies', in *Power/Knowledge: Selected Interviews and Other Writings 1972–1977 by Michel Foucault*, ed. Colin Gordon. New York: Pantheon Books, 134–45.

FOX, TED, 1986: *In the Groove: The People Behind the Music*. New York: St Martin's Press.

FRITH, SIMON, 1988: 'Video Pop: Picking Up the Pieces', in S. Frith (ed.), *Facing the Music*. New York: Pantheon Books, 88–130.

FROW, JOHN, 1995: *Cultural Studies and Cultural Value*. Oxford: Oxford University Press.

GAROFALO, REEBEE, 1997: *Rockin' Out: Popular Music in the USA*. Boston: Allyn and Bacon.

HENNION, ANTOINE, 1981: *Les professionnels du disque: une sociologie des variétés*. Paris: Editions A. M. Métailié.

HENRY, RALPH AND KEITH NURSE, 1996: 'The Entertainment Sector of Trinidad and Tobago: Implementing an Export Strategy'. Port-of-Spain: Industry and Trade Division, TIDCO, unpublished manuscript.

HILL, DONALD, 1993: *Calypso Calaloo: Early Carnival Music in Trinidad*. Miami: University of Florida Press.

JACOB, DEBBIE, 1998: 'A SuperBlue Time'. *Sunday Express* (Trinidad), 22 February: 2.

LAING, DAVE, 1998: 'Economic Importance of Music in the European Union'. Euromusic: EMO: http:/ /www.euromusic.com/EMO/eumusic/index.html

LIVERPOOL, HOLLIS URBAN LESTER, 1986: *Kaiso and Society*. Charlotte Amalie, St Thomas: Virgin Commission on Youth.

——, 1993: 'Rituals of Power and Rebellion: The Carnival Tradition in Trinidad and Tobago'. Ph.D. dissertation, University of Michigan.

NEGUS, KEITH, 1992: *Producing Pop: Culture and Conflict in the Popular Music Industry*. London: Edward Arnold.

——, 1996: *Popular Music in Theory*. Cambridge: Polity Press; Hanover: Wesleyan University Press.

NURSE, KEITH, 1996: 'Trinidad and Tobago's Carnival: Towards an Export Strategy'. *Caribbean Labour Journal*, March.

——, 1997: 'The Trinidad and Tobago Entertainment Industry: Structure and Export Capabilities'. *Caribbean Dialogue* 3 (3): 13–38.

——, 2000: 'Copyright and Music in the Digital Age: Prospects and Implications for the Caribbean'. *Social and Economic Studies* 49 (1): 53–81.

PETERSON, RICHARD AND DAVID BERGER, 1975: 'Cycles in Symbol Production: The Case of Popular Music'. *American Sociological Review* 40: 158–73.

ROBINSON, DEANNA CAMPBELL, ELIZABETH B. BUCK AND MARLENE CUTHBERT, 1991: *Music at the Margins: Popular Music and Global Cultural Diversity*. London: Sage.

ROHLEHR, GORDON, 1990: *Calypso and Society in Pre-Independence Trinidad*. Port-of-Spain, Trinidad: published by the author.

THÉBERGE, PAUL, 1997: *Any Sound You Can Imagine: Making Music/Consuming Technology*. Hanover: Wesleyan University Press.

WALLIS, ROGER AND KRISTER MALM, 1984: *Big Sounds from Small Peoples*. London: Constable.

SECTION IV

Place, space and power

The 1990s saw a shift in the way that social and cultural theorists understood geographical space, and the influence of this change was strongly felt in debates about popular music. Much work had reported on the particular ways in which music cultures related to nations, or particular locations (see, for example, Wallis and Malm, 1984; Robinson, Cuthbert and Buck, 1991) and this emphasis continued into the 1990s, with work on local scenes in such locations as Liverpool (Cohen, 1991) and Austin, Texas (Shank, 1994) and on the ways in which genres such as rap were adapted in different countries (e.g. Mitchell, 1996; Krims, 2000; Mitchell 2001). There was an increasing emphasis on the way in which music helped to constitute a sense of place as well as how it reflected local identities (see Leyshon, Matless and Revill, 1997; Román-Velázquez, 1999; Bennett, 2000). Informed by tendencies in social thought more generally, there was a growing interest in the concepts of diaspora and globalisation in popular music studies. An especially influential treatment of music in relation to locality and space was Paul Gilroy's *The Black Atlantic* (1993), one of the few works of social and cultural theory since Adorno which has placed music at the centre of its analysis.

The influence of the shift towards questions of diaspora and globalisation can particularly be seen in chapters here by Román-Velázquez and Hosokowa. Patria Román-Velázquez questions the way that salsa has been treated as a music which 'belongs to' or originates from a specific place, be it Cuba or Puerto Rico. Salsa is international, but Román-Velázquez emphasises that salsa is not a place-specific music which was later internationalised: it was 'dislocated' from the very beginning. Salsa, she argues, needs to be thought of as a form continually undergoing processes of location and relocation. Vital to understanding these processes is the commercialisation of salsa as a dance form, and the perception in non-Latin places of salsa as exotic, which in turn feeds off wider and long-standing media representations of Latin music and dance. Shuhei Hosokawa also explores the power relations involved in the journeys and movements of musical styles, outlining three waves of Japanese responses to black music from the United States (blues in the 1960s, doo wop in the 1980s and rap in the 1990s). Hosokawa's aim is neither to celebrate these responses as the latest in a series of Japanese borrowings of foreign culture (as Japanese nationalist history might have it) nor to see them as mere imitation or appropriation. The point, suggests Hosokawa, is to explore how, through such adaptations, meaningfulness is created in local contexts.

Yet for all the movements of musical sounds across the world, particular places do still have distinctive musical cultures. Nabeel Zuberi's contribution follows the work of other writers (e.g. Manuel, 1993) on Indian musical culture, who have emphasised the special importance of film and (later) of cassettes. Zuberi updates this work by analysing the impact of television, under the neo-liberal marketisation of Indian media in the 1990s. Zuberi shows that the 'cultural imperialism' model is inadequate for understanding these recent developments: Indian media companies are increasingly powerful media players themselves. However, Zuberi suggests that music is increasingly part of a system that is encouraging the growth of brand-name consumerism, as media companies of various kinds try to encourage greater genre awareness and artist loyalty amongst their audiences.

The concept of power is lurking within these analyses of place and space, and indeed in many of the contributions to the book as a whole. Up to the mid 1990s, when power was theorised explicitly it was usually according to a neoGramscian notion, developed in cultural studies, whereby popular culture (and therefore popular music) was part of a constantly unresolved struggle between different social classes for hegemony, for control of culture and ultimately for social and political domination. This was a useful theory for many writers, whether focused explicitly on music (notably Middleton, 1990) or on cultural practices more generally (e.g. Hall, 1986), in that it paved the way for analysis of the imbrication of culture with power, while recognising the relative autonomy of culture from economic, political and social realms. However, by the early 1990s this framework was coming under critical scrutiny. The shift away from class politics to an interest in various other forms of social identity (often labelled 'difference') was key here. Many writers found post-structuralist (especially Foucauldian) or Habermasian theories more adequate to deal with questions about culture and power. In his chapter here, Motti Regev outlines and argues against the neo-Gramscian heritage and proposes an alternative account, drawing on the work of Max Weber and Pierre Bourdieu. Regev focuses on how the institutionalisation of certain musical forms relates to the emergence of new collective identities, and how rock/pop culture in particular facilitates a battle for legitimacy, whereby certain sections of the middle class struggle to legitimate their cultural preferences at the expense of others. The implication of this argument is that we should pay much more attention than before to those institutions that are involved in the legitimisation of these forms. This could entail thinking critically about rock criticism, popular music museums, televised popular music documentaries, university curricula, scholarly conferences and, ultimately, books such as this one. While not everyone will agree with Regev's formulation, we have chosen to end the book with it, because it encapsulates very cogently the concerns of popular music studies which we identified in the general introduction – the triad of power, meaning and value. It also challenges us to continue to reflect critically upon the assumptions and circumstances which inform our choice of research subject and on the potential consequences of our research activity.

References

BENNETT, ANDY, 2000: *Popular Music and Youth Culture*. Basingstoke and London: Macmillan.

COHEN, SARA, 1991: *Rock Culture in Liverpool*. Oxford: Clarendon Press.

GILROY, PAUL, 1993: *The Black Atlantic*. London: Verso.

HALL, STUART, 1986: 'Gramsci's Relevance for the Study of Race and Ethnicity'. *Journal of Communication Inquiry* 10 (2): 5–27.

KRIMS, ADAM, 2000: *Rap Music and the Poetics of Identity.* Cambridge: Cambridge University Press.

LEYSHON, ANDREW, DAVID MATLESS AND GEORGE REVILL (eds), 1997: *The Place of Music.* New York and London: The Guilford Press.

MANUEL, PETER, 1993: *Cassette Culture.* Chicago: University of Chicago Press.

MIDDLETON, RICHARD, 1990: *Studying Popular Music.* Buckingham: Open University Press.

MITCHELL, TONY, 1996: *Popular Music and Local Identity.* London and New York: Leicester University Press.

——(ed.), 2001: *Global Noise.* Hanover: Wesleyan University Press.

ROBINSON, DEANNA, ELIZABETH B. BUCK AND MARLENE CUTHBERT (eds), 1991: *Music at the Margins.* London: Sage.

ROMÁN-VELÁZQUEZ, PATRIA, 1999: *The Making of Latin London.* Aldershot: Ashgate.

SHANK, BARRY, 1994: *Dissonant Identities.* Hanover: Wesleyan University Press.

WALLIS, ROGER AND KRISTER MALM, 1984: *Big Sounds from Small Peoples.* London: Constable.

13

Locating salsa

Patria Román-Velázquez

As a music practice salsa raises a series of questions about location and dislocation, for it is as much about the New York *barrio* experience as it is a transnational dance form. The internationalisation of salsa has led to it being constantly located, dislocated and relocated and therefore continually in a process of transformation. This process, however, is also marked by the maintenance of certain codes and conventions. The complexity of the dynamics involved, although implicit in most of the academic literature, seems to be obscured or neglected as various writers try to locate and fix salsa as either Puerto Rican or Cuban.

It is my intention in this chapter to discuss the ways in which salsa has been claimed by different groups as either Cuban, Puerto Rican or, more generally, Latin. I will indicate some of the political motives for adopting such perspectives and suggest that such viewpoints lead to essentialist arguments about the relationship between music, place and identity. In contrast, I suggest that a focus on the location/dislocation/relocation of salsa might bring another tone to the politics of music, place and identity: one that moves away from the idea of music belonging to one place. This argument might lead us from salsa as a place-specific music and move us towards a perspective on the porous relationship of music to place – one that considers music in its relationship to other places, and thus salsa as belonging to more than one place simultaneously. This, however, does not occur evenly. As salsa travels around the world, so are different power relations at play. Understanding these power relations might involve considering the migration of Caribbean and other Latin American groups to the United States, the commercial strategies of the music industries in expanding to other markets in the name of 'globalisation', and a growing interest in salsa amongst wider audiences. The first part of this chapter will concentrate on how the production of salsa has been claimed for specific ethnicities and locations; the second part will consider how a similar process influences dancing to salsa.

Claiming salsa

Salsa developed in New York City as a hybrid and eclectic creative practice that incorporated different music cultures. If literally translated into English, salsa means sauce, a term employed to signify a blend of stylistic forms and rhythms that are arranged around a rhythmic matrix, called 'la clave'. More than just a music form or a rhythm, salsa has been described as a 'manner of making music' which is a flexible blend of many genres and which is continually reblended and given slightly different 'flavours' in different locations (Quintero-Rivera and Alvarez, 1990). An argument repeatedly made in works about salsa (Quintero-Rivera, 1992, 1999; Manuel, 1991; Boggs, 1992; Calvo Ospina, 1995) is that this music is the product of the consequence of a blending of the many cultural manifestations of an 'ethnic amalgam' that took place in the Caribbean. The recordings made by Celia Cruz, Willie Colón and Rubén Blades during the late 1960s and early 1970s are usually cited as examples of 'classic' salsa, with writers often stressing how their lyrics address the experiences of Latin communities in the United States (see, for example, Manuel, 1991; Padilla, 1989; Duany, 1984; Quintero-Rivera, 1999).

Salsa's development and further spread across the world cannot be separated from the history of migration. Initially associated with the Spanish Caribbean populations of Cuba and Puerto Rico, salsa was soon claimed as the voice of the New York City *barrio* and as representative of the experiences of the Latino community in the United States. Even though salsa has its roots in New York City and has further developed and evolved from the ability of musicians to incorporate a variety of rhythms and melodies from around the world, salsa seems to be claimed by musicians, dancers, fans and academics alike as either Cuban or Puerto Rican. In a similar way, salsa incorporates a wide variety of music styles emanating from genres as diverse as cumbia, rock and jazz; nevertheless most academic work tends to prioritise and recognise musical elements present in the Cuban son and the Puerto Rican bomba.

Numerous writers agree that salsa is the result of a complex series of interactions which occurred in New York City during the 1960s and which had as their impetus the migration of people from Caribbean islands and other parts of Latin America, and the movement of aesthetic forms. These people, forms and practices met in New York City, a metropolitan centre with a long history of being facilitator to the cultural meetings and interactions which led to the emergence of various forms of jazz and popular song throughout the twentieth century. However, whilst numerous writers agree that salsa emerged as a result of the movement and meeting of musical styles, cultural identities and social practices in this city, they diverge in their attempts to attribute a distinct social identity and a time and place of its roots or origins. So, for example, for certain writers salsa is 'Cuban'. Although produced outside the Caribbean island itself 'salsa is essentially Cuban music' (Steward, 1994: 485), or, as it is based musically on the son and the clave, salsa is derived from what are thought of as essentially Cuban styles (Roberts, 1979). Peter Manuel (1991, 1994) has even gone further by suggesting that salsa is an essentially Cuban music that has been assimilated by Puerto Ricans in New York City. According to Agustin Gurza, the Cuban influence continued into the middle of the 1990s, when he declared that 'Cubans have emerged as the progressive vanguard of salsa music, a style rooted in the island's fertile blend of African and European cultures. And they've done so, mercifully, at a time when much of the mainstream salsa made outside of Cuba is stamped with mediocrity' (1996: 53).

In contrast to the emphasis placed on Cuba, others have wished to prioritise Puerto Rico. Angel Quintero-Rivera (1999) has recognised numerous rock, jazz and blues, and more generically 'Latin', 'black' and 'mulatto' music elements within the 'free combination of forms' which constitutes salsa, but sustained an argument that Puerto Ricans have played the 'leading role' in its development, arguing that other musicians (e.g. of Jewish-American descent) were secondary to this influence and 'working or expressing themselves within the (im)migrant Puerto Rican community' (2001). He even goes further by suggesting that non-Caribbean groups like the Japanese Orquesta de la Luz have gained international recognition largely because of their dependence on 'Caribbean creativity and/or mastery of salsa' (2001). In referring to Japan's Orquesta de la Luz, Quintero-Rivera privileges the role of their sound producer – Sergio George – and explicitly refers to his ethnicity as 'a black Puerto Rican from New York' (2001). Jorge Duany (1984) has also acknowledged that salsa is a 'hybrid genre' and in a similar way has suggested that the Cuban elements were less significant than the contribution made by Puerto Ricans. For Duany, when salsa emerged it was able to express 'the unmistakable voice of the Puerto Rican barrio. It reflects the sorrows and the dreams of the rapidly growing urban proletariat of the last four decades' (1984: 198). Duany argues that 'salsa, then, is the product of a semi-nomadic population perpetually in transit between its homeland and exile' (1984: 197). Likewise, Felix Padilla (1989; 1990) also acknowledged that salsa had Cuban elements but argued that the music was created as an 'ethnic-specific' Puerto Rican style before becoming 'a cultural expression of Latino consciousness' (Padilla, 1989: 28–9). Padilla's broader identity claims are similar to those of Fania Records, the company which first began using the term 'salsa' for commercial promotion and which was responsible for actively constructing salsa as a 'Latin' genre from the middle of the 1960s. These suggestions of Latin unity also acknowledge that soon after its 'origins' salsa had become a form that was important for a sense of identity in Venezuela and Colombia, with musicians and dancers from both of these countries contributing to its style (Rondon, 1980; Ulloa, 1992; Waxer, 2001).

In claiming salsa for one group, and in privileging certain musical elements, the fluidity of this aesthetic form is collapsed into a stable category in much the same way that the music industry used the category of salsa to stabilise a complex mixture of musical elements as a new 'Latin' genre. Salsa was the term which was used at a particular moment to catch a series of musical dynamic interactions; it was a label used to capture a movement, an unstable blend of stylistic forms and music rhythms. Nevertheless, various academic writers and commentators have sought to categorise salsa as primarily Puerto Rican, Cuban, Latin-Caribbean or more broadly 'Latin'. Trying to label salsa in such a way can be viewed as an attempt to claim it for a singular identity, to fix its rather fluid character and to limit its capability to be transformed as it travels.

In many ways, these claims are understandable as political statements. One claim works as a gesture of political sympathy for the Cuban people who have long been marginalised and excluded from participation in academic, musical and literary forums in the United States due to the sanctions imposed by the US government. An explicit example of this position is taken by Peter Manuel (1991), when asserting his purpose for publishing a book on Cuban music 'dealing with music in Cuba proper, but also with contemporary derivative genres that flourish in New York City' (vii). Manuel writes that 'it is an explicit goal of this volume to challenge and surmount, in however tentative and limited a manner, this information blockade which has inhibited Cuban studies and mutual understanding in both countries' (viii). Salsa is also used as an assertion of identity and pride for the rather ambivalent Puerto Rican population in the United States, who despite being US citizens by birth and having lived there for over three generations are still treated as a 'minority' or immigrant community parallel to other Latin American groups.

There have also been occasions when salsa has been used by the Cuban and Puerto Rican governments as a tool to attract tourism, or to assert a sense of national identity, respectively. Cuban embassies have sponsored local Cuban bands to travel across the world as a tool to promote tourism to Cuba. At times this has been accompanied by the distribution of tourist brochures during bands' performances. In this context salsa is being claimed by state institutions as Cuban. The Puerto Rican government have also used salsa to promote tourism whilst asserting a sense of national identity. This was the case during the quincentennial celebrations held in Seville in 1992, at which Puerto Rico was presented with the slogan 'Puerto Rico is salsa' (Otero-Garabís, 1996). Juan Otero-Garabís (1996) suggests that to claim salsa for national identity purposes in the 1990s and not in the 1970s when 'salsa represented an essential bastion of cultural resistance and community expression' (25) responds to salsa's survival as a romantic form that homogenised 'its rhythms and its thematics to satisfy the requirements of the market' (26). In this sense he argues that salsa was adopted as a national emblem only when it became displaced from the community and class it was formerly used to address.

This came at a time when the shift towards romantic salsa (or *salsa romántica*) seemed to be at its peak. The early 1980s marked the shift from classic salsa or *salsa dura* – as early salsa productions are often called – to *salsa romántica*. Many studies concentrating on early versions of salsa's lyrics have focused on songs with an explicitly political content and the ability of *salseros/as* to communicate the experiences of the *barrio* life (see Duany, 1984, for example). *Salsa romántica* is often critiqued for its lack of political comment and aesthetic innovation. As Otero-Garabís argued, salsa was adopted as a sign of national identity by the Puerto Rican government only when it became depoliticised and therefore more readily available to the middle classes. However, as further studies have demonstrated, this shift does not necessarily mean the abandonment of politics altogether.

From studying the salsa dance scene in Cali, Colombia, Lise Waxer (2001) has also demonstrated how:

> in contrast to 1960s/70s salsa, which was strongly tied to the working class and to leftist university students, salsa romántica was marketed throughout Latin America as a glamorous product for the middle classes. Following this trend much of the Caleño audience for this new style hailed from the city's growing new rich, and also from Caleño middle-class youth (73).

Whilst some researchers have focused on the way in which this aesthetic turn can be related to class differences amongst salsa's audience, Frances

Aparicio (1998) has focused on gender. Aparicio's research on how salsa music is listened to by women of different class backgrounds shows how this aesthetic change allowed more women to enjoy the genre and how a large female audience were able to adopt different listening and interpretation strategies, challenging in this way the public–private/male–female distinction which informed the interpretation of classic salsa as a live, public and male form. Aparicio's argument also relates to Keith Negus's (1999) observation that the fact:

> that salsa can no longer be identified with the urban barrio and male worker does not mean that it is no longer 'political'. When salsero Mark Anthony took the stage in front of 20,000 people in New York's Madison Square Garden in September 1998 and performed draped in the flags of the Dominican Republic and Puerto Rico, he was simultaneously raising awareness of, generating cash for and inspiring solidarity with those in the Caribbean who had suffered the consequences of Hurricane Georges (137).

In this sense, salsa's lyrics might no longer communicate the daily struggles of the *barrio* experience but this shift does not necessarily mean that the genre lacks a political content.

Despite salsa's stylistic variation and 'semi-nomadic' character, academic writing has been concerned with trying to locate salsa by proving it is either Puerto Rican or Cuban in origins. The claim that salsa articulates the ethnic amalgam of the Caribbean has also been tied to class groups: it was only when salsa moved away from its origins that a more middle-class audience started to appropriate it and be identified with it. These attempts to fix salsa seem to contradict the arguments for salsa as a 'free combination of rhythms, forms, harmonic patterns and melodic phrases of numerous genres' (Quintero-Rivera, 2001). That salsa music developed in New York City out of the interaction of the different groups and music cultures that merged in this metropolitan centre is not disputed in the existing academic literature. It is rather the location/dislocation of salsa that seems to be the core of the arguments and that I think should be critically questioned. This argument seems to drift away into a fruitless attempt to prove beyond doubt that salsa is essentially Puerto Rican or Cuban. And here I can only leave unresolved questions which lead to sociological issues outside the range of this chapter. Why is it that salsa has to be placed? Why is the placement of salsa important? Why is it that the placement of salsa has to be so contested? What does it have to tell us about the Cuban–Puerto Rican relationship – either in exile, or in and across the Islands?

Despite attempts to locate salsa and to privilege certain forms over others, salsa music has been internationalised, raising perhaps further questions for an argument about the simultaneous location/dislocation/relocation of salsa.

The internationalisation of salsa

The spread and distribution of music around the world has mostly been approached first through the cultural imperialism thesis and the argument that cultural forms contribute to economic inequality, and subsequently through arguments about globalisation, where the time-space movement of music is considered to be less related to power relations. Even though 'Anglo-American' recorded music has been assumed to be the dominant style in both theoretical approaches, salsa has been one of those music styles that has travelled the world, though still not on equal terms with its Anglo-American counterparts. This phenomenon, however, is not new or exclusive to salsa. As Georgina Born and David Hesmondhalgh (2000) have stated:

> Throughout the twentieth century, even in the era when Anglo-American repertoire seemed to be dominating the world market, some non-Western popular musics have been successful in the West, whether in the guise of styles adopted by Western musicians, or in the importation by record companies and promoters of recordings and stars which could then be repackaged and sold on to consumers (25).

This was the case with, for example, tango's appeal during the 1920s in places like France and Japan.

The movement of salsa around the world should involve a consideration of the commercialisation of salsa by the music industries, the growing number of Latin American people migrating to other parts of the world, the changing musical tastes of non-Latin American people (dancers, musicians and disc jockeys), the interest of independent record labels, and the sponsorship of borough councils and embassies around the world. Thus, the internationalisation of salsa cannot be explained by focusing on one aspect alone, but by considering a combination of factors that have contributed to and created the possibilities for salsa to spread around the world. These processes are important for understanding the development and routes of salsa from New York to the Spanish Caribbean, and to other Latin American countries such as Venezuela and Colombia, and also for considering the later routes of salsa to other countries around the world such as Japan, France, Italy, Switzerland, Holland, Germany, Canada and England.

My research on salsa music clubs in London (1999) has shown how the migration of Latin Americans to the UK during the 1970s made an important contribution to the spread of salsa music. Latin Americans brought with them, or asked their relatives to send them, the music that they had listened to in the countries they came from, and this was played during house parties or gatherings at local community centres. However, the spread of salsa music was not simply due to the presence of Latin Americans. There was also a growing interest in the music amongst non-Latin American people. Dancers, musicians, disc jockeys and entrepreneurs all contributed to the further circulation of salsa across Britain, Western Europe and beyond. Musicians, for example, started playing outside of their gig circuits which were mainly in London and began performing at different venues throughout England, Scotland and continental Europe. Disc jockeys were also gaining information from international music magazines and charts, and establishing links with other music scenes across the world by attending music carnivals and conventions in Latin America, Europe and the United States, most significantly those events held in Tenerife, Colombia and Miami. The routes of salsa into and across metropolitan London were also influenced by the simultaneous efforts of music industries, record shops, magazines, radio stations, embassies, solidarity campaigns and music clubs. Although acting for their own objectives and purposes, the networks developing from these different interests aided the development of a local salsa scene in London whilst incorporating it into a wider international music network.

As a result of this movement, outside of New York and other Latin American countries salsa began to be promoted and sold (by music and media industries and record shops) as 'Latin', 'world' or 'international' music. Several articles in trade magazines like *Music Business International* and *Billboard* pointed to the importance of Latin American popular music as a market in Europe. In addition, world music magazines, for example *World Music* and *Global Music and Culture: Rhythm Music Magazine*, began to refer to salsa as world music, a term created for specific marketing reasons and sometimes used as an inclusive label for all non-English-language foreign music. Whether salsa, Latin, world or international these marketing categories and their related practices signal the way in which the categorisation and placement of salsa in record shops is dependent on geographical boundaries and definitions.

Keith Negus's (1999) research on the Latin music industry in the United States has shown that even though salsa is mainly produced and purchased in the US, and as such it could be considered a 'domestic' genre, it is nevertheless located in a separate Latin department within the companies' international divisions. Negus (1999) argues that the structural location of the Latin division within the North American companies 'gives an indication of how the industry initially shapes the production and distribution of salsa by defining it as "international" (basically as a "foreign" music within the US)' (142). He elaborates this argument by acknowledging that neither structural arrangements within a company nor commercial and marketing strategies alone can 'provide a complete account of how salsa, or any other genre, is circulated and given meaning' (145). He suggests that the circulation of salsa and its subsequent meanings are shaped within a 'cultural matrix'. He uses this term to explain the 'commercial webs' connecting the music industries in New York City, Miami and Puerto Rico and other not so institutionalised webs emerging from the production of salsa by artists from Venezuela, Colombia, other regions of the US and from Cuba. These webs extend even further when the activities of musicians from other parts of the world are considered.

As salsa is placed geographically in different locales around the world so are different localised identities created, represented and experienced. Salsa, like numerous other musical styles, moved outwards and onwards, and was adopted and appropriated in different ways by musicians and dancers in various parts of the world. For example, as Shuhei Hosokawa (1999) has shown, in Japan salsa enabled the aesthetic and social articulation of some of the dilemmas associated with being Japanese in the modern 'global' world. It expressed, in part, the particularities of a Japanese relationship to the Caribbean and Americas, and also a search for a specific type of ethnic 'authenticity' through which contemporary forms of recorded popular music are legitimated. Research on salsa music has also shown how non-Latin American salsa musicians are usually questioned about their authenticity and ability to perform or play an instrument that is usually not associated with their ethnic group. This is the case when, for example, Larry Harlow's contribution to salsa is immediately followed by remarks about his Jewish-American descent, as if this is an odd occurrence. Questions about the relationship between music and ethnicity are also present for salsa musicians outside New York and preconceptions about ethnic background and musical ability are still present in the way some salsa musicians are treated. In my research I found this to be the case with English and Scottish musicians who performed in the United States: their ethnic background was questioned by others who maintain essentialist ideas about a link between Latin identity and musical competence. As an English conga player commented when comparing London and New York:

> Over there, because there are so many Latin musicians, it is more difficult to be accepted. I mean, it is just that people are not used to hearing or seeing non Latin people playing that kind of music. Of course they don't believe that is possible . . . That was not a problem here because there is not that many Latin musicians.

> (in Román-Velázquez, 1999: 134)

The relocation of salsa involves commerce and industry as well as the migration of different populations and music styles across the world. The relocation and subsequent meanings of salsa are not unchallenged. Thus, exploring the relationship between music, place and identity should include questions about the power relations across the different institutions and social groups involved in the construction of Latin identity. In my research on salsa clubs in London I analysed how the geographical location of the clubs and the activities of participants across salsa clubs contributed to the creation of particular Latin identities. For example, salsa music has become popular along with Latin food and themed bars and there has been a growth of commercially run clubs, bars and restaurants and a simultaneous increase in fiestas, concerts and cultural events sponsored by local governments and community organisations. Some events have produced sites for the meeting and mixing of musicians, dancers and DJs, the sharing of experiences between Latin and non-Latin people, and the potential for the forging of new cultural identities. Yet other places constructed with a Latin identity have presented salsa within the context of a contrived environment attempting to signal the mythical ambience of pre-Revolutionary Cuba or amongst stereotyped images of beaches, palm trees, sunny holidays and hot Latin lovers, both deliberately seeking to attract wealthy, middle-class Londoners with disposable income.

More concealed are many working-class cafés and clubs run by Latin Americans, who have been struggling to establish a presence and be recognised in the city since the 1970s. Hence understanding the Latin identity constructed at salsa clubs involves considering the social and political position of Latin American groups in London, together with their migratory status and position within the local economy. To draw from Doreen Massey (1993), it is important to retain an awareness of the power geometry through which the movements of people, culture and capital become possible, and how people are placed and assume a position in relation to a politics of mobility, access, international migration, transportation, ethnicity and gender.

The multiple locations of salsa

In certain respects, salsa could be considered as a 'global' form that is given particular localised forms of identity. In this way, salsa would not be exceptional. It would be like numerous forms of music which have been 'globalised' and been given what are thought of as localised forms of identity. But salsa is slightly different and it is misleading to think of it as a place-specific music which has simply been 'globalised', or moved from one locale to another. As I suggested earlier, salsa has been conceived simultaneously as a located and a dislocated music practice since its inception; this is something which the attempts to claim salsa both emphasise and deny. As an example of this paradox, the Senegalese group Africando claims that:

> It is no secret that Cuban dance rhythms – the heartbeat of salsa – originated in Africa, but the other side of the Afro-Cuban connection has only recently come to light. From Zairean soukous to Senegalese mbalax, modern Afro-pop evolved largely out of Latin music, as each African nation re-traditionalised the salsa sound along its own ethnic lines.

(Birnbaum, 1993)

To put it another way, the claim has been one of returning salsa to its roots by stressing its African heritage. In this sense Africando are seen as 'completing the Afro-Cuban circle and bringing the music back home' (Birnbaum, 1993). This argument has also been made by Al Angeloro (1992):

> Several centuries ago, a human tragedy brought about an amalgamation of African rhythms and European instrumentations in the countries whose shores the Diaspora touched upon. As time moved on, various musical amalgamations arose and became an integral part of the countries' national identities. Later these new rhythms and dances went 'back to Africa', and were incorporated into indigenous African rhythms (305).

He refers to this process of musical change and movement as 'reverse transculturation'. To simply view salsa in terms of the global and the local is to ignore the continual dynamics of location and relocation through which the genre has been formed and transformed. Hence not only is it misleading to view salsa as place-specific, it is equally misleading to think of it in terms of the globalisation of cultural forms.

Salsa cannot be thought of as localised in the same way as other forms of song-based dance music such as rock, reggae and rap, which have tended to be appropriated and sung in local languages. Whether played in Los Angeles, London, Tokyo or Berlin salsa is mainly sung in Spanish. Perhaps the most internationally recognised non-Latin bands are Africando, a Senegalese band that sings some songs in Wolof and Spanish, and Orquesta de La Luz, an all-Japanese salsa band, whose lead singer, Nora, despite not being able to speak the language, sings all their songs in Spanish. It is perhaps ironic that the internationalisation of salsa, whilst contributing to its transformation by blending and mixing with different local styles, has also led to the maintenance of certain generic codes. That is to say, whilst rap is adopted and blended with local rhythms in Turkey and sung in Turkish, for example, salsa is almost universally sung in Spanish, frequently by people who cannot speak

Spanish and who only have a vague idea of what the lyrics mean. In this context salsa has not been able to go beyond the language barrier. It is worth highlighting that Willie Colón, an important contributor to 'classic' New York salsa during the 1970s, composed and sang in Spanish, even though his first language was English. For Willie Colón, a Newyorican – a New York-born Puerto Rican – to compose and sing in Spanish was a political statement in the United States during the 1970s. For Nora, Orquesta de la Luz's lead singer, singing in Spanish involved adhering to the conventions of the genre. My research on salsa clubs in London (1999) suggested that being able to sing in Spanish and having the right intonation was crucial for getting a job as a lead singer in a salsa band, and moreover these were important elements for conveying a sense of generic Latin musical identity.

The internationalisation of salsa is significantly related to its commercialisation as a dance form. Whilst salsa bands can be found making recordings and performing throughout the world, salsa's spread has been particularly connected to the increasing popularity of salsa as a dance (rather than a musical style). Internationally, salsa has become more a music to be danced to, rather than a music that is produced. The movement of salsa around the world has involved the creation of local salsa dance scenes (Román-Velázquez, 1999; Waxer, 2001), which have been specifically connected to the importation of recordings, the formal organisation of salsa dance lessons and the establishment of salsa clubs by entrepreneurs who prefer hiring disc jockeys rather than booking bands for their Latin nights. In this respect Waxer (2001) has shown that, for those wishing to learn how to dance salsa, recordings have become more important than live performances. Also, as Aparicio (1998) suggests, a lot of academic work has focused on salsa as a live form and has neglected the fact that it is far more common for people (and women in particular – as her focus was on women) to interact with recordings rather than to attend live concerts and gigs.

The internationalisation of salsa as a dance music has also involved the maintenance of certain generic codes. Salsa is danced to in clubs around the world where it is generally recognised as a 'Latin' music, but often without any awareness of the political or romantic significance of the lyrics nor of the history of the style. Salsa is one of most popular forms of recorded dance music, which is heard in dance lessons and clubs amongst people who actively participate in maintaining the genre but who do not necessarily purchase the recordings or even have a strong interest in the backgrounds of performers, the contexts of production and the semantic meaning of the lyrics. Dance lessons play a crucial role in maintaining salsa within a very particular set of discursive practices. Unlike many genres of contemporary electronically recorded music, to dance to salsa requires knowledge of very specific rules, codes and conventions. It is danced in couples, unlike reggae, rap and rock. As a dance form salsa is given particular meanings through the encoding of specific gender relations. When taught, salsa is presented in terms of leading and improvising for men, and following and being led for women. It is a dance in which men have the control and in which women dance for men (Román-Velázquez, 1999).

These linguistic and gender codes are maintained, even though the internationalisation of salsa as a dance form might also involve stylistic mixing and blending as research on dancing styles in Colombia has highlighted. Lise Waxer (2001) has shown how:

> During the 1960s and 1970s, Caleños developed a unique style of dancing, charac-
> terised by a rapid, 'double-time' shuffle on the tips of the toes. In Colombia this idio-
> syncratic local style is still known as the *el paso caleño* (the Cali dance step). It is
> distinct from the way that salsa is danced in the rest of Latin America (and in other
> parts of Colombia, for that matter), where the basic 'short-short-long' step developed
> from Cuban son is the norm. High kicks and rapid footwork also became a hallmark
> of Caleño salsa dancing. The Caleño style was a hybrid of elements from Cuban
> guaracha and mambo, along with North American popular dances such as jitterbug,
> twist and charleston (69).

This process of mixing and blending has enabled the development of localised dancing styles that are communicated in dance lessons throughout the world. These localised forms of dancing seem to have been institution-alised through dance lessons, so that it is not unusual for a London dancer to refer to dancing salsa in a 'Cuban' or 'Colombian' way (even though the style may only be specific to certain parts of Cuba or Colombia). In some ways this attribution of a place-specific dancing style is how dance teachers assert their authenticity when seeking to attract dancers to their classes and not those of their competitors.

On this point salsa is also appropriated, interpreted and perceived as exotic. Jane C. Desmond's (1997) research on dance, and in particular Brazilian dance forms in the United States, has shown how most dance labelled as 'Latin' or 'black' is 'represented and promoted in terms of the dance's sexual allure'. What is promoted and considered a 'hot' Latin style turns into an 'Anglo-Latin' dance style for which 'meaning arises from and contributes to the larger dialectic between these two social and political entities and their current political and economic relations' (48). This, she argues, is the case with almost every dance craze in the United States that is promoted to the non-Latin population. This argument could be extended to London, where I found that dancers perceived salsa as sexy and as 'natural' to Latin Americans. Latin Americans were perceived as generally sexy and having a 'natural sense of rhythm' by those attending classes or reporting on them for the media (Román-Velázquez, 1999).

The media have contributed to these images and ideas about Latin identity. Significant here has been the use and representation of Latin American music and dance in advertisements and films. As Ana M. López's (1997) research has demonstrated 'Rhythm has been – and continues to be – used as a significant marker of national ethnic difference: the cinema locates and placates Latino/as and Latin Americans rhythmically' (340). Jane C. Desmond (1997) has also acknowledged the role of the mass media in facilitating the spread of music and dance styles. However, she argues that these mediated images tend to simplify complex dances into a series of dance steps isolated from the social practices, contexts and communities of performance that these are part of. She writes that:

> Such representations are a key factor in the reworking of the meanings of these
> movements as they travel. Further, the identities once attached to certain styles of
> moving (associated with 'black' or 'white' or 'mestizo' populations in Brazil, for
> instance) become genericised in the transportation, standing now for an
> undifferentiated 'latinness', with original markers of class, racial identity, and
> national specificity all but erased (50).

The internationalisation of salsa as a dance form has also involved a sense of Latinness in a reductive way – only this time it is the dance steps/styles (rather than the aspects of production and the performers) which have had their multiple identities 'erased'.

I started this essay with reference to the complexity of salsa's musical blending and the creative mixture which has facilitated its productions, and noted how, rather than the complexity of this being addressed, there has been a tendency to reduce salsa to a Puerto Rican, Cuban or generically Latin form. I have ended with dance practices, involving numerous people, Latin and non-Latin, in different places, which also seem to be reduced to Cuban, Colombian or a generically 'hot' and 'natural' type of Latin dancing. Throughout I have highlighted various aspects or dimensions of the power geometry through which salsa has continued to move outwards from its moment of 'Latin' origin (wherever that is assumed to be). Salsa, like many genres of popular music, occupies multiple locations simultaneously. It is produced by a wide variety of people who are labelled in different ways, it is danced to by different groups, yet it continues to be perceived, claimed and maintained as a Latin style. I have suggested that there is a complex dynamic to both the production and the consumption of salsa, yet this complexity has too often been evaded, as authors, dancers and musicians alike seek to claim it for one place and one ethnic group.

References

ANGELORO, A., 1992: 'Back-to-Africa: The Reverse Transculturation of Salsa/Cuban Popular Music', in BOGGS (1992: 299–306).

APARICIO, F., 1998: *Listening to Salsa: Gender, Latin Popular Music, and Puerto Rican Cultures*. Hanover: Wesleyan University Press.

BOGGS, V. W. (ed.), 1992: *Salsiology: Afro-Cuban Music and the Evolution of Salsa in New York City*. New York: Excelsior Music Publishing Co.

BORN, G. AND D. HESMONDHALGH (eds), 2000: *Western Music and its Others: Difference, Representation and Appropriation in Music*. Berkeley: University of California Press.

BIRNBAUM, L., 1993: Africando, *Trovador*. Vol. 1, Stern's, Africa (sleeve notes).

CALVO OSPINA, H., 1995: *Salsa: Havana Heat, Bronx Beat*, trans. Nick Caistor. London: Latin American Bureau. First published 1992 as *Salsa: 500 jaar optimisme, liefde en ritme*. Antwerp: EPO.

DESMOND, J., 1997: 'Embodying Difference: Issues in Dance and Cultural Studies', in C. Fraser Delgado and J. Estaban Muñoz (eds), *Everynight Life. Culture and Dance in Latin/o America*. Durham, N.C.: Duke University Press, 33–64.

DUANY, J., 1984: 'Popular Music in Puerto Rico: Toward an Anthropology of Salsa'. *Latin American Music Review* 5 (2): 186–216.

GURZA, A., 1996: 'Salsa Wars. Revolution and the New Sound of Cuba'. *LA Weekly*, 26 April – 2 May: 53.

HOSOKAWA, S., 1999: 'Salsa no tiene frontera: Orquesta de la Luz and the Globalisation of Popular Music'. *Cultural Studies* 13 (3): 509–34.

LÓPEZ, A. M., 1997: 'Of Rhythms and Borders', in C. Fraser Delgado and J. Estaban Muñoz (eds), *Everynight Life: Culture and Dance in Latin/o America*. Durham, N.C.: Duke University Press, 310–44.

MANUEL, P. (ed.), 1991: *Essays on Cuban Music: North American and Cuban Perspectives*. Lanham, MD: University Press of America.

——, 1994: 'Puerto Rican Music and Cultural Identity: Creative Appropriation of Cuban Sources from Danza to Salsa'. *Ethnomusicology* 38 (2): 249–80.

MASSEY, D., 1993: 'Power-Geometry and a Progressive Sense of Place', in Jon Bird, Barry Curties, George Robertson and Lisa Tickner (eds), *Mapping the Futures; Local Cultures, Global Change*. London and New York: Routledge, 59–69.

NEGUS, K., 1999: *Music Genres and Corporate Cultures*. London and New York: Routledge.

OTERO-GARABÍS, J., 1996: 'Puerto Rico is Salsa: Propositions, Appropriations and Interpretations of a Popular Genre'. *Journal of Latin American Cultural Studies* 5 (1): 25–31.

PADILLA, F., 1989: 'Salsa Music as Cultural Expression of Latino Consciousness and Unity'. *Hispanic Journal of Behavioural Sciences* 11 (1): 28–45.

——, 1990: 'Salsa: Puerto Rican and Latino Music'. *Journal of Popular Culture* 24: 87–104.

QUINTERO-RIVERA, A. G., 1992: 'El tambor en el cuatro: La melodización de ritmos y la etnicidad cimarroneada', in *La tercera raíz: La presencia africana en Puerto Rico*. San Juan, Puerto Rico: CEREP and ICP, 44–55.

——, 1999: *¡Salsa Sabor y Control! Sociología de la música tropical*. Mexico: Siglo XXI.

——, 2001: 'Big Sounds (or Movements?!) from *Small Peoples*? Salsa, Globalisation and Worldvisions'. Unpublished manuscript.

QUINTERO-RIVERA, A. G. and L. M. ALVAREZ, 1990: 'La libre combinación de formas musicales en la salsa'. *David y Goliat: Revista del Consejo Latinoamericano de Ciencias Sociales (CLACSO)* 19 (57): 45–51.

ROBERTS, J. S., 1979: *The Latin Tinge: The Impact of Latin American Music on the United States*. New York: Original Music.

ROMÁN-VELÁZQUEZ, P., 1999: *The Making of Latin London: Salsa Music, Place and Identity*. Andover: Ashgate.

RONDON, C. M., 1980: *El libro de la salsa: crónica de la música del Caribe urbano*. Caracas: Editoral Arte.

STEWARD, S., 1994: 'Dancing With the Saints: The International Sound of Salsa', in S. Broughton, M. Ellingham, D. Muddyman and R. Trillo (eds), *World Music: The Rough Guide*. Harmondsworth: Penguin.

ULLOA, A., 1992: *La Salsa en Cali*. Colombia: Ediciones A. Ulloa del Valle.

WAXER, L., 2001: 'Record Grooves and Salsa Dance Moves: The *viejoteca* Phenomenon in Cali, Colombia'. *Popular Music* 20 (1):61–82.

14

Blacking Japanese: experiencing otherness from afar

Shuhei Hosokawa

Imitation produces nothing. Imitation is no expression of life. Following the other people's expression of life is no culture. Imitating another's style is already an insult to hip hop culture.

(By Phar the Dopest, from *Woofin'* vol. 2, *Music Life Special*, August 1997: 56).

Blues is blues, whether played by blacks or whites. So there is no need to call it 'white blues' just as it is not 'yellow classical' when Japanese play Western classical music. It is not odd that blacks and whites play the same music because both are in essence the same human being.

(a reader's letter, *New Music Magazine*, July 1969: 79)

The intercultural and interracial transgression on a global scale of African-American music, or 'black music' as it is colloquially called (and adopted hereafter), is among the best examples of the astonishing mobility of musical performers, commodities, information and sounds. This music has been well embraced by Japan as is apparent in the frequent tours of African-American performers, countless issues and reissues of CDs, and numerous domestic artists of black and black-inflected music. There is of course nothing comparable to the socio-cultural intercourse of the 'black Atlantic' in terms of complexity and reciprocity. It is not massive migration but communication and commercial trade (and the travel of a select few) that characterise the cultural connections between the two distant countries.

But this does not mean that Japan has been passive in its reception of black music. After all, nothing is immune from the effects of cultural travel. By examining various aspects of the adaptation, appreciation and appropriation of black music and blackness, my chapter will discuss the transnational and translocal connections of music culture. My emphasis is on how black history has been interpreted, on how mimicry is ambiguously tied with locality, and on how a 'foreign culture' is domesticated and absorbed, according to local institutions, ideology and language.

Mimicry is a key process by which a cultural form is transferred from one place and person to another, and by which the boundaries between the original and the copy, the desired object and the mimicking subject, are blurred (Bhabha, 1994). It takes place in many locations at different moments for different cultural reasons. The term 'influence' always connotes a certain degree of imitation and mimicry. In the strong words of anthropologist Michael Taussig, 'world history cannot be thought of outside the mimetic faculty itself' (1993: 70). Starting from this assertion, he argues for a relationship between the colonial power game and the primitivism-shamanism involved in it. He also underlines the fundamental force of reproductive (or mimetic) technologies such as photography and phonography. It seems to me that his theory can be applied to the process of cultural appropriation outside the colonial context.

More than literature, film, stage dance and theatre, popular music has played a key role in disseminating African-American culture because it is as easily portable as it is immediately sensible. Whether as broadcasts or recordings, music from the Bronx or Mississippi can travel vast distances and is instantly consumable by dancing, listening, collecting or performing. Due to this ubiquity and to its intimate connection with fashion, image and the body, popular music is crucial for the globalised African-American culture as a whole. Among the variety of foreign musics Japan has received, black music has a special significance because of its commercial potential, musical specificities and racial ambiguity. In this chapter I will discuss three separate instances of Japanese appropriation of black music: blues (1960s), doowop (1980s) and rap (1990s). While I focus on several specific moments in each instance, space does not allow me to pay full attention to the historical development of each genre. Nor is there room for me to discuss important styles such as rhythm and blues, gospel, New Orleans-style brass bands, dance/pop and other important facets of African-American music in Japan.

Toru Mitsui once noted that the Japanese country and western community 'is significantly characterised by a lack of self-consciousness in terms of tradition' (1993: 289). This is also true of black music. Japanese performers and listeners are conscious of their position outside the 'tradition' of the music, namely, its authentic location and history. To overcome their 'exterior' position, listeners use the rhetoric of an affective connection that makes the particular appeal of a musical style universally relevant. Respect and passion are usually the two affective forms that create a bridge with which to link the universal with the particular. Respect and passion are both social and material, political and historical, and they are structured by, and embedded in, lived experience. This experience is mediated by social organisation, politics, ideology, discourse, body, image and sound. Through ideas of respect and passion, aficionados interiorise otherness, while reconfiguring their own social reality. A cogent metaphor for this play between the interior and the exterior, for the ambiguous self and other, and for the expression of otherness is *ventriloquism*. It is an illusory performance of the audible and the visual, the animate and the non-animate, the subject and the object. A monologue suddenly and mischievously becomes dialogue between the puppet and the self. One may wonder in whose voice the ventriloquist speaks.

Black is a colour of resistance

It was jazz in the 1920s that first drew serious attention to black music. From this early period on, Japanese contact with American musics has been mediated by the white-dominated international cultural industries, because recordings, films and journalism were pivotal for the Japanese reinterpretation of American sounds. To put this differently, Japan receives music that has already 'crossed over' ethnic and racial boundaries. After the Second World War, the channels of American music became more complicated due to the presence of American military bases, the increasing number of Japanese going abroad, the imported recordings available and the widening network of mass media.

With the arrival of bebop in the 1950s, Japanese jazz fans and musicians became more aware of attributed links between 'race' and styles of jazz. Some believed that black jazz was more authentic than white jazz. In the late 1960s some critics started discussing the racial and political aspects of jazz after reading Langston Hughes, Frantz Fanon, Leroi Jones, Charles Keil and others. It was the first time that music critics took the political 'message' of jazz (Max Roach and Charles Mingus, for example) seriously. To them, supporting black jazz meant a rejection of white America (see also Russell, 1992: 306; 1998: 120). Jazz critic Hisato Aikura, in his preface to the translation of Charles Keil's *Urban Blues*, noted that 'the violence of the urban guerrilla and blues have much in common' (1968: 7). Blues was thus regarded as a symbol of resistance and revolution, and the listening experience was expected to establish political solidarity (ibid.: 4).

The politicisation of jazz history coincided with a change in the meaning of blues, a change triggered by a blues revival in the US and UK. Previously blues designated, on the one hand, a format prevailing in jazz and rock'n'roll, and, on the other hand, it indicated Japanese songs based on a slow foxtrot which the British social dance world had traditionally (and erroneously for black music fans) called blues. The blues revival reached Japan through imported records and books. Sound and ideology came hand in hand. They were lucky enough to hear the blues, a genre hardly broadcast on television and radio, and they had the language skills to understand the lyrics (many blues fans and musicians in Japan had a college education). Jeff T. Titon's retrospective assertion that the blues revival in white America 'was remarkably oriented to records and the record-listening experience' (1993: 225f) is very much true in Japan, where no African-American bluesmen performed until B. B. King in 1971, and Sleepy Joe Estes in 1974.

Leroi Jones's poetic concept of a 'blues impulse' appealed to many leftist critics and readers so deeply that some even searched for a 'Japanese blues impulse'. For example, Tôyô Nakamura, founder of *New Music Magazine* (*Nyû Myûjikku Magajin*), the first critical popular music journal in Japan (1969–present), praised singer-songwriter Nobuyasu Okabayashi's 'Sanya Blues' (Sanya is Tokyo's largest underclass neighbourhood; see Fowler, 1996) as a sign of a Japanese blues impulse. Okabayashi's inspiration was clearly Bob Dylan, yet his guitar and vocal style scarcely resembled an

American delivery. Moreover, in contrast to many of his peers, who were influenced most strongly by translations of new American folksongs, Okabayashi's main influence seemed to be his volunteer activities in Kamagasak, the Osaka counterpart of Sanya.

Nakamura urged his readers to grasp blues not merely as a 'hip' style but as music that can enhance international solidarity. Sanya, he argued, represented the most intense conflicts of the Japanese capitalist economy, much like the slave economy in the US. Hence 'Sanya Blues' in some ways intersected with the music of Paul Butterfield, Canned Heat, John Mayall and John Lee Hooker. Nakamura's conclusion revealed his intention of adapting the blues to the Japanese context: 'We are going to find a new meaning in blues as an affective bond bridging us, Sanya and America' (1969: 46).

'Finding meaning' was in its own right an alternative direction in popular music criticism. Nakamura's transposition of blues to Sanya anticipated the attitude of Japanese conscious rappers (discussed below). In retrospect, the political interpretations of the late 1960s can be seen as a narrative designed to steer the imagination of listeners. Precisely because they are so far removed from American reality, Japanese aficionados of black music tend to be bound by an ideological connection to the scene. As was the case with their American counterparts, they regarded blues as a 'symbol of stylised revolt against conservative politics and middle-class propriety' (Titon, 1993: 223). This ideological convergence may be an outcome of the white mediation of black music in Japan.

Around 1968 some Japanese musicians performing in American military bases started emulating British blues rock. Many reached Mississippi and Chicago via London and wrote their songs in English, a 'universal' language, rather than in Japanese, a parochial one (see Hosokawa, 2000). One of the early blues bands, the Blues Creation (later the Creation) sang of their passion for blues in (somewhat odd) English as follows:

I'd just turned sixteen
When I got into the blues scene
I got a hold of a guitar
No longer could I listen
To the songs playing on the radio

Fell in love a several times
And now I have a home on my own
Pains I had to go through
My guitar saved me
I am yellow – there's blues in this country, too

Today I am not what I used to be
Creating many sounds, I'm into the world at last
People anticipating the East
I'm dreaming of the West
The world is one, people are one

Creation is my life, and blues is my soul
Right on, Buddy Guy, man
You can find Empire State Building even her[e] in Tokyo

('Blues from the Yellow', from *Creation Twin Best*)

The lyrics tell how blues distanced the first person 'me' from pop music (symbolised by 'songs playing on the radio') and, more importantly, how blues became 'my soul' even though 'I am yellow'. To justify their adaptation, the Blues Creation needed to proclaim the universality of blues ('The world is one, people are one').[1] Similarly, another early blues band, West Road Blues Band (sometimes the West Road) confessed their total reliance on 'black-eyed blues' (akin to 'blue-eyed soul'): 'I need a vaccination for the black eyed blues / A total fascination for the colour I choose / ... A certain declaration to the black eyed blues / A total destination for the colour I choose' ('Black Eyed Blues' from *West Road Live in Kyoto*, 1975).

What is striking is the way Japanese biological traits seem to justify the 'colour' of the music they have 'chosen'. Although the logic is somewhat forced, it does at least signal their recognition of racial difference. The blackness of blues makes Japanese performers more conscious of their *racial* status than rock and new American folksongs. It is hard to imagine Japanese rock bands singing about their skin colour. This is probably because rock is regarded as 'white' music, or as music unmarked by the concept of race (though there are rock bands named Yellow, Yellow Monkey and Yellow Magic Orchestra). It is blackness, not whiteness, that matters to Japanese musicians.

Chanels: blackface

The most impressive black music group in Japan may have been the blackface doowop group Chanels (or Shanels, today's Rats & Star). They consisted of four blackface vocalists with exaggerated lips, white gloves and greased hair, and six non-blackface instrumentalists. Despite the absence of blackface minstrelsy in Japan, some Japanese regarded them as offensive, as was fiercely expressed by a reader of *Asahi Shinbun*, one of the largest national newspapers:

> Is painting [one's face] black 'for business' a kind of racial discrimination? They [Chanels] can wash off the black. But I hear that black-skinned children at the Elisabeth Sanders Home [an interracial orphanage] tried to rub their skin to whiten up. What do they think of Chanels? I can accept blackface as a theatrical prop [for spoken dramas] but singers don't need to do it.

> (*Asahi Shinbun*, 26 June 1980)

To counter this opinion, another reader defended them:

> They [Chanels] are enchanted by black music and they started painting their faces in order to become black people at least while singing. This doesn't mean they have a racist consciousness in their minds.

> (*Asahi Shinbun*, 1 July 1980)

Is blackface racism or respect? For the leader of the band, blackface is a stage device to show their 'respect for black people' and to 'get as close to black people as possible'. In the words of their regular lyricist Reiko Yukawa,

'They want to be black. They keep on blacking up their faces till it sinks into the skin' (*Josei Jishin*, 24 July 1980: 208). They decided to black up their faces to make a sensation (*ukenerai*) when they participated in a national amateur band contest in 1978 (*Shûkan Myôjô*, 23 March 1980: 38–43). The band was aware of the comical effect of their appearance and of how it communicated via the use of black stereotypes. There were two reasons for Chanels' use of blackface: to stand out and to pay respect to black music (see also Condry 2000: 175).[2] Through blackface, they shared with the audience a racial fantasy. According to a report on their early stage show, 'they walk and move their hands just as the blacks do' (*Shûkan Myôjô*, 23 March 1980: 38–39). Their gestures were thus in conformity with the spectators' preconceived notion of blackness.

Cultural historian John Szwed notes that 'The fact that, say, a Mick Jagger, can today perform in the same tradition without blackface marks the detachment of culture from race and the almost full absorption of a black tradition into white culture' (quoted by Lott, 1993: 7). Although white culture has absorbed many aspects of black tradition, the detachment of culture from race is not fully complete, as shown by the media presence of Chanels.[3] However, it should be also noted that there are no other blackface groups. It is as if they patented this gimmick. By contrast, contemporary R&B singers such as Yuki Koyanagi and Toshinobu Kubota often tan the skin. To transform one's dermatological pigments and to paint one's face with facial cream are two completely different ways of 'turning black'. Following the contemporary colour code, these singers seem to be rejecting the use of facial cream as clownery.

Blackface not only exploits blackness. It also makes whiteness salient as a liminal sign, rather than masking it. Just as orientalism perversely unveils what constitutes the 'occidental' (here) rather than the oriental (over there), blackface in an American context reveals how 'white subject formation and subjectivity' (Lott, 1993: 35) has been ambiguously forged by displaying the contested other. By the same token, Chanels illustrate Japanese subject formation and subjectivity because they are situated on a delicate colour line in Japanese popular culture. Chanels constitute a 'contact zone' (Mary Louise Pratt) or an 'interstitial passage' (Homi Bhabha) that separates one territory from another, as well as binding them together. Chanels evoke the mixed reaction of approval and refusal, affirmation and anxiety. Such ambivalence is tied to the presence of their ineffaceable Japanese physiognomy, behind the black facial cream.[4] A weekly magazine called them 'fake blacks' or 'Japan-made blacks (*wasei kokujin*)' (*Shûkan Myôjô*, 23 March 1980), and the public too was fully aware of the falseness of their appearance. As W. T. Lhamon Jr. notes, blackface is not a replacement of one identity with another because 'Assimilation is negotiated in a moving ratio that always retains traces of the previous identity' (1998: 108).

Such ambiguity is in part inherent in a Japanese tradition of spectacle as is found in the practices of cross-racialising (cross-ethnicking) and cross-gendering. Japanese troupes allied with European naturalism (*shingeki*) usually use white facial powder to simulate a white persona. The spectators do not see them as unnatural but as fictional. Likewise, cross-gendered actors/actresses/singers are constitutive of *kabuki*, *Takarazuka revue*, and *enka* ballad (see Robertson 1998: chap. 2) and are not seen as misusing femininity (or masculinity). A subgroup of female enthusiasts of rock groups with heavy makeup ('visual-*kei*') organises fancy-dress parties (*kosupure*) where they pompously appear in the guise of male Gothico-Baroque rockers. Chanels' cross-racialisation can be interpreted in terms of these masking/self-morphing practices. Such examples are not, however, subversive of the established gender order because the deviation is only tolerated in a spectacle governed by utterly different sets of laws and values than those of everyday life. The blackface of Chanels is regarded by audiences as a similarly codified, and therefore tamed transgression.

However, their presence has another aspect, an aspect tied to their class position. One may wonder why Chanels learned a nostalgically sweet harmony style just as hip-hop was emerging. The members of Chanels, educated to high school diploma level at most, grew up in the industrial Keihin area (Tokyo–Yokohama axis). When the band formed, they were working as a latheman, gas station man, truck driver and so on. Some of them were affiliated with motorcycle gangs, the heroic and emblematic group of the working-class male community (see Sato, 1991). As Masahiko Ohyama notes, 1950s classics were popular throughout the 1970s among Japanese working-class youth (2000: 69–70). The 'obsolescence' of the music offered a way for the working-class youth to differentiate themselves from middle-class and university-graduated youth who were largely inclined to the latest hard rock, country rock, progressive rock, soul and other categories.

The first band that broke into the national media from the Keihin working-class community was Carol. As the band's name suggests (in a homage to Chuck Berry's 'Carol'), the greased hair and leather jacket are evidence of their close association with the rebel image of 'wild ones'. Their 1972 debut literally shook the national rock scene, which had been dominated by hippie-like groups. Carol were said to discharge the primary energy of rock'n'roll uncontaminated by sophisticated lyrics and performing technique. Their links with motorcycle gangs became a hallmark for the 'anti-establishment' position of rock (see Sato, 1991).

The obsolescence of fifties' music and fashion thus provided a new meaning in which these working-class youths could invest. Doowop and blackface were to Chanels what rock'n'roll and leather jackets were to Carol. The 'blacking up' of the former unknowingly evoked the 'underclass alliance' (Lhamon, 1998: 152) between whites and blacks in the nascent stage of American minstrelsy (*c.* 1820s–1840s) when blackface was concerned with the practice of 'cross-racial mutuality' (187) to mock the middle-class (segregationist) rebuke that ultimately formed today's standard view of blackface as racist. However, it has been an ambiguous and conflictual mode of expression because it grafts an individual's chosen affiliation onto his/her biological self, but does not erase the latter. The playfulness operates in the mischievous in-between space, in the spectacle of race.

A set of audio-visual symbols chosen by Chanels and Carol are related to a 'detour through fictive identities' or a 'strategical switching of identities', a strategy of uttering interests in a disguised voice when not allowed to address them directly (Lipsitz, 1994: 62, 75). However, one has to be wary about the less strict correspondence between economic status (class) and the cultural expressions in Japan than in many European and American countries. Though an economic and educational disparity certainly affects Japanese lifestyles, it does not always result in clearly distinguishable marks, as is the case of many genres of popular music around the world (this is part of the supposed evidence used to support the idea that Japan is a 'homogenous nation'). In other words, the class boundaries concerning cultural expressions are generally more blurred in Japan. Therefore the underclass connotation of Chanels as described above should not be overstated. This may explain their easy acceptance outside the working class.

Rap, rhyming and r.e.s.p.e.c.t.

In 1999, the English-loaned word of *risupekuto* (respect) became fashionable in Japan as a result of the globalisation of hip-hop jargon (along with 'posse', 'crew' and 'sucker!' amongst others). The word became so fashionable that the *Asahi Shinbun* glossed it for non-initiated readers. A sociologist explained that while 'respect' in African-American hip-hop is a powerful statement of a non-assimilative attitude, in Japan it merely expresses an 'empty moral'. The article criticised stylish but politically insensitive rappers from Japan who neutralise the political significance of hip-hop (*Asahi Shinbun*, 11 December 1999).

Immediately Shirô Sasaki, the member of Rhymester whose 1999 album *Risupekuto* (*Respect*) was mentioned in the article, responded angrily, saying that the album's cover (three rappers in pre-Meiji military uniform, or the mixture of samurai sword and Western apparel) was intended not, as the newspaper suggested, as a 'return to feudalism', but rather as a statement of affiliation with the creative chaos just before the Meiji Restoration, a period before cultural syncretism between Western civilisation and the vernacular system came to be institutionalised. The *Asahi* article, Sasaki continued, portrayed Japanese hip-hop as fakery, in contrast to the supposed authenticity of 'message' rap made in the ghetto (Sasaki, 2000).

There have been recurrent debates over imitation and authenticity in Japanese performers from tango to jazz (Atkins, 2000; Hosokawa, 1998; Savigliano, 1995: chap. 5). As illustrated in the words of Sasaki, few Japanese performers believe themselves to be imitators. Though they admit to heavy 'influence' from outside sources, they are trying hard in myriad ways to make their performance meaningful in local contexts.

In the relatively short history of hip-hop in Japan, the use of Japanese from around 1985–86 marks a dividing line (Gotô, 1997: 43ff). Not only did it make the music more accessible; it also brought about a conscious attempt to adjust foreign sounds to an indigenous milieu. Unlike pop and rock songs, the 'cover' – commonly the first practice of learning and adapting imported popular music – is so inconceivable as to be unfeasible in the case of rap (see also Dai Griffiths' contribution to this volume), though of course the use of quotation in the form of samples is very common. In other words, writing one's own words is a priority for rappers.

In the mid-1980s some Japanese experimented with writing English rap songs, but gained little audience approval. English lyrics, rapper K-Dub Shine recalls after his unsuccessful trial, can never 'represent' (*repezen* in Japanese hip-hop jargon) his Japanese community (*Front*, January 1998: 16). However, finding an appropriate way to write Japanese words to a beat intimately tied to African-American oral poetics and alien to Japanese intonation was much harder than finding the 'rare grooves' used by African-American DJs. Moreover, rhyming was alien to Japanese lyrics. The technical incompatibility between the phonetics and grammar of the Japanese language and the rap style has been gradually overcome by those who have learned by experience the techniques of rhyming and flow, two essentials of rap, in their native language. The years around 1995–96 saw the widespread, though not nationwide, recognition of Japanese-language rap.

The Japanese rap scene is roughly divided into two subcategories: 'party rap' and 'hardcore hip-hop' (see Condry, 2000: 176ff). It is the latter group that draws most ostensibly on African-American culture. Rhymester evidently belongs to this category. Shirô Sasaki admits that economic gaps and racial segregation are less visible in Japan, where oppression against ethnic minority groups and non-conformists has generally gone unnoticed (Sasaki, 2000). For example, the rapper A-Twice (1975–2000), son of an African-American father and a Japanese mother, was known for his straightforward expression of an unstable identity and a marginal position in Japanese society (Eguchi, 2001). Japanese hip-hop can potentially provide a voice for such 'spiritual minorities' who are seeking their own home place under the pressure of rigid political, social, economic and educational systems. Some Japanese rap songs critique school bullying, minority crime, drug use, schoolgirl prostitution, and other social problems closer to their reality than segregation, gang fights and other issues which feature in North American rap.

How to treat Japaneseness is a conundrum for any hip-hopper. Some sample from traditional music, but others (a majority) hesitate to do this, because 'Japanese music' does not sound familiar to contemporary youth and is too alien for the sonic texture they want. Japanese DJs seldom play Japanese records on their turntables. In the words of DJ Krush,

> Though I was born in Japan by chance, I don't know what Japaneseness is, do I? To use the shakuhachi [bamboo flute] because I'm Japanese is out of the question. So, we had better think about what one can do not as a Japanese but as an individual. Foreigners have [fixed] images of Japanese. They superficially associate Japanese with the shakuhachi. We do exploit it [foreigners' received idea] and express what is beneath and deeper inside, Japanese blood. But I don't know what it is.

> (*blast*, February 2000: 61)

The absence of Japaneseness in deejaying makes rapping in Japanese even more crucial for local B-boys to anchor performance in their reality. Fashioning their colloquialisms in disruptive rhyme and flow needs playful craft and a set of quick-witted ruses unprecedented in local popular music. More than DJs, therefore, rappers are conditioned by local thinking.

The lyrics of 'hardcore' hip-hop often pinpoint the opposition between 'us' and 'them'. Such a binarism has led to the practice of 'representing' in hip-hop. Just as African-American rappers represent their 'hood' and community (Forman, 2000), Japanese rappers shout out the names of their posse and locality with pride. The idea of 'representing' is new to Japanese popular music, where references to 'Japan' and 'Japanese'-ness have been almost completely absent. This is because some rappers are susceptible to the kind of criticism seen in the *Asahi* example quoted above. For example, the Rhymester's album in question, *Respect*, includes the following lines:

Risupekuto shitokubeki	You should respect
Japanese hip-hop scene	Japanese hip-hop scene
Mass ga utsutsu nukasu	Blow away
chaban fukitobasuze	The burlesque mass get mad
Oretachino future funk	Our future funk
Korezo sekaini hokorubeki	This is what we should be proud of
Made in Japan as no. 1	Made in Japan as no. 1.

('King of Stage')

Alluding to Ezra Vogel's bestseller of the 1970s (*Japan as Number 1*), Rhymester lauds the 'Japanese hip-hop scene', situated outside mass society. Lines directed against white-collar domination – 'the target is Nippon Corporate Company / The tie and white shirts that tie up your heart' ('Mic no shikyaku' ('An Assassin with a Microphone')) – characterise some of the hardcore hip-hop songs. Such a defiant attitude is not typical of Japanese popular music. For example, oppositional punks in the 1980s sometimes spat on middle-class hypocrisy (ex. Inu's 'Don't Eat Meal', Stalin's 'Stop Jap'), but the punk aesthetic, at least in Japan, had little cultural practice that corresponded to 'representing' in hip-hop.

Among Japanese hip-hoppers 'with attitude', the notion of 'respect' provides a means of connecting themselves with the African-American idea of 'nation'. It makes the local hip-hop community more than a taste-based niche fan circle existing throughout Japan, because it strengthens an emotional and ideological bond with an object of esteem, a bond more explicit than mere fondness. Respect also dictates certain types of behaviour. Through *practising* respect (sampling, fashion, gesture, etc.), hip-hoppers can acquire imaginary 'citizenship' in the African-American 'nation'. K-Dub Shine, for example, states his philosophical alliance with Afrika Bambaataa's Zulu Nation: 'I identify myself as part of the Zulu Nation. I rap as a Zulu nation' (*Front*, January 1998: 19). Twigy, another MC, titled his first album *Al-khadir* ('Green Lord'), a clear reference to his learning of Islamic thought from the New York hip-hop circle. To become part of the translocal hip-hop nation, one does not need to become black any longer: 'we [the hip-hop generation] don't think we wanna be black' (*blast*, August 1999: 15). Here he criticises the fad of (artificially) tanning the skin among contemporary R&B fans and performers. Some DJs despise the use of tanned skins, dread hairstyles, and other 'hip-hop fashions' because hip-hop is not a fashion but a way of life, a state of the spirit (DJ Yutaka, *Front*, October 1998: 79). Yet, many hip-hop fans are strikingly sensitive to American 'street' fashion. Appearance is both irrelevant to the philosophy of hip-hop and crucial as a tribal marker.

If the largest community that African-American rappers represent is determined by a colour line, that of Japanese sympathisers is configured by 'Japan'. In Twigy's words, 'I say, I represent Japan but people misunderstand the meaning. All Japanese represent Japan. The representatives of Japanese' (*Front*, October 1998: 70). Such a way of positioning oneself consciously in Japan is too defiant and too deviant for the conventions of party rap and pop/rock. However, what hardcore rappers call for is not alignment with a nation state named Japan but with a translocal 'hip-hop nation'. As the Rhymester raps, A delicate touch with sincerity, geniuses without glory / A requiem from me to them, hymn of the unbeatable / Pay loyalty to this flag *regardless where you were born and have grown up* / Go to the Promised Land with life skills and wisdom to survive in the mud' ('B-Boyism', emphasis mine). The tropes of flag and hymn evoke a certain type of state nationalism but their imaginary nation goes far beyond the usual borders.

There is no such clearcut entity as 'nation' in the Japanese hip-hop scene but posse, crew, club, magazine, record label and studio all provide spatial and affective territoriality for the members. As outsiders they elusively fantasise about the Bronx or Compton, yet, as Simon Frith notes, music 'both articulates and offers the immediate *experience* of collective identity', experience of 'alternative modes of social interaction' (1996: 273, 275). Sharing the sound experience means sharing emotional reality. It is clear that experiencing a certain collective identity does not instantly alter one's social and cultural identity. But some devotees such as the rappers quoted above may start seeing themselves and their reality from alternative angles. Musical production and consumption allow participants to experience ideal forms of the social, the sexual and the racial/national. Such a self-projection onto a significant (black) other through music is *real* to the participants of a scene, no matter how one may interpret the 'message' or 'feeling' embodied in the language, gesture, fashion, style and sound of otherness. Black music fuels the emotional state of listeners/performers with imaginative and imaginary resources precisely because it comes from outside – socially and racially.

Experiencing blackness is not limited to an erotic/exotic desire as American detractors claim, but is open to an exterior zone where mimicry allows, to use Eric Lott's succinct phrase about blackface, 'one culture's ventriloquial self-expression through the art forms of someone else's' (1993: 92). In whose voice does a ventriloquist speak? One voice in two bodies or two voices in one body? Ventriloquism is an art of borrowed/borrowing voice which presents the dialogue between the ventriloquist and 'double', or the monologue of the fictively divided self. Chanels clearly represent ventriloquial ambiguity through the deliberate *mise-en-scène* of cross-racialisation. Blackface is, to be sure, an extreme case of this ambiguity, but a similar cultural uncertainty is more the rule than the exception in our age of transnational and translocal conjunctures and disjunctures.

Conclusion

In the US, the 'social unconscious' (Lott, 1993: 234) is set as well as disturbed by the concept of, and the cultural practices surrounding, race. But in Japan, the notion of race (*jinshu*) has played a lesser role in the social unconscious than that of nation (*minzoku*). Indeed, it was not until the end of the nineteenth century that the term was invented. It was disseminated by the earliest Japanese anthropologists, who established their discipline after studying abroad (Tomiyama, 1994). As in Europe, the term cannot be dissociated from imperial politics and it is used in various political and (para-)scientific contexts, especially in discourses concerning the confrontation of Japan or 'Asia' with the West (yellow v. white discourse) and the origin of Japanese (northern vs. southern race discourse). It is undeniable that race is important but it is somehow exterior to the inner self. This aradicalised self may have helped to bring 'sheer ignorance' in Japan about race and racism (Russell, 1998: 173).

Instead of *jinshu*, the term of *minzoku* (translation from German *Volk*), literally 'people-collective', has been more persuasive and predominant in the social unconscious in modern Japan. Born from the same anthropological/ethnological cradle as *jinshu*, *minzoku* assumes shared origins, the historical continuity and affective unity, rather than the measurable biological traits fundamental to the notion of race (see Oguma, 1995). To put this schematically, *minzoku* represents culture, and *jinshu* nature. The concept of *minzoku* is almost interchangeable with that of nation and the conflation of them generated the ideology of a single-*minzoku* nation state, an ideology notorious in the age of multiculturalism and affirmative action. (It is curious that the term of 'single-race nation state' has not been current.) Many Japanese claim that their country has no racial segregation and some Japanese politicians make blatantly racist statements, and yet this is less an indication of misrecognition of racial others than it is a demonstration of how their national subjectivity is formed *without* race as a 'complex lived social reality' (Lott, 1993: 35). 'Race thinking' is thus foreign to Japanese national and individual identity. However, its absence has incited rather than hindered the self-reflexive (sometimes parodic, sometimes sincere) appropriation of black music for several generations. Whereas American history textbooks cannot dispense with slavery and abolition, Japanese national-history classes cannot neglect the serial encounter and adaptation of 'advanced' foreign civilisations, from the Chinese writing system to European science. They usually treat receptivity as part of an overall national character. What matters throughout Japanese history, according to this official version, is the melting pot of overseas civilisations, not the promiscuity of races. This narrative celebrates the national cultural power of 'digesting' the non-indigenous. Whether writing systems or computers, Japanese can absorb anything without detriment to their identity. Thus, hybridity is genuinely Japanese. If such 'borrowing' itself is part of Japan's national heritage, then it is difficult to stand out in mainstream society by using such alternative symbolism as black music. The Japanese adaptation of black music is more a one-sided love affair than a mutual communication, because the majority of the performers play mainly in Japan, except for occasional recordings and tours in the US. Their audience and market are predominantly Japanese. Experiencing blackness from afar has already had more than a half-century's history in Japan and the people passionately and respectfully committed to it have little reason to think that they would be rejected by the object of their empathy. Few of them feel any exclusion, certainly not alienation from black heritage. My aim is not to celebrate Japan's cultural cannibalism nor to bemoan the futility of cultural ventriloquism. Instead, I have underlined the need to research processes of adaptation and the production of new meanings, in the discursive, histori-cal and material contexts that enable and condition the individual and collective experience of music.

Acknowledgements

The author thanks David Hopkins, Reiichi Kimoto and Ian Condry for their critical suggestions.

Notes

1. On the similar tactic of celebrating the universality of the particular by a Japanese band, see Hosokawa (1998: 514).

2. According to sociologist Hideki Toyota, NHK (the Japanese Broadcasting Association), when transmitting the music show *Kôhaku Utagassen* to the US, auto-censored the part with the Rats & Star (Chanels) (Ichikawa, 1998: 219). This incident indicates NHK's concern about American acceptance of the band. This of course does not preclude them from excluding the band from the domestic programme.

3. John Russell's remark that 'a tradition of theatrical mimicry of blacks does exist in Japan' since Commodore Perry's minstrel show in 1853 seems to me overstated (1998: 141). The photograph of blackface Japanese (*c.* 1870) he reprinted could have been taken by a photographer in a studio and may not be related to theatre. Russell tried to put the 'Japanese obsession with "blackness"' in a historical context but his rationale is some-times too far-fetched. For example, to prove the roots of 'white supremacy', he quotes Japanese sayings about the beauty of the white female body (1992: 297; see also Cornyetz, 1994: 122). However, traditional 'white' complexions have aesthetically little to do with Caucasian skin colour.

4. Nina Cornyetz and John Russell are among the strongest Anglophone critics of the anti-black racism prevailing in Japan. Focusing upon the sexuality and burlesque of black stereotypes detected in 'negrophile' and 'negrophobic' novels, television and other cul-tural forms, they regard the Japanese either as ignorantly manipulated by the racial prej-udice borrowed from the West (Russell) or as itchingly excited by the flaunted eroticism (Cornyetz). For Russell, 'the popularity of rap music among Japanese youth would seem to lie less in the subversive content of its sociopolitical message than its counterfash-ion...statements and danceability...all of which ultimately serve to confirm black stereotypes' (1992: 316). Apoliticized reception of hip hop is not only characteristic of Japanese mindless youth but is found even among American White students (see Panish, 1997, p.145).

References

AIKURA, H., 1968: 'Kaisetsu: Blues to Kokujin' ('Notes, Blues and the Black People'), in C. Keil, *Toshi no Kokujin Blues*. Tokyo: Ongakunotomosha, 2–9 (translation of *Urban Blues*, Chicago: University of Chicago Press, 1966).

ATKINS, E. T., 2000: 'Can Japanese Sing the Blues? "Japanese Jazz" and the Problem of Authenticity', in T. Craig (ed.), *Japan Pop! Inside the World of Japanese Popular Culture*. Armonk and London: M. E. Sharpe, 27–59.

BHABHA, H. K., 1994: *The Location of Culture*. London and New York: Routledge.

CONDRY, I., 2000: 'The Social Production of Difference. Imitation and Authenticity in Japanese Rap Music', in H. Fehrenbach and U. G. Poiger (eds), *Transactions, Transgressions, Transformations. American Culture in Western Europe and Japan*. New York and Oxford: Berghahn Books, 166–84.

CORNYETZ, N., 1994: 'Fetishized Blackness: Hip Hop and Racial Desire in Contemporary Japan'. *Social Text* 41: 113–39.

EGUCHI, Y., 2001: *Rafra, 24 Sai no Yuigon. Aru Rapper no Shôgai* ('Rafra's Testament of a 24 Year Old. The Life of Rapper'). Tokyo: Poplar Sha.

FORMAN, M., 2000: '"Represent": Race, Space and Place in Rap Music'. *Popular Music* 19 (1): 65–90.

FOWLER, E., 1996: *San'ya Blues: Laboring Life in Contemporary Tokyo*. Ithaca: Cornell University Press.

FRITH, S., 1996: *Performing Rites: On the Value of Popular Music*. Oxford: Oxford University Press.

GOTÔ, A., 1997: *J-rap Izen. Hip Hop Culture wa Kôshite Umareta* ('Before J-rap. How Hip-Hop Culture Was Born'). Tokyo: FM Tokyo Shuppan.

HOSOKAWA, S., 1998: '"Salsa no tiene frontera": Orquesta de la Luz and the Globalisation of Popular Music'. *Cultural Studies* 13 (3): 509–34.

——, 2000: 'Rock and National Language: The Japanese Case', in T. Mitchell and P. Doyle (eds), *Changing Sounds. New Directions and Configurations in Popular Music*. Sydney: Sydney University of Technology, 98–101.

ICHIKAWA, S., 1998: *'Chibikuro Sanpo' no Shuppan wa Zek Hika* ('Is the Publication of the "Story of Little Black Sambo" Good or Bad?'). Kyoto: Kitaôji Shobô.

LHAMON, JR., W. T., 1998: *Raising Cain: Blackface Performance from Jim Crow to Hip Hop*. Cambridge, Mass. and London: Harvard University Press.

LIPSITZ, G., 1994: *Dangerous Crossroads: Popular Music, Postmodernism and the Politics of Place*. London and New York: Verso.

LOTT, E., 1993: *Love and Theft: Blackface Minstrelsy and the American Working Class*. New York and Oxford: Oxford University Press.

MITCHELL, T., 1996: *Popular Music and Local Identity: Rock, Pop and Rap in Europe and Oceania*. London and New York: Leicester University Press.

MITSUI, T., 1993: 'The Reception of the Music of American Southern Whites in Japan', in N. V. Rosenberg (ed.), *Transforming Tradition: Folk Music Revivals Examined*. Urbana and Chicago: University of Illinois Press, 275–293.

NAKAMURA, T., 1969: 'Koenaki Blues no machi Sanya' ('Sanya, the Voiceless Blues Town'). *New Music Magazine*, April: 42–6.

OGUMA, E., 1995:*Tan'itsu Minzoku Shinwano Kigen. Nihonjin no Jigazo no Keifu* ('The origin of The Myth of the Homogeneous Nation'). Tokyo: Shin'yosha.

OHYAMA, M., 2000: 'Rock'n'Roll, Dancing and Motorcycles: An Ethnography of a Motorcycle Gang in a Small Japanese Town'. *Perfect Beat* 5 (1): 67–80.

PANISH, J., 1997: *The Colour of Jazz: Race and Representation in Postwar American Culture*. Jackson: University Press of Mississippi.

ROBERTSON, J., 1998: *Takarazuka: Sexual Politics and Popular Culture in Modern Japan*. Berkeley, Los Angeles and London: University of California Press.

RUSSELL, J. G., 1991: *Nihonjin no Kokujin Kan. Mondai wa 'Chibikuro Sambo' Dakedewa Nai* ('Japanese View on Black People. The Problem Is Not Just "Little Black Sambo"'). Tokyo: Shin Hyôronsha.

——, 1992: 'Race and Reflexivity: The Black Other in Contemporary Japanese Mass Culture', in G. Marcus (ed.), *Rereading Cultural Anthropology*. Durham, N.C. and London: Duke University Press, 296–318.

——, 1995: *Henken to Sabetsu Wa Donoyôni Tsukurareruka. Kokujin Sabetsu Han Yudaya Ishiki Wo Chûshin Ni* ('How Are Prejudice and Segregation Made? With an Emphasis on Black Segregation and Anti-Semitic Consciousness'). Tokyo: Akashi Shobô.

——, 1998: 'Consuming Passions: Spectacle, Self-Transformation, and the Commodification of Blackness in Japan'. *positions* 6 (1): 113–77.

SASAKI, S., 2000: 'Asahi Shinbun Nishida Kensaku Kisha eno Tegami' ('A Letter to the Asahi Journalist Kensaku Nishida'). *blast*, February: 118–19; March: 132–5.

SATO, I., 1991: *Kamikaze Biker: Parody and Anomy in Affluent Japan*. Chicago: University of Chicago Press.

SAVIGLIANO, M. E., 1995: *Tango and the Political Economy of Passion*. Boulder, San Francisco and Oxford: Westview Press.

TAUSSIG, M., 1993: *Mimesis and Alterity: A Particular History of the Senses*, New York and London: Routledge.

TAYLOR, T., 1997: *Global Pop: World Music, World Markets*. New York and London: Routledge.

TITON, J., 1993: 'Reconstructing the Blues: Reflections on the 1960s Blues Revival', in Ned V. Rosenberg (ed.), *Transforming Tradition: Folk Music Revivals Examined*. Urbana and Chicago: University of Illinois Press, 224–40.

TOMIYAMA, I., 1994: 'Kokumin no Tanjô to "Nihon Jinshu"' ('The Birth of Nation and the "Japanese Race"'). *Shisô* 845 (November): 37–56.

15

India song: popular music genres since economic liberalization

Nabeel Zuberi

The complexities involved in Indian popular music illustrate that it, and popular culture in general, are best understood as arenas in which heterogeneous class and regional forces are negotiated. Future studies, it is hoped, will be able to concentrate in greater detail on specific genres and aspects, for popular culture has become too important a feature of modern Indian society to be ignored.

Peter Manuel (1988:175)

India is not non-West; it is India.

Ashis Nandy (1983: 73)

Indian music in a global economy

Indian sounds and images permeate the history of 'Western' popular music and its recorded archive. Sitars drone and twang through Beatles songs and countless psychedelic tracks; Madonna chants a Sanskrit mantra over a glossy synth-and-sequencer wash; rapper Missy Elliot's rhymes try to catch a tripping tabla beat; dance duo Basement Jaxx apes Indian film song sequences in music video; and musicians of the South Asian diaspora weave the sounds of Indian classical, popular and folk music into their rock and dance recordings. The economies and technologies, institutions and discourses that characterize globalization have accelerated musical traffic between India and other parts of the world. World music sections in retailers incorporate significant India collections, and digital technologies put Indian images and sound sources at the fingertips of musical producers and consumers. India has itself become increasingly open to the influences of contemporary music from elsewhere.

This chapter examines Indian popular music culture since the introduction of 'economic liberalization' policies in the early 1990s. Though deregulation of domestic industry and foreign loans increased during the 1970s and

1980s, the Congress government's New Economic Policy (NEP) of 1991 is commonly taken as the point when liberalization began in earnest. Facing a mounting debt crisis, the government was persuaded by the World Bank and International Monetary Fund to allow greater foreign investment into the country and make other necessary 'structural adjustments' (Bhaduri and Nayyar, 1996). Both the left-of-centre United Front (UF) and Hindu nationalist Bharatiya Janata Party (BJP) coalition governments continued the shift toward increasingly market-driven policies in the 1990s. Pro-liberalization economic discourse – now dominant in government, business and the media – has stressed the importance of consumerism for domestic and imported goods among the growing middle classes as a major force in stimulating national economic growth (Varma, 1998: 170–1).

With a population of over 1000 million, India is potentially an enormous market for music products. India's share of the global pop purse is US$250 million – about one-sixth of 1 per cent of the world's music. According to entertainment trade weekly *Screen* (7 April 2000: 17), the national industry's combined turnover has multiplied more than 60 times in the last decade. By 2000, official Indian Music Industry (IMI) figures valued turnover at Rs 1200 crore (1 crore = 100 lakhs = 10 million; 1 lakh = 100 000) and predicted the industry would be worth Rs 2200 crore by 2005. However, piracy still accounts for 35–45 per cent of current turnover. Indian and foreign companies wish to destroy piracy, extend the market for international pop music in India, and increase sales of Indian music overseas. The IMI, formed in 1994, now includes the Indian divisions of Universal Music, BMG, Sony Music International and Virgin Records, along with Indian companies such as Saregama India Ltd (HMV/Gramophone Company of India), Tips, Venus, Magnasound, Milestone and Times Music.

In a transnational economy marked by the rising trade value of cultural goods, India is a major culture-producing nation with global ambitions. For example, a magazine advertisement for the Music Forum 2000 organized by Sony Hi-Fi Audio, MTV and music retailer Planet M featured a large photograph of Punjabi pop star Daler Mehndi in his turban, kurta and shalwar flanked by similarly dressed but diminutive bodies with the superimposed heads of Michael Jackson, Mariah Carey, George Michael, Madonna, Sting and Elton John. Referring to Mehndi's bhangra pop hit 'Tara Rara', the underlying caption read 'Ab Duniya Bole Tara Rara' ('Now the world will say Tara Rara'). The ad further elaborated in English: 'We have music that cuts across languages and cultures. Performers with a style that's unique and popular. So why aren't we up there with the best in the world? Many such questions will be raised and answered at the MTV & Planet M Music Forum. Come and learn how to sing a global tune.' Indian media organizations already exert considerable economic and cultural power in national and regional markets, including South Asia, South-East Asia, Africa and the Middle East/Western Asia. South Asian diaspora populations in these regions and Europe, North America and Australasia also consume Indian cultural commodities. A consideration of Indian music must be aware of music production in India, its export and the presence of Indian sounds in international music, as well as the influence of international music in India. India is undergoing a new stage of integration into the global economy that cannot simply be accounted for by the largely one-way traffic denoted by the term 'cultural imperialism' (Hesmondhalgh, 1999; Frith, 2000). However, changes in the media industries, especially cable and satellite television, also contribute to India's 'development' into a consumer society.

The impact of television

The new deregulated television culture has had a massive impact on the texture of everyday life. Many Indians may now watch as many domestic and foreign channels as are commonly available in Western Europe and North America. Commercial networks like STAR TV and Zee have challenged the centralized control of broadcast news and information by state broadcaster Doordarshan. In entertainment programming, drama serials debate women's roles in middle-class urban India. Game shows like STAR's enormously successful *Kaun Banega Crorepati* (a version of *Who Wants to be a Millionaire?* hosted by film megastar Amitabh Bachchan) combine the Indian love of general knowledge quizzes with a post-liberalization consumer desire for wealth and celebrity. These shows and the ubiquitous commercial films and music videos occupy most air time on the privately owned and now semi-commercial state channels (Page and Crawley, 2001; French and Richards, 2000; Singhal and Rogers, 2001; Thomas, 1999). *Cassette Culture* (1993), Peter Manuel's excellent study of the enormous impact of cassettes on Indian music during the 1980s, should now be supplemented with a consideration of music television as technology and cultural form. In particular, MTV India has shaped the sound and look of popular music and provided novel modes of address to the Indian listener-viewer-consumer. MTV has also become a key institution in defining the direction of India's media culture. Music television has been so influential that those who have come of age in the post-liberalization era are routinely described as part of the 'MTV generation'. Music channels like MTV and Channel [V] have been instrumental in producing new styles of popular music.

Music genres

My focus on music genres in this chapter is primarily informed by approaches in media and cultural studies. Richard Middleton (1999: 145) argues for a conception of genre 'as analogous to a discursive formation, in the sense that in such a formation there is regulation of vocabulary, types of syntactic unit, formal organization, characteristic themes, modes of address (who speaks to whom and after what fashion)'. Genre analysis considers the triadic relationship between audience, musical text and industry. Genres embody sets of conventions, the meanings of which are negotiated between industry, the media and consumers. Keith Negus (1999: 4) defines genre as 'the way in which musical categories and systems of classification shape the music that we might play and listen to, mediating both the experience of music, and its formal organization by an entertainment industry'. I discuss the sound of the music and its visualization, but also how these forms are affected by the mediation of emergent consumer-citizen lifestyles in the post-liberalization state.

Indian popular music lacks the wide plurality and rapidly accumulating distinctions that mark international pop culture and its genre consciousness. If genre is a form of product differentiation, then the Indian marketplace encompasses relatively few categories: film songs, Indipop, international, devotional/religious, ghazal and regional folk music. The distinction between the two most commercially successful types – film and Indipop – results more from media industry location than the sonic characteristics of the music. In February 1999 when I interviewed Mishaal Verma, then director of programming at MTV India, he said that when the network asked viewers about their musical tastes, the audience's most popular categories were 'film', 'fast' and 'slow'. Media industries aim to overcome such troublesome consumer 'naivety' by gradually moulding tastes and prejudices. According to Verma:

> In the Asian market, success lies in localization. There are two things a channel needs to do. It needs to survive and lead. While we reflect audience tastes with Hindi film music, there is a consolidated effort by the industry and the channel to play International, to educate the consumer. There's a huge youth market in this country and an increasing listener base.

Song culture and the hegemony of the Hindi film song

Because film songs have been the dominant commercial music since the 1930s, Indian popular music has had an integral visual component. In this chapter I focus on genre change in Hindi film music and Indipop (non-film music). Music television has provided the crucial visual space and promotional medium for Indipop and international pop. I do not examine significant bodies of Tamil, Malayalam and other 'vernacular' language film and pop music, though the hegemonic pan-Indian, indeed pan-South Asian Hindi film song form exerts a powerful influence on these traditions too.

Film songs (filmi geet) with their catchy hooks and beats percolate through the landscape, pumping out of shops, paan/betel vendors, cars, radios and television in both public places and private residences. An array of activities maintain song consciousness in everyday life. Live amateur song performance remains a stronger element in Indian public and private life than in Britain and North America. Indians sing and hum to themselves in public and in private during work and leisure activities. Song melody is integrated into the rhythms of daily routine. More ritualized singing takes place collectively at parties, weddings and many kinds of social gathering. Film songs dominate 'live' and mediated soundscapes.

The song has a mobile identity in public life and the commodity form, but it comes first, before the artist, songwriter, producer or film. Films may have been long forgotten, while their songs continue to circulate in popular memory. This also leads, like vintage Jamaican riddims still played in the

Kingston dancehall, to a certain temporal ambiguity about the song's history. Even if it was recorded 40 years ago, the song enlivens the present, as a resource to be drawn upon repeatedly. The popularity of Antakshari, a party game that is now a successful television show, testifies to the public's desire to continue performing the repertoire of film songs.

Songs are packaged in a multiplicity of commodity forms: under the singer's name, the film title, the name of the actor who lipsynched the lyrics, the lyricist, the music director (composer), and sometimes even the film's producer. In the marketplace, the song's belonging or identity moves across these various individuals and media sites. However, consumer loyalty is much greater to the song than any individual or film. The song's identity supersedes its authorship or any of its origins. This makes it more flexible to promote across the multiple identities involved in its manufacture, but also harder to pin down in any one of those identities.

The changing film song: the 'decline' of lyrics and ascendancy of repetitive beats

The filmi geet has always been – whatever its musical form – simply a song from a film. With the advent of talkies in 1931 actors were chosen for both their acting and singing abilities. But by the late 1940s the employment of the 'playback' singer had become the norm. Vocals were recorded by a professional singer in a studio. On film the actor lipsynched the words in the song 'picturization'. From the outset the film song was a generic hybrid, mixing and matching Indian and Western instruments in small groups and then larger orchestral arrangements. Composers liberally mixed classical raag forms and indigenous folk music with Western musical structures such as foxtrots and waltzes. The Hindi film song remains a case of what Arnold (1988) calls 'mass-market musical eclecticism'. There also persists a division of labour in song composition. The music director writes, conducts and usually produces the music, while a lyricist writes the words. Collaboration between lyricist and music director has decreased since the 1950s as the separation of these professional tasks has become more marked.

During the 1960s the studio orchestra on a film song recording grew in size. Elaborate arrangements and breaks allowed strings to soar and gave wider scope to recording effects such as reverb and echo. Songs became longer as the formats of vinyl singles, EPs and LPs replaced the 78 r.p.m. disc. Despite these technological changes, film and radio (after the late 1950s) were the primary means through which most Indians listened to recorded popular music.

By the mid-1970s, the introduction of electronic instruments such as synthesizers began the downsizing of film music production in the studio. The electrification of film music included the use of rock and funk-influenced wah-wah guitar and more abrasive, metallic tones such as the drum machines used in European and American disco music. For example, R. D. Burman's music for *Shaan* (1980) resembles Giorgio Moroder's erotic disco productions with Donna Summer. The more beat-driven and raucous Western sounds had usually found their visual home in the Bombay/Bollywood film's nightclub or 'cabaret' scenes, but electronic instrumentation and foreign musical textures have burst out of these cinematic spaces into many kinds of song picturization.

The ascendancy of the beat since the 1970s (synonymous for most Indian critics with Western rock and pop influences) has been matched by the perceived decline of the lyric. The generation of Urdu (and mainly Muslim) ghazal poets, such as Kaifi Azmi and Sahir Ludhianvi, who wrote Hindustani (a hybrid of Hindi and Urdu) lyrics was first dislocated by Partition in 1947 and then gradually disappeared after Hindi film's 'golden age' in the 1950s. Today the weak cultural currency of Urdu has been replaced with a sentimental nostalgia for Indian Muslim affect at the same time that populist Hindu nationalism has attempted to erase the living contemporary signs of secular Muslim culture. Only the screenwriter-turned-film lyricist Javed Akhtar and director-lyricist-poet Gulzar continue to significantly connect the Urdu ghazal to Hindi film song, though in somewhat diluted version. Despite much touted ghazal revivals, today's commercial artists such as Jagjit Singh and Pankaj Udhas perform ghazals that lack the multiple levels of lyrical meaning – romantic, erotic, spiritual and political – essential to the non-film ghazals of, for example, the nineteenth-century poet Ghalib and the twentieth century's Faiz Ahmed Faiz.

The oft-repeated melancholic refrain 'where have all the lyrics gone?' articulates not only a yearning for bygone Urdu/Hindustani lyricism, but anxiously responds to the greater presence of vernacular banter in song. The tension between the more poetic Hindustani or Hindi lyric and urban vernacular has animated film songs for many years, often as the basis for humour about class differences. But the contrast appears more aggravated since the late 1980s. This may be due to the changing constituency of film audiences in the period. Movie theatres experienced decreasing audiences, as middle-class film viewers retreated to their domestic VCRs. The urban working-class audience had less time for 'poetry', preferring bump-and-grind numbers and the 'vulgar' vernacular of contemporary urban life. The conflict in lyric styles is embodied in the difference between the upper-class romantic hero Shah Rukh Khan and his working-class comedy counterpart Govinda in Hindi films during the last decade (Inden, 1999).

Urban vernacular in popular song lyrics may also be more prominent due to the influence of television. As networks 'Indianized' their programming in the 1990s, the unofficial language of the cities entered media spaces through news and entertainment programming. The greater frequency of English words and phrases in song lyrics also reflects Zee, STAR and MTV's acknowledgement and encouragement of a hybrid urban language – Hinglish – a composite of Hindi and English (Thussu, 2000). Despite these changes to the linguistic register of film songs, most critical discourse (popular and academic) still places greater value on the more 'poetic' and romantic lyric with a strong melody.

Many critics see the increasing emphasis on rhythm as a regretful encroachment on song structure. Synthetic dance beats have, according to this view, upset the fine balance between words and music in the filmi geet. For example, the eminent musicologist Ashok D. Ranade (1998: 297) writes of post-MTV film music: 'The contemporary musico-cinematic structures are relying on strong rhythms and loud sounds – the two musical components, traditionally and universally pressed into service, to replace individuals with a collective mass, and thinking and questioning minds, with obedient organisms.' Ranade goes on to quote Plato's injunction that changing the rhythms of the state will lead to anarchy. Such shrill claims and the fears that dance music will make young women more physically expressive and sexually independent are reason enough to analyse the impact of 'repetitive beats' on the MTV generation.

Hindi remix

The prevalence of dance rhythms can be attributed to changes in technologies of musical production, exposure to more international pop through television, and the new leisure practices of the middle and upper classes in urban India. Hindi remix has emerged as one of the new genres or market categories in the last decade. The style consists of largely well-known Hindi film songs remixed or re-recorded with greater emphasis on electronic drums and bass frequencies. Hindi remix is a compromise between the resilient lyric and melody of the older Hindi film song and the rhythms of contemporary global dance music genres.

One of the significant influences on the formation of Hindi remix was the success of British producer Bally Sagoo's *Bollywood Flashback* album (Sony, 1992). Sagoo re-recorded well-known Hindi film hits with ragga, rap, house and electro rhythms. In the early 1990s, he appeared on MTV India's *Club MTV*, mixing his Western beats with Hindi film songs 'live' on the studio set. But Hindi remix also has a pre-history in the cheaply produced cassette versions of famous hits recorded by Gulshan Kumar's T-series label.

Kumar revolutionized the music industry in the 1980s through low-cost production and pricing of cassette music (Manuel, 1993). Unknown vocalists would record cover versions of old songs that were sold using the name of the original artist and image in bold print; the new vocalists were listed in small print. The cassette *Hits of Kishore Kumar* might bear the image of Kishore on its cover, but all the songs would be performed in the style of Kishore by a newcomer. T-series was able to profit from this practice because consumers were duped. But these tapes were also successful because Indian consumers remain primarily devoted to the song, not the artist. In the mid-1980s some music lovers dismissed these cassette cover versions or jhankaar tapes as 'truck driver music'. Ironically, many of the singers who began recording cover versions with T-series (such as Kumar Sanu and Sonu Nigam) are now major recording artists and playback singers.

Improvements in cassette technology helped disseminate Hindi remix, a format that appears to give value for money with a continuous stream of at least 20 'non-stop hits'. The sound quality of the Indian cassette (still the most affordable and thus dominant format) and its longevity have historically been very poor; the tape did not run smoothly and its plastic carriage fell apart easily. Vinay Sapnu, chief of programming at Polygram India, points out the multiple attractions of the Hindi remix cassette for consumers and producers:

> Today's generation wants nothing but the best in terms of sound quality. When you remix a popular song of the 50s or 60s with advanced technology you give them a good quality product which is rich in lyrical content. It is like enhancing an already popular product. And what is more, not only the new but even the older generation enjoys it.

(Wagle, 1997a: 33)

The improvement in technical quality has meant that music companies can differentiate their official releases from pirated copies and thus justify raising the price of cassettes. Between 1994 and 1996 over 100 Hindi remix albums were issued in India. T-series began releasing its Mega Mix collections in 1994. HMV (the Gramophone Company of India), which had a virtual monopoly for much of Indian recording history, has a vast back catalogue available for remixing. Remixes such as *Yeh Mera Dil/This is My Heart* and *The Greatest Dance Music Selection* each sold over 300 000 (3 lakh) units. Playback singer Asha Bhosle's *Rahul and I* album, a re-recording of some of her best-known 1960s and 1970s collaborations with her late ex-husband, music director R. D. Burman, sold 5 lakh units in 1996. R. D. remixes themselves constitute practically a sub-genre. HMV remixes constitute just one part of a broader programme of re-releasing old songs in new packaging, under the sign of the singer, music director, film title and period. The latter has introduced a relatively novel sense of historical consciousness with which to frame film music.

The remix aesthetic relies on a playful camp sensibility as old film song clips are recontextualized in music television schedules. MTV and Channel [V] adopt an ironic but affectionate posture to these old clips, cutting and mixing them DJ-style. Post-Sagoo, the Hindi remix phenomenon has developed other directions through UK-based South Asian musicians, many of whom routinely sample snatches of Bollywood dialogue and orchestral string breaks in their music. The London-based label Outcaste's *Bollywood Funk* and *Bollywood Breaks Sampler* both present Hindi film music for the dance floor filtered through a sensibility informed by camp and the fan connoisseurship of Afro-American genres like soul, funk and hip-hop. These Brit-Asian soulboys indulge in funky trainspotting as they plunder the past, wilfully obscuring the discographical sources of the music like an exclusive DJ intent on the uniqueness of their set and the anonymity of their white label vinyl. A postmodern perspective also informs the Hindi remix of Northern California-based DJ Shadow and the Automator on *Bombay the Hard Way: Guns, Cars and Sitars*, their 'treated' compilation of 1970s film music (not songs) by music directors Anandji-Kalyandji. Fragments of English dialogue from these Bollywood 'brownsploitation' movies add an extra frisson to the original recordings. Unlike the original film soundtrack albums, such revisits to the Bollywood sound archive do not just reissue the song, but include incidental, non-vocal music and Hinglish dialogue.

There is not a huge gap between these 'foreign' reconstitutions of Hindi film music and Hindi remix in India itself. Increasingly, contemporary film and Indipop feature Hindi vocals with ragga rhythms, Jamaican-style toasting and US-style rapping, albeit in crude form without the vocal skills of their sources. The Hindi remix aesthetic has become so pervasive that new releases of film music are keenly followed weeks later with a dance remix version of the soundtrack's songs on cassette and CD. In the last few years, Hindi remixes have been joined by dance mixes of Indipop, Goa trance, Latin pop and Euro-disco. In fact, dance mix tapes increasingly feature a combination of tracks from all these genres. The juxtapositions in these mix tapes reflect the mix of music found on Channel [V] and MTV. The brand identities of music television networks feature prominently on cassettes and CDs, which are released in association with music companies. The music channels have also been active agents in creating a broader DJ culture through dance programming and corporate-sponsored DJ competitions in the major metropolises.

Indipop

Music television has played an essential part in the formation of non-film popular music as a significant if still minor music category (in commercial terms). The term Indipop can encompass any non-film music from bhangra and Indian rock to regional folk-influenced ballads. For example, the Sony/Virgin compilation *Now That's What I Call Indipop* (1999) features female vocalist Shubha Mudgal with a heavy rock song, the Bombay Vikings with Hindi dance pop featuring Jamaican Patois toasting, Alisha Chinnai singing over a Latin Caribbean rhythm, Punjabi bhangra artist Malkit Singh and Pakistani 'Sufi' rock group Junoon.

For many analysts, Indipop is a step towards creating more long-term and stable music industry practices, less beholden to film producers with short-term economic goals and criminal underworld influences. This expectation centres on the growth of Indipop as a genre and market segment. Sales of Indipop have increased – not per unit by a particular artist, but across more artists – potentially democratizing musical production. At a July 1998 music forum organized by MTV, Shashi Gopal of Magnasound reported that Indipop constituted over 3 per cent of the 21 000 titles sold in India. Industry executives professed hopes that the Indipop market share would reach 30 per cent early in the next century. However, this goal has failed to materialize. Hit albums by Indipop artists such as Alisha Chinnai, Daler Mehndi and Colonial Cousins have been followed by market flops. The Indian music industry has failed to regulate the procedures of artist and repertoire (A&R) and marketing departments in any long-term way. The pressure to produce the hit that will persuade the public to buy the cassette or CD has resulted in huge production budgets of up to Rs 25 lakh for music videos that require exotic locations, models and dancers to meet the thematic conventions and production values of music television. Such capital outlay has not guaranteed success. Many film music composers and singers record Indipop albums for the sake of their own artistic identities, free of the formulaic constraints of the Bollywood masala picture. But the record companies still cannot match the high one-off payments film producers can make to in-demand musicians. Even A. R. Rahman, a successful artist in both film and Indipop – his patriotic 1997 *Vande Mataram* is the best-selling Indipop album – has gradually done more work overseas, frustrated with the lack of artistic autonomy as a film composer.

The media industries and music into the twenty-first century

Film producers and their banners (companies) still dominate the music industry. Cassette sales have become increasingly vital to a film's financial success. Since the late 1980s, some film soundtrack albums have been more profitable than the films themselves. Cassettes now routinely receive their official launch with lavish parties and press junkets some weeks before the film is released in theatres. Music companies like Tips and T-Series have ventured into film production. However, large multinationals like Sony have been in a stronger position to purchase the expensive domestic and increasingly lucrative international rights from a handful of successful film producers.

Film companies also have bigger budgets for film-song picturizations than music companies have for music videos. These elaborate sequences absorb a disproportionate amount of the film's total budget, given their relatively small screen time. Only fragments of these picturizations are released to the music channels before the film's release, since film producers fear that exposure to the whole song on television will dissuade viewers from going to see the film at a theatre. A symbiotic, if uneasy relationship has developed between Bollywood and music television. The MTV style suffuses the mise-en-scène and editing of Hindi films like *Dil To Pagal Hai/My Heart is Crazy* (1997). Film-song picturizations and music videos feature the same models and dancers, choreographed like the dance music videos of R&B and pop artists in Europe and America. Indian choreographers have still not got over the impact of Michael Jackson's *Thriller* video and the aerobic workouts of sister Janet's rhythm nation. In a single five- or six-minute song sequence, the film may cut between foreign locations in Scotland, South Africa, New Zealand, Switzerland, Canada and India. Filmed songs continue to offer vicarious tourism for Indian audiences and, in the post-liberalization era, present spectacles of conspicuous consumption with their brand name clothes and accessories.

In the post-liberalization period Indian media industries look outwards. They seek to maintain dominance in the South Asian region and use the diaspora market as a base to expand their influence. Music companies forge alliances with Western-based transnationals in order to both expand the market for Indian sounds and sell English-language pop to India (which currently accounts for 10 per cent of the national market). Super Cassettes, the owners of T-series which controls about 65 per cent of the film music and Indipop market, has forged an alliance with Time Warner to market music in the South-East Asian region. T-series is converting its extensive back catalogue into MP3 files as it goes online with one of the many Silicon Valley companies run by new Americans of Indian descent. Much of the business rhetoric in the move to online music sales targets the more profitable NRI (non-resident Indian) or diasporic sector rather than the Indian market. According to the *Indian Express* in January 2001, a nation of one billion people still only has 4.3 million PCs. The telephone network still has chronic infrastructural problems. E-commerce is unlikely to be significant in the near future because credit cards are still rare. India's capacity for international telecom traffic remains only 780 megabits per second (mbps), a mere 1.4 per cent of that available in China. Internet access continues to be most widespread amongst the 18–24-year-old age group, mainly in the middle and upper classes. Given the relatively high costs of music production, distribution and consumption through these new technologies, the cassette will remain the dominant music technology in India for some time to come.

Indian consumers will continue to want their music visualized. The most popular new stereo systems feature all-in-one cassette, CD and VCD (video compact disc) players. Films and compilations of song picturizations can be bought and rented on VCD in neighbourhood bazaars as video becomes an extinct technology in urban India. Music television's visualization of popular music sounds may lead to a proliferation of language-specific genres, as Channel [V] and MTV venture into regional territories, broadcasting in languages such as Tamil and Bengali. This might see an expansion of vernacular non-Hindi popular music, though the history of the film song suggests that the musical form will be pan-Indian, with language not music providing the major differences between the regions.

Music and the middle classes

Music television and record companies concentrate on an urban, middle-class youth market. For the first time in its history, India has as many people living in its towns and cities as in rural areas. Surveys estimate that the 'consuming classes' include anywhere between 200 million and 500 million people. There has been some ambiguity in defining the middle class in India. Ashis Nandy (1983: 5) argues that the 'Indian upper-middle class may have some of the economic features of an elite, but it has not tried to distance itself from the culture of the lower-middle class', while 'the lower-middle class is shot through with fears of demotion to the proletariat and lives with the anxieties associated with that fear and with the standard hopes and ambitions of the middle class. It cherishes its political-cultural links with the upper-middle class.' Writing in her ethnography of women viewers of Indian television, Purnima Mankekar (1999: 9) suggests that those 'who were barely middle class nonetheless aspired to middle-class status via the acquisition of consumer goods; by their efforts to attain middle class "respectability" such as through the ways in which they socialized and disciplined their daughters and daughters-in-law; and in how they positioned themselves as citizen-subjects of the Indian nation'. Nandy (1983: 6) makes the larger claim that the 'passions of, and self-expressions identified with the lower-middle class – for that matter, the middle class as a whole – now constitute the ideological locus of Indian politics'. And Arjun Appadurai and Carol Breckenridge (1995: 7) also stress that in 'the society of consumption' in India, the 'middle class – both actual and potential – is the social basis of public culture formations'. Pro-liberalization discourse has tended to amplify the buying power of the mid-dle classes as the machine of 'development', even though its consumption patterns for most durable goods still lag behind South-East Asia, Latin America and China. As Varma (1998: 182) points out, this is still a middle class in a post-colonial nation with a minimum of 250 million Indians still going hungry every day, and 290 million Indians who cannot read or write.

At the same time, there might not be as huge a gap as we imagine in the genre mix of music heard across social classes in urban India. MTV's Mishaal Verma describes a lower-class neighbourhood in Bombay in 1999:

> There's a basti [neighbourhood] in front of me, across from my place. Every day those bastards would get up and start their bhajans at 5:30 in the morning and then play their music which was Hindi film music. Then it was Ricky Martin. Of course, it's a pirated cassette. Now you hear Daler Mehndi, 'Macarena', Ricky Martin's 'Un dos tres – the Maria Song', and Aqua's 'Barbie Girl'.

The CD DJs at exclusive dance parties, hotel discotheques and clubs play a similar blend of international, Hindi film and Indipop hits. At one private New Year's Eve dance party I attended in Ahmedabad (around the same time of year that Verma was being woken up by his neighbourhood sounds), a couple of hundred young men and women in designer clothes danced around a swimming pool with silent MTV projected against a cloth screen to accom-pany the CDs. Most of these music enthusiasts may not yet have been aware of the vast spectrum of musical genres in 'the West'. They could still not distinguish between hard house and deep house, techno and trance, rock and post-rock. But they already understood the significance of labels such as Tommy Hilfiger, Calvin Klein, Benetton and Levi Strauss and, thus, the elaboration of distinctions vital to consumer capitalism.

Acknowledgements

I would like to thank Shuchi Kothari for her crucial insights into Indian music and film culture and Dave Hesmondhalgh for his invaluable editorial help during the writing of this chapter.

References

APPADURAI, A. AND C. A. BRECKENRIDGE, 1995: 'Public Modernity in India', in C. A. Breckenridge (ed.), *Consuming Modernity: Public Culture in a South Asian World*. Minneapolis: University of Minnesota Press, 1–20.

ARNOLD, A., 1988: 'Popular Film Song in India – A Case of Mass Market Musical Eclecticism', in P. Oliver (ed.), *Popular Music in India*. New Delhi: Cambridge University Press/Manohar, 177–8.

BHADURI, A. AND D. NAYYAR, 1996: *The Intelligent Person's Guide to Liberalization*. New Delhi: Penguin.

BROSIUS, C. AND M. BUTCHER, 1999: 'Introduction: Image Journeys', in C. Brosius and M. Butcher (eds), *Image Journeys: Audio-Visual Media and Cultural Change in India*. New Delhi: Sage, 11–39.

FRENCH, D. AND M. RICHARDS (eds), 2000: *Television in Contemporary Asia*. New Delhi: Sage, 59–68.

FRITH, S., 2000: 'The Discourse of World Music', in G. Born and D. Hesmondhalgh (eds), *Western Music and its Others: Difference, Representation and Appropriation in Music*. Berkeley: University of California Press.

HESMONDHALGH, D., 1999: 'Globalisation and Cultural Imperialism: A Case Study of the Music Industry', in R. Kiely and P. Marfleet (eds), *Globalisation and the Third World*. London and New York: Routledge, 163–83.

INDEN, R., 1999: 'Transnational Class, Erotic Arcadia and Commercial Utopia in Hindi Films', in BROSIUS AND BUTCHER (1999), 41–66.

MANKEKAR, P., 1999: *Screening Culture, Viewing Politics: An Ethnography of Television, Womanhood, and Nation*. Durham, N.C. and London: Duke University Press.

MANUEL, P., 1988: 'Popular Music in India: 1901–1986', in P. Oliver (ed.), *Popular Music in India*. New Delhi: Cambridge University Press/Manohar, 157–76.

——, 1993: *Cassette Culture: Popular Music and Technology in North India*. Chicago and London: University of Chicago Press.

MIDDLETON, R., 1999: 'Form', in Bruce Horner and Thomas Swiss (eds), *Popular Music and Culture*. Malden, Mass.: Blackwell, 141–55.

NANDY, A., 1983: *The Intimate Enemy*. New Delhi: Oxford University Press.

NEGUS, K., 1999: *Music Genres and Corporate Culture*. London and New York: Routledge.

ODELL, M., 2001: 'Singh the Merciless'. *Q* (March), 54–6.

PAGE, D. AND CRAWLEY, W., 2001: *Satellites over South Asia: Broadcasting Culture and the Public Interest*. New Delhi, Thousand Oaks and London: Sage.

RANADE, A. N. 1998: *Essays in Indian Ethnomusicology*. New Delhi: Munshiram Manoharlal Publishers Pvt. Ltd.

RICHARDS, M. AND D. FRENCH, 2000: 'Globalisation, Television and Asia', in FRENCH AND RICHARDS (2000), 13–27.

SINGHAL, A. AND E. M. ROGERS, 2001: *India's Communication Revolution: From Bullock Carts to Cyber Marts*. New Delhi, Thousand Oaks and London: Sage.

THOMAS, A. O., 'Up-Linked yet Down-Played: Understanding Transnational Satellite Television in Asia'. *Media Asia* 26 (3): 132–8.

THUSSU, D. K. 2000: 'The Hinglish Hegemony: The Impact of Western Television on Broadcasting in India', in FRENCH AND RICHARDS (2000), 293–311.

VARMA, P., 1998: *The Great Indian Middle Class*. New Delhi: Viking.

VASUDEVAN, R. S., 2000: 'Introduction', in R. S. Vasudevan (ed.), *Making Meaning in Indian Cinema*. New Delhi: Oxford University Press, 1–36.

WAGLE, J., 1997: 'Remixes Move up the Charts'. *Screen*, 25 July: 33.

16

The 'pop-rockization' of popular music

Motti Regev

The question of 'rock', 'pop' and popular music seems to haunt popular music scholars and commentators. Two issues tend to be at the focus of attention in this context. One is the relationship between 'rock' and 'pop', and the other the place of 'rock' in popular music history. The confusion about the terms 'pop' and 'rock' can be illustrated by several quotes. Here, for example, is a quote from a scholarly handbook of popular music:

> Rock'n'roll was created by the grafting together of the emotive and rhythmic elements of the blues, the folk elements of country & western music, and jazz forms such as boogie-woogie. Pop is seen to have emerged as a somewhat watered-down, blander version of this, associated with a more rhythmic style and smoother vocal harmony.

> (Shuker, 1998: 226)

Shuker echoes here the familiar distinction between 'rock' as the more 'authentic' or 'artistic' sector of popular music, and 'pop' as the more 'commercial' and 'entertainment' sector (see also Hesmondhalgh, 1996). The following quote, from an album review by a leading New York popular music critic, represents a different view:

> Americans enticed by talk of 'rock'-dance fusion should bear in mind the cultural deprivation of our siblings across the sea. Befuddled by the useless 'rock'–'pop' distinction, they believe 'rock' is something that happened in the '70s. The more inquisitive among them are aware of Pearl Jam and Nirvana, but if they've ever heard of Los Lobos or Hüsker Dü they probably think they're 'pop'.

> (Christgau, 2000: 321)

For Christgau, there is no real difference between 'pop' and 'rock' – they are interchangeable. Sometimes 'popular music' as an all-encompassing term is preferred over the two. But 'popular music' is not the same as 'pop'.

> While the use of the word 'popular' in relation to the lighter forms of music goes back to the mid-nineteenth century, the abbreviation 'pop' was not in general use as a generic term until the 1950s when it was adopted as the umbrella name for a special kind of musical product aimed at the teenage market.

> (Gammond, 1991: 457)

Gammond goes on, in this encyclopedic entry on 'pop', to exemplify the term by referring mostly to the history of 'rock'. The issue, in other words, is far from being settled.

The place and role of 'rock' in the history of popular music is another source of confusion and disagreement. Negus provides here a useful discussion of the issue (Negus, 1996: 136–63). Developing an argument against the division of popular music history into 'eras', and especially against what he believes is an overemphasis on the 'rock era' (as exemplified in Frith, 1981; Grossberg, 1992; Wicke, 1990), he argues that rock was not as revolutionary as some scholars have believed it to be. Drawing on Lipsitz (1990) and on Van Der Merwe (1989), Negus demonstrates that rock was largely based on a logic of 'dialogue' with various musical genres that preceded it, and in fact was (just) one additional moment in the history of popular music. Pointing to the fact that the most commercially successful album during the 1960s – the peak of the 'rock era' – was the film soundtrack *The Sound of Music*, he also argues that the 'rock era' (approximately 1955–80) was not necessarily dominated by 'rock'. In the same vein, Negus rejects the notion that rock 'died' in the late 1970s, as suggested by some scholars (Grossberg, 1986; Frith, 1988) and points to the fact that there are several histories of rock, not one. Negus, in other words, makes a strong case against the conventional belief, widely accepted as historical and cultural truth by most writers on popular music, that the emergence of 'rock' in the mid-1950s stands as a 'great divide' in the history of popular music (see Peterson, 1990), and that after 1980 'rock' lost its genuine meaning.

The preoccupation with the relationship between 'rock' and 'pop' and with the historical role of 'rock' is obviously laden with value judgements and ideological concerns, which sometimes seem to be of interest to aficionados only. But this is not a matter for pop and rock pundits alone. Given the cultural place popular music holds within late modern culture, a proper sociological understanding of its role is certainly necessary.

Such sociological understanding requires a descriptive interpretation of the field of popular music. My point is not to clarify the exact relationship between 'pop' and 'rock' (I do not think this is really possible), but rather to portray one phenomenon, which I call 'pop/rock', that came to dominate popular music, or rather the conceptualization of popular music, in the second half of the twentieth century. In what follows, 'pop/rock' is delineated by three major characteristics that underlie its current condition: a typical set of creative practices, a body of canonized albums, and two logics of cultural dynamic.

The rock aesthetic

A major characteristic of popular music is the interrelatedness of most, if not all, of the genres and styles of which it consists. While it is true that popular music consists of many different styles and genres, each one of them perceived sometimes as an articulation of a specific micro or macro identity, it is also true that a large proportion of these genres are interconnected in their histories and stylistic genealogies. There is a cultural logic that allows us to group together, under the umbrella term of 'pop/rock', names such as Britney

Spears, Metallica, Public Enemy, Oasis, Khaled, Joni Mitchell, Aphex Twin, Bob Marley and the Who, while at the same time excluding names such as Dean Martin and Ethel Merman – and, indeed, *The Sound of Music* soundtrack. Put differently, there is an institutional convention that gathers genres such as rap/hip-hop, electro-dance, mainstream pop, heavy metal, alternative rock, reggae, 'classic' rock, and others, into one web or meta-category called 'pop/rock'. 'Pop/rock' may be interpreted of course as a cultural construct, produced and sustained by interests in the field of popular music, of which those of the music industry are the most salient. But knowing that a phenomenon is a cultural construct does not diminish the reality of its existence. This is a basic sociological truth. Within the contemporary cultural reality of popular music, the meta-genre of 'pop/rock' became an institutional fact. The question, therefore, is not whether we may or may not refer to 'pop/rock' as one phenomenon, but rather what is the nature of the connection between all the genres 'pop/rock' is made of.

I think that what connects the many different styles and genres of 'pop/-rock' into one web or meta-category is the fact that they all share the same set of production, or rather creative practices. This set of practices consists of extensive use of electric and electronic instruments, sophisticated studio techniques of sound manipulation, and certain techniques of vocal delivery, mostly those signifying immediacy of expression and spontaneity. I want to call the set of creative practices around which 'pop/rock' is organized the *rock aesthetic*.

The *rock aesthetic* is a set of constantly changing practices and stylistic imperatives for making popular music based on the use of electric and electronic sound textures, amplification, sophisticated studio craftsmanship, and 'untrained' and spontaneous techniques of vocal delivery. It should be stressed that these practices include sampling and turntabling. It means that styles of popular music largely based on electronics that emerged in the 1980s and 1990s (hip-hop, house, techno, etc.) are also based on the use of the *rock aesthetic*. The use of this set of practices gives all styles of 'pop/rock' a certain common denominator. They all use more or less similar sonic textures in order to convey their specific meanings, typical rhythms and melodic structures. The use of this set of practices renders all genres of 'pop/rock' participants in one sonic idiom, in one semiotic system. As such, the semiotic system of 'pop/rock' is not exactly the same as that of 'popular music' (or 'music', for that matter). The creative practices of 'pop/rock', as outlined above, exclude from this meta-category pre-'rock' genres such as 'big-band' and 'traditional popular song', and their inheritors during the 'rock era'. Bing Crosby and Ethel Merman, Dean Martin and Peggy Lee, and also Andy Williams and Barbara Streisand are performers whose work does not typically fall within the 'pop/rock' meta-category. However, central to the *rock aesthetic* is also an eclectic logic that encourages the application of these practices to any musical style. This means that any musical style, or indeed any musical work, has the potential to become 'pop/rock' if sampled or 'electrified'. Thus, for example, the application of the rock aesthetic to non-Western music idioms has created the 'pop/rock' styles known as 'ethno rock' or 'world beat' (and at the same time tended to exclude from 'pop/rock' those styles and genres of 'world music' based on devoutness to sonic images of ethnic or folk purity). This point will be further discussed below.

The reason I call this set of music-making practices by the name 'rock aesthetic' is that the socio-cultural context known as 'rock' has been the site in which these components were institutionalized as creative and artistic means for making contemporary popular music. Their institutionalization took place through the canonization of the so-called 'classic' Anglo-American rock albums and artists of the 1960s and 1970s, and their inheritors in later decades. Indeed, a final point about the *rock aesthetic* that should be stressed is its tendency to emphasize and put high value on the authorship of performers. It constructs a status hierarchy in which musicians perceived as authors of their works (either in terms of traditional authorship, or in terms of 'technological' authorship – i.e. DJs, musical producers, etc.) are placed above musicians regarded as only performers. But the issue of authorship, hierarchy and canonization is in fact the second characteristic of popular music which I want to discuss.

The 'pop/rock' canon

The other characteristic that came to underlie popular music in recent decades is the canonization of a specific body of musical works. There is a body of musical works that stands in the collective memory of consumers and musicians in industrialized countries (and in many other countries as well), as the 'great art works' or 'masterpieces' of 'pop/rock', sometimes even of 'popular music'. Each one of these works is an album of recorded music, containing several shorter units (mostly songs, but sometimes longer 'works') and typically lasting for 35 minutes to one hour. The authors of these albums are thought of as the most important and best musicians in 'pop/rock', or indeed in 'popular music'. Many, although not all, of these albums were recorded in the 15 years between 1965 and 1980. The names of these albums and their authors are very well known. Some of the most obvious examples include the Beatles' *Revolver* and *Sgt. Pepper's Lonely Hearts Club Band*, Bob Dylan's *Blonde on Blonde* and *Blood on the Tracks*, the Velvet Underground's *The Velvet Underground and Nico*, Marvin Gaye's *What's Goin' On*, Stevie Wonder's *Songs in the Key of Life* and Joni Mitchell's *Blue*. Some salient additions in the 1980s and 1990s include Prince's *Sign 'o' the Times*, Public Enemy's *It takes a Nation of Millions to Hold Us Back*, Nirvana's *Nevermind* and Radiohead's *The Bends*. The list is of course much longer and, as with any artistic canon, it is always contestable and susceptible to changes. In fact, the constant and never ending arguments about the 'best' albums reveal the existence of the core canon, the albums whose high place in it hardly change, and the importance of this canon in the tastes of popular music consumers. The 'pop/rock' canon finds its best expression in the 'best albums lists' published by magazines, newspapers and other publications (see, for example, Marcus, 1979; 'Rock Library: Before 1980' in Christgau, 1990; Larkin, 2000; see also the website http://www.rocklist.net/). The fact that even general newspapers such as the UK's *Guardian* repeatedly publish such lists testifies to the fact that the status of top-ranking albums in such lists is not just an affair of devoted cognoscenti.

Of course, artistic canons are produced and erected by interested parties, and the 'pop/rock' canon is not different. It has been constructed by a particular group of professionalized fans (mostly male, it should be noted) – that is, by rock aficionados who became professional critics (Regev, 1994). But, again, knowledge of the social agents who produced the canon, or of the power dynamics involved in the process of canonization, does not minimize the cultural fact of its existence, of the belief, shared by generations of casual consumers and aficionados alike, in its value. The sociologically interesting question concerns the reasoning behind the canonization and the artistic ideology surrounding it.

The artistic ideology that has been producing the 'pop/rock' canon is essentially a permutation of the traditional ideology of autonomous art. Based on this traditional logic, it attempts to accord the canonized albums a status not dissimilar to that of any other 'great' art works (Regev, 1994). It does so by interpreting the albums as being embodiments, or fulfilments of two elements. The first is the potential of the practices involved in the production of popular music to be genuine expressive and creative tools – that is, of being artistic tools. Contrary to a conservative view that understands these practices as technological gadgets facilitating music making for people without talent, the artistic ideology of rock portrays these practices as new and unique means of musical expression. In the right hands and talents, electric and electronic instruments, studio production techniques, sampling and turntabling, and of course 'spontaneous' vocal delivery can be used in highly original ways to create authentic, expressive music. The canonized albums serve as cultural proof of this point. The second is the fact that there is an authorial presence behind the operation of these practices. Again, it serves to contradict a traditional understanding of music making, which sees all popular music as a product of cultural assembly lines in which various professionals contribute components for a musical artefact made for the market. Within the context of the 'pop/rock' artistic ideology, the canonized albums provide the proof and evidence that either in the form of individuals that conceive and master all components of popular music making (that is, composition, writing of lyrics, singing, playing of instruments), or in the form of collective creative entities (bands), popular music is (sometimes) made by authors – that is, by genuine artists.

In other words, the canon of albums discussed here serves as the standing evidence that 'pop/rock' is in effect a genuine art form, the art of recorded (popular) music, or the art of making records. The canon also creates within 'pop/rock' a realm of sacredness, a mythology of its own history. By erecting this canon in a process that lasted several decades, the artistic ideology of rock has attempted – and one is tempted to say succeeded – to transcend the mid-century conventional view of popular music as a lesser musical art form. The initial erection of this canon in the 1960s and 1970s has generated an artistic hierarchy in the field, and has set in motion dynamics of change.

'Pop-rockization': logics of change

The constant emergence of new styles and genres, applications of the rock aesthetic to 'non-rock' styles and genres, and addition of new entries to the canon are three phenomena that exemplify the logics of change, or the cultural dynamics underlying the development and change of 'pop/rock'. These logics are essentially twofold. One is the logic I want to call *commercialism*, the other is *avant-gardism*. It should be stressed at the outset that, despite their difference, their outcome tends to be of a similar nature: the expansion of 'pop/rock', so it comes to consists of more styles, genres and variants.

Commercialism refers to a cultural logic driven by market interests or organizational isomorphism (see DiMaggio and Powell (1983) for this concept). It is essentially a practice of mimicking and copying rock aesthetic practices that have been proved successful either in terms of sales or artistic value. Interest to replicate commercial success, belief that the audience at large likes the 'new sounds', a wish to adhere to new conventions and a belief that it will improve the artistic quality of music are some of the typical reasons behind the practice of commercialism.

The cultural dynamic of commercialism is by no means unique to popular music. But it has been a major force in this field since the 1950s, contributing dramatically to the expansion of 'pop/rock'. Famous early examples of this pattern are the so-called 'high school' singers of the late 1950s in the USA, whom producers attempted to present as 'rock'n'roll' singers, that is, as the equivalents of Elvis Presley, Chuck Berry and Buddy Holly; and bands such as the Monkees that were formed by the industry in the wake of the Beatles and other rock bands of the mid-1960s. Other examples include the emergence of 'new wave' in the wake of punk in the late 1970s, and the adoption of electronics by a whole range of musicians during the 1990s, most notably Madonna.

An important case of commercialism is the adoption of elements of the rock aesthetic by so-called mainstream or middle-of-the-road popular music styles. It is important because the introduction of electric and electronic instrumentation into styles and genres traditionally thought of as 'light music' but not necessarily 'pop/rock', has blurred the difference between 'pop/rock' and other forms of popular music. The case of the Eurovision Song Contest is exemplary: the songs performed in this competition were gradually 'electrified' during the 1980s, becoming by the 1990s almost completely 'pop/rock' – in sharp contradiction to the 'popular song' tradition that dominated this competition until the late 1970s.

'Avant-gardism' refers to a cultural logic of inventiveness. It is associated with the notion of 'breaking new grounds' of sonic textures and affective meanings, of creating new expressive possibilities and musical languages. Avant-gardism may take various different forms within 'pop/rock'. The most common and salient is the exploration of new sonic textures offered by technological developments in sound-generating machines and studio technology. 'Researching' the expressive possibilities of the electric guitar or the synthesizer, constructing complex music layers and 'effects' in the studio and piecing together sound samples, are some of the techniques that gave authors such as Jimi Hendrix, the Beatles, Brian Eno, New Order, Public Enemy and, most recently, DJ Shadow their aura as important artists (see Theberge (1997) and Jones (1992) on technology and 'pop/rock').

Another tactic of avant-gardism is that of hybridity. The logic here is to apply the rock aesthetic to non-rock styles, or to hybridize different 'pop/rock' styles into something else. Some examples of the first type include the application of the rock aesthetic to various folk or ethnic musical idioms, thus creating the genres known as *folk rock* (the work of Richard Thompson, for example) and *ethnic rock* (or *world beat*; the list of examples here is world-wide: see Taylor, 1997; Mitchell, 1996; 2001), and the mixing of rock with art (i.e. 'classical') music, creating thereby *progressive rock* (Macan, 1997). Examples of the second type include the mixing of rock, soul and jazz to create *funk* in the 1970s, the merging of *disco* and *alternative rock* by various musicians during the 1980s (New Order should be mentioned again here), the fusion of *punk* and *heavy metal* into *grunge* in the early 1990s; and the hybrid of guitar-based rock with electronics recently explored by various musicians.

The artistic ideology of rock has traditionally tended to value avant-gardism more than commercialism as the preferred logic of change. But in the 1980s and 1990s this tendency has been replaced by a wider notion of newness that values innovations made under commercialism as well. In fact, one of the paths adopted by avant-gardism in the 1980s and 1990s has been to 'rehabilitate' styles, genres and musicians previously thought of as 'commercial' and therefore 'non-art': *lounge* and *easy listening* are cases in point here.

The working of these two logics of cultural dynamic in the field of popular music since the 1950s has gradually produced the plethora of styles and genres of 'pop/rock'. In their flow chart of 'marketing trends and stylistic patterns in the development of pop/rock music', Chapple and Garofalo (1977) argue that by 1974, 85 per cent of the total output of the popular music industry in the USA was 'pop/rock'. By the turn of the century, 'pop/rock' is a global meta-category of popular music (Regev, 2002, forthcoming). The expansion of the rock aesthetic, its becoming the taken-for-granted musical professional knowledge, technical skill and artistic sensitivity for making popular music, has marginalized popular music styles and genres that do not use it, and has caused the 'pop-rockization' of popular music. It is therefore useless, in a sense, to try and clarify or dismantle the exact relationship between 'rock', 'pop' and 'popular music'.

The use of the rock aesthetic, the belief in the 'pop/rock' canon and its artistic logic as source of inspiration, and the logics of change have made 'pop/rock' into a cultural entity whose styles, genres and musicians are intricately interwoven. There are many different questions to ask about this cultural entity, concerning various dimensions and elements. One major question that I want to address briefly in what follows is the theoretical account of its emergence and institutionalization.

Pop/rock theorized

Taken together, 'pop/rock' became by the 1980s and into the 1990s an art world (Becker, 1982) consisting of various and different genres and styles organized around a core set of creative practices, and held together by a belief in a canon of works and their authors as the constituting works and most valuable creations of this art world. Put differently, 'pop/rock' became an institutional formation that dominates the late modern cultural form of popular music.

Given this cultural condition, what is the proper socio-cultural account of its emergence? What is the cultural and social logic behind the emergence and institutionalization of this state of things in the field of popular music? In what follows, a brief outline of the major account that has dominated the theorization of 'pop/rock' is presented and criticized. It is then followed by an outline of an alternative sociological explanation.

Neo-Gramscianism

The standard theoretical narrative in popular music studies for describing and explaining popular music, and especially 'pop/rock', has been inspired by neo-Gramscianism. According to this perspective, the key element that initially facilitated the emergence of rock music was the socio-political meaning of the music. 'Pop/rock' music has been widely perceived as an expression of rebellion, subversion, resistance and critique. While critics and audiences typically found these meanings in the music itself, including the lyrics, neo-Gramscian scholarly readings of 'pop/rock' tended to emphasize its resistant meanings in the relationship between audience and music, in the acts of reception and consumption. Focusing on the production and consumption of 'pop/rock' styles within the collective entities known as subcultures (Hebdige, 1979; Wicke, 1990), on the 'empowering' function of 'pop/rock' at the individual level of consumption (Grossberg, 1984), or on both (Frith, 1981), 'pop/rock' scholarship was largely based on its understanding as a cultural expression of revolt and subversiveness against dominant culture. This theoretical emphasis made the contradictions between rock being 'a mass-produced music that carries a critique of its own means of production ... [and] a mass-consumed music that constructs its own "authentic" audience' (Frith, 1981: 11) the single most important issue in popular music studies. Neo-Gramscianism, in other words, has been occupied with the question of 'pop/rock''s 'sell out'. Thus, in addition to analyses of how critique and resistance are articulated by and in 'pop/rock', this theoretical perspective has been also examining how 'pop/rock' has or has not been absorbed into hegemonic culture. On the one hand, it has produced pessimistic readings of the relationship between 'pop/rock' and hegemonic culture, in which the total 'co-optation' of rock by the dominant culture has been proclaimed (Chapple and Garofalo, 1977), or in which the critical essence of rock has been declared 'dead' (Grossberg, 1986; Frith, 1988). On the other hand, neo-Gramscianism has been preoccupied, in a rather optimistic vein, with analyses and examinations of styles that have been found to be re-invigorations of the resistance and the critical power of 'pop/rock'. Heavy metal (Walser, 1993), hip-hop (Rose, 1994), house (Rietveld, 1998) and world beat (Garofalo, 1992) are some of the genres in which empowerment and subversiveness have still been found to exist in the 1980s and 1990s. In fact, with Grossberg's notion of *authentic inauthenticity* (1992), empowerment and critique are potentially found in almost every genre and style of popular music.

In the final analysis, neo-Gramscianism arrives at either one of two assertions about 'pop/rock', each one of them problematic. By interpreting almost all post-1980 'pop/rock' as co-opted, incorporated music that serves the interests of the music industry only and of the capitalist regime, it closes ranks with the Adornian legacy of popular music as 'mass deception'. It thus empties 'pop/rock' from any cultural meaning except that of being affirmative culture. Its reading of 'pop/rock' connotes an aura of a cultural 'failure', the bankruptcy of critique and resistance.

But the cultural position of 'pop/rock' is anything but a cultural 'failure'. It has an immense presence in contemporary culture, and plays an enormous role in the sense of identity of individuals and collectivities. By any measure, the emergence and institutionalization of 'pop/rock' has transformed popular music, and in fact music at large. These assertions are not intended as valorizations of 'pop/rock', but as simple observations of its impact.

On the other hand, neo-Gramscianism sometimes takes to the other extreme, of interpreting almost all 'pop/rock' as resistant. Frith (1996), in what seems to be a certain shift of his theoretical position, nicely criticizes this point: 'What was once an argument about cultural class, race and gender conflict, has been translated into a kind of celebratory political pluralism' (14). And also: 'The populist assumption is that all best-selling goods and services are somehow the same in their empowering value' (16). Frith's critique of the populist variant of neo-Gramscianism leads him to a lengthy analysis of judgement and discrimination practices in popular music. He implies a different interpretation of the social role of taste in 'pop/rock': not so much that of empowerment, as that of distinction and cultural capital.

In the light of these reservations, a different theoretical framework for understanding the emergence and institutionalization of 'pop/rock' is outlined below.

Weberianism

What I wish to propose is an alternative sociological account of the institutionalization of 'pop/rock'. It follows a tradition in the sociology of culture whose origins are in the work of Max Weber, especially his discussion of prestige, lifestyle and status groups (Weber, 1946). It is a sociological perspective that looks at the use and consumption of art and culture in terms of their function for the self-definition of collective entities and their quest for status, prestige and power. It is a tradition that has been greatly enhanced through the work of Pierre Bourdieu. By applying this perspective to popular music, I want to look at 'pop/rock' as a cultural form whose emergence is associated with the rise, in late modernity, of new collective actors, who struggle for status and legitimacy. 'Pop/rock' is seen here as a cultural tool, used by these rising collective entities and identities, to define their sense of cultural uniqueness and difference. The institutionalization of 'pop/rock', its becoming a major contemporary cultural form, signifies therefore the success of (some of) these new collective actors to gain legitimacy, even dominance, in contemporary society.

Bourdieu's understanding of the role of culture might be divided in two: a theory of 'distinction' and cultural capital, and a theory of the fields of art. The theory of distinction outlines the role of cultural capital in the production and maintenance of inequality, superiority and prestige. The theory of the cultural field delineates the cultural dynamic whereby the content of dominant cultural capital is constantly refined and redefined. Bourdieu points to a certain homology, an unintended correspondence, between the struggles within art fields, that constantly invent and re-invent art genres and styles, and the emergence of class fractions and sub-fractions demanding recognition and legitimacy. That is, he points to the fact that the success of new genres and styles to legitimize themselves as respected positions in a given art field serves the interests of rising class formations to construct their claim for social position, for power, around their self-definition as specific taste cultures and lifestyles. Or, as he puts it: 'by obeying the logic of the objective competition between mutually exclusive positions within the field [of art], the various categories of producers tend to supply products adjusted to the expectations of the various positions in the field of power, but without any conscious striving for adjustment (Bourdieu, 1993: 45).

But Bourdieu tends to limit his own analyses to older types of class structure and cultural capital, based on traditional 'high' art and its institutions. Except for some hints and occasional remarks, he hardly ever addresses the change in the status, position and prestige of the contemporary cultural forms known as 'popular culture' (film, television, popular music). Referring to emerging styles and genres, or, one should speculate here, to new and emergent cultural forms, he does, however, assert that:

> Without ever being a direct reflection of them, the internal struggles [in the field of art] depend for their outcome on the correspondence they may have with the external struggles between the classes...When newcomers...bring with them dispositions and *prises de position* [i.e. genres, styles, cultural forms] which clash with the prevailing norms of production and the expectations of the field, they cannot succeed without the help of external changes. These may be...deep-seated changes in the audience of consumers who, because of their affinity with the new producers, ensure the success of their products (57–8).

In the light of these remarks, the emergence of 'pop/rock' and its institutionalization should be understood as corresponding to the emergence of new collective entities and identities in the second half of the twentieth century. But who are these new collective entities and identities? Frow (1995) provides in this respect a useful discussion of the 'new class', and tends to call it 'the knowledge class'. Lash (1990), elaborating on Bourdieu, describes and indeed associates the emergence of late modern cultural sensibilities with the groupings he calls 'the new middle classes':

> It is the newer, post-industrial middle classes, with their bases in the media, higher education, finance, advertising, merchandising, and international exchanges, that provide an audience for postmodern culture...[They] have a whole range of different sources of identity than the older groupings and are likely to perceive their own 'ideal interests' in terms of a whole different range of symbolism and a whole different range of cultural objects than do the older groupings...Bourdieu speaks of battles for hegemony in terms of 'classificatory struggles'. This new post-industrial middle class thus could be entering into this sort of struggle with older dominant groupings in order to impose their own classificatory schema, which is comfortable with and valuates postmodern cultural objects, as hegemonic for the whole society (20).

'Pop/rock' should be understood as one of the cultural forms (together with film and television), that has been serving the self-definition of such entities along parameters of taste and lifestyle, and their social interests to gain recognition, legitimacy and power.

Indeed, as Peterson and associates have demonstrated (Peterson, 1992; Peterson and Simkus, 1992; Peterson and Kern, 1996), 'pop/rock' genres have become a major component in the taste patterns that emerged in the 1980s and 1990s among high-status professionals on the one hand, and lower-status technical professionals on the other – the 'omnivorous' and the 'univorous' cultural consumers, respectively. While the latter tend to adhere to one genre as a way of signalling their identity, the first groupings tend to consume 'everything': that is, many and various types of 'pop/rock' genres, among them those genres consumed by lower-status groupings. Status marking, the display and experience of distinction, has thus shifted from exclusivity and from *what* is consumed, to modes of interpretation through knowledge supplied by intellectuals – that is, to *how* culture is consumed (this point is also demonstrated in the case of Australia by Bennett, Emmison and Frow, 1999).

But the new collective entities of late modernity whose sense of identity is based on aesthetic sensitivities associated with contemporary cultural forms are not only class-based. They consist also of various other forms of identity.

> these same social groupings also form in large part a constituency for the new social movements. Their habituses or identities can thus also be constructed importantly along lines of gender, minority ethnicities, minority sexual practices, enviromentalism…that is, along lines of difference rather than of invidious distinction.
>
> (Lash, 1990: 22)

Late modernity, in other words, is characterized by a constant growth in the number and sophistication of actors in the market of collective identities. The claim of each one of them for cultural uniqueness and social legitimacy generates demand for constant emergence, development and sophistication of artistic styles and genres based on new aesthetic sensibilities. 'Pop/rock' fits here squarely. By being perceived essentially as a late modern cultural form, and with its inner logic of eclecticism, it has become a major supplier of such styles and genres. Starting with early rock'n'roll, consolidating in the 1960s and 1970s with the music now regarded as its essential canon, and then further expanding with funk, punk, disco, reggae, metal, hip-hop, alternative, house and techno – to name just the most obvious styles and genres – the history of 'pop/rock' has been marked by a series of styles and cultural contexts. Their initial appearance has taken the form of scenes or subcultures, where they have been articulated as expressions of specific ethnic-, class- or gender-based collective entities. But as these collective entities gained legitimacy, the 'pop/rock' scenes proved to be, in fact, social and cultural workshops in which aesthetic forms, meanings, contents and cultural practices were explored, tested and formulated, in order later to be adopted as components of the shifting cultural capital.

Conclusion

In conclusion, let me contextualize the cultural position of 'pop/rock' as follows. World society, and in particular Western countries, have undergone a deep social and cultural change during the second half of the twentieth century. This has been most symbolically reflected not so much in the actual descriptions, analyses and explanations of the new epoch, as in the tendency to name it. Names such as postmodernity, late modernity, reflexive modernity, the information age, network society and others have been used to emphasize certain dimensions of the contemporary era, or to describe and analyse it in its totality. Among the many aspects that most social and cultural theorists point to as key elements of contemporary world society – the 'time-space compression', the abundance of visual signification practices and their massive permeation of everyday life, the weakening of the nation state, economical globalization and cultural glocalization – a salient one is the emergence of a multitude of new collective actors, who struggle for recognition and legitimacy within and across nation states. These collective actors are professionally based or lifestyle-based class formations, gender-based identities, ethnic identities, and any combination of these variables. Like any other collective identity in history, an essential component in the production of these identities' sense of specificity, of uniqueness, has been the use of expressive cultural forms or, more precisely, art forms, genres and styles. As a way of distancing themselves from earlier collective entities, and emphasizing their 'newness' and their being present-day phenomena, these new collective actors have tended to use for the production of their uniqueness contemporary cultural forms such as film, television and popular music, and specific genres and styles within them. Consequently, the struggle of these new collective actors for social recognition and legitimacy has gone hand in hand with, and in fact is inseparable from, the struggle to recognize the artistic value of and legitimize their tastes for contemporary art forms, better known as 'popular culture'.

In other words, the second half of the twentieth century witnessed a classificatory struggle over the contents of legitimate cultural capital. In what should be understood as a homology with the struggle of new collective actors for legitimacy, power and prestige, a cultural struggle has been aiming to redefine the artistic status, prestige and legitimacy of contemporary cultural forms, especially those associated with 'popular culture'. Success of this struggle meant legitimizing contemporary art forms, thereby making them appropriate elements of tastes that define new types of social identity. The emergence of 'pop/rock', its institutionalization and continuous changes and refinements, are major embodiments of this cultural process.

It all means, among other things, that the wider social significance of the professional production of meaning in popular music – the work of critics, reviewers, writers, radio DJs and music editors (see, for example, the work of Lindberg et al., 2000), as well as that of public bodies such as museums, education, honorary prize committees, etc. – should be given much more emphasis than hitherto by popular music scholarship. The attributions of meaning and value to past and present, old and new styles, genres, artists and works, including practices of classification, should be analysed in terms of the social interests they stand for. The sociological question is not whether 'pop' is inherently different than 'rock', but what are the social and cultural forces working in this or any other classificatory practice in the field of popular music.

References

BECKER, HOWARD, 1982: *Art Worlds*. Berkeley: University of California Press.

BENNETT, TONY, MICHAEL EMMISON AND JOHN FROW, 1999: *Accounting for Tastes*. Cambridge: Cambridge University Press.

BOURDIEU, PIERRE, 1993: *The Field of Cultural Production*. Cambridge: Polity Press.

CHAPPLE, STEVE AND REEBEE GAROFALO, 1977: *Rock'n'Roll is Here to Pay*. Chicago: Nelson-Hall.

CHRISTGAU, ROBERT, 1990: *Christgau's Record Guide: The 1980's*. New York: Pantheon Books.

——, 2000: *Christgau's Consumer Guide: Albums of the 90's*. New York: St Martin's Press.

DIMAGGIO, PAUL AND WALTER POWELL: 1983: 'The Iron Cage Revisited: Institutional Isomorphism and Collective Rationality in Organizational Fields'. *American Sociological Review* 48: 157–60.

FRITH, SIMON, 1981: *Sound Effects*. New York: Pantheon Books.

——, 1988: *Music For Pleasure*. New York: Routledge.

——, 1996: *Performing Rites*. Cambridge, Mass.: Harvard University Press.

FROW, JOHN, 1995: *Cultural Studies and Cultural Value*. Oxford: Clarendon Press.

GAMMOND, PETER, 1991: *The Oxford Companion to Popular Music*. Oxford: Oxford University Press.

GAROFALO, REEBEE (ed.), 1992: *Rockin' the Boat*. Boston: South End Press.

GROSSBERG, LAWRENCE, 1984: 'Another Boring Day in Paradise: Rock and Roll and the Empowerment of Everyday Life'. *Popular Music* 4: 225–58.

——, 1986: 'Is There Rock after Punk?' *Critical Studies in Mass Communication* 3: 50–74.

——, 1992: *We Gotta Get Out of This Place*. New York: Routledge.

HEBDIGE, DICK, 1979: *Subculture: The Meaning of Style*. London: Methuen.

HESMONDHALGH, DAVID, 1996: 'Rethinking Popular Music after Rock and Soul', in James Curran, David Morley and Valerie Walkerdine (eds), *Cultural Studies and Communications*. London: Arnold, 195–212.

JONES, STEVE, 1992: *Rock Formation*. Newbury Park: Sage.

LARKIN, COLIN, 2000: *All-Time Top 1000 Albums*. London: London Bridge.

LASH, SCOTT, 1990: *The Sociology of Postmodernism*. London: Routledge.

LINDBERG, ULF, GESTUR GUDMUNDSSON, MORTEN MICHELSEN AND HANS WEISETHAUNET, 2000: 'Amusers, Bruisers and Cool-Headed Cruisers: The Fields of Nordic and Anglo-Saxon Rock Criticism'. Århus (Denmark): Research report.

LIPSITZ, GEORGE, 1990: *Time Passages*. Minneapolis: University of Minnesota Press.

MACAN, EDWARD, 1997: *Rocking the Classics: English Progressive Rock and the Counterculture*. Oxford: Oxford University Press.

MARCUS, GREIL (ed.), 1979: *Stranded: Rock and Roll for a Desert Island*. New York: Knopf.

MITCHELL, TONY, 1996: *Popular Music and Local Identity*. London: Leicester University Press.

—— (ed.), 2001: *Global Noise: Rap and Hip Hop Outside the USA*. Hanover: Wesleyan University Press.

NEGUS, KEITH, 1996: *Popular Music in Theory*. Cambridge: Polity Press.

PETERSON, RICHARD, 1990: 'Why 1955? Explaining the Advent of Rock Music'. *Popular Music* 9: 97–116.

——, 1992: 'Understanding Audience Segmentation: From Elite and Mass to Omnivore and Univore'. *Poetics* 21: 243–58.

PETERSON, RICHARD AND ROGER KERN, 1996: 'Changing Highbrow Taste: From Snob to Omnivore'. *American Sociological Review* 61: 900–7.

PETERSON, RICHARD AND ALBERT SIMKUS, 1992: 'How Musical Tastes Mark Occupational Status Groups', in Michele Lamont and Marcel Fournier (eds), *Cultivating Differences*. Chicago: University of Chicago Press, 152–86.

REGEV, MOTTI, 1994: 'Producing Artistic Value: The Case of Rock Music'. *Sociological Quarterly* 35: 85–102.

——, 1997: 'Rock Aesthetics and Musics of the World'. *Theory, Culture and Society* 17: 125–42.

——, forthcoming: "Rockization": Diversity within Similarity in World Popular Music', in Ulrich Beck, Natan Sznaider and Rainer Winter (eds), *Global America?* Liverpool: Liverpool University Press.

RIETVELD, HILEGONDA, 1998: *This is our House*. Aldershot: Ashgate.

ROSE, TRICIA, 1994: *Black Noise*. Hanover: Wesleyan University Press.

SHUKER, ROY, 1998: *Key Concepts in Popular Music*. London: Routledge.

TAYLOR, TIMOTHY, 1997: *Global Pop*. London: Routledge.

THÉBERGE, PAUL, 1997: *Any Sound You Can Imagine*. Hanover: Wesleyan University Press.

VAN DER MERWE, PETER, 1989: *Origins of the Popular Style*. Oxford: Clarendon Press.

WALSER, ROBERT, 1993: *Running With the Devil*. Hanover: Wesleyan University Press.

WEBER, MAX, 1946: 'Class, Status and Party', in *Max Weber: Essays in Sociology*, trans. H. H. Gerth and C. Wright Mills. Oxford: Oxford University Press, 180–95.

WICKE, PETER, 1990: *Rock Music: Culture, Aesthetics and Sociology*. Cambridge: Cambridge University Press.

Index